THE ANTI-JACOBIN NOVEL

The French Revolution sparked an ideological debate which also brought Britain to the brink of revolution in the 1790s. Just as radicals wrote 'Jacobin' fiction, so the fear of rebellion prompted conservatives to respond with novels of their own, indeed, these soon outnumbered the Jacobin novels. This is the first survey of the full range of conservative novels produced in Britain during the 1790s and early 1800s. M. O. Grenby examines the strategies used by conservatives in their fiction, thus shedding new light on how the anti-Jacobin campaign was understood and organised in Britain. Chapters cover the representation of revolution and rebellion, the attack on the 'new philosophy' of radicals such as Godwin and Wollstonecraft and the way in which hierarchy is defended in these novels. Grenby's book offers an insight into the society which produced and consumed anti-Jacobin novels, and presents a case for re-examining these neglected texts.

M. O. GRENBY is Hockliffe Research Fellow in the English Department at De Montfort University. He recently held the Fulbright-Robertson Professorship of British History at Westminster College, Fulton, Missouri. He has written for a number of scholarly journals, and has been a regular contributor to *History: the Journal of the Historical Association*. This is his first book.

CAMBRIDGE STUDIES IN ROMANTICISM

This series aims to foster the best new work in one of the most challenging fields within English literary studies. From the early 1780s to the early 1830s a formidable array of talented men and women took to literary composition, not just in poetry, which some of them famously transformed, but in many modes of writing. The expansion of publishing created new opportunities for writers, and the political stakes of what they wrote were raised again by what Wordsworth called those 'great national events' that were 'almost daily taking place': the French Revolution, the Napoleonic and American wars, urbanisation, industrialisation, religious revival, an expanded empire abroad and the reform movement at home. This was an enormous ambition, even when it pretended otherwise. The relations between science, philosophy, religion and literature were reworked in texts such as *Frankenstein* and *Biographia Literaria*; gender relations in *A Vindication of the Rights of Woman* and *Don Juan*; journalism by Cobbett and Hazlitt; poetic form, content and style by the Lake School and the Cockney School. Outside Shakespeare studies, probably no body of writing has produced such a wealth of response or done so much to shape the responses of modern criticism. This indeed is the period that saw the emergence of those notions of 'literature' and of literary history, especially national literary history, on which modern scholarship in English has been founded.

The categories produced by Romanticism have also been challenged by recent historicist arguments. The task of the series is to engage both with a challenging corpus of Romantic writings and with the changing field of criticism they have helped to shape. As with other literary series published by Cambridge, this one will represent the work of both younger and more established scholars, on either side of the Atlantic and elsewhere.

For a complete list of titles published see end of book.

CAMBRIDGE STUDIES IN ROMANTICISM 48

THE ANTI-JACOBIN NOVEL

THE ANTI-JACOBIN
NOVEL

British Conservatism and the French Revolution

M. O. GRENBY

CAMBRIDGE
UNIVERSITY PRESS

PUBLISHED BY THE PRESS SYNDICATE OF THE UNIVERSITY OF CAMBRIDGE
The Pitt Building, Trumpington Street, Cambridge, United Kingdom

CAMBRIDGE UNIVERSITY PRESS
The Edinburgh Building, Cambridge CB2 2RU, UK
40 West 20th Street, New York, NY 10011-4211, USA
10 Stamford Road, Oakleigh, VIC 3166, Australia
Ruiz de Alarcón 13, 28014 Madrid, Spain
Dock House, The Waterfront, Cape Town 8001, South Africa

http://www.cambridge.org

First published 2001

Printed in the United Kingdom at the University Press, Cambridge

Typeface Baskerville Monotype 11/12.5 pt.   *System* LATEX 2$_\varepsilon$ [TB]

A catalogue record for this book is available from the British Library.

Library of Congress Cataloguing in Publication data
Grenby, M. O. (Matthew Orville), 1970–
The anti-Jacobin novel : British conservatism and the French Revolution /
M.O. Grenby.
p.   cm. – (Cambridge studies in Romanticism)
Includes bibliographical references and index.
ISBN 0 521 80351 9
1. English fiction – 18th century – History and criticism.   2. France – History –
Revolution, 1789–1799 – Literature and the revolution.   3. English fiction – 19th century –
History and criticism.   4. Conservatism – Great Britain – History – 18th century.
5. Conservatism – Great Britain – History – 19th century.   6. Political fiction, English –
History and criticism.   7. English fiction – French influences.   8. Romanticism –
Great Britain.   9. Conservatism in literature.   10. Jacobins in literature.   I. Title.   II. Series.
PR858.F7 G74   2001
823′.609358 – dc21   2001025521

ISBN 0 521 80351 9 hardback

To my parents

Contents

Preface

Numerous novels appeared in Britain in the years after 1789 addressing the debate on the French Revolution and the ideas emanating from it. Some novels sympathising with the radical cause have received significant scholarly attention, but those which took a conservative line have so far escaped any sustained analysis. These were the anti-Jacobin novels.

Close to two hundred late eighteenth- and early nineteenth-century novels have been consulted in my quest to identify the extent and varieties of the conservative fiction published in Britain in the decade or so on either side of 1800. Yet this survey still covers only a small fraction of the fiction produced in the period. There are, therefore, almost certainly many more anti-Jacobin novels, of varying degrees and types, which remain undetected. Finding those anti-Jacobin novels which do appear in the following pages has been essentially a three-stage process. First, there are several existing works of scholarship which, together, have discerned between fifteen and twenty anti-Jacobin novels, and these form the foundation of this research. These 'tip-offs' sometimes occur in unlikely places: in biographies of figures who were maligned by the anti-Jacobins, perhaps, or in studies of the early Evangelical movement. Second, and in the attempt to place this survey on the basis of at least a degree of nominal comprehensiveness, I have made a thorough search of the major periodicals of the age – the *Monthly*, the *Critical* and the *Analytical Reviews*, the *British Critic* and the *Anti-Jacobin Review* – all of which contain a mixture of reviews and short notices of recently published novels, and which have proved invaluable for pointing out previously unknown conservative fiction. The latter two publications, of course, delighted in finding new anti-Jacobin novels, and so proved especially useful.

The third, and much less scientific, method of hunting anti-Jacobin novels is to track them down in the places in which they congregate – the forgotten holdings of the major research libraries – where they can be traced by means of clues in their titles, imprints or attributions. This might most properly be characterised as serendipity, but access to new CD-ROM databases of publications and library catalogues, with their powerful search engines, has enabled a slightly more systematic approach. Promising-looking titles can be picked out, located and read, and although many have proved to be false leads, several important finds have been made. Any success achieved with this method of detection must always be accompanied by a degree of frustration, however, for the more anti-Jacobin fictions one finds by chance, the stronger the suggestion that there remain many more as yet undiscovered.

This survey might have been larger than it currently is, but I have decided not to include novels translated into English even though they might contain much that is anti-Jacobin. I have, though, included works published by Americans in America as well as some novels which are no longer extant. For the latter I have had to rely on contemporary reviews, with their extensive quotations. Where I have done this, I have endeavoured to make this clear. It should also be pointed out that I have paid more attention to the less well-known novels of the period. There is much that might usefully be said, and in some cases has been said, of the political orientation of the novels of Ann Radcliffe, Frances Burney, Jane Austen, Maria Edgeworth, Matthew Lewis and so on, but I have opted to bring more obscure material (at least to the modern reader) to light.

In most cases, I have preserved the traditional attributions of works by anonymous authors, using the names supplied, often for no obvious reason, by the major library catalogues. Indeed, I have spent little time investigating the authors, or supposed authors, of the novels which I consider, preferring, as will become apparent, to see the anti-Jacobin novel as a coherent body of texts rather than as a collection of novels by separately motivated individuals.

Some of the novels under consideration in the following chapters are of much literary merit, and do, I feel, deserve to be rescued from the obscurity into which they have fallen. The same cannot be said for all the novels. But in any case, this book is not the place to make claims for them as great literature. Rather I have sought to use these neglected novels as a lens through which to examine the ideological fabric of British society in the age of revolution.

Acknowledgements

This research began as a PhD, generously funded by the British Academy, at the University of Edinburgh. I was able to bring the project to fruition in large part because of the support offered to me by my subsequent employers – the University of Edinburgh, the British American College London and De Montfort University. I would also like to express my thanks to those who founded and fund the Fulbright-Robertson Visiting Professorship in British History at Westminster College, Fulton, Missouri, through whose liberality I was able to canvass my opinions in the United States before committing them to print.

A version of my Introduction has already appeared in *History: the Journal of the Historical Association*, volume 83 (July 1998). I am grateful for the permission of its editor to reproduce it here.

I would like to record my gratitude to those who encouraged and advised me in this research at various stages in my academic career – to the late Paul Edwards, to Nick Phillipson, Frances Dow, Geoffrey Carnall, Gary Kelly and Iain McCalman, and above all, to Harry Dickinson, a model tutor, post-graduate supervisor and mentor.

It has been pointed out to me – and I know it to be true – that these acknowledgements would not be complete without recognition of those who have given me friendship and support, sometimes accommodation, and usually only mild harassment about what I have been doing all this time. Thank you to Henry, Jenny, Lizzie, Patricia and Stephen in Edinburgh, to Hugh, Liz, Malcolm, Mary and Tim in London, to Dave, Rebecca and Sam in Fulton, and to my family in St Albans.

Introduction

I beg Pardon for being so prolix; but as I have the Subject very
much at Heart, I know you will excuse this Effusion of Loyalty
                    Ann Thomas, *Adolphus de Biron. A Novel* (1795?)

Between 1791 and 1805 as many as fifty overtly conservative novels were
published in Britain. Others contained distinctly conservative elements.
These were the anti-Jacobin novels. They were written in opposition to
what their authors believed, or perhaps affected to believe, were the principles of the French Revolution. The implicit assumption behind these
books was that these Jacobin principles were establishing themselves in
Britain where they threatened to undermine all that had enabled Britain
to flourish and thrive. Some of the novels may certainly be considered
propaganda. What is perhaps most revealing though is that others lacked
an explicitly didactic intent. They seem to have absorbed and recapitulated conservative sentiments almost by default. How and why this
happened is one of the subjects of this book. But however it was that so
much fiction became aligned with a conservative agenda, these novels
provide a very valuable insight into the society which created, commissioned and consumed them. Each novel is interesting in itself, but when
read in aggregate, as if they constituted one single text, they take on a
greater historical significance as a very direct manifestation of the British
response to the French Revolution. And indeed, the two qualities which
the late eighteenth-century novel has routinely been regarded as displaying – 'popularity as a form of entertainment and . . . inferiority as a
form of art'[1] – provide a transparency in the relations between production and reception, and thus the link between literature and the society
which generated it, which is seldom available. Their popularity, and their
tendency to reproduce the familiarly conventional, endow these novels
with a representativeness which entitles them to be thought of as a vital key to the understanding of British society in an age of crisis and as

I

perhaps the most historically meaningful literary response to the French Revolution and its aftermath.

Yet both literary historians and critics have been reluctant to explore the conservative fiction of the decade or so on either side of 1800. Partly this is due to an embarrassment of riches. Few of the paramount figures of literary romanticism had qualms about engaging directly with the political issues of their day. The reactions of these eminent figures undoubtedly conduce to our understanding of the period, and, in particular, the famous recantations of support and sympathy for the Revolution made by Coleridge and Wordsworth in the late 1790s do still act as fixed points of reference in the history of the response to the Revolution. But whether these are in any way typical of society as a whole is a very different question. The audience for new poetry was, after all, limited and specific. The readership of novels, by contrast, was almost certainly expanding. And scholars working on the novel of the 1790s and 1800s have also been spoiled for choice. The resurgence of historicist criticism has demonstrated just how many previously non-canonical authors now demand scholarly attention.[2] Perhaps understandably, research has tended to focus on those works which are significant either in literary terms or because they exhibit doctrinal originality. Conservative novels, at least at first glance, seldom fall into either category. Indeed, the fullest attempts to chart the extent and diversity of anti-Jacobin fiction remain the single chapters (or less) allotted to them by Allene Gregory in 1915, J. M. S. Tompkins in 1932 and Marilyn Butler in 1975.[3]

Although none of these studies identified more than about a dozen anti-Jacobin novels, when in fact at least three times as many were produced, it is hardly fair to criticise them for the underestimation since none of their authors actually set out to provide full surveys of conservative fiction.[4] Yet they have contributed to the creation of the impression that there were more, and more important, radical novels published in the 1790s than conservative. The claims of critics who asserted that the political novel of the late eighteenth century was 'usually associated with radical ideas' or that 'surely few novelists, except Jacobin ones, ever hoped that their performances would conduce to the happiness of their readers by any other means than by entertaining them' have remained largely unchallenged.[5] The reality was that anti-Jacobin novels outnumbered Jacobin fictions and outlasted them too. Even including the more dubiously Jacobin novels there were still only about twenty radical novels produced, with only a very few of them appearing any later than 1796. The forty-plus conservative novels reached a peak of production only in about 1800 and fresh works were still appearing five years later. Anti-Jacobin fiction as propaganda may not have actually won the Revolution debate itself, but it was certainly on the winning side.

However, rather than recognising the dominance of anti-Jacobin fiction in the literary marketplace by the later 1790s, critics have sought to question the oppositional relationship of conservative and radical fiction. Claudia Johnson, for instance, has contended that

Most of the novels written in the 'war of ideas' are more complicated and less doctrinaire than modern commentators have represented. It does not suffice to denominate writers as 'conservative' or 'radical' according to whether they were 'for' or 'against' the French Revolution. By the mid-1790s, with France and England at war and the Revolution and Terror *faits accomplis*, there were few English 'Jacobins' around, and among professed 'anti-Jacobins', there is far more disagreement than first meets the eye.[6]

In keeping with this attempt to downplay the disparity between radical and conservative fiction recent critics have variously argued that both were together engaged in the process of establishing new middle-class values or the attempt to revise the limits of gender propriety.[7] Certainly, these attempts to revise the notion of a heavily polarised debate provide an important caveat to older assumptions and a valuable warning not to interpret novels too glibly according to their ostensible political orientation. Several authors are much more problematic than has often been thought and do defy easy political stereotyping. But crucially the majority of politicised popular novelists manifestly did not seek, nor achieve, any degree of ideological ambiguity in their fiction, but rather attempted exactly the opposite. Most of those of a broadly conservative orientation certainly thought of themselves, and were keen to promote themselves, as frank and forthright anti-Jacobins, routinely constructing their writing on the basis of their enmity towards the opposing tendency.[8] Charles Lucas, for instance, was perfectly candid in his retrospective discussion of his anti-Jacobin novel *The Infernal Quixote* (1801). 'The work was written to counteract the *revolutionary* mania among the community at large,' he remembered; it was 'avowedly written against the modern principles of atheism and licentiousness, disguised as philosophy'.[9] Indeed, many conservative novelists were aware, and delighted to admit, that they were contributing to an established and coherent genre. Both Jane West and Elizabeth Hamilton, whom Claudia Johnson holds up as ideologically conflicted authors, acknowledged their novels' similarity and indebtedness to earlier anti-Jacobin fictions, using their prefaces to exonerate themselves from the charges of plagiarism which they feared their novels might naturally attract.[10]

Moreover, if reception rather than production is taken into account when assessing fiction's political alignment then it seems much clearer that many novels were regarded as either Jacobin or anti-Jacobin when they were first produced, no matter how much modern scholars have sought to problematise their taxonomy. Not only the witch-hunting of the *Anti-Jacobin Review* or *British Critic* bears testimony to this, although their paranoid identification of exactly what was Jacobin and anti-Jacobin remains a useful indicator. Those contemporary reader-responses to which we have access proclaim that an awareness and acceptance existed of two literary camps, conservative and radical. The literary pundit Hugh Murray, for example, exhibited no unease whatsoever about identifying two distinct and cogent genres of 'Philosophical romances' which had made their appearance in the years leading up to 1805. 'Some of the first,' he wrote, 'were written with the view of supporting some very ill-founded and dangerous principles' – the Jacobins – but 'of late', he continued, 'several very ingenious works have been produced, with the view of counteracting the bad effect of those above alluded to.'[11] Most of all, though, the way in which the anti-Jacobin novel became formularised into a convention, a process which I shall be examining in some detail, demonstrates that a coherent anti-Jacobin genre undoubtedly existed for contemporaries, a genre within which only a very few of the best works displayed any substantial degree of difference and, thence, ideological ambiguity.

That even new historicist literary critics have still by and large been seeking to identify and investigate radical authors, novelists whose work posed some kind of a challenge to the prevailing structures of society, is all the more surprising since recent historians have increasingly been turning their attention to the forms, and prevalence, of conservatism in the Britain of the 1790s and beyond. Those who first opened up the study of the British response to the French Revolution overestimated the strength of radicalism in the 1790s.[12] Their enthusiasm was first replaced by more balanced assessments of the Revolution debate.[13] And more recently it can seem as though the heirs of Burke have entirely driven the heirs of Paine from the pages of historiography.[14] This new emphasis on the conservative represents something more than a mere oscillation in scholarly fashion. It is essentially a recognition that loyalty, patriotism and even a quite specifically targeted anti-Jacobinism, were much more significant elements in British society – affecting more people more deeply – than any radical impulse had ever managed to become. Radicalism, it is now generally recognised, only ever appealed to a relatively small section of society, and, in its appeal to a mass constituency in mainland Britain, was a transitory phenomenon. Those converts it did make in the early 1790s – that largely (but not exclusively) urban, sophisticated, subordinate élite which joined the corresponding societies and read Price, Paine and perhaps even Godwin – quickly, by about 1795, returned to their former political quiescence. Partly this was because new laws – Pitt's 'terror' – compelled them to do so. Perhaps also the propaganda campaign of the early 1790s (of which anti-Jacobin novels, at that time, were only a small part) had an effect. But most of all, events on the Continent turned Britons against the Revolution. The regicide, the Terror and the Edict of Fraternity which promised French support for insurgency in Britain, all played their part in 1792–3. The military victories of the Revolutionary armies in late 1792, which proved the Revolution might survive and export itself, and the interference with British trading interests in the Low Countries which it brought, added to British misgivings. And when the National Convention declared war on Britain in January 1793, the Revolution and the Jacobinism which was supposed to animate it were not only discredited in the eyes of most Britons, but were transformed from something with which an enlightened Briton might sympathise into something deserving nothing less than the most thorough execration, from something from which many had derived a satisfying sense of *schadenfreude* into something which shattered British complacency and seemed to demand concerted opposition. The 'Revolution debate', the 'war of ideas', withered away, not because every champion of radical doctrine had been utterly converted by the logic of the conservatives, but because few of them, with just one or two exceptions, could be found who wished to defy a near unanimous and highly militant anti-Jacobinism to put forward what had suddenly become dangerously unorthodox opinions.

This is not to say that the radical threat had entirely dissipated by the mid 1790s. Some lone radicals were still travelling the country at the turn of the century attempting to whip up support for their cause. More worryingly, the mutinies in the Royal Navy in 1797 were undeniably exacerbated by radical rhetoric. There were serious food riots in 1800-1 and labour disturbances throughout the period, possibly with an accompanying insurrectionary purpose in the case of the Yorkshire Black Lamp conspiracy of 1802. Nor did the great Irish Rebellion of 1798, or Emmet's Irish rising of 1803, materialise from nowhere or achieve their frightening – albeit limited and temporary – successes without a network of radical agents, both Irish and British, behind them. And there were many informed Britons who worried about the likelihood of a French invasion of the mainland, let alone Ireland, well into the 1800s (a well-grounded anxiety, as was proved by the attempted French landings in Wales and Ireland in 1796, 1797 and 1798).[15] Yet so much of the evidence pointing to a continued revolutionary underground enduring until the re-emergence of a confident and vocal radicalism after about 1807 derives from the reaction to that perceived threat by the establishment rather than from the threat itself. Government spies and state prosecutors were kept busy throughout the period creating a culture of state repression which, in retrospect, seems totally out of proportion to the level of danger. We do not know, for instance, if Colonel Despard's 1802 conspiracy would ever have come to fruition (let alone have been successful), because Home Office measures forestalled it. But what we do know is that Henry Addington was sufficiently worried about the information he was receiving to instigate prompt and decisive action.

Such swift government action, along with runs on banks, hoarding of specie and anxious letters to newspapers are symptoms of panic but not proof of imminent revolution *per se*. Whether or not the virtual conservative hegemony of which some historians talk had been established by the mid 1790s then, the important point remains that there was no dispersal of the sense of crisis in Britain even after the Treason Trials (1794) signalled the beginning in earnest of the government's clamp-down and the corresponding and constitutional societies had organised their last mass meetings (1795). Rather, as the orators of conservatism found they had fewer and more reticent voices against which to compete they simply became more strident and bombastic. Certainly, few could compete with the grandiloquence which Burke had achieved as early as 1790 in his *Reflections on the Revolution in France*. But after the period of genuine debate which followed, as the followers of Burke and Paine sparred with one another – a time when the fate of the Revolution in France still hung in the balance and when the rhetoric of conservatism had become a little muted – Burke's impressive chords were struck once again with all the told-you-so triumphalism of a party which had been vindicated.

For various reasons, it was in the interests of these vocal anti-Jacobins to maintain the spectre of the Jacobin threat. Some still genuinely believed Britain to be in peril. Others, particularly those influenced by Evangelicalism, thought their business only half completed. Though they might feel that they had seen off the immediate threat of a French-inspired revolution, they still found Britain possessed of a brittle social structure, riddled with corruption, which, if not quickly shored up, might collapse at any moment and achieve that which French agents, arms and principles had thus far found impossible. But besides the triumphalism and the genuine anxiety, there were two other important elements which sustained the sense of a 'Revolution crisis' after the real danger had subsided. First, it is impossible not to notice the sort of communal psychosis which permeated British society in the 1790s and beyond. The analogue is the astonishingly pervasive anti-communism of more recent times, and the anti-Jacobinism of the late eighteenth century is just as difficult precisely to account for. Undoubtedly it had its roots in the anti-Gallicanism and anti-Catholicism which had dominated the psycho-ideological composition of British identity for many decades. But it was also fed by propaganda of various sorts which encouraged the British public to comprehend the wholly unprecedented events in France as a catastrophe of quasi-biblical proportions, not as a series of political incidents but as a great moral offence against virtue, nature and God. Jacobinism, although it was also much more than this (for it was also often represented as having tangible effects too, such as depriving the people of food and rendering profitable business impossible), became a dreadful synthesis of assaults on queens, killings of kings, of priests hanging from lamp-posts, streets deluged in blood, and of cannibalism, incest and unrestrained sexual licence too. Jacobinism, in other words, was a gestalt with no set definition, and thus provided the perfect basis for the sense of crisis which developed and perpetuated itself in the 1790s and early 1800s. It was a crisis during which the challenge Britons felt they faced amounted to much more than the sum of its parts would have seemed if ever rationally appraised.

Second, though, there were numerous individuals and groups who deliberately maintained and exacerbated the idea of a Jacobin menace, using it as a stalking horse for their own, more narrowly targeted campaigns. Evangelicals like Hannah More or the members of the Eclectic Society used Jacobinism as a pretext for forcing through their vision of a moral reformation.[16] Contrariwise, Jacobinism could also be used as a stick to beat any and all movements for reform, of whatever complexion, and ultra-reactionaries had no hesitation in doing so. Anyone from the followers of Fox and the Society of the Friends of the People to the enemies of the slave trade or those who, like Hannah More herself, sought to establish Sunday schools, could be labelled as Jacobins, and frequently were by the *Anti-Jacobin Review*, the individuals who made up its staff and many others of like mind. They too were able to do this because Jacobinism had no fixed meaning.

It would be impossible to propose a precise definition of Jacobinism. Contemporaries used the word frequently, and often deliberately, without any exactness, purely to stigmatise their opponents. Jacobinism was simply a label for all that conservatives found detestable within society. Robert Bisset's attempt at a definition demonstrates this negative postulation and the almost limitless scope of attack: 'Whoever is the enemy of Christianity, and natural religion, of monarchy, of order, subordination, property and justice, I call a Jacobin.' They were the enemies of every established institution Bisset could think of, in other words, and, by an easy extension, of any which he could not.[17] By the same token anti-Jacobinism was its opposite, undefined but still an abiding moral and political imperative which, by the middle of the 1790s, permeated almost the entirety of British society.

This opposition to Jacobinism and the Revolution manifested itself on two levels. The majority of the nation became possessed, or in most cases continued to be possessed, of a sort of residual and passive conservatism, a political acquiescence which had always been largely based on anti-Gallicanism and had no difficulty incorporating a newer anti-Jacobinism into its constitution. But second, there were those who became active anti-Jacobins. Some confined themselves to signing loyal addresses or attending loyalist demonstrations – both astonishingly common diversions – but many also joined the army, the Volunteers, or more specifically dedicated organisations such as the Association for the Preservation of Liberty and Property Against Republicans and Levellers, the largest political organisation in the country at its height in 1792–3.[18] It is to the latter group of active conservatives that the first anti-Jacobin novelists belong. Figures such as Edward Sayer, Ann Thomas or Henry James Pye, who published strongly anti-Jacobin novels in the first half of the 1790s, were 'doing their bit', were volunteering for duty every bit as ardently as their more military-minded comrades. They believed that, as Hannah More put it in 1793, 'it is not so much the force of French bayonets, as the contamination of French principles, that ought to excite our apprehensions'.[19]

Indeed, it is immediately clear that anti-Jacobin novelists exactly fit the pattern that historians of conservatism have recently established for other forms of militant loyalism in the 1790s, a concurrence which, again, makes it all the more surprising that anti-Jacobin fiction has so far received so little attention. Having surveyed almost every manifestation of popular conservatism other than fiction, for instance, Harry Dickinson, has contended that,

In mounting a more sustained response to the radical challenge, the conservative defenders of the existing constitution in church and state matched every action to be taken by the radicals and usually did so on a larger and more impressive scale. In its strategy and its tactics militant loyalism copied and improved upon those adopted by its radical opponents.[20]

This could not more precisely apply to the anti-Jacobin novelists who not only expropriated the form of the novel from the radicals for their propagandistic purposes, but absolved themselves of all anxiety about pressing a popular form into political service by continually restating the fact that the Jacobins had villainously commandeered it first (see chapter one for examples of this rhetoric).

Similarly, Dickinson and others have pointed out that popular loyalism was independent and never under the control of the governing élite. Again, this is a characteristic which anti-Jacobin fiction shares. Elizabeth Hamilton may have received a pension from the King and Pye may have been Poet Laureate, but they were exceptions and, in any case, their anti-Jacobin novels were in no sense commissioned by the government.[21] Novels were never a form of state propaganda, and nor, in one important sense, were they propaganda at all. As Dickinson suggests, most conservative publicists 'were clearly reinforcing and tapping prejudices which already existed'.[22] So too were novels – not creating, nor even seeking to create, an anti-Jacobin rectitude in their readers, but writing to reinforce existing convictions. Fiction was perfectly adapted to reinforce anti-Jacobin nostrums without appearing to ram them home. But moreover, as a commodity in a competitive market, they would have been unable to do anything else – unless their authors or publishers were prepared to sustain large financial losses. The small active group of anti-Jacobin novelists within the population, in other words, relied for their existence on that much more substantial residual, passive conservatism in which almost the entirety of British society was involved by about 1794–5. If propaganda, by definition, seeks to provide its receivers with something they do not already possess, so anti-Jacobin literature, since it sought no converts and relied for its existence on a market which already shared its beliefs, cannot be regarded, in the strictest sense, as propaganda.

Anti-Jacobin fiction was two things successfully merged. It was a political campaign aiming to repulse Jacobinism. And it was a product, requiring a market for its existence. It was able to achieve both these things at once by retailing a sort of confirmatory anti-Jacobinism, bolstering the conservative convictions of its readers and simultaneously establishing a remunerative niche for itself. The fact that Jacobinism was almost extinct by the mid 1790s, therefore, gave strength to the anti-Jacobin novel rather than depriving it of its purpose, for as the threat of revolution receded anti-Jacobin fiction was able to build on the ideological unanimity of the population to expand its market and, by reaching more people, most of whom had become increasingly predisposed to accept it, to enhance its potency as an agent of conservatism.

It is when viewed in this light that anti-Jacobin fiction can best help to clarify the nature of conservatism as a whole in Britain in the late eighteenth and early nineteenth centuries. Anti-Jacobin novels appeared in dribs and drabs in the early 1790s. By 1794–7 a handful had materialised. But by 1798 the trickle had become something approaching a torrent, with some thirty highly conservative novels published between then and 1805, years when a French invasion seemed conceivable, but when radicalism had receded to its lowest ebb. Anti-Jacobin novels might have had subtitles like *The Philosophy of the Day* (1802), *A Tale of the Day* (1801) or *A Tale of the Times* (1799), but in fact they were tales of times then past. Indeed, Mary Anne Burges' *The Progress of the Pilgrim Good-Intent*, subtitled '*in Jacobinical Times*', was no less out of sync with the age it professed to concern itself with in 1822, when it reached its tenth edition, than it had been when it was originally published in 1800.

Most obviously, by following the contours of success of anti-Jacobin fiction much is revealed about the chronology and duration of anti-Jacobinism as a whole. Anti-Jacobin novels would not have been produced in such numbers in 1800, or in 1805, if there had been no market for them. Clearly, this supports the conception of anti-Jacobinism as a phenomenon only tangentially linked to the Revolution itself or to any actual manifestation of radicalism in Britain, both of which were well past their apogee by the time the anti-Jacobin novel reached its zenith. What it also suggests, though, is that anti-Jacobinism picked up speed as the 1790s wore on, almost in an inverse proportion to the threat actually posed by Jacobinism. It is apparent that the same pattern holds true of the most militantly loyalist periodicals and non-fictional publications too, but enterprises such as the *British Critic* (1793), the *Anti-Jacobin* (1797–8) or the *Anti-Jacobin Review* (1798–1821), or the investigations of the 'Illuminati conspiracies' published by William Playfair, the Abbé Barruel and John Robison (1795–8), or even such exercises as the Cheap Repository

Tracts (1795-8), cannot claim to be representative of the overall disposition of the British public in the same way that the novels can, for they were the work of committed, not to say fanatical, individuals who would probably have published, whatever they judged the reception of their work likely to be. The anti-Jacobin novels were different. They owed their existence, at least when they are regarded as a coherent class of novels and not a series of individual texts by individual authors, to a perceived desire amongst the public for such works. They required if not a guaranteed consumption, then an obvious and established appetite, before they would be able to make their appearance. This was the bottom line, however much they might also have been genuinely hopeful of encouraging the conservative orthodoxy of their readers.

Moreover, these anti-Jacobin novels enable a more detailed analysis of the conservative context within which they appeared because their authors, as a group, identified specific areas of strength in their campaign, concentrating on targeting the existing fears of readers with arguments with which they already sympathised. Those areas which anti-Jacobin fiction particularly aimed at, in other words, may be regarded as the areas of particular centrality to the conservatism of the nation as it had developed during the 1790s. These were the issues which constituted the anvils upon which that all-pervasive conservatism had been forged. And these remained the subjects around which the anti-Jacobinism of the post-Jacobin era still coalesced. For these reasons they are also the areas which I shall be investigating in detail.

In fact, what emerges when anti-Jacobin novels are taken as a single, aggregate text is a surprisingly coherent strategy. Three specific fronts were opened up in their campaign. To display the Revolution in France in all its horror was one obvious technique. France's descent into barbarity was a truth universally acknowledged, continually reinforced by ostensibly objective reportage, and perfect for a little fictionalisation so as to present an incontestable argument against Jacobinism. A second key tactic of the novelists was to caricature the 'new philosophy' of the British radicals, to show their utopian schemes as, first, chimerical, and second, productive only of evil. The proponents of such schemes they portrayed as only out for individual gain, simply exploiting any fool thoughtless enough to fall into the ambit of the new philosophy. The novel of the late eighteenth century, with its cast of victims and quixotes, rakes and manipulators, could not have been better suited to this purpose. And thirdly, novelists could appeal directly to the fears of their overwhelmingly middle- and upper-class readers, possessive of their prosperity and

jealous of their social standing, by exposing Jacobinism as a ruthless assault on hierarchy, status and wealth. Jacobinism was presented as nothing but the cover for levellers, social climbers and corrupt nobles – three
groups long detested by, and inimical to the interests of, the dominant
socio-economic groups around which anti-Jacobinism gravitated.

These were the three principal avenues of attack of the anti-Jacobin
campaign in fiction, each explored in further detail in chapters two
to five. Before this analysis begins I have sought to examine the literary context in which the novels made their appearance. A picture of
a deep-seated contempt for novels and especially political novels will
quickly emerge, and it was a context which had a direct formative effect
on anti-Jacobin fiction. This feeds in to what is probably the most important question surrounding the novels, a question to which I propose
an answer in the final chapter: why were anti-Jacobin novels written?
There were clearly a number of individual, highly committed authors
who produced anti-Jacobin fiction in the hope that it would nullify the
threat they genuinely thought was being posed by Jacobinism. But not
all anti-Jacobin authors were such fanatics, and the fact that many either
grew into their anti-Jacobinism from a previously neutral or even radical
position, or produced novels which were distinctly conservative in some
important respects, but clearly lacked the motivating zeal of the more
committed anti-Jacobins, suggests that anti-Jacobinism was not only an
acquired trait but one which many authors were highly anxious to acquire and to display, often as prominently as possible. The argument
made in chapter six that anti-Jacobinism became not merely fashionable,
but also something of a prerequisite for literary success, is a contention
that underlies all the chapters in this book. That the conventions of the
anti-Jacobin novel were appropriated for the fundamentally non-political
fiction of the ensuing, post-Revolutionary age goes some way to demonstrating that anti-Jacobinism in fiction, though it may have started as a
crude attempt at propaganda, quickly became something much more
than the work of a few isolated individuals. It developed into a coherent species of novel, and one which distinctly reflected the values of the
society which commissioned and consumed it.

CHAPTER I

Novels reproved and reprieved

It was said by Fletcher of Saltoun, 'Let me make the ballads of a nation, and I care not who makes the laws.' Might it not be said with as much propriety, Let me make the novels of a country, and let who will make the system?

Anna Lætitia Barbauld, *An Essay on the Origin and Progress of Novel Writing* (1810)

A rhetoric of opposition to the spread of reading, and to the educational and distributive processes that seemed to facilitate it, grew steadily throughout the eighteenth century. This was generally a rather petulant and sporadic resentment against the trickle down of a literary competence, but it occasionally found a tighter focus. Institutions which could be painted as inventions only of the present iniquitous age were seized upon as simultaneously causes and symptoms of the problem. Chief amongst these were the circulating library, the Sunday or charity school, and the novel. In the conservative imagination, the Sunday school taught the illiterate to read; the circulating library enabled them to do so affordably; and the novel enticed into the habit those who had previously been unwilling. What these institutions have in common is that they could all be arraigned for spreading the reading habit to new sections of society, to the lower orders, to women, to children.[1] It was the spread of literature to these inexperienced and susceptible readers which was to be condemned, conservative commentators were careful to point out, not reading itself, which few Protestants, few believers in the past glories of English literature, and few who read themselves, would be prepared to do. New readers were, they insisted, not sufficiently discriminating to distinguish between the wholesome food and the poison into which literature had always been divided.

This suspicion and hostility to reading and its agencies received new impetus from the French Revolution and the British radical response to it. The bout of conservative introspection brought on by the Revolution

crisis of the 1790s endowed by then established attitudes to the trickle
down of the literary habit with a new urgency. Education of the poor,
and the dissemination of reading materials to them, had consistently
been condemned because they unfitted them for their station in life.
Humphrey Repton's 1788 perspective was typical, not least in its vague-
ness: 'I contend that some degree of ignorance is necessary to keep them
['the lower orders'] subordinate, and to make them either useful to others, or happy in themselves.'[2] But by 1797 this had become a distinctly
political concern:

A man of no literature will seldom attempt to form insurrections, or plan an
idle scheme for the reformation of the State. Conscious of his inability he will
withdraw from such associations; while those who are qualified by a tincture
of superficial learning, and have imbibed the pernicious doctrines of seditious
writers, will be the first to excite rebellions, and convert a flourishing kingdom
into a state of anarchy and confusion.[3]

In an age when 'every pen was raised in the cause of freedom and
equality' and 'a new system every day broke from the groaning press', as
one novelist was convinced, any broadening of literature's constituency
must be dangerous.[4] In an age when Paine's quick-acting poison was
reputed to have reached one in ten Britons, it was only natural to conclude
that it would be better if no one could read at all than that they should be
able to read the *Rights of Man*.[5] A little learning created 'a predisposition
for the reception of nonsense, and especially innovating nonsense', and
'Tom Paine's book was wonderfully adapted for circulation'.[6] A reading
public had become a revolutionary public.

Because of its formulation as simply the opposite of all that was good,
Jacobinism itself did not have to do anything to draw literacy, education
and reading into its orbit. It was conservatives who cast them there, influenced as they were by the all-encompassing conspiracy theories of the
day, and the general sense of crisis which seemed to induce the detection
of Jacobinism in all things in any way offering a challenge to the old
order. Thus Samuel Horsley could claim in the House of Lords, with no
obvious evidence, that 'schools of jacobinical religion, and of jacobinical
politics; that is to say, schools of atheism and disloyalty' were appearing 'in
the shape and disguise of charity-schools and Sunday-schools, in which
the minds of the children of the very lowest orders are enlightened; that
is, taught to despise religion and the laws, and all subordination'.[7] The
extent of such paranoia is astonishing. The treatment of Hannah More
serves as an example. After her *Village Politics* (1792), the authorship of

which was soon discovered, her *Remarks on the Speech of M. Dupont* (1793) and the Cheap Repository Tracts (1795–8), few could seriously have suggested that More was actively sponsoring Jacobinism. Yet allegations made during the Blagdon crisis of 1800–3 clearly made the accusation. In establishing her contentious Somerset schools dedicated to teaching the poor to read the Bible she had, after all, endowed them with a literary competence, dangerous since they were held to be inexperienced and precipitate enough not to be able to discern those books of appalling tendency which everyone agreed existed. Even schools devoted purely to the propagation of religion must become suspect: 'if a disposition for reading is *in any degree* indulged,' wrote one reluctant critic of education, 'the sublimity of the Sacred Scriptures is perhaps bartered for the effusions of some superficial or political pamphleteer'.[8]

In fact, Hannah More was as deeply horrified by the books readily available in the 1790s to even the lowest class of readers as anyone alive. 'Vulgar and indecent penny books were always common', she knew, but the 'speculative infidelity' which she saw 'brought down the pockets and capacities of the poor', she thought formed a 'new æra' of depravity in history.[9] It was More who, perhaps more than anyone else, was responsible for the recognition that the damage could not be undone and that the peril had somehow to be countered. Fascinatingly, she dramatised her own realisation of this in her Cheap Repository Tract 'The Sunday School' (probably 1795). The prevailing defeatist conservative stance on reading, with which she could empathise but not agree, is represented in the tale by Farmer Hoskins. Her own reinvigorated optimistic faith in the power of reading to preserve the old order is represented by Mrs Jones, who is attempting to found a school. They start poles apart. 'Of all the foolish inventions and new-fangled devices to ruin the country,' says Hoskins, 'that of teaching the poor to read is the very worse.' 'And I, farmer,' rejoins Jones, 'think that to teach good principles to the lower classes, is the most likely way to save the country. Now, in order to do this, we must teach them to read.' She soon wheedles out of the Farmer the real, and familiar, reasons for his anxiety. In More's approval of these fears, and her careful rebuttal of them, we witness the reclamation of reading, and education, for the conservative cause:

'I am afraid my own workmen will fly in my face [protests Hoskins] if once they are made scholars; and that they will think themselves too good to work.' 'Now you talk soberly, and give your reasons,' said Mrs Jones, 'weak as they are they deserve an answer. Do you think that man, woman, or child ever did his duty the worse, only because he knew it the better? ... Now, the whole extent of learning which we intend to give to the poor, is only to enable them to read the Bible ... The knowledge of that book, and its practical influence on the heart is the best security you can have, both for the industry and obedience of your servants. Now, can you think any man will be the worse servant for being a good Christian? ... Are not the duties of children, of servants, and the poor, individually and expressly set forth in the Bible? ... Will your property be secured so effectually by the stocks on the green, as by teaching the boys in the school, that *for all these things God will bring them unto judgement?* Is a poor fellow who can read his Bible, so likely to sleep or to drink away his few hours of leisure, as one who *cannot* read? He may, and he often does, make a bad use of his reading; but I doubt not he would have been as bad without it; and the hours spent in learning to read will always have been among the most harmless ones of his life.'[10]

Convinced by this, Hoskins becomes a supporter of the school. It thrives, and needless to say, the village community flourishes in harmonious tranquillity.

In fact, More, in her own activities, went further than her *alter ego* Mrs Jones. Her whole Cheap Repository scheme was in itself an attempt to use the written word as a weapon to fight Jacobinism, and an attempt to spread a sense of political urgency throughout the nation. This is not to say that More wished for a *debate* on the Revolution, encouraging any actual *opinions* amongst the people.[11] But she did realise that it was the appeal of popular literature that, just as it had been its undoing, could make it positively useful. When we read the key résumé of More's activities by William Roberts, her first biographer, this becomes clear. 'As the school of Paine had been labouring to undermine, not only religious establishments, but good government, by the alluring vehicle of novels, stories and songs,' he asserted, 'she thought it right to encounter them with their own weapons ...'[12] Other conservatives were recognising this too. Their utilisation of institutions and techniques that had formerly been deemed the province of the enemies of the state opened an active front for the conservative campaign. The tactics which had been used with such effect by the forces of radicalism, as it seemed to many conservatives at least, once appropriated, enabled the protectors of the *status quo* to face their enemies on battlefields chosen long ago, and until the mid 1790s, left almost entirely undefended against the advance of the Jacobins. There had long been a general recognition that the great effectiveness of radical propaganda was derived not only from the persuasiveness of its message (obviously, no conservative could believe the substance itself would be convincing), but from the way in which it was delivered in an appropriate and seductive form and from the means by which it was disseminated. As much had been said at the trial of Paine for

Seditious Libel, when the Attorney General had warned the jury to 'be pleased to take into [their] consideration the phrase and manner as well as the matter'.[13] For More, and other like-minded conservatives, imitation of this formula was naturally the next step to take in their crusade. Together with other parallel conservative endeavours, like the tracts of the Association for the Preservation of Liberty and Property, the Cheap Repository securely established a tradition of conservative pamphlets which both outnumbered and outclassed the radical publications which had provided the initial inspiration. Exactly the same pattern was to recur with the novel. A fear of a reading public, and a fear of radicalism's ability to capture those readers, would suddenly combine to enable and encourage the anti-Jacobin novel to flourish.

As has been well documented, during the last three or four decades of the eighteenth century the novel form had been subjected to a welter of censorious criticism unbalanced by any serious or sustained apology.[14] The substance of this abuse is too well known to require repetition, however delectable the put-downs by reviewers, or provocative the self-righteousness of moralists' warnings. But the key characteristic of this fear of fiction, as with the attacks on Sunday schools and circulating libraries, is that it was built not on concern about the novel in itself, but rather on the question of who was reading it. The apprehension that novels were particularly adapted to those on the edge of the apparently widening circle of readers – that is to say the lower orders and especially women – was what chiefly motivated the denunciation of fiction. Criticism of the novel, effectively, had become a stalking horse for addressing a deeper malaise in society, the formation of an educated, literate, unsettled and ambitious tendency amongst those who ought to have occupied humbler and more submissive places in society. This was the anxiety which led commentators to suggest that a tax should be placed upon novels to elevate them beyond the reach of the poor, or – only half in jest – that 'none should be permitted to peruse a novel unless possessed of an estate of seven hundred a year'.[15]

As we have seen, such a readership was putatively dangerous because it was undiscriminating, unable to distinguish between that literature that was safe or even useful, and that which, either by an author's malicious design or through simple irresponsibility, was hazardous. Fiction in particular was supposed to be guilty of conjuring up a chimerical vision of life, as full of heroes, heroines and easily acquired fortunes as it was empty of the harsh realities of life, a utopian no-place in which a naïve reader might erroneously place his or her faith. Such consternation, although couched, as it often was, in the more specific ridicule of the gothic novel, is familiar to us from *Northanger Abbey* and other such 'anti-novels'. Whatever the specific and immediate targets of these satires, the principal lesson to be learned was that vouchsafed by the sensible Mr Mordaunt at the close of Mary Charlton's satire on novels, *Rosella, or Modern Occurrences* (1799). He hopes, he says, Rosella's 'past danger will henceforth teach her to pay a little more deference to the established usages of society than I hear she has lately done'.[16] The novel, in other words, was impeached principally because it putatively encouraged readers to disregard customary practices and values.

Crucially, the new philosophy of French and British Jacobins was, according to both its own proponents' definitions and those dispensed by its antagonists, a system which likewise deliberately clashed with established usages. It can be no surprise then that attacks on new philosophy followed the pattern of attacks on novels. Directly out of the traditional concern about novels' effect on naïve readers and about their fabrication of a chimerical, parallel system of values, a more overtly political concern about the chimerical delusions of the new philosophers evolved in the 1790s. Naturally, no conservative could ever accept the veracity of the apologies made for Revolutionary France, nor the logic of the stance taken by Price or Paine, Godwin or Wollstonecraft, so in assessing the threat of the Jacobin position, they were forced to conclude that its danger stemmed only from its plausibility. Since its principles were obviously and necessarily false, its charisma was its threat, and thus, its propagation its crime. Whilst those able to discern its fallacies would dismiss it, the undiscriminating reader might fall under its spell. This was especially true if it were placed before them in the captivating terms of a novel, decked out in the bewitching forms and debonair language which fiction could deliver. A new, more political reprehension of fiction fitted snugly into the tradition of criticism already well established. So while fiction had been consistently censured for 'painting vice and folly in their most gaudy colours' to 'allure the innocent and seduce the unwary', 1790s conservatives simply elaborated on the theme by condemning 'those seditious, yet dangerous *because plausible*, publications with which the press at this period groaned'.[17] Jacobinism added a new urgency to the incrimination of the novel, but built upon already existing structures, without, as it were, the necessity of any new legislation being added to the statute book.

But did Jacobin novels actually exist? In fact, despite some manifestly Jacobin productions, the most obvious testimony of their existence is provided by its opponents rather than exponents. Whether this often hysterical identification of the inexorable menace of Jacobin fiction is accurate is questionable. As we shall see, it could be used as the perfect apology for an apprehensive novelist's own authorial endeavours. Prefaces from the early 1790s and for the next fifteen or twenty years abounded in lamentations, like this one from 1805, that 'Novels and Romances have, of late years, been too frequently rendered the vehicles of revolutionary and infidel principles', the threat being alarming enough for some anti-Jacobin zealots to dedicate years of their life and thousands of pages, to exposing it.[18] Most vigorous of those who diagnosed this Jacobin disease was T. J. Mathias. In the first part of his *Pursuits of Literature* he could not restrain himself. 'The time for discrimination seems to be come,' he said, and offered a series of stark warnings against Jacobin novelists: 'Mrs Charlotte Smith, Mrs Inchbald, Mrs Mary Robinson, Mrs &c., &c.,' he cautioned, are all 'too frequently whining or frisking in novels, till our girls' heads turn wild with impossible adventures', – and departing from this very conventional criticism – 'and now and then are tainted with democracy.'[19] This was a charge taken up, as one would expect, by Robert Bisset, whose novel, *Modern Literature* (1804), was fundamentally another careful, and calculatedly horrific, dissection of Jacobinism's cancerous growth within the literary body. Fictionalising many of Mathias' concerns, Bisset had his heroine rencounter with 'Jemima', evidently Mary Wollstonecraft, who reveals her plans for a hierarchy of women to disseminate her principles. With herself as primate and one 'Mary' – Hays by her description – as her 'archbishop', it only remained to pick, from the many available candidates, twenty-four 'bishops'. When those selected are 'chiefly the writers of sentimental and loving novels', and yet are largely composed of authors who, both to posterity and their contemporaries, have appeared lacking in any genuinely radical credentials, we can see anti-Jacobin literary paranoia at its height. Relying on Bisset to identify Jacobins is rather like asking Senator McCarthy to point out communists.[20]

Whatever the reality of the Jacobin novel it is the panic endemic in its reception that is most significant. It seems never to have occurred to those berating the Jacobin novel that the reading public might not have actually wanted to read radical literature, something that, as the 1790s progressed, seems increasingly likely to have been the case. The 'widened circle' of readers was regarded as purely passive in the eyes of the anti-Jacobins, a body without a volition of its own, and who were so undiscriminating as to be won over by whoever produced the most alluring and available fiction. It was without their knowing it that these guileless readers would be drawn into iniquity, which made not Jacobinism itself, however reprehensible, the primary object of reproach, but its transmission through fiction. Nowhere is this made clearer than in *Modern Literature*, the hero of which, William Hamilton, reads the philosophical treatise of one 'St Leon' – that is to say Godwin's *Political Justice* – and, being an educated and sensible man, immediately spots its many errors. The danger only arises when a narrative – *Caleb Williams* – appears in its support:

> Subtle sophistry alone could hardly establish the inutility of criminal justice, but an affecting fable, setting forth the punishment of innocence and escape of guilt, strongly interests the feelings; *and the emotions of the heart are mistaken for the conclusions of the head.* A fictitious tale of an individual case is so skilfully managed, as, to many, to appear a fair and general exhibition of penal law, and its operation.[21]

Fiction was dangerous because it was able to engage the reader and to appear to prove a point without requiring any recourse to reason. If it was well written, by an author of talent like Godwin, so much the worse, for it would be that much more proficient in its aims. But also, Bisset implies, the danger arose because novels were read by those who would not read philosophical treatises. Jane West even appeared to remember with fondness the long gone days when 'Deistical tenets' were 'enveloped in the thick pages of some metaphysical treatise', before they became routinely 'insinuated into novels' and 'lowered to every capacity, or degree of leisure and information'.[22]

The idea that the novel was being enlisted by Godwin and his fellow Jacobins for the furtherance of their principles did have some basis in fact. Godwin had admitted his tactical use of fiction in the 'Preface' to *Caleb Williams* and in his letter to the *British Critic* of July 1795.[23] Gilbert Imlay acknowledged that he had chosen the novel form as the most effectual way of drawing his readers into his radical views.[24] It was this deliberate strategic deployment of the novel that most incensed Jacobinism's opponents, and provoked a response. Mixed with the angry denunciation of Jacobin novels, a determination to reply *in kind* quickly became evident, just as Hannah More had done with her Cheap Repository Tracts. For them to have spontaneously politicised their novels would have been an unthinkable dissemination of an ideological debate to many whom they considered unequipped to participate in it. Indeed, many held that novels had a particularly unfitted constituency for political disputation. So it was only when this constituency was assailed by Jacobinism, contaminated by debate, that a conservative political novel could be contemplated. Anti-Jacobin fiction, for the great majority of its exponents, existed only as an antidote, never as spontaneous and self-contained propaganda.

Certainly, by the middle of the decade, several novelists were asserting how morally and politically incumbent upon them it was that they should rush to aid their country in its distress. Not only did they produce anti-Jacobin texts, but, usefully to the historian (although it in fact reflected their anxiety about pursuing this course), they frequently depicted or dramatised their own conversion to this actively anti-Jacobin literary campaign. Typical was Ann Thomas, who excused her anti-Jacobin novel by having one character, the wise Mr Stanley, explain that, 'When turbulent Men are so industrious in disseminating Sedition through the Land, every good Subject, and every true Patriot ought to be as vigilant to incite in himself, and in his Neighbour, that Obedience to the Laws, and Respect to the chief Magistrate, which may secure and promote Concord and Quiet.'[25] Her novel was her answer to her own call to arms. For many, such writing by women, possessed of a political tendency, would previously have constituted a glaring transgression against the very strictest codes of gender propriety.[26] But so powerful was the anti-Jacobin rationale – that it was incumbent on each individual to do their utmost in support of Church and King – that it could exonerate not merely fiction, but also political fiction, and even its production by women. Thomas was attempting to vindicate her literary endeavours by declaring their necessity, or rather having a trustworthy character affirm it for her. Without the benefit of the distancing device, she had felt obliged to be rather more reticent, articulating only the trepidation about producing political fiction which would prompt the subsequent attempted justification: 'If an Apology be necessary for the political Part of the Novel,' she ventured nervously, 'permit me to declare, that I could not lose the Opportunity of expressing my Gratitude for that Protection which every Individual enjoys under the BRITISH CONSTITUTION.'[27] In claiming only a rather passive rectitude, instead of the very active anti-Jacobinism that she was actually to produce, Thomas demonstrates what a pivotal position she occupies. In 1795, a few anti-Jacobin novels had already been published, but they had been characterised either by a diffidence which still appreciated the temerity and danger of any political fiction or a defiance which set at nought the tradition of criticism of fiction. It was not until the later 1790s that anti-Jacobin fiction began to feel comfortable with its rôle. Before turning to its zenith, however, its origins, which literary history has altogether passed by, merit some investigation.

No more strident anti-Jacobin novel would be published than Edward Sayer's 1791 *Lindor and Adelaïde*, but in some respects this is little more than one of the author's political tracts and, for a novel of so early a date, its unembarrassed anti-Jacobin assault was exceptional. Two novels of 1793 exhibit a much more typical trepidation. For the author of *The Minstrel*, a conviction that politics in a novel is dangerous, because of fiction's likely readership, is still very apparent. In her preface she insisted that 'though necessarily led, by the personages of her drama, cursorily to introduce some subjects lately much agitated', she had no intention whatsoever of joining 'her feeble voice to either of those parties which, at present, divide a large proportion of Europe'. And yet, as well as offering some distinctly political opinions on the Revolution in France (a general sympathy with the French typical amongst those observing developments in France in early 1792), she also proffered a lucid, and almost prescient, warning to British Jacobins, so confident that it seems almost anachronistic. That a native of Britain, she wrote, 'should wish to throw off the mild government of its king, free himself from the salutary restraint of its laws, subvert all order, annihilate all subordination,' only to see the nation ruled by 'the caprice of a lawless mob' must, she went on, 'be deemed the most glaring insanity. Far be it from the author of THE MINSTREL,' she concluded, 'to spread such a detestable mania, or contribute to its baleful effects.'[28] Only in this last sentence do we return from the obvious anti-Jacobinism to the apology from which we started out. Clara Reeve's *Memoirs of Sir Roger de Clarendon* also evinces a degree of reluctance about brazenly introducing political concerns into her fiction, but it tilts the balance further in favour of a positive political didacticism. Reeve's preface defines the purpose of her tale in orthodox terms, speaking of her wish to inculcate wisdom, encourage reform and to discourage complacency about the present day, comparing it with Britain's half-legendary past – certainly a political statement in itself, of course, in the light of what Burke had said in the *Reflections*. But she shatters any vestige of ideological neutrality by proposing that her fiction might be of service in demolishing British radicalism. Her chief stimulus in writing the novel, she admitted, was 'to give a faithful picture of a well-governed kingdom, wherein a true subordination of ranks and degrees was observed, and of a great prince at the head of it'. For, she added,

The new philosophy of the present day avows a levelling principle, and declares that a state of anarchy is more beautiful than that of order and regularity. There is nothing more likely to convince mankind of the errors of these men, than to set before them examples of good government, and warnings of the mischievous consequences of their own principles.

In the novel itself Reeve still sheltered behind her allegory, apparently unwilling to labour a political point, but the possibility of a positive conservative agenda for fiction had been established and, most momentously, by a female, popular, novelist, with a well-founded reputation for absolute propriety, and whose novels and treatises had done much, in her own words, 'to point out the boundaries' of the form.[29]

That there was no outpouring of conservative novels between 1793 and the last one or two years of the century is a matter requiring attention. The mid 1790s were, after all, the years of the most vituperative debate and conflict, or rather the years when an ecumenical anti-Jacobinism established itself as the dominant ideology and did not shrink from pushing home its advantage through tracts, sermons and associations, as well as legislation. A few anti-Jacobin novels made their appearance in the middle of the decade, but in nothing like the numbers in which they would be published after about 1798. Probably the most important factor in delaying the rise of the anti-Jacobin novel was the fact that Jacobin fiction, from which it drew its *raison d'être*, did not reach its apogee before the mid 1790s at the earliest. Essentially, it was only these Jacobin novels, and not Jacobinism *per se*, that allowed the anti-Jacobin novel to flourish. The Jacobin fictions which appeared most menacing, and for most conservatives symbolised all Jacobin novels, were Godwin's *Caleb Williams* (1794) and *St Leon* (1799), both of which launched flotillas of rejoinders and allowed the anti-Jacobin novel to define itself in terms of what it was not. This is conspicuous in the attempts of Sophia King and Henry Pye to continue to attempt to exonerate their political fiction with reference to Godwin's novels even after they had both already produced successful anti-Jacobin novels.[30]

Perhaps the clearest statement of what almost all the anti-Jacobin novelists were doing is to be found in the dedication to George Walker's *The Vagabond* (1799). He wrote his political novel, he said, as 'an attempt to parry the Enemy with their own weapons; for no channel is deemed improper by them, which can introduce their sentiments'.[31] It is from this determination to fight fire with fire that the unanimity of anti-Jacobin fiction derives. Jane West even employed the same metaphor as Walker, expressing a similar slightly ersatz hesitation about entering the fray in 1799. Since 'the most fashionable, and perhaps the most successful, way of vending pernicious sentiments has been through the medium of books of entertainment,' she wrote, then it must be 'not only allowable, but necessary, to repel the enemy's insidious attacks with similar weapons'.[32] She was still using the same formula in 1802, presenting herself (falsely) as having *recently* been converted to this opinion. Her apology to the public forms such a comprehensive summary of the anti-Jacobin approach that it is worth quoting in full:

The rage for novels does not decrease; and, though I by no means think them the best vehicles for 'the words of sound doctrine'; yet while the enemies of our church and state continue to pour their poison into unwary ears through this channel, it behoves the friends of our establishments to convey an antidote by the same course; especially as those who are most likely to be infected by false principles, will not search for a refutation of them in profound and scientific compositions.[33]

This last phrase provides what was the clinching, and continually recurring, argument.[34] It was an argument of surprising sophistication, since not only did it encompass the notion that all new philosophy was necessarily fallacious, ready to be dispelled by the first puff of genuine reason, but by justifying their fiction as having popular appeal, conservative novelists had managed to appropriate a well-rehearsed and long-standing criticism of novels and turn it into a justification for their own fictional sallies. What is more, the potency of fiction which had been so thoroughly execrated because of its alliance with vice, infidelity and sedition, could now not merely be rehabilitated, but extolled as a positive virtue. Not only would anti-Jacobin fiction provide a prophylactic against the evils contained in radical novels, reaching an audience not likely to turn to treatises for the illumination that could dispel the Jacobin fantasy, but it could proselytise, obtaining converts to a proactive conservatism with its own fascinating language and without having to engage the reader in a debate on the matter which might prove both off-putting and ill-advised. This realisation was fiction's reprieve.

Seen retrospectively then, the flowering of the anti-Jacobin novel seems to have proved Charlotte Smith correct in her assertion of 1792, that only 'those who object to the matter' of novels would 'arraign the manner, and exclaim against the impropriety of making a book of entertainment the vehicle of political discussion'.[35] Once conservatives had realised the potential boost the novel could give their cause, they were content to cease attacking it and even to endorse it. As we shall see in chapter six, many reviewers changed their opinion of the genre. Even Hannah More, the form's greatest foe, came round, producing *Coelebs in Search of a Wife* in 1809.[36] But what is suspicious is that prefaces continued to testify to the grave threat posed by radical fiction, and the need to retaliate in kind, well into the nineteenth century, after both the Revolution crisis and the production of Jacobin novels had largely subsided. The preface to a novel was also the traditional site for an author's sycophantic attempts to propitiate the critics, and there must be a suspicion that some authors were emphasising the political mission of their fiction merely in the attempt to acquire a degree of respectability in excess of what they might otherwise have been able to hope for. So manifest was their deep ideological commitment, that it would be outrageous to suppose that the likes of More, West or Hamilton were jumping on an anti-Jacobin bandwagon merely for the chance it offered them to absolve their fiction's entrance into a public sphere. But as women, who felt they had an urgent political message to impart to the public but few opportunities to do so without violating their own, and others', sense of gender propriety, the Jacobin novel was an invaluable invitation into the literary mêlée. For novelists such as Smith and Walker, and perhaps Mary Robinson, all of whom had once produced basically Jacobin novels, the prospect of expiating their past crimes by the production of conservative fiction must have been tempting indeed. It might not have wiped their slates entirely clean, but at least it made them less vulnerable to renewed criticism of their politicisation of fiction. But it is with authors possessed of a very clear and pre-formed personal agenda that one cannot help feeling that the Jacobin novel was an excuse, and soon a cliché, frequently commandeered merely as a serviceable horse on which to ride into their own private battles. Sir Samuel Egerton Brydges, for instance, prefaced the second edition of his novel *Arthur Fitz-Albini* (1799) with talk of a crisis in which 'the circulating libraries have inundated the kingdom with a flood of novels, by half-witted writers', and a resolution that 'it seemed no useless task to attempt to stem this torrent of seduction', but, not put off his stride in the slightest, he then got on with dealing with the same concerns that had dominated his life and works until then, and would continue to do so, that is to say his veneration for rank and loathing of new wealth.[37]

Whether genuinely felt, or designedly constructed, however, enmity towards Jacobin novels remained an essential component of the anti-Jacobin novel long after its dominance had been established. It was its *raison d'être* and its vindication, and it never forgot it. Indeed, this same enmity also continued to be extended to fiction in general. Except in the case of their own work, anti-Jacobin authors clung to the notion that all modern novel-writing was intrinsically Jacobin. Henry James Pye, for instance, thought all contemporary novelists guilty of what he called '*novellism*', a crime possessed of a distinctly Jacobin tendency even though it did not advance an overtly radical agenda. Echoing Burke, he explained that 'In fiction as well as reality, the age of chivalry is past', meaning that in modern novels 'the sentimental philosopher takes the place of the warrior' as hero, and that he 'must be always deprecating the glories of the field, and must brand with infamy the sword of patriotism, though it glows with the blood of those who draw theirs against everything most dear to him'. Heroines were just as bad – they had turned 'manly', and were so determined to get whatever they wanted that they curse 'All laws but those which love has made'. Worst of all, if such a wife finds her husband 'disagreeable, inattentive, or absent though on service of his country, or in acquiring wealth for her, she is allowed to solace herself with some gentle youth, whom the hand of sensibility dresses out in the most bewitching garb, while insidious lust in the specious form of refined delicacy strews his false roses over the violated marriage-bed'.[38]

In Elizabeth Hamilton's *Memoirs of Modern Philosophers* (1800) novel-reading is likewise represented as the sure road to Jacobinism. She portrays two novel-addicts, representatives of the reading public Hamilton wished to warn. Bridgetina Botherim, having selected only novels and metaphysics for her entertainment, has, as a result, lapsed into new philosophy before the novel opens, but Hamilton does depict the fall of Julia Delmond for our instruction. Her seduction by Vallaton is designed to demonstrate that Jacobinism and all the traditional errors arising from the reading of fiction are inextricably intertwined. Vallaton woos Julia by appealing to her love of novels, convincing her that he is a foundling, a hidden aristocrat in all probability, and then undermining her piety, filial duty and chastity with his talk of reason, enlightenment and necessity. He unites these two techniques perfectly, simultaneously drawing on Godwin and Wollstonecraft, and the tradition of *Clarissa*, when telling Julia that it is a '*tyrannical prejudice*' that her father will not countenance their marriage and wants her to marry the respectable Major Minden. 'Thus was she on the eve of one of those cruel persecutions with which so many heroines have been tormented,' she muses. She beholds Minden as 'the hateful Solmes' and her father as acting 'with all the cruelty of all the Harlowes'. 'But never, (she resolved) never would she disgrace the principles she had adopted, by a base submission to the will of an arbitrary tyrant.'[39] The consequences are salutary. Julia is beguiled from her home, left to penury, imprisonment, attempted suicide and prostitution in London, followed by a contrite death. For Hamilton, novels and new philosophy had the same effect, and when combined together proved all too lethal. Even in 1800 Hamilton, along with many other anti-Jacobins, saw herself as writing in opposition to both Jacobinism and the main current of modern fiction. This leads to an important paradox. Anti-Jacobinism had done much to rehabilitate the novel in the eyes of many of its former critics. In part, the new respect which the nineteenth-century novel commanded was earned, like the spurs of an aspiring knight, through its service during the Revolutionary crisis. But the anti-Jacobin novel was itself the product of the traditional contempt for novels every bit as much as of a more historically specific contempt for Jacobinism. By the late 1790s, in fact, they had become tantamount to the same thing.

CHAPTER 2

Representing revolution

Go, Englishman, and tell your countrymen the things that thou hast witnessed. Things which eye hath not seen, nor ear heard, nor the heart of man conceived. How then shall men describe? Let example speak what precept would fail to enforce, and may the misfortunes of this hapless pair prevent the misfortunes of others.

> Edward Sayer, *Lindor and Adelaïde, a Moral Tale. In which are exhibited the Effects of the Late French Revolution on the Peasantry of France* (1791)

I own the King's situation must be interesting, horribly interesting, but it is an interest that pervades the globe, and I believe few bosoms in Paris have more lively feelings on the subject than it excites in those of England.

> R. C. Dallas, *Percival, or Nature Vindicated. A Novel* (1801)

Representing revolution was the most straightforward means of infusing an ideological purpose into fiction. That we tend to think of the ideological novel of the 1790s as a novel of *ideas* is simply the residue of the over-emphasis on Jacobin novels in the literary response to the Revolution. When Edmund Burke wished to execrate recent events in France, even before events there turned irredeemably vicious, he chose a pseudo-fictional form which, in large part, depicted, rather than reasoned, the Revolution. It was a decision for which he was roundly ridiculed by his opponents, but the *Reflections on the Revolution in France* (1790) was nevertheless hugely popular, as well as successful in its polemical aims, and it certainly influenced numerous novelists. Many quickly realised that a narrative provided the scope to illustrate a philosophy from its origins, through its progress, to its effects, and to cover protagonists in satirical contempt, or glowing eulogy, according to their opinions. Even those authors not attempting didactic fiction could benefit, the Revolution providing their fiction with a contemporaneity and weightiness that could make a claim for an increased

28

regard for a novel, so often regarded as the least worthy of literary forms.

This is not to say that novelists of the 1790s and 1800s all felt obliged to slot the Revolution into their fiction. Some even went so far as pointedly to set their plots in an apparently contemporary France, but without a revolution, a political statement in itself of course, although it is stretching a point to suggest that such a decision necessarily constituted a deliberate and thought-through anti-Jacobin stance as at least one commentator has done.[1] The anonymous author of *The Invasion; or, What Might Have Been* of 1798 could even write a novel dealing with the invasion of southern England by a nameless foreign power in an unspecified present without the least indication of an awareness of any contemporary relevance. But even if not deliberately disingenuous, it was certainly naïve for a novelist to expect to deal with these kinds of subjects – an invasion, a mob, the storming of a gaol, the fall of a cruel despot – without inciting a recognition of contemporary events amongst the novel's readers. And before such novels are allowed to undermine our notions of an all-pervasive Revolution crisis, it should be made clear that this kind of nonchalant novel was the exception. Indeed, this kind of idiosyncrasy rather highlights the fascination of the majority of novelists with the Revolution, or rather with revolution in general and with riot or invasion too, whether in France, Britain, the abstract, or the traditional geographical and historical no-places of so much fiction. Quite apart from anything else, the turmoil of a revolution or war, as the author of *The Invasion* must have noticed, provided a perfect setting for the adventures of a daring hero or the tribulations of persecuted lovers. The Revolution itself, as Burke's luxuriously gothic description of Marie-Antoinette's adventures in his *Reflections* had amply demonstrated, was made for the novelist, being already replete with a full cast of brave heroes, susceptible heroines and dastardly villains. The French Revolution as E. J. Clery has emphasised, was itself 'being written, and consumed by a paranoid British public, like a gripping romance translated from the German', and those novelists who ignored the Revolution were passing up a glorious opportunity.[2] That many did not let this chance pass them by meant that, to refine Clery's contention, a large number of novel-reading Britons were also reading the Revolution actually *in* a novel (gripping or not).

Yet the question of why it was that authors were inserting the Revolution into their fiction must remain. Was it a genuine and considered anti-Jacobinism, or was it a desire to imbue their novels with the manifold advantages – a certain contemporaneity, a ready-made wardrobe of elegant, gallant and gothic clothes – that put the Revolution into the novel? Were these representations of revolution propaganda? And, if some were written as much as ten or twenty years after the events that they were describing, must they be considered 'historical novels', in the same class as those of Scott or Dickens, a connection which at least one scholar has made?[3] This is a question to which I shall be returning at the end of the chapter. Before that, I shall give a general outline of the ways in which, and the purposes for which, revolution – both of the 'real' French (and Irish) variety, and its more abstract analogues – was used in fiction. Through this, the nature of the relationship between representation and didacticism may begin to become a little more distinct.

Even if the representation of the French Revolution was not always used for a deliberately anti-Jacobin purpose, it was certainly not a weapon that British Jacobin novelists chose to take up to any significant extent. Their determination to show things as they were, with the implication that things were not as they ought to be, was limited very much to Britain. This was a policy which made sense, since Godwin, Holcroft and others were ostensibly pointing out the abuses of the British *ancien régime*, rather than their 'post-revolutionary' emendation, which they might conceivably have claimed to have been achieved in France. Of course, as the Revolution descended into Terror, its portrait, however well drawn, would not have helped the radical cause in Britain a great deal anyway, and the best of Jacobin fiction was not to be written until after the guillotine, the regicide and the outbreak of war between Britain and France had rendered approval of the continuing Revolution almost unthinkable. Yet even before these developments, while there could still be a debate on the Revolution, in that strange lacuna between Burke's *Reflections* and the events of 1792–3 which would appear to prove him a prophet of remarkable accuracy, it is rather surprising that the representation of the Revolution was not chosen as a battleground on which to contest the issues. It was after all, debatable land, reports from France varying enormously, a situation which seemed made for fiction to step in and shape perceptions of the Revolution.

Charlotte Smith's *Desmond* of 1792 is just the kind of novel one would expect to have been written by many more supporters of the Revolution before about 1793 – an exercise in literary radicalism attempting to vindicate French feats of liberty by depicting them in all their glory. It gives a favourable, and reasonably factual, description of the Revolution as seen by a hero attempting to submerge his love for a married woman in the 'new dawn' across the Channel, his enthusiasm only slightly tempered by the caution of his correspondent in Britain. But Smith deliberately shied away from the sort of polemical fiction which she might so easily have produced. Her preface avowed as much, claiming that she had not attempted to argue in favour of any one party in the novel but had sought to represent accurately and objectively the Revolution and the debate surrounding it. If the veracity of this statement seems somewhat doubtful, her depictions of the Revolution do actually support the claim. They are not really fictionalised, and they are not polemical, or at least not *very* polemical, but have the genuine character of letters from an eyewitness in Paris, written to disabuse misled Britons. 'I can now... assure you,' writes Desmond in a letter dated 14 July 1790,

that nothing is more unlike the real state of this country, than the accounts which have been given of it in England: and that the sanguinary and ferocious democracy, the scenes of anarchy and confusion, which we have had so pathetically described and lamented, have no existence but in the malignant fabrications of those who have been paid for their misrepresentations.[4]

Desmond is apparently speaking of the Feast of the Federation, a peaceful celebration of the Revolution's successes that took place at the Champ de Mars on 14 July 1790. From his complaint, though, it seems likely that Smith was confusing this with the massacre at the Champ de Mars, which followed the next anniversary of the Bastille's fall in July 1791. In any case, what is clear is that Smith was attempting to seize the moral high ground, claiming that she was dealing only with truth whilst others – the fanatical enemies of the Revolution whom she claims have been paying to have events in France misrepresented – are forced to fictionalise that which they wish to condemn. It was doubtless this same faith in the power of truth, and distrust of falsification, that convinced other radically inclined authors not to attempt vindicatory fictionalised representations of the Revolution.

This reluctance is in marked contrast to the anti-Jacobins, for Smith's claim that there were 'malignant fabrications' abroad was far from being merely empty rhetoric. Edward Sayer's *Lindor and Adelaïde*, of a year earlier, was surely one of them, and does provide, in contrast with *Desmond*, the first appearance of a rival strain of Revolution fiction. There is no hard evidence to suggest that Smith was specifically referring to Sayer's novel when she made her accusation, but it is still illuminating that *Lindor and Adelaïde* professed to depict the France of late July and early August 1790, just as this particular section of *Desmond* had been doing, and that

Sayer's novel revolves around a special day of ceremony and celebration of the Revolution in the village of Ermonville, a sort of rural Feast of the Federation. Whilst Smith had depicted real events, which she had obviously researched with some care, Sayer uses imaginary incidents to fulfil his purpose, and a very obvious purpose it is. The festivities quickly plunge into violence and riot, our hero is killed by the mob, our heroine is sexually harassed by their leader and soon dies having heard the lone villager, faithful to the memory of the kind aristocrats, tell the tale of the outrages of the mob. As if impelled by some terrible force, the mob had converged on the chateau, and in his description Sayer provides one of the best, as well as the earliest, portraits of the revolutionary crowd:

When arrived we found a great multitude already assembled and committing every possible excess. Their riot increased with their numbers, and distorting themselves with various noises and notions, they were soon spread over every part of the ground that surrounded the house. At last, they seemed as if by mutual consent, or the command of some superior, to gather close together before the great gates. Many women and children were then seen hurrying out of the house, each bearing in their arms a part of the furniture, tables, chairs and any thing that could be moved. Just at that moment, a flame burst forth out of two of the lower windows towards the left; at the sight of which, the people sent forth a hideous shout of acclamation. Some calling out, Perish the aristocrats! While others screamed aloud, *Vive la Nation, Vive la Nation* . . .[5]

In certain respects, Sayer was claiming to depict accurately events in France – a note maintains that 'the Author has endeavoured throughout, to adhere as strictly as possible to French names and manners of expression' – but the sources for his history, though we cannot be sure of course, seem to come more from his imagination than any creditable account. This was exactly the same method employed by Burke, Sayer's stated model, who had furnished his *Reflections* with fictionalised illustrations. Thus Sayer provides us with the story of the late Lieutenant Governor of Marseilles, 'lately torn to pieces by the mob', not as a recorded fact, but as an anecdote related by an English visitor who happens to wander into Ermonville, and who, having dined with the Lieutenant Governor the night before, rose the next morning to see 'the head of my friend, streaming with blood and disfigured by blows, borne upon a pole and carried in barbarous triumph by a long train of furious and insolent rabble'.[6]

Ultimately, it was Sayer's method of representation that was to win out over the sort of event-based understanding and depiction of the Revolution that Smith purported to present. Sayer's representations, though, were severely limited by his willingness to admit that he was openly writing fiction with a purpose, that the novel he was producing was essentially propaganda. Though anonymous, Sayer proudly announced the novel to be 'By the Author of "Observations on Doctor Price's Revolution Sermon"' and used his 'Advertisement' to recommend Burke's great work – the *Reflections* – of which his own novel, he said, could only be a pale imitation. Moreover, he filled his narrative with long disquisitions, much longer than the whole of his *Observations* in fact, supposedly given in character, but so obviously out of keeping with the form that he was using that he felt obliged to offer apologies for at least some of them. 'Prepare yourselves' – says the venerable Prieur to our protagonists (and us readers), before launching into one particularly tightly argued eighty-five-page essay on the evils of the Revolution, the adequacy of the French *ancien régime* and the perfection of the British constitution – prepare yourselves 'for a discourse of some length, and of some nicety, but I trust not unworthy of your attention, nor impossible to understand'.[7] This sort of gauche didactic fiction could surely not have been particularly effective. Its explicit propagandising is condescending and alienating, and one can almost sense a ghostly feeling of disappointment clinging to the book from all the readers who felt betrayed into such dull political precepts by a novel with such an alluring title as *Lindor and Adelaïde*. There were certainly many more thrills in Burke's *Reflections*.

The way that this clumsiness was overcome, and the way the real achievement of anti-Jacobin fiction's representations of revolution was arrived at, was by the mating of the methods of Sayer and Smith. *Desmond's* apparent historicity was the perfect antidote to Sayer's sententiousness, its supposed objectivity the perfect corrective to his condescension. What made it the obvious way forward for those seeking to write anti-Jacobin fiction, though, was probably not any conscious emulation of Smith, but rather the change in the course of events in France.

Smith, for her part, had been still sticking to her empirical analysis of the Revolution, her *Banished Man* of two years after *Desmond* being written on the same principles. It was certainly a recantation of sorts, but accompanied by none of the retrospective re-evaluation of old convictions indulged in by, say, Coleridge, and the change in her opinions was manifestly still as a result of *events* in France in 1792 and 1793, events which obliterated the promise of the early Revolution.[8] 'Englishmen must execrate the abuse of the name of liberty which has followed;' she wrote in July 1794; they must have had their opinions changed by events, having contemplated with mingled horror and pity, a people driven by terror to commit enormities which in the course of a few months have been more destructive than the despotism of ages – a people who, in place of a mild and well-meaning monarch, have given themselves up to the tyranny of monsters, compared with whom Nero and Caligula are hardly objects of abhorrence.[9]

Even such a comprehensive statement as this of a personal revolution in the estimation of the Revolution causes little surprise since it was undergone by such a substantial portion of that part of the British population that took an interest in affairs across the Channel. As Clara Reeve was insisting a year earlier in 1793, interjecting some contemporary 'further remarks on the untimely death of princes' into her tale of the fourteenth century, the *Memoirs of Sir Roger de Clarendon*, 'the impartial and unprejudiced part of mankind, will draw the line of distinction between those men who effected the revolution, and framed the first constitution; and those who overturned it, and trampled upon all laws, divine and human'.[10] Once this condemnation could be assumed, objectivity was something to be wholeheartedly welcomed by anti-Jacobin novelists, and by the mid 1790s the Revolution was indeed no longer debatable ground, one report competing with another to answer the question of whether it should be welcomed or not, but a battlefield already taken. The events of 1792–4 in France proved only one thing: the iniquity of the Revolution. Thus the ostensible impartiality of Smith, who attempted to convince her readers that she was relying only on reported facts, could, because it was so confidently preordained, be added to representations of the Revolution like those of Sayer, who had openly fictionalised the subject. Future anti-Jacobin novels would continue with Sayer's technique of fictional representation, but would court at least the appearance of candid and objective description for it played into their hands to do so.

Understandably then, anti-Jacobin novels delighted in chronicling the descent from a Revolution which had at first augured well, seeming to aspire only to the perfections of the British constitution, into a perversion of itself that self-evidently proved its own transgression. Henry James Pye almost gloated at the 'Amiable and pardonable error' of the pro-Revolutionary protagonists of his *The Aristocrat* (1799), delighting in charting their disillusionment due to 'the excesses of the most sanguinary people on earth'.[11] John Moore, author of one of the best-known and not wholly unsympathetic historical accounts of the early Revolution, in his later novel *Mordaunt* (1800) was explicit about the way in which an events-driven disenchantment made support for France not just impolitic but impossible, eradicating even long-held radical opinions:

Their cruelty to the king and royal family shocked the hearts of all humane republicans, and roused a spirit of loyalty, which for some years preceding the French Revolution seemed rather benumbed all over Europe. . . The democratic bias, which had been gaining ground, was by the tyrannical and rapacious conduct of the French, checked in all the countries of Europe, particularly in Great-Britain. The very chimney-sweeps in London have become aristocrats, from their hatred to their brethren the blackguards and sans-culottes of Paris.[12]

How these chimney-sweeps gained their putative knowledge of the Revolution is a matter of some interest to the historian. Presumably, unlike the protagonists of Pye and Moore they, as with most Britons, had not had the opportunity to travel through France and observe the Revolution at first hand. Like most Britons, the chimney-sweeps relied, in other words, on representations of revolution, perhaps of the representations of novelists every bit as much as journalists or returning travellers, representations which, from *Desmond* and *Lindor and Adelaïde* onwards, many novelists evidently believed could best be achieved by sending a character or two off to see France for themselves.

But even more illuminating of the almost magical power of just the merest glimpse of the Revolution to banish folly and inspire wisdom in the onlooker are the attempts of various British Jacobin characters to prevent their dupes from witnessing anything happening in France for themselves. Thus, the 'new philosophers' who ensnare the political quixote in *The History of Sir George Warrington* (1797) are ever mindful of the need not only to hide their own typically licentious and avaricious motives, but also 'as much as possible the horrible consequences which had ensued, and would still ensue, from the French Revolution'. And whilst they argue our hero out of his proposed trip to France (depriving us of another depiction of the horrors of the Revolution), for they were 'too sensible that at this period the waters of the Seine . . . had a powerful effect in curbing the republican mania when it attacked Englishmen', we see his true friends attempting to lift the veil from his eyes by putting in his way the newspapers of the day.[13]

If newspapers very speedily effected the reformation of George Warrington, the political quixote, the light of truth suddenly bursting in upon him, for most other characters inhabiting the sort of novel whose plan did not include a lengthy tour of France, letters from correspondents witnessing unfolding events across the Channel served just as well for the enlightenment of protagonists and readers alike. It was not a new technique, of course; the advantages of the epistolary novel for depicting snippets of a complex picture without the necessity of a thorough description or explanation were well known and easy to use. It took no great ingenuity on the part of an author to send an expendable character or two off to France, have one of them be 'seized by the sbirri of Robespierre's party' perhaps, and the other send a letter home bearing the news from Paris 'of the poor fellow's having paid the forfeit of his life, for daring to speak sincerely of the sanguinary party, which after spilling the blood of the too inoffensive Louis, can have no compunction in wading through that of every Frenchman who was attached to him'.[14] Often, though, these letters did not form part of an overall epistolary scheme, but were isolated nuggets of anti-Jacobinism, often rather awkwardly inserted, giving the recipients of the letter a pre-packaged and very succinct 'knowledge' of the Revolution. A letter from Marchmont, eponymous hero of Charlotte Smith's novel, who has been packed off to France on the pretext of escaping his persecutors and meeting up with a distant relative (which is to say that he has been sent there to allow Smith another opportunity to rewrite her opinion of the Revolution), informs his mother, sisters and fiancée, awaiting his return, of the 'scene of phrenzy and of horrors' witnessed in Paris, and of the folly and the ferocity of the people, which excite his contempt and abhorrence respectively.[15] What do the women, sitting at home, make of it? Very little, for they blithely accept Marchmont's account, shake their heads in sorrow and congratulate each other on being British. One cannot help but suspect that in doing so they were representing what, according to the novelists, was exactly the right sort of reaction to the Revolution, expected of readers of the novels as much as readers of the letters. Indeed, Marchmont's womenfolk might well be seen as representing the stereotypical class of novel-readers in the 1790s – genteel, educated and refined, of moderate wealth, and with the lace-making business in fashionable Margate they have just established putting them almost on a par with the proverbial novel-reading milliners. We novel-readers, like the recipients of the letter, are told, in simple terms, exactly what we need to know, and no more, and the Revolution is distilled into comprehensibility.

Take, for instance, a letter received by Charlotte de Cordet bearing news from Paris in Helen Craik's novel *Adelaide de Narbonne* (1800). The purpose of our narrator in detailing the contents of the letter, of having it sent in the first place, has little to do with the plot, but edifies both Charlotte and the reader of the novel simultaneously. It contained, we are informed, 'a very frightful description' – too frightful to be vouchsafed verbatim it seems, and thus another displacing layer is inserted between the events and their reception – 'of the anarchy which prevailed, and the atrocities that were committed in the metropolis' and of 'the sanguinary proceedings of the bloody Roberspierre [*sic*] and the no less infamous Marat', who 'were perpetually sounding the tocsin to devastation and murder' and encouraging 'the most impious ceremonies, and the actual practice of every vice under the face of Heaven!'[16] Charlotte's response to the letter is not recorded (although it would be less than a volume before she would get round to assassinating Marat), but if we wish to know how a recipient of such a letter was expected to react, we need only turn to Ann Thomas' *Adolphus de Biron* (1795?) and Miss Hamilton's observably 'female' comments, full of novelish sensibility. 'How often am I astonished at being told,' she says, presumably meaning by those returning from having seen the Revolution (which happens a good deal in the novel),

that so many obdurate Hearts, so many savage and barbarous Hands, could be found in one City! But O! when one figures to the Imagination the various Sufferings of the unhappy Victims, as well as the complicated Woes of their surviving Friends, what awful Thoughts does it excite! And yet, Sophia, there are People who speak highly of the French Revolution.[17]

In effect, our response has been controlled through the response of our representative reader of the Revolution in the narrative. Thomas has led the reader of her novel quickly and firmly from a picture of the Revolution to an opinion of it, prescribing the correct response to reports of the Revolution so that any response not fitting the template which her character supplies becomes almost inconceivable, and certainly so for any reader aiming to emulate the sort of sensibility and refinement exhibited by her heroines.

J. M. S. Tompkins has pointed out that in Charlotte Smith's treatment of the French Revolution 'it is chiefly suffering, deprivation and exile, which attracts her', and it is an observation that applies equally to almost every other anti-Jacobin author.[18] This is a representational strategy which essentially writes the reader (whether inside or outside the fiction) out of the need for, and even possibility of, an individual response. The Revolution is cut and dried, the suffering, deprivation and exile it causes allowing only one response – a revulsion so deep that it denies the possibility of debate. Although this may be usefully analysed as a literary strategy, it is also a reflection of the 'real' historical debate going on outside fiction in 1792–4, the debate that British radicalism would lose with the knock-out blow delivered by Robespierre, the Terror, the Edict of Fraternity and the outbreak of war, and of which Smith's 1794 literary recantation was a symptom. The most memorable passages of her *Banished Man* are those in which her *émigré* hero, D'Alonville, returns to France and wanders amongst the desecration, witnessing scenes of carnage, wilful destruction, the dead lying unburied and the population almost all unhappy and half starved – the same unanswerable arguments, in other words, that were winning the actual debate.[19]

Smith was depicting events of late 1792 and 1793, a year or so before the novel was written, but scarcely enough to make *The Banished Man* an historical novel. But the same cannot be said of those anti-Jacobin novels which would continue to depict the same Revolutionary tableaux over the following ten or so years. Well over a dozen novels, of virtually every year of the decade from 1794, were all set squarely in the midst of events in France of 1792 to 1794, so that they form a seemingly seamless sequence with those novels which absolutely must be regarded as falling into the genre of 'historical novels', written after Waterloo and throughout the nineteenth century. This obvious fascination perfectly demonstrates how important these events had become in formulating not only the conservative, but the literary, response to the Revolution. But, in fact, what we see is a bundle of pre-packaged incidents of the Revolution becoming far more important for what they signified than what they actually were. Events became emblems, and even without adopting a semiotic approach it must soon become obvious that the Revolution in the later 1790s came to be represented in terms only of a series of powerful and only loosely historically accurate motifs, which both separately and together epitomised and represented the iniquity into which France had fallen.

Of course, the practice of depicting the Revolution purely in rather a-historical signifiers was not new, and Ronald Paulson has admirably shown Burke to have been the master of the technique, most famously with the *Reflections'* fundamentally fictional treatment of the Parisian mob's assault on Marie-Antoinette on 6 October 1789.[20] Amongst many other incidents, novelists were quick to employ very similar synecdoches to those of Burke. In Mary Charlton's *Parisian* of 1794, for instance, the subtitle of which proclaimed it to be comprised of *Genuine Anecdotes of Distinguished and Noble Characters*, there is an episode which tells us all we need to know about the Revolution in which we see a French mob surrounding a delicate and defenceless heroine. In one phrase, our narrator establishes the Revolution as everything that persecutes the innocence and loveliness to whose charms it is insensible. 'Her beauty and extreme youth moved a few who were near her, to something resembling compassion, or her death would have been instantaneous', we are told, before seeing the mob drag her off to an interrogation 'which was meant to be a form of trial', but at which the sentence of death would certainly have been pronounced had not our hero appeared in the nick of time to effect a rescue.[21]

If the persecution of beautiful innocence was perhaps the most obvious motif running throughout the novels, portrayals of revolutionary 'justice' at work were only slightly less incessant and insistent. Whilst Charlton had shown the mob about to enact their 'form of trial' on her heroine, it was the Revolutionary Tribunal that was more usually seen visiting its brand of justice on an innocent victim. Both Craik's *Adelaide de Narbonne* and Moore's *Mordaunt*, for example, dealt with the juridical persecutions inflicted on Princess Elizabeth, Louis XVI's sister, a sort of surrogate Marie-Antoinette. Moore produced a wonderful description, both touching and grimly comic, of the tribunal in action. The scene is recounted by 'la Marquise', whose account of her own persecution fills up much of one of the novel's volumes. She finds her former dancing-master on the tribunal, a man so asinine that, despite his power, the Marquise's mother cannot help but ironically mock his judgements:

'And the princess Elizabeth!' exclaimed my mother – 'she was also a bloody-minded tyrant – Was she not?'
The commissioners stared.
'Or, what was her crime?' resumed my mother, with an animation of look approaching to wildness.
The commissioner looked first at one, then at the other, of his brethren.
He who had spoken last said that 'Elizabeth was certainly suspected of being an enemy to the revolution.'
'She certainly was,' added the chief commissioner.' And then looking to the dancing-master, he added – 'Did you not tell me, brother, that one who attended the Temple informed you that he had overheard her praying very fervently, and that her prayers were anti-revolutionary?'
'It was you that said that they were anti-revolutionary,' replied the dancing-master. – 'I only told you that the man had said that she was overheard praying for the *reformation* of the king's enemies.'
The two commissioners looked at each other without speaking.
The person who sat at the bottom of the table, and acted as clerk, had formerly been a priest, and had distinguished himself as a casuist: he now opened his mouth for the first time, and said, with a solemn tone, 'By *reformation* she meant *destruction*.'

'Ay, she certainly meant destruction,' rejoined the first commissioner.

'And if the prayer should ever be granted,' resumed the clerk, 'it is more likely to be according to the *meaning* than the expression of the petition.'

'Most assuredly,' said the chief commissioner.

...

'It follows, therefore, as a necessary consequence, that the princess Elizabeth's prayers were anti-revolutionary,' confirmed the casuist, 'and might have been the cause of oversetting the revolution: and to overset the revolution by dint of prayers is just as treasonable as by any other means: for, when the revolution is overset, where is the difference?'

'None! none!' exclaimed the commissioner.

'That being the case,' said the clerk,' it is clear that the princess Elizabeth was a bloody-minded tyrant, and merited death.'

'Ah! the monster,' said my mother ... bursting into tears as she uttered it.[22]

If this seems a trifle sardonic, there are several more ardent treatments of similar scenes elsewhere. In Smith's *Banished Man* the revolutionary judges of D'Alonville, in what must be admitted to be a very skilfully handled twist in the plot, turn out to be the two most contemptible characters we have so far encountered, the hero's apostate brother and the Abbé Heurthofen, whom we know to be despicable villains from their earlier appearances, and whose Jacobinism is evidently merely a costume worn to facilitate their general malevolence, especially their hatred of D'Alonville. He is locked away in the deepest dungeon, and then made to witness mass executions, every minute expecting to take a more active part in them (an almost identical episode was described by Maria Edgeworth fifteen years later).[23] Likewise, in Mary Robinson's *Natural Daughter* (1799), we trace the progress of our heroine, Martha Morley, who, with her husband, is arrested in Paris, thrown into the Abbaye gaol ('where every horror and every insult convinced them, that their peril was no less imminent than certain'), and taken, with all due suspense, before her 'barbarous, and unrelenting judge'. This turns out to be none other than 'the abandoned Julia', Martha's sister, current mistress of Robespierre, and the would-be lover of Mrs Morley's husband, whom she promises to free if he will only return her passion.[24] This is a neat trick and shows how successfully Robinson, like Smith, had been able to integrate the process of Revolutionary justice into the plot and character definition of her novel. Just as our already subsisting contempt for the Revolution fuels our contempt for Julia, or the Abbé Heurthofen, so what we already know of them deepens our response to the Revolution, each response feeding off the other.

Smith could sometimes take a more subtle approach to showing just why the Revolution should be anathema to the British. Her description of Revolutionary Paris in *The Banished Man* was less horrific than usual, in the sense that there was less blood swilling around the gutters, but perhaps more *frightening* in its canvassing of what the middling Briton might expect from the Revolution – economic stagnation. D'Alonville 'saw the once-flourishing tradesman of Paris sitting in his almost deserted shop, looking pensively on bales of goods which had lain unfolded, and unasked for, for more than two years: he saw the class of manufacturers without employment'.[25] But such attempts to target specifically representations of revolution were rare. Above all, it was an all-pervasive portrayal of the sheer abomination of the Revolution, the offences committed in its name and reaching their climax during the Terror, the period so persistently depicted, which dominated the Revolution in the novels. If a single passage had to be chosen to stand for many, it could well be from *The Natural Daughter* again, not a classic anti-Jacobin novel by any means, for Robinson criticises the tyrannical 'prejudices' still to be found in Britain and was considered by many to be a Jacobin, but possessing some flawlessly formulaic depictions of Robespierre's France. A typically second-hand description, as our heroine elicits the recollections of a friend, provides us with all the intelligence necessary to condemn the Revolution:

On our arrival in Paris, we found every thing wild and licentious. Order and subordination were trampled beneath the footsteps of anarchy: the streets were filled with terrifying *spectacles*; and the people seemed to be nearly frantic with the plenitude of dominion; while the excess of horror was strongly and strikingly contrasted by the vaunted display of boundless sensuality.[26]

This seems rather purple prose, quite powerful even, but the vitality of Robinson's language belies its conventionality. More or less the same evocations appear over and over again, not only within this one novel, but in a dozen other fictions too. The same images continually recur, surfeiting the imagination with vast numbers of descriptions of life ebbing away in the prisons of L'Abbaye or La Force, of the guillotine cutting a swathe through the population of France and the Revolutionary Tribunals trying their hardest to keep pace with its appetite.

Read in numbers, the plain fact that so many of these depictions are so similar, that they shared such a limited representational vocabulary, nicely emphasises the increasingly emblematic rôle that these descriptions were playing. By 1807, for instance, the Revolutionary Tribunal is reduced to comic cliché, though still performing a clearly didactic function, merely a place where 'members were rather in the habit of ordering prisoners to execution without the ceremony of a trial' and whose judges 'were attired in strict conformity to the etiquette of a Jacobin toilette; whereof I suppose soap was not an article'.[27] And the offences of which the Revolution is guilty are similarly distilled, quickly becoming nameless deeds, merely recounted to us as 'horrors' or 'atrocities'. We see this clearly when the innocent Swiss have to flee from the French invaders in Hugh Murray's 1804 novel *The Swiss Emigrants*. They speak only of 'those calamities which might be too certainly expected from the ravages of such an enemy as this is described to be', and one feels that Murray was either unwilling, or unable, actually to describe the specific atrocities which the French were threatening to unleash on peaceful Switzerland. When he tries, the French having arrived, he can only come up with the disappointingly vague 'frantic scenes of riot and plunder' perpetrated by men whose 'monstrous delight was in the destruction and misery of their species'.[28] Although such signifiers of carnage were all that was strictly speaking required, a few gory details could still be thrown in for good measure. 'I want language to express the feelings of horror with which this observation inspired me', concedes Edward Mangin's narrator, having witnessed a fight between two factions which has left him the only survivor in one quarter of Paris, but we should not take him at his word, since he could still describe himself picking his way through 'a vast area strewed with carcasses', and could not resist throwing in aural confirmation with 'the pealing of the distant tocsin, and the frequent roar of an agitated populace'.[29] The tropes with which he could overcome his speechlessness came easily to hand, pre-packaged as clichés already taken up by other novels, his 'distant tocsin', just to take one example – not bell, but tocsin – occurring more or less every time an intimation of Parisian massacre was needed to liven up plot or prose.

Nor can the vivid barbarity of which the anonymous *Memoirs of M. De Brinboc* (1805) speaks in its portrait of the Revolution obscure its reliance on well-rehearsed, and decidedly Burkean, images, trenchant through their symbolism not their freshness. The 'immense multitude . . . bearing in front two bloody heads stuck upon pikes, with the sight of which these bloody monsters had been agonizing the feelings of the king and other royal captives' is an image that bears a remarkable, but unsurprising, resemblance to a description in Sayer's *Lindor and Adelaïde* already cited, and which no longer makes much of a pretence of veracity.[30] Even more revealing is the author's scene-setting, citing the period at which these memoirs commence, thirteen years before the novel was published, as 'precisely that moment when France ... had undergone that terrible concussion which annihilated an ancient monarchy, and threatened ruin to every thing connected with it'. And as the novel opens, we are immediately confronted by a cut and dried assessment of the Revolution, relayed only in the series of trigger-words. Our hero's father, we are told, for example, 'did not live to witness the *horrors* with which his country was *afflicted*, nor the *calamities* which befell his own race', or, 'Not a week passed over in which they had not to *deplore* the commission of some *atrocious* deed, or the departure of some acquaintance who was driven into exile in order to escape a greater *misfortune*.'[31]

By the time we reach the next generation of novels describing the early Revolution, Louisa Sydney Stanhope's *The Nun of Santa Maria de Tindaro* of 1818 say, the process is complete. The Revolution is only blood and death, blood and rapine, blood and savagery, something absolutely requiring execration, but never explanation. In passages which seem synopses of the events of some twenty-five years earlier inserted for the benefit of her younger readers, Stanhope gives the appearance of being the Revolution's historian, but, in fact, remains its prosecutor, citing only a series of hackneyed but potent images as her evidence:

Alas! devastation still raged in the capital: under the plea of patriotism, her citizens were butchered, and the minds of the people fomented by the most nefarious artifices; ruffian emissaries of jacobin clubs usurped the title of executive power, and every falsehood which could alarm, inflame, and agitate the populace, were circulated and believed. Nightly did the dreadful tocsin sound the signal for slaughter, and daily was the earth saturated with blood: convents, hospitals, and prisons, were alike devastated; sacrilege and profanation overthrew the altars, and Europe viewed with dismay the studies of human depravity.

. . .

[E]ach struggle of party was marked with blood and death: bold and hardened adventurers seized the helm of power, whose only aim at competition was to outvie each other in enormity, and alternately did the Jacobins and Girondists blaze like firebrands of the earth.[32]

Stanhope may have retained a few historically specific details, the Jacobins and the Girondins for example, which just about tie her portrayal to 1790s France, but in fact her scene could just as well have been taken from any revolution, or any other scene of carnage at all, revolutionary or not. The motifs in which Stanhope was dealing had become so ingrained as to supersede the events which they had originally been conjured up to represent. If this was an historical novel, then it was a novel based not on history but on novels which had represented that history.

The representations of revolution we have been examining aimed at exciting an emotional response which would damn the Revolution on the basis of its manifest, and increasingly assumed, horror. It was undoubtedly a powerful technique, and working in conjunction with pamphlets, graphic prints and other forms of propaganda, seems to have succeeded, convincing all but a few Britons that France, after about 1792, was indeed a land of abomination. Frances Burney, for instance, herself responsible for a novel portraying France 'during the dire reign of the terrific Robespierre', characterised herself as accepting utterly fiction's depiction, before, that is, she herself crossed the Channel, following the Peace of Amiens, in April 1802. She was amazed to find the inhabitants of Calais civil, genteel and prosperous, noting in her journal, 'I cannot say how much this surprised me, as I had conceived an horrific idea of the populace of this Country, imagining them all transformed into bloody monsters.'[33] But of course, even this sort of testimony will never tell us for sure how genuinely Burney, and others like her, actually believed in the sort of picture cheerfully supplied by Smith, Craik, Robinson and the rest. Might they not simply be acquiescing in a myth which provided an easy and appealing way of coming to terms with an event so complex as the Revolution? After all, representations of its savagery, its sheer horror, provided one, and perhaps the best, nucleus around which events in France and their implications for Britain could be organised, understood and reassuringly neutralised by that understanding. Indeed, beyond those descriptions of the Revolution which sought to excite revulsion through portrayal only, other representations of revolution had perhaps their most powerful effect in rewriting events so as to account for them, to explain exactly why they were so contemptible and thus to rationalise a reprehension.

One such attempt to reason out a response to the Revolution is evident in the conspiracy theories, explaining the Revolution in terms of the Illuminati and the Freemasons, which found favour in Britain in the 1790s. Regardless of whether the Abbé Barruel, William Playfair or John Robison, the authors of the most notorious exposés of the supposed conspiracy, really believed that these quasi-supernatural forces had been behind the Revolution from the very beginning, it seems clear that they enjoyed such a wide currency because, as their historian has pointed out, such interpretations provided a much appreciated 'attempt to impose some order on the bewildering variety of changes which suddenly showered on Europe with the Revolution and its aftermath'.[34] The same quality was shared by the techniques anti-Jacobin novelists were using to rationalise the Revolution through their slowly evolving representations. The Illuminati played a dual rôle in the propaganda campaign, first organising the Revolution into something which could be nailed down to specific causes (however implausible), so that once comprehended it could be addressed, and second, denying it the status of a legitimate political movement, requiring a reasoned and serious political response. The presentation of the Revolution's brutality, as we have seen it emerge in so many novels, played an analogous rôle, simultaneously giving the Revolution a unifying theme and denying it the status of a genuine expression of political opinion. But there were also more sophisticated ways in which novelists sought to comprehend the Revolution and thus to circumvent any need to engage directly with its real political meaning.

In order to discredit the Revolution, the first task was to arraign and indict its stated aims, namely its initial revolt against the French *ancien régime*, irrespective of the fact that this had long been the detestation of every true Briton. This was what Burke had attempted with his *Reflections*, and it was what his loyal disciple, Edward Sayer, also strove to achieve with his *Lindor and Adelaïde*. Why Sayer's response stands out amongst anti-Jacobin novels is because his vision of the *ancien régime* France that the Revolution had displaced, was, like his mentor's, an almost entirely perfect idyll, a standpoint which, however useful for an anti-Jacobin responding to events of 1789 and after, sits rather uneasily with the sort of anti-Gallicanism which was axiomatic for so many conservatives before, as well as after, the Revolution. In Sayer's fiction, the Revolution prompts a recasting of the French *ancien régime* in the British mould. It becomes the fertile, prosperous, harmonious place that we recognise from, say, de Rochefoucauld's descriptions of affluent England, or the British arcadias painted by Hannah More or Elizabeth Hamilton for their own didactic purposes, a place where, as Sayer put it, 'The peasant paid the easy and honourable tribute of respect with willingness, nay with zeal, while he received in return, the solid advantages of security and peace.' Sayer even devotes a sizeable portion of his novel to having his sagacious Prieur carefully rebut each charge so often laid against the *ancien régime*, even up to and including the *lettres de cachet* so symbolic of despotism's abuses.[35]

This was unusual, and never an entirely convincing strategy, even in Burke's attempt, for so much of British opinion had greeted the initial Revolution with sympathy, welcoming French attempts to catch up with British liberty. More typical, and durable, was the sort of representation to be found in another novel of 1791, the anonymous *Siege of Belgrade*, which mixed reprehension of the *ancien régime* with an equal disdain of the Revolution. As well as exemplifying what we know to be the British response to the Revolution, *circa* 1791, and attempting to relate the Revolution to the less than perfect Bourbon régime, it appears rather prophetic. Couched as second-hand reportage as it is, and using very familiar vocabulary, it is also another early example of the sort of representation of the Revolution to which readers would become used.

At dinner the conversation turned principally upon the French revolution; and the Viscount Leinster, who had been a witness to all the sanguinary proceedings, in the beginning of that extraordinary event, related some circumstances, which had never publicly transpired. The assassination of both King and Queen, and a change of the succession, he mentioned as objects actually intended by the Duke de – , of whom he spoke in language of great severity. But, although he censured the violence committed upon this great occasion, he very forcibly described the abstract virtue and necessity of reformation: alleging, that the spirit of the constitution, and the indispensable rights of men, had been totally absorbed in a blind and slavish obedience to despotism. The unparalleled injustice of letters de Cachet, the incredible horrors of the Bastile [*sic*], and other state prisons; the oppressions of the Ministry; the venality of judges; the wretchedness of the peasantry; the wanton cruelty and barbarism of vassalage and feudatory power; the waste of public wealth; and the abuse of prerogative; he, not only described, but illustrated in colours, strong, glowing, and natural.[36]

The key-stone phrase here, holding in place the whole architecture of the response to the Revolution, is Leinster's simultaneous censuring of the violence committed on this 'great occasion', whilst forcibly describing the necessity of reformation. The reconciliation of these potentially antithetical responses was an achievement that would underlie all future anti-Jacobin representations of the Revolution.

To exhibit the evils of the *ancien régime* quickly became a highly serviceable ploy for British anti-Jacobins, allowing them to compare their notion of an initial, mild and well-meaning resistance against tyranny, with the Revolution's subsequent demonstrable fall into an absolutely indefensible Terror, a fall made all the worse not by the paradise lost, but by hopes of a redemption from corruption betrayed. But this could only be the result of a complacency yielded by events of the mid 1790s,

allowing British conservatives the luxury of formally recognising the corruption of the tyrannous *ancien régime*, and concomitantly admitting, in
theory at least, a degree of esteem for the first, 'British-style', Revolution.
Thus the novel-reader of the 1790s was presented with a procession of
edifying émigré aristocrats who had initially favoured the aims of the
Revolution but had since learned, to their own personal cost as well as
that of the nation, of the perfidy of its protagonists. Charles Lucas' 'Duke
de Meritè' is typical, admitting to the world, when he finally emerges
from the Welsh well in which he had taken refuge after fleeing France,
that 'I conceived that I should be the grand means of making five and
twenty millions of people happy, and I rashly helped to overturn the old
fabric, that crushed us all in its fall.'[37] Smith's D'Alonville is even more
explicit in formulating a paradigm in which contempt for the Revolution
does not rely on praise for the *ancien régime*, but rather draws strength from
the comparison:

these are the boasted blessings of that liberty for which they have for four
years been contending – infatuated, misled people! The taille, the gabelle, the
corvés, even the feudal services, however heavily imposed, what were they when
compared with the oppressions under which you now labour! If ye had burthens
under the government of an arbitrary monarch, ye danced gaily under them;
but the yoke ye have put on yourselves weighs ye down to the earth – its iron
points are stained with blood, and dipped in poison![38]

As we shall see, it became a central theme of anti-Jacobin fiction to
represent the Revolutionary régime as nothing more than a restatement
of traditional French despotism, but at this point, the point at which
novels began to integrate *ancien régime* abuses into their novels of the
Revolution, another question theoretically began to arise. If the *ancien
régime* was to be accepted as corrupt, and deserving of reform, could
rebellion then be justified?

In fact, this was not so much a question, as a chance to demonstrate
that rebellion, however justifiable the evils of the existing régime might
appear to make it, could never be legitimate. Including the *ancien régime's*
corruption in their fiction gave novelists the opportunity to show
how even seemingly warranted insurgency would necessarily bring, as
D'Alonville had been explaining, far worse evils than could have been
previously dreamt of, and this, of course, was a message carefully attuned
for domestic consumption, and shrewdly developed in fictional representations of revolution. In a few novels there did appear something
approaching a genuine sense of debate on the long-standing problem, at

the centre of the Price–Burke controversy which had opened the British debate on the Revolution, of whether tyranny justifies resistance. In Mary Robinson's *Hubert de Sevrac* (1796), for example, we see a typically benevolent Marquis, forced to flee the Revolution, frankly disputing with his daughter on the question of whether 'Anguish the most acute' – the Revolution – 'is preferable to lingering misery' – the *ancien régime*.[39] But such open debate remained a rarity. Indeed, *Hubert de Sevrac* was also unusual because it addressed the debate in the context of the Revolution itself, and not in the sort of crucible which a novel could so easily provide in which revolution might be presented in the abstract.

Looking back to *The Siege of Belgrade*, for instance, although the novel was set in 1789 and touched on the Revolution in France, the author chose to site his or her demonstration of the evils of insurrection, as predicted by Viscount Leinster in the French context, in a vague Serbian setting. The Prince Czerskaskoi is quickly established as the representative of the *ancien régime*, and the analogical representation of Revolution proceeds from there. So it is that we quickly learn that everyone agreed with Leinster's strictures on the old, corrupt order in France, save only the Prince, who was 'unable to endure doctrines so adverse to his own tyrannical ideas of government'. Still more overtly our author confides, with some relish, that 'The Bastinado, the Katze, the batogen, the single and double knout, were in unremitted use through every part of his extensive government; and, such was his tyranny, that the people notwithstanding their natural insensibility, were ripe for revolt and retribution.' Yet when this inevitable rebellion arrives, and Czerskaskoi's 'prodigious gothic pile' is attacked by the oppressed peasantry, Leinster's attitude to it is unequivocal. However legitimate the grievances of the people, their insurgency simply cannot be tolerated, and the course of action incumbent upon him is plain. 'Under circumstances such as these, no time was to be lost,' we are told, and

compassion must give place to duty. The arrival of Leinster was soon known, and submission as soon demanded; but the rage was too fervent and headstrong to be immediately suppressed; and the troops were, though reluctantly, commanded [by Leinster] to fire. Many of the furious assailants were killed and wounded; some fled; and others, inflexible, resolving on resistance, stood their ground, and seemed to defy the consequences: a second unavoidable discharge of musquetry, however, shewed them the folly of opposition; and they dispersed precipitately into the country.[40]

This might seem somewhat ruthless – and lest, in seeing this as a repeat of the St George's Field Massacre or as a sort of prefigurement of Peterloo, we forget that Leinster was the friend of the people, our author does remind us that under his succeeding government, the laws were respected so that 'love began to reign ... the gloomy hills of Wiatka to exult, and the vallies to smile in gladness!' – but the moral had been made crystal clear.[41] The Revolution is an illegitimate enterprise; the one prop that it could conceivably use to support itself – that it was an attempt to redress the abuses of the *ancien régime* – was systematically taken from it.

And it was a point made time and again, in settings as various as the highly gothicised medieval Madrid of Matthew Lewis' *The Monk* (1796), with its famous description of the mob venting its vengeance on a community of nuns, trampling the Prioress to a pulp before bringing the walls of the convent down on their own heads, or contemporary Jamaica, where a slave insurrection in Elizabeth Helme's *Farmer of Inglewood Forest* (1796) is reprehended by one of our narrators when his fellow slaves start to redress their grievances by 'killing their tyrants, and deluging the estates with the blood of their oppressors'.[42] Most often though, these fictionalisations of the illegitimacy of rebellion, and its inevitable ill-consequences, were sited in a thoroughly British context which could only have made more explicit this rationalisation of revolution as always an unjustifiable act.

The Revolution already had its analogue, of course, in that eighteenth-century British institution, the mob, and numerous novelists would delight in demonstrating its inherent iniquity. One striking example is Robert Bage's *Hermsprong, or Man As He Is Not* (1796), generally regarded as one of the breed of Jacobin novels, in which the hero explains to the mob in both words and blows, why even institutionalised poverty cannot justify revolt.[43] More narrowly the Church and King riots of the early 1790s, especially the Birmingham riot of 1791 in which, notoriously, Joseph Priestley's laboratory was destroyed, provided a very specific motif for the representation of an uprising of the people, in a just political cause, though still utterly reprehensible. The heroine of Helena Wells' *Constantia Neville; or, the West Indian* (1800) has no love for Priestley and his principles, but she clearly explains to a party of travellers (one of whom turns out to be Mrs Priestley) that,

the populace of Birmingham did not go the right way to work; the philosophical apparatus and the Doctor's manuscript works on Chymistry, could not have assisted in revolutionizing this country. For my own part, though I should not like his religious tenets to be spread, nor do I conceive any man is warranted in propagating opinions that are subversive of the fundamental doctrines of Christianity, I yet think the treatment he received at Birmingham, will ever be an indelible disgrace to the inhabitants, and throw odium on the country at large.[44]

Thomas Skinner Surr's *George Barnwell* (1798) was surely also deliberately summoning up the memory of the Priestley riot, and explaining its futility, when he has the mob surround the house of Mr Mental, known to own a large and secret laboratory full of obscure electrical and chemical apparatus, known to be an exponent of the new philosophy and suspected to be a member of the Illuminati. Yet when they are on the point of pulling down his house, Surr's rewriting of the riot stays their hands as he sends the local magistrate to search the house, find no incriminating evidence and disperse the mob.[45]

Clearly this sort of lesson was not addressed to the mob it was describing, but if it was lacking in that kind of direct propagandism, it was still an attempt, through representations, to *explain* revolution, French and British, real and abstract, in the reassuring form of an illegitimate and doomed expression of complaint and, moreover, something which could be halted by the intervention of a respected individual representing legitimate authority. Furthermore, it was comforting to find how different a British mob was from those of France, a point made glaringly clear by a passage in *The Chances; or, Nothing of the New School* (1803). Sir Charles Sommers has been imprisoned in a private madhouse, as symbolic of the abuse of the law in Britain as *lettres de cachet* were for France, and when word of this villainy gets out, the indignant mob gathers. In their shouts we can hear just how closely they are allied to their French counterparts; in their dispersal we can see the difference:

The populace, to an incredible number, had assembled before the outer gate, threatening to demolish the Asylum. With one voice the multitude shouted out, 'Down with the bastile! [*sic*] – down with the bastile! – no bastiles for Englishmen!'

The magistrate, apprehensive of mischief, caused a chair to be brought out of the house, mounted the rostrum, and harangued the crowd. He admonished them to order, and to allow the law to revenge the cause of the injured gentleman.[46]

Could the Parisian revolutionaries of July 1789 have been as easily routed, we are forced to ask. No, and it is in that recognition, and the solace it brings, that lies a principal motivation for anti-Jacobinism's representation of revolution.

In the Britain of the novels, of course, there was no oppression or, if there was, it could be eradicated by legal means, but it remains clear that the main thrust of conservative fiction, perhaps all fiction, in presenting the mob, the revolutionary crowd, even the plantation slaves of

Jamaica, was to show them unjustifiable in their insurgence, no matter how grievous the oppression under which they had been forced to exist. A stage further, however, was to show those grievances themselves to be a sham, to be no more than a pretext for the machinations of miscreants desirous only of pursuing their own agenda through the incitement of the crowd. If revolutionary activity was truly threatening, after all, it was because it had a genuine motivation, a real and understandable agenda demanding consideration. For George Walker, the campaign to show that the mob never had any semblance of an appreciable agenda could extend to rewriting the Gordon Riots of 1780, which (with a few contemporary modifications) featured in his *Vagabond* of 1799. While the mob is shouting 'No Popery!' and 'Lord George Gordon for ever', its leaders are attempting to enlist Frederick, our philosophical protagonist, in their cause by revealing that their real motives have nothing whatsoever to do with their anti-Catholic bombast. 'It is our watch-word,' confides the revolutionary. 'The ignorant believe they are fighting for religion, but we guide them and direct where the storm shall fall. The passions of men must be raised, their rational senses must be confounded with terrific reports, before the mass can be roused.'[47] And we find the same exposé of the gulf between revolutionary rhetoric and the real reasons for rebellion in *The History of Sir George Warrington* (1797), the hero of which is duped into leading a crowd apparently bent on securing the higher wages which their standard of living evidently necessitates. It turns out, though, that the incendiary Davenport has shown Warrington only the hovels of those made poor by their own debauchery and immoderation. Indeed, the mob soon becomes ungovernable, and, despite Warrington's protests, sets off to attack the house of the local squire, Mr Annesley, with no intention other than wilful vandalism. This is exactly as Davenport had planned, for the whole scheme has been designed by him only to revenge himself on Annesley. Both the mob and its pilot, Davenport, have their own motivation, neither of which has the least connection with their stated aim of relieving the poverty, which in fact does not even exist.[48]

Characteristically, not only is the mob in *George Warrington* led by ill-designing individuals, but, having no will of its own, it disperses when Warrington is felled in a duel, his conqueror, a Captain Montague, apparently having only to appear for the mob to vanish. These were two parallel techniques, both of strategic significance for anti-Jacobinism's attempt to undermine the validity of revolutionary activity. If it was comforting to find that mobs could be effortlessly dispersed by individuals, generally the representatives of legitimate authority, it was equally reassuring to show the mob as merely a tool of villainous individuals, manipulating it for their own ends. By decoding the mob as nothing but the mask for individual wickedness, a much more comprehensible crime, and one which had always been, and could continue to be, opposed with a solid front of reprehension, novelists were able to emasculate revolution, certainly as a coherent ideological expression of discontent. With the succession of powerful historical figures coming to dominate the Revolution in France, and at just the point when Terror chased out hope, this was a method that novelists could easily apply also to events across the Channel. Marat, and more especially Robespierre, frequently figured in fiction, the *sans-culottes* becoming little but an extension of their wills. John Moore even opened his *Mordaunt* with the assertion that the Revolution, like the St Bartholomew's Day massacre before it, had not been the result of the mob as had so often been pretended, but of the malevolence of a few individuals, the Jacobin leaders and Catherine de Medici respectively, merely using the pretence of liberty and religion – ideas designed to appeal to a mob.[49] Exactly who Moore thought had been pretending that the mob had been at the forefront of the Revolution is difficult to imagine. Certainly it was not Burke, who gave his readers a few *banditti* but no organised revolutionary crowd, nor was it any of the other respected contemporary commentators on the Revolution (Moore included) since, as has often been pointed out, it was only really following Carlyle's *French Revolution* (1837) that the mob became an independent entity and the chief agent of the action. If it was anyone, it was the anti-Jacobin novelists who placed the mob at the centre of the Revolution in the 1790s, and yet, in almost every case, behind every mob, a depraved villain lurked.[50]

Indeed, Charles Lucas had no doubt that all the evils of the Revolution stemmed from that one moment when 'private villains undertake to manage public good', but it is Charlotte Dacre who provides perhaps the most vivid picture of this kind of trespassing by nefarious individuals with private purposes into the public sphere of French politics, a transgression that had brought on all the horrors of the Revolution. 'You remind me,' says the object of a libertine's attempt at seduction in *The Confession of the Nun of St Omer* (1805),

of those sanguinary rebels who sought to hurl a peaceful monarch from his throne to establish a monster of their own creation, whose vices and whose indolence render them obnoxious to society, and who willingly profited by the general devastation to attain a guilty eminence on the mangled bodies of their fellow creatures; blood alone could satisfy their thirsting souls; heated by dwelling on the fancied injustice they experienced, they longed to wade through the purple current, to gorge their hearts with murder, and sink to their own gloomy level those whom they could not rise to equal.[51]

She can see, in other words, no distinction between private and public vice, the one inevitably leading to the other. And in the anti-Jacobin novelists' rewriting of it, the Revolution became a series of events that came about purely because Marat craved the love of Adelaide de Narbonne (he forces through legislation 'compelling women of rank, birth or riches, to engage in marriage with persons of the lowest origins' – like himself – on pain of death), or because the *ci-devant* Marquis de Chevreville desired Eugenie de Brinboc (he persuades the Republic's executive committee to imprison her and force her to submit to him or 'bow to the statue of liberty').[52] Revolutionary legislation, the guillotine, the Terror, were all merely means to these ends.

Above all, the manipulation of the mob by individual villains showed that nothing had changed with the Revolution, that the same crimes were still being perpetrated by the same men, and sometimes women, only the means being slightly different. In *The Parisian* (1794), for instance, we see the mob playing more or less the rôle of a *lettre de cachet*. The malevolent Comte pins the murder of the mob's darling on our hero, knowing that they will lynch him.[53] And, lest we should be tempted to think that it was unusual for a nobleman to manage the Revolution like this, Moore provides an explanation. His count, in *Mordaunt*, we first encounter as 'one of the most furious against any kind of concession on the part of the government, or the least redress of any of the grievances complained of ... He declared that nothing ought to be granted to the *canaille*; and he considered nine-tenths of the nation as *canaille*.' But once the Revolution broke, or gained an unstoppable momentum rather, he changed his language and his attire: 'This alteration was more and more remarkable in the progress of the revolution, until at last the change was so complete, that those whom he had formerly stigmatized as *canaille* he now distinguished by the title of *peuple souverain*. He altered his dress as well as his language, and assumed in both the style of the *sans-culottes*. . .'[54] It hardly needs to be noted that the changes were cosmetic only, and as the story of the beautiful Marquise whom the Count has been persecuting, develops, it becomes equally obvious that what his new language and clothing signify – the rule of the people – is also no different from the previous state of affairs. Not only could villainy thrive under both old and new régimes, but both régimes, as if the Revolution had never occurred, were in themselves equally corrupt, equally brutal and equally tyrannical.

No one made this clearer than Moore, who having already shown aristocrats metamorphosing into democrats to suit their own ends, was also quick to present the process in reverse, Jacobins becoming, once in power, merely a reiteration of the tyrants they had ostensibly sought to overthrow. In one of the periodic potted histories of events in France scattered through *Mordaunt*, Moore has his hero offer the vision of a full 360 degree revolution between *ancien régime* and Terror. 'What could be more apparent than the grievances of the ancient government of France,' Mordaunt asks, before detailing the stages of the Revolution as if it were a relay race, the baton passing from 'those who attempted to remedy them' to the Girondins, many of whom, though inexperienced, 'meant well to their country', and eventually to 'a gang of the most horrid ruffians that ever were let loose on any nation'; so that 'France within the space of a few months, experienced greater calamities than she had suffered in the course of centuries.'[55] Charles Lucas took up the theme, arguing in an odd little message-in-a-bottle history of the Revolution set into his *Infernal Quixote* (1801) as a paper found by a character in the lining of a new portmanteau, that each article found wrong with the *ancien régime* had been superseded, but by a worse oppression. The 'old, rusty fetters' had gone, but were replaced by others, 'new and gilded, which rankled to the very bone'; the 'tedious formalities of the law' had been supplanted by a state in which suspicion was followed by death without a word, and in which 'slow justice' had been replaced by 'hasty murder'; and in the place of days of voluntary fasting and other 'unmeaning ceremonies' of the Church, France now has nothing but ridiculous rites and days of starvation made obligatory by want.[56] France's monarchy, as Smith put it in *The Banished Man*, 'was exchanged for anarchy infinitely more destructive and more *tyrannical*', a word echoed by so many anti-Jacobin novelists, and surely deliberately meant to jar with the stated aims of the Revolution, and a point she illustrates by having her hero discover a victim of the revolutionaries left to that most despotic of fates, a slow death in an oubliette.[57] Perhaps, rather oddly, it is Sayer, writing in 1791, who provides the best statement of this attempt to represent the Revolution as undeserving of our concern or sympathy, let alone support, because of its return to despotism. His paranoid prediction that when 'distinctions are abolished, degrees are levelled, and a whole body of established nobility is ... exchanged for another, whose sole pretension to preference consists in their own assertion', then 'Amurath succeeds Amurath, the tyrant is changed but the tyranny continues', perfectly sums up the attempt to rationalise the Revolution out of any possibility of being countenanced by showing it to be nothing more than a restatement of the *ancien régime*, the loathing of which had long since become habitual to the true Briton.[58]

The character making this observation was in fact an Englishman, a representative of Sayer and his readers, witnessing on their behalf events in France. Or rather he was not attempting an accurate account of the Revolution, nor even what Sayer thought was happening, but was articulating what Sayer thought his readers ought to be told was passing in France, and, additionally, prescribing how they ought to respond. Sayer's onlooker was not a solitary voyeur, but comprised part of what must have been a sizeable community of fictional Britons abroad in France, all saying much the same sort of thing, establishing what their authors must have hoped would shape the impression their fiction would make on their readers. This should remind us that the object of any anti-Jacobin novelist depicting the Revolution was, above all, to encourage their readers to deplore the example the French had set and to appreciate the contrasting state in which they were living. This purpose is plainly demonstrated by the peroration to *Lindor and Adelaïde* in which the worthy Prieur tells an Englishman about to return home to bid his countrymen compare the scenes of Revolutionary France Sayer has presented with 'the blessed and peaceful state of their own country'. Let them contrast,

their riches with our poverty, their strength with our weakness, their credit with our distrust, their security with our fear; and though last, not least, the sacred and inviolable majesty of the law, with the savage and tumultuous wilderness of licensed injustice. Let them cast their eyes over a country, whose rich and fertile prospect gratifies them with a view of unbounded prosperity; prosperity, that almost realizes the prophecies of heavenly bliss, bliss not yet to be enjoyed by man; a land flowing with milk and honey!

Let them ponder these things well in their minds, and from a sense of our misfortunes, learn to place a just value on their own happiness.[59]

We should remember, in other words, that representations of the French Revolution, and insurrection elsewhere, in the decade or so following its actual occurrence were essentially a screen on which could be projected domestic anxieties.

Of course, this fits in rather neatly with Gerald Newman and Linda Colley's suggestions that notions of Frenchness helped to define British or English self-identity. Newman has noted that anti-Gallican 'perceptions' around 1800 bore scant affinity to any genuine observations, but were primarily useful 'as a convenient and uniquely powerful icon in domestic political, moral and social debate', a point splendidly borne out, as we have been seeing, by the anti-Jacobin novel.[60] But we have also seen that there were two distinct methods authors were using to represent revolution to a British audience, both of which were designed to encourage a vociferous anti-Jacobinism. On the one hand, it was the common attempt of many authors to diminish the threat posed to Britain by the French and their Revolution, and in particular, its ideological menace. Novelists attempted to deprive the Revolution of its status as a legitimate, coherent or even revolutionary movement and on occasion went so far as to fill their fiction with confident assertions that what they saw in France could never have happened in Britain. In as apprehensive a novel as *Lindor and Adelaïde*, Sayer strove to spur British resolve by having a French *émigrée* record that 'the English are, and always have been affectionately attached to their Monarchs, and loyal to a degree of enthusiasm', so that, following infractions in 1649 and 1688, this patriotic fervour 'is now revived in a manner that protects the Throne from every attack'.[61]

On the other hand, there were those novelists who were anxious to display the very real danger of the Revolution, both ideological and physical, in a way designed to dispel complacency and incite a salutary anxiety. The horrors of the Revolution, which we have already seen represented so hysterically, were recruited precisely because they could serve so effectively as a grim warning to Britons. 'Let Britain shudder at the scene before her, and grasp her blessings the closer' was the message Clara Reeve was proud to be propagating through her fiction in 1793, a sentiment periodically reappearing in prefaces, or the statements of sagacious Frenchmen – as in *Adolphus de Biron*:

Look, therefore, ye Sons of Britain, on the awful Scene, which France now presents to your View, with Sentiments worthy of your Character. Regard the passing Events in awful Silence, and turn our Calamities to your own Advantage, by a due Thankfulness to Providence for the Blessings you enjoy under your well-formed and excellent Constitution.[62]

What these blessings were, precisely, was a point open to debate, different authors suggesting different candidates to be extolled as the single thing that had done most to keep Britain revolution-free. Whilst the liberal Mary Robinson thought it was free speech, the more puritanical George Walker thought it Britain's strict, and possibly even a little repressive, legal process and the evangelical John Cunningham was sure it was an established religion.[63] But the point was that these precious institutions, whatever they were, needed to be maintained and bolstered, no matter what some foolish reformers might be saying.

This was very necessary scaremongering, but would distanced depictions of revolution in France or any fictionalised other-place be sufficient to jolt Britons out of their complacency? Perhaps not, and although many novelists continued to scruple to depict revolution ravaging Britain – still a dangerously intoxicating theme, especially given the novel's supposed readership – representations of revolution were gradually brought closer and closer to home. The novel-reader was ultimately never actually vouchsafed a quite *contemporary*, or quite *British* revolution, but several novels came close. Naturally, the most immediate trope that presented itself, without setting revolution quite in the present, was that of the Gordon Riots of 1780, the last great explosion of anything resembling revolutionary activity in Britain. In George Walker's *Vagabond*, it is immediately obvious that he was aiming to show his audience exactly what they, and not some fictional French aristocrat, had to fear from revolution. The scene was London, fire ravaging every part of it, 'the flames chasing the distracted people from street to street' – and we readers flee with them, taken on a grisly tour by the lurid imagination of Frederick,

to see the rage of lust despoiling those disdainful beauties, whose love heretofore was only to be won by cringing; to see trembling tyrants biting the dust, and drinking their own blood as it mingled in the kennels; to hear amidst the uproar the thunder of cannons, the whistling of bullets, the clashing of swords, the tumbling of houses, the groans of the wounded, the cries of the conquerors; and see, amidst the blazing and red-hot ruins, the sons of Freedom and Liberty waving the three-coloured banners dripping with the blood of their enemies, and hailing the everlasting Rights of Man!!![64]

This was powerful stuff, and meant to tell the reader that, if he loved his wife and daughter, if she cherished her husband and son, if they wished to preserve their life, property and virtue, then there could be no quarter given to even those mild 'new philosophers' like the misguided Frederick, for they were traffickers in revolution.

Though Walker was nominally depicting the Gordon Riots, not the French Revolution, the parallel was obvious, not least because of his concentration of the one specific incident that they had in common – the storming of Newgate, or nine years later, of the Bastille. Ronald Paulson has made the point that for many in Britain, the Fall of the Bastille *was* the French Revolution, but this was not the only reason for its being taken up as the perfect synecdoche of revolution by a number of novelists, for it was an incident, which perhaps more than any other in the course of the Revolution, brought home the real menace of insurrection to the average British novel-reader.[65] The image of the state's chief prison being attacked by the mob, its prisoners, a nation's most depraved criminals, being let loose into the night, was exceedingly potent (whether it had actually happened or not). Partly, this was because it had taken place in Britain as recently as 1780, and so if any kind of revolutionary activity was conceivable, then this was it, but also, its propagandising potential lay in the fact that convicts freed from prison could be in no way considered philosophical or political, but were just ordinary lawbreakers, common criminals, whom anyone and everyone might denounce without compunction.

Walker chose to bring home the realities of revolution to his readers by demonstrating how much they had to lose in terms of property, for the dregs of society released from Newgate in *The Vagabond* set off to burgle London on a massive scale. The anonymous author of *Dorothea; or, A Ray of the New Light* (1801), however, determined that even this threat was not sufficiently alarming to startle her readers out of any thought of a replica revolution. First, she brought the revolutionary scene even more up to date, her reiteration of the Bastille's fall set in a vague mid 1790s Ireland, although of course bearing unmistakable echoes of the Irish Rebellion of 1798. Then she showed her readers the miniature revolution in all its gory detail, starting with the crowd preventing justice from being carried out by seizing from the scaffold several rebels sentenced for their insurgent activities, and from there, proceeding to yet worse outrages:

The populace exulting in their conquest, no longer knew any bounds to their fury; charmed with this first effort they resolved to proceed in the great work of emancipation; and for this purpose, turning their whole strength against the doors of the prison, the barriers gave way, and the inhabitants whom prudence, policy, or justice had secluded within its walls, being freed from their thraldom, so many more citizens were added to the population of Kilkenny.

As if this was not unsettling enough, these ruffians, like the common criminals they are, a point explicitly emphasised, escape into the country determined to pillage the first house they come to. It is a pretty cottage, the very seat of domestic felicity and bucolic contentment. Having picked up a smattering of Jacobin philosophy, their leader encourages their plan – 'the good things of the world are common stock, upon which one man has as valid a title as another, to draw what he wants' – and they quickly resolve to 'exemplify their doctrine on the poor farmer', killing the only man amongst them who objects. Having stormed the house and stolen its contents, in a genuinely shocking scene, they murder the farmer, his wife and their three children, a crime given no Jacobinical justification whatsoever, emphasising the evil, rather than the folly, of anyone abetting revolution.[66]

The Irish Rebellion was the starkest portent a novelist could brandish in front of his or her too nonchalant readers. By sending their villainous new philosophers from mainland Britain, the real sphere of their plots against government and heroines alike, to Ireland to foment revolution, authors were demonstrating, at just one remove, the inevitable results of their schemes should they remain unchecked. Charles Lucas' *Infernal Quixote* (1801) showed this even more overtly than *Dorothea*. Its anti-hero, Lord James Marauder, adopting the pseudonym Patrick McGinnis, involves himself in the Irish Rebellion, and Lucas uses his story to investigate and expose just how close to revolution Ireland, and by implication Britain, came in 1798. Lucas uses McGinnis' involvement with the United Irishmen to reveal everything about them, all frighteningly efficient, from their organisation – half a dozen pages explaining the structure of their executive and its sub-committees – to their propaganda, which thankfully, Lucas says, helped to betray their plans to the ministry. Through McGinnis we discover their 'real intentions', hidden from their followers and known only to the leaders, which of course transpire to be only 'the introduction of that no-principle of the French'.[67] And through all this, Lucas seems to have just two objectives – to display what ordinary people had to fear from rebellion, and just exactly how close Ireland had come to full-scale revolution. Thus we learn of how, under McGinnis' leadership, 'large parties of the natives sally forth at night, and plunder their helpless neighbours'; of the thousand well-disciplined men, with McGinnis at their head, seated on as fine a horse as any in the King's service, who can sack any town they choose in their search of arms and ammunition; and thus we find that it was only the pusillanimity of their high command that prevented the rising becoming general. As Lucas pointedly puts it, 'the ambitious prospects of the hero seemed to meet with no check but the timidity of his own party', a rebuke to Government and the British people alike.[68]

Dorothea and *The Infernal Quixote* drafted in the Irish Rebellion in 1801, enlisting it in their campaign to preserve Britain from the threat of revolution. Over a decade later, the Rebellion of 1798 was still providing an exhilarating backdrop for fiction, but manifestly without the same degree of didactic intent. Caroline Lamb's *Glenarvon* of 1816, for instance, was set in Ireland in the late 1790s and featured a rather ill-defined mob of United Irishmen, apparently bent on revolution, fading in and out of the action according to the exploits of the protagonists of the novel, the leaders and adversaries of the mob (as and when, that is, they could take time off from their more pressing domestic tribulations). And if in Lamb's novel the Rebellion was little more than an historical landscape around which the heroes and heroines could wend their way, in Eaton Stannard Barrett's *Heroine* of 1813 the rebels made their incursion into the fiction for predominantly comic effect, appearing as a huddle of 'gentlemen with rusty superfine on their backs, and with the longest words in the world', which they used to inveigle the honest Jerry Sullivan into their plots, as he later recounted, persuading him 'that old Ireland was going to ruin; I forget how now, but I know I had the whole story pat at that time; and the end of it was, that I became a United Irishman'.[69]

Since it seems so unlikely that either Lamb or Barrett was representing revolution for any overtly ideological purpose, especially when we contrast their fiction with that of Lucas or the other ardent anti-Jacobins of the two or three years on either side of 1800, certain questions naturally arise. Given that revolution or rebellion could seemingly be presented in the 1810s without any overt didacticism, should any representation of revolution a decade or so earlier be regarded as a necessarily ideological or didactic statement? Is it, in other words, over-interpreting these texts to insist that any representation of the horrors of Revolution in France, or elsewhere for that matter, whether in 1801 or a dozen years later, must, or even can, be assessed as a deliberate expression of anti-Jacobinism? Ultimately, of course, short of finding the explicit testimony of the authors, we will never be able to discover which novels were overtly and primarily anti-Jacobin and which employed representations of revolution for other, perhaps more purely *literary*, purposes (and even such testimony would not guarantee that readers complied with these authorial intentions). To search for an answer remains a valid undertaking however, and an illuminating one, for though it must fail to reveal a clear dividing line between deliberately didactic, and what we might call 'scenic', anti-Jacobin depictions of revolution, a certain symbiosis quickly becomes apparent, which once identified, appears to be a characteristic of all, even the most propagandistic, conservative fiction of the 1790s and 1800s. Additionally, and perhaps more importantly, it also becomes perceptible that once representations of revolution had come to be drafted into an anti-Jacobin campaign, they stayed enlisted, even in that fiction which lacked the conspicuous and wilful didacticism which had originally inspired their appearance.

Firstly, though, it might be helpful to consider when, if indeed it did occur, the overtly anti-Jacobin import of these fictional representations of revolution could be deemed actually to have drained away. It is interesting to find that as early as 1804, and from as committed an anti-Jacobin as Robert Bisset, there is an example of the Irish Rebellion being used in a combination of the purely plot-assisting manner of *Glenarvon* and the comic vein of *The Heroine*, both of which uses are conspicuous in the adventures of Roger O'Rourke, the rather picaresque villain of his *Modern Literature*. Fleeing from the law, Roger, the sometime Jacobin and Methodist, winds up in Ireland in the early 1790s, where he declares himself a Catholic, and 'ready and willing to become an united Irishman'. He pursues his career of infamy, pretending to be a Catholic priest, but reverting to Methodist minister when it suits him, traversing the country 'confessing the women; and exhorting the men to what he called the emancipation of Ireland', but just as often defrauding widows of their last pennies or perpetrating highway robberies, for which offence he is at last apprehended, tried and hanged.[70] Roger's stint in Ireland has been both diverting and has allowed Bisset to dispose of his villain, as the plot demanded, quickly, easily and even with an edifying moral. It has also been broadly didactic in the context of the Revolution crisis, linking the rebels, targets of many aspersions, with a rogue in the traditional mould. It is, in other words, a half-way house between the propaganda of Lucas, say, and the ambivalence of Lamb.

So too was Frances Burney's *Wanderer* of 1814, as the work of Margaret Doody has intimated. She calls it 'in a sense a novel of the '90s', an ideological novel, but also likens it to the 'modern historical novel' of Scott and later authors. Burney evidently fills her novel with a distinctive kind of anti-Jacobin didacticism, but as Doody's analysis reveals, also saw the Revolution as providing the novelist with an invaluable source of incidents, opinions and indicators, which could be no end of use to their plots, characterisations and moral purpose.[71] It goes almost without saying that the Revolution could, as was the case with *The Wanderer*, provide a wonderful basis for a novel, propelling a forlorn, friendless and fascinating heroine into the wilderness of mixed dangers and delights which constituted the natural province of the novel. But it also provided authors with a marvellous opportunity to test the mettle of their protagonists, to delineate their moral worthiness as it intermeshed with events in France, and to add colour, weightiness, a certain thrill and a firm historical location to their fiction. Stanhope's *Nun of Santa Maria di Tindaro* combines all this perfectly, the Revolution impinging on the novel only as it affects its protagonists, tearing our hero away from his beloved when he returns to France to avenge the fate of the 'hapless Louis', and marking out quickly and simply just who deserves our sympathy. The heroes we find exalted for a special type of loyal sensibility: 'Individual sufferings are nothing,' exclaims Eugenius, 'as the tears of anguish rolled down his cheeks; loyalty and patriotism ought to be the *first* feeling which warms, and the *last* feeling which expires in the heart of man.'[72] The vestiges of anti-Jacobinism very clearly remain, but subservient to the literary advantages which could accrue to novelists through their recruitment of the Revolution. It was no coincidence that the horrors of the Revolution became a frequent subject of fiction in an age renowned for its fascination with the 'horrid novel', a point borne out by Catherine Morland's famous conflation of the two in *Northanger Abbey* (1818).[73]

It was, however, in this very space between propaganda and the non-partisan novel (however abstract a concept that may be) that, to varying degrees, all the fiction we have been considering was positioned. Just as even the most apparently disinterested novelist to include revolution in his or her fiction could not do so without making some kind of ideological commitment inherent in its production, let alone its reception, so not even the most vehement, or blatant, of anti-Jacobin novelists could include anti-Jacobin propaganda without it being in some way enmeshed in the fiction. The balance between an apparently calculated and an apparently inadvert anti-Jacobinism did tilt over the decade or so after 1800, but even the most determinedly anti-Jacobin novelists had been content to include representations of revolution for the 'literary', rather than ideological, benefits that could accrue. For instance, if in *The Wanderer* and *The Nun of Santa Maria di Tindaro* we saw the French intruding into the fiction only to designate the virtues of the protagonists, there could be no more flagrant example of this same literary exploitation of the political climate than in Pye's classically anti-Jacobin *Aristocrat* of 1799. As a consequence of his Frenchified education, Sir Edward Eaglefield has on a number of occasions been embarrassed by his inability to perform the offices expected of an Englishman (which consist of fixing saddles and rescuing damsels), but he is determined to learn these necessary skills, becoming particularly fired at the idea of soldiery. His chance to prove himself reformed comes not, as before, when a saddle slips or a companion falls down a cliff, but when a party of French 'corsairs' (this is *circa* 1792) lands a mile or two from his residence in Scotland, loots the house and takes the whole party staying there hostage aboard their ship – save for Sir Edward, who fled on their approach. Or so, to our heroine's chagrin, it had appeared. But in fact, he had run off to summon a local detachment of the Royal Navy, who, together with Sir Edward, capture the ship, and save his friends and their possessions. His reformation is complete.[74]

No more contrived episode could be conceived, yet this should not surprise us for the Revolution as plot device was a constant component of the most committed anti-Jacobin fiction, bearing a didactic burden, but often very evidently primarily designed with the intention of shaping the storyline rather than the readers' political convictions. Occasionally it shows through with astonishing blatancy. 'By this time the troubles in France had gained such a crisis,' writes Sarah Wood, when it was time to pitch her protagonists off to Britain, 'that it was necessary for every friend to order, for every lover of peace and religion, to leave that ill-fated nation', and it is only as if as an afterthought that she adds a few explanatory details: 'The principles of the Illuminata [*sic*] triumphed; anarchy, confusion and bloodshed succeeded.'[75] The same generalised but highly reprehended Revolution was used by Mary Pilkington in her *New Tales of the Castle* (1800), a novel for children, which starts with a brief description of the awful fate of Louis XVI and his family before launching the young and ingenuous protagonists off into the series of *émigré* adventures which make up the book.[76]

Even specific events could be used to hurry along the storyline. The fall of Robespierre, for instance, was a recurrent plot device, used in Robinson's *Natural Daughter* to secure our heroine's release from a Parisian prison and to punish her sister, the last of Robespierre's mistresses. In a novel of almost ten years later, the anonymous *Memoirs of Female Philosophers* (1808), the fall of Robespierre is again appropriated to release one of its allegorical heroines, Allegrina, from the Abbaye prison (although bizarrely she and her fellow inmates had enjoyed their time behind bars, Allegrina having taught them to dance and draw, and forbidden them to mention the guillotine).[77] And in Mangin's *George the Third* (1807), the same frivolous note also sounds. Its hero, George Ardent, gets himself imprisoned in Revolutionary France (there are so many prisoners that his gaol is an ex-cathedral), finds himself selected, seemingly at random, for the guillotine, is stripped and bound, taken to the Place de la Révolution, even to the foot of the scaffold – but all the time seems more bemused than frightened or horrified – and then reveals:

This was, in short, a day never to be forgotten in the annals of Paris, or in mine; – the memorable one which produced the downfall of Robespierre, gave security to the National Convention, and life to the son of the rector of Oakley [i.e. Ardent]. Somebody else, however, must write the history of the French people, whilst I proceed on my own.[78]

Despite its light-heartedness, this was still the Revolution in all its horror, lacking in explicit didacticism perhaps, but still definitely anti-Jacobin. And this was true of more or less all novels representing the Revolution ten or so years after it happened. They might have been historical novels, because they were depicting events of several years previously and because they had left behind the sense of crisis which had originally put the Revolution into fiction, but they were still, implicitly in their depictions, ideological novels, having absorbed unchallenged the anti-Jacobinism of previous representations.

In fact, the balance between ideological representation of revolution and merely 'scenic' depictions constitutes a sort of dynamic equilibrium, constantly shifting within novels, and from one novel to another, as well as over time. At one end of the scale is *Lindor and Adelaïde* or *Adolphus de Biron*, perhaps, and at the other, *Glenarvon* or *The Nun of Santa Maria di Tindaro*, with all the other novels somewhere in between. Never did anti-Jacobin didacticism come completely to dominate a novel to the exclusion of plot, character or the conventions of fiction, but nor, for a generation, could that anti-Jacobinism entirely fade away. A knowledge of the horror of revolution could be presupposed not only because the Revolution in France *circa* 1792–4, historically speaking, had self-evidently proved itself an abomination, but because this interpretation had become enshrined in fictionalised representations of it, had actually *become* the Revolution, to all intents and purposes, for authors and audience writing and reading in the twenty years after the Terror had subsided. This was the success of the anti-Jacobin novel. Representation of revolution remained imbued with conservatism long after those authors including it in their novels had forgotten why it had originally been put there.

CHAPTER 3

The new philosophy

This volume to the reader's eye displays
The infernal conduct of abandoned man;
When French Philosophy infects his ways,
And pours contempt on Heav'n's eternal plan;
Reversing order, truth, and ev'ry good,
And whelming worlds, with ruin's awful flood.
Epigraph to Sarah Wood's *Julia, and the Illuminated Baron.*
A Novel (1800)

Anti-Jacobinism, insofar as it can be ascribed a coherent identity at all, was more propaganda than ideology. This, indeed, was its great tactical strength, for in defining itself purely in terms of what it was not, in terms of what it was opposed to, its protagonists evaded the necessity of having to formulate any doctrine of their own, a doctrine from which independently minded members of its potentially vast constituency might demur. Any attempt to assess anti-Jacobinism, then, immediately finds itself trying to define what that Jacobinism was that provoked anti-Jacobinism into being, or rather what conservatives thought it was. It is at this point that the seeming simplicity of the apparently polarised debate on the Revolution in France begins to dissolve.

Much has been written about radicalism in Britain in the 1790s, but this is not to say that a congruous ideology of radicalism has ever been discerned. Indeed, Jacobinism's heterogeneity is the most recurrent theme of those surveys which have been undertaken.[1] Certainly, no single conception of Jacobinism has been found that might have been cheerfully subscribed to by both radicals and conservatives. Gary Kelly's suggestion that British Jacobinism was, like anti-Jacobinism, defined by its opponents, though observably true, only complicates the issue still further, formulating an equation which runs neither way, a notional anti-Jacobinism defining Jacobinism and a notional Jacobinism

65

defining anti-Jacobinism.[2] The result was a sort of war of shadows, the anti-Jacobins in particular starting at a spectre of their own imagining, a spectre which portended a significantly more revolutionary destiny than almost any corporeal radical would actually have sought.

Jacobinism, from anyone's point of view, was less an ideology than an insult. If not entirely meaningless, then it was so broad a term that it could encompass any transgression against the institutions or manners of the *status quo*. In religious terms only, for instance, denominations right across the spiritual spectrum could be reviled with the label. Thus, whilst Robert Bisset in 1800 claimed that Jacobinism and the strict *Calvinism* of the Scottish 'seceders' were united, Samuel Horsley could insist in the same year that 'The Jacobins of this country, I very much fear, are at this moment making a tool of *Methodism*', and George III dismiss the idea of *Catholic* Emancipation a year later as 'the most Jacobinical thing I ever heard of!'[3] Even in the reign of the next monarch but one, the original Jacobins by then an extinct species and 'revolutionary' political reform actually about to materialise, the word was still in use, not merely as a meaningless insult, but as a sin grave enough to be transmitted through three generations to deny Ben Brierley a dish of beef stew at the charity feast laid on to celebrate William IV's coronation, simply because 'thy gronfeyther's a Jacobin'.[4]

Back in 1799, when Francis Wollaston had seen fit actually to attempt a definition of Jacobinism, he came up with a matrix of all that was nefarious. The evolutionary process he charts, evidently much influenced by the Illuminati conspiracy theories of the time, reads like a travesty of a thoroughbred's pedigree, or some infernal formula for conjuring a demon:

To the liberty and equality of original free-masonry; to the fierce rancour of Voltaire and his self-called philosophers against Jesus Christ and his religion; to the democratic principles of Rousseau, and his visionary schemes about the origin of all government; these delegates [he is talking of the Illuminati] added, the rage of Weishaupt and his pretended more enlightened followers, against all kings, or rather against all who under any title bear any rule among men. The fiery spirit of the French, kindled at once into a Flame. The names of free-mason, of philosophers, of friends to a social compact, of illuminé or enlightened, were from that instant all absorbed in the one name of Jacobin.[5]

Two things are apparent here that are fundamental to any understanding of the Jacobin threat. Wollaston's identification of many different but interconnecting strands of Jacobinism is one, and had its expression most commonly in the envisaging of Jacobinism as Hydra-headed, both in the sense that the menace emanated from so many directions, and that the monster seemed to grow more fearsome the more it was fought. A second point to note is that Wollaston was ostensibly, although rather vaguely, talking of the authentic Jacobins, the militant Revolutionaries who had originally met in the Dominican Monastery of St Roch, and thus was doing his best to provide a text-book anti-Jacobin answer to the question of what caused the Revolution in France. Revolution, in other words, was caused by Jacobinism. Revolution was not an evil to be combated in itself so much as an effect to be prevented by striking at the cause – Jacobinism.

Nowhere do we see both these convictions more fully than in Mary Anne Burges' highly schematised novel, *The Progress of the Pilgrim Good-Intent, in Jacobinical Times* (1800). In her Bunyan-inspired topographical representation of the ideological stresses of the times, revolution is a mountain, dangerous and forbidding indeed, but neutral in itself and always having existed, and it is only when the forces of Jacobinism scale the mountain that its horrors become apparent and palpable. Moreover, Burges' design, again like Wollaston's matrix, features Jacobinism – or rather 'Mr JACOBINISM' – as only one part of the project to overset all that is good, albeit its leading influence. All the forces of iniquity combine to launch their assaults, as on 'Mount *Sabbath*', for instance:

in front it was attacked by the army of BLOOD-MEN, led on by JACOBINISM, their chief captain, who brought battering-rams and scaling-ladders to take it by storm; on one side a troop of the followers of FASHION assailed it from a great distance with missile weapons; and on the other, Mr PHILOSOPHY himself, at the head of a company of pioneers, was at work on a mine, whereby he hoped to sap the foundations, and overthrow the walls.[6]

Here we see three of the principal heads of the Hydra – the 'BLOOD-MEN', who in Burges' scheme are those villains who lead the ascent of 'Mount *Revolution*' simply for the love of discord (the names of a few of their chiefs are 'RAPINE', 'EXTORTION', 'OPPRESSION' and 'MURDER'), the devotees of 'FASHION' (amongst whom are numbered 'AMUSEMENT', 'EXCESS', 'PRODIGALITY' and the other inhabitants of the 'groves of *dissipation*'), and 'Mr PHILOSOPHY', patron of all the vices and keeper of the temples of 'ATHEISM' and 'ANARCHY'. This dreadful phalanx, determined to precipitate the revolution, is implicit in the work of all the anti-Jacobins. For most authors though, these elements are fused, not individually identifiable as they are in Burges' highly schematised rendering.

Indeed, this fusion of the elements of Jacobinism into one mythic, but not quite imaginary, monster is central to the anti-Jacobin campaign as it took shape in the majority of novels. They had a name for it too – new, or sometimes modern, philosophy – an umbrella term to describe, or rather comprehend without describing, Jacobinism as it appeared to them in Britain. It was a term that came to cover all the strands of the Jacobin matrix, all the varieties of poison that Wollaston had identified in France, and which were seeping into Britain. Just as Wollaston had identified Voltaire, Rousseau and Weishaupt – philosophers all – as the main springs of Jacobinism in France, so it was philosophers in Britain who were found guilty of importing the lethal French toxin, who were cast as the real indigenous exponents of Jacobinism and became, in effect, the metaphorical equivalents of Robespierre, Danton and their associates, the original Jacobins of France. Such figures, as we saw in the last chapter with novelists' portrayals of their French counterparts, might be Jacobins either out of deluded conviction or selfish malice, but their currency, the rhetoric of their propaganda, was still philosophy. In the next chapter I shall be examining those Jacobins whom novelists depicted as having adopted new philosophy merely because it suited their transient needs and desires. Here, though, I shall be surveying what this new philosophy actually was, and indeed, this is a question which ought chiefly to concern us, for what must immediately become apparent is that no anti-Jacobin had any clearer idea of what new philosophy was than they had of what constituted a Jacobin. The relationship between the thought and writing of Rousseau and Voltaire, Price and Paine, Godwin and Wollstonecraft, and novelists' conception of new philosophy was stretched to say the least. New philosophy was the creation of anti-Jacobinism, and as such it displays, in the most cogent form we have available to us, the concerns of conservatives in the grip and aftermath of the Revolution crisis.

One of the factors that grants the anti-Jacobin novel the status of a significant and coherent class of novel, and allows the many individual texts which comprise that class to be usefully treated in aggregate, is the extensive use of the term and concept of 'new philosophy'. Furthermore, so implicit, and therefore so vague, are the delineations of new philosophy given by individual authors that it is only by amassing their separate hints on the subject that a distinct definition begins to emerge. There undoubtedly existed a whole host of different ideas on the subject of what new philosophy was – as many as there were anti-Jacobin authors indeed – but the basic ingredients remained constant, only the specific aversions of individual authors determining exactly how the concoction would taste.

To give a flavour of the mixture, we might start with Joseph Wildman's recipe, composed in 1799. Both the constituents of his conception of new philosophy and the concerns he expresses about their effects, are fairly typical. Only his accusation against Gibbon, as he attempts to piece together the lineage of what is a veritable international conspiracy, seems rather idiosyncratic:

> Hume and Gibbon took the lead in England – Voltaire and Rousseau in France – and Goethé [*sic*] (the author of Werther) in Germany; – these pernicious scepticisms and sophistical delusions, from their fascinating stile [*sic*], and animated diction, obtained many readers: – and those, unaccustomed to the higher pursuits of literature, in which Hume and Gibbon moved, were accessible through the medium of novels, in which were disseminated the most dangerous of principles: – principles which corrupt the heart and debase the understanding: – giving to vice the charms of virtue – to infidelity the specious colourings of superior intellectual attainment – to crimes, the shameful sophistry of irresistible necessity – and to self-destruction the delusive argument of a right in the creature to resign his existence when it ceases to afford him happiness, and the reasonableness of escaping misery.[7]

What we can notice immediately is that Wildman does not actually name the opinions he condemns, allowing them to remain as nameless 'pernicious scepticisms and sophistical delusions'. And nowhere does he single out particular arguments to oppose, seeming rather to avoid engaging with them. He mentions 'irresistible necessity' say, which the tutored eye recognises as a reference to Godwin's political philosophy, and he alludes to Goethe's *The Sorrows of Young Werther* (1774), but he leaves the references to stand alone and implicate themselves. For Wildman, and indeed for anti-Jacobin novelists as a whole, the names or terms cited with opprobrium are cultural and ideological references, not bodies of ideas or arguments, just as the notice he takes of the supposed wave of Jacobin novels published to introduce new philosophy to the supposed 'novel-reading masses' is, as we noticed in chapter one, largely a rhetorical construction with only a hypothetical basis in reality.

Elizabeth Hamilton's *Memoirs of Modern Philosophers* of 1800, though its very title claims an intimacy with the school of new philosophy, reinforces this reliance on an entirely notional 'understanding' of the ideological debate of the 1790s. When we ask what the modern philosophy was to which her vain and foolish characters subscribed, no clear-cut answer presents itself. Although she cites Godwin, Rousseau, Hays and Wollstonecraft, and shows us a radical debating society and the genesis of a pantisocratic programme, *Modern Philosophers* never becomes a satire of ideas but remains a satire of individual characters who merely represent, and in very loose terms, those ideas, and then only in pastiche. What is most significant about this is that Hamilton assumes a knowledge of what modern philosophy is, assumes that the same conception of it is shared by herself and her readers. Such an approach was entirely typical, new philosophy pre-understood as necessarily wicked, a crucial *donnée* underlying anti-Jacobin fiction. Naturally, this was a highly effective strategy, and by obviating any need for description or analysis of philosophical or political propositions, it served both literary and ideological purposes. That the novel was not the place for philosophical disquisitions was an opinion not merely artistic, but, for conservatives, an article of ideology, debate being a privilege reserved for a very few, if any, and least of all to be encouraged amongst those sections of society widely supposed to be reading novels. Moreover, for anti-Jacobins actual debate on the Revolution was an evil to be avoided wherever possible, as Mark Philp, in the context of pamphlet propaganda, has argued.[8] There was, in fact, an almost oppositional relationship between any hint of genuine ideological *debate* and the intentions of the anti-Jacobin campaign as a whole. However tempting it may be to think of the years following the French Revolution as a time when a 'war of ideas' was playing itself out, this must be something of a misnomer, at least at the level of fiction. After all, one side in this war, and by far the stronger, as well as ultimately victorious side, was determined to avoid any encounter with the enemy if it was to be fought on their terms, in the field of ideas.

Second, denying new philosophy any serious treatment in fiction, as Hamilton and the anti-Jacobin novelists were doing, was a powerful comment in itself. Crucially, new philosophy was an ironic designation. Philosophy was a good, *new* philosophy should be better, but, in fact, was a perversion. The irony could only be understood by those who already knew that 'new philosophy' was a cipher for Jacobinism, and that Hamilton could confidently trust that the irony of her title, *Memoirs of Modern Philosophers*, would be comprehensible to anyone seeing it on the shelf of a bookseller or circulating library is indicative of the accuracy of this assumption by the turn of the century. In fact, by 1805 and *Memoirs of M. De Brinboc*, it was no longer only *new* philosophy that was a signifier of iniquity, but as one character well versed in the ways of the world laments, 'the very name of philosophy, though originally a very respectable one, now fills me with a sensation of horror which I cannot possibly describe'.[9]

Indeed, the changing uses of the term 'philosophy' are interesting, and although the term was employed differently by individual authors, Charles Lucas' proposition that there ought to be a distinction made between what he calls 'philosophers' – good – and 'PHILOSOPHISTS' – bad – was common, at least implicitly. He distinguishes between 'common philosophy' and the 'new philosophy' of the philosophists by defining the latter as 'A species of Wisdom, which man discovers by the aid of his own individual powers, corporeal and mental, without owning the aid of any superior Being'.[10] This sounds a rather Burkean criticism (especially if we disregard, for the moment, the religious dimension) with its emphasis on the error of any opinion that sets itself up in opposition to the wisdom of the ages, and one cannot help thinking that for Lucas, the evil was concentrated more in the 'new' than the 'philosophy'. Similarly Burkean concerns are evident in numerous anti-Jacobin novels, new philosophy being responsible for the annihilation of chivalry for instance, although more usually being pressed into service as the symbolic opposite to the 'entailed inheritance' of political and religious institutions which, according to Burke and conservatism as a whole, each generation had a duty to abide by and preserve.[11] In Ann Thomas' *Adolphus de Biron* (1795?) for instance, one protagonist compliments another on a discourse in defence of the old order with the aid of one of Burke's favourite images: 'you have justly compared the Stability of the British Constitution to the Growth and Firmness of Oaks', contrasting this with the challenge of new philosophy: 'Our freedom was not founded on chimerical Notions, nor spun from Cobweb Systems, but it was formed on Principles which have produced her Safety and Superiority.'[12]

Following Burke, what Thomas and numerous other anti-Jacobin novelists rely upon is a putative 'old philosophy', successful, and thus laudable, by virtue of its evident results (the perfections of the present day), but never actually explained. Since neither this old nor new philosophy was ever defined, the point at issue was merely the newness, the innovation, the wholesale transformation (or deforestation, as Burke might have put it) of the political landscape, something utterly condemnable, and something that comes across well in Thomas Skinner Surr's *George Barnwell* (1798). Surr evidently felt it both inadequate and inappropriate merely to make his new philosopher, Mr Mental, the opposite to

Sir James, the local squire and 'a whig of the old school, and a high church-man', since,

By the opposite to a whig, used to be formerly understood a tory; and by the opposite to high-church, low-church was suggested. Now Mr Mental was neither whig nor tory, nor a high, nor low church-man; yet were his principles more at variance with Sir James than a Jacobite presbyter's: the latter only differed with the knight as to the person of a king and the modes of religion. Mr Mental was supposed to be equally averse to all kings, and to all religion.[13]

A new epoch of iniquity had dawned, and all previous delinquency had apparently been rendered obsolete, but the new challenge had no vocabulary of its own, and we clearly see Surr seeking to avoid the necessity of defining what he meant by the new philosophy to which Mental subscribed. His first endeavour was to define it in terms of its opposite, and although he admits himself unsuccessful in finding an 'old philosophy' which could form a direct counterpart, he still enlisted an already established political lexicon (kings, religion and rebellion), a strategy which remained the only method of proceeding for anti-Jacobins.

In other words, though numerous novels include what seem like attempts to define new philosophy, or provide what appear to be recipes for the manufacture of a new philosopher in their accounts of a character's progress towards his or her iniquity, closer inspection reveals almost all such definitions to be couched purely in negatives. Henry James Pye's description of Sir Edward Eaglefield, the misguided protagonist of *The Aristocrat* (1799), demonstrates this perfectly. A trip to the Continent with his philosophical tutor furnishes him with 'a mind amply stored with all the secrets of the new philosophy', merely meaning, we are told, that, 'He could expatiate learnedly on the horrors and inhumanity of war, the bigotry of priests, the tyranny and fraud of governments, the pedantry of ancient learning, and the rude and unpolished manners that disgraced his own countrymen' – not that he had anything to put in its place.[14] Similarly, the new philosophy of Charles Lucas' Marmaduke Pendragon, in *The Castle of St Donats* (1798), though he calls himself 'a violent assertor of the cause of freedom, in other words, a democrat upon the French scale', actually consists only of pretending 'to disbelieve every thing, religious or moral, that did not suit his own turn'. In fact, the metaphysics with which he both entertains and frightens our hero is comprised only of a 'jumble of law terms, political cant, London phrases, pieces of orations heard at the spouting clubs and other public meetings, with gleanings from the playhouse, and extracts from the pamphlets of the day

... a complete mixture of absurdity, impudence, and folly'.[15] That new philosophy is in fact *no* philosophy is the premise that, as we shall see, underlies the entirety of the anti-Jacobin strategy.

However, three years later, Lucas did decide to venture, if not quite a definition, then a survey of new philosophy, an enterprise that took up almost a hundred pages of his *Infernal Quixote* (1801) and which must be considered as one of the strangest endeavours of the whole anti-Jacobin campaign. He divides the 'infernal quixotes' by whom Europe is beset, and by which he seems to mean new philosophers in both France and Britain, into nine distinct categories, although individual modern philosophers, Lucas points out, may belong to more than one sect. It is a curiously idiosyncratic exercise in taxonomy which seems designed simultaneously to excite the consternation of readers by showing the depth and breadth of the threat they were facing, and to reassure them that, now it was detected, measured and classified, the threat could be neutralised. The apparent comic intent of some of the categories also bespeaks a rather surprising degree of frivolity in the satire, making Lucas seem a sort of literary Gillray.

First, he presents to our anxious imagination the 'Stoics or Insensibles', who criticise society as it is and will not have their arguments contradicted. They are soon won over to the Revolutionary cause in France, and almost as soon have their heads cut off. The 'Epicureans', his second category, reject both government and religion because both interfere with the gratification of the senses, the sole purpose of life. There are many men on both sides of the Channel that belong to this sect, including even the Prince of Wales, Lucas hints, but, of course, 'There is scarcely a female Philosopher to be found that is not an EPICUREAN.' Next come the 'Peripatetics or Busy Bodies', men, mostly, who dally in new philosophy under the impression that it will make them appear wise or fashionable, or simply because they have nothing else to do. They do not think for themselves, but affect their sympathy with sedition. The 'Virtuosos or lovers of wonder' embrace anything novel or interesting, particularly anything engaging for its antiquity, a description that brings to mind the ancient constitutionalism of some strands of late eighteenth-century radicalism but seems more an attack on the dilettantism of a William Beckford or William Hamilton. The category of 'Illuminati or Wiseacres' likewise suggests a serious Jacobin target but falls into more general satire. They think the present generation, that is to say themselves, infinitely wise, and profess a Godwinian faith in the perfectibility of man, but the examples Lucas furnishes us with include, as well as the discernibly 'Jacobin' notion of the possibility of avoiding illness and death by strength of will, a belief in such apparently ideologically neutral projects as vaccination and animal magnetism.

Sixth in Lucas' scheme come the 'Libertarians or champions of liberty', contrary figures who, despite their grandiose name, object to anything merely for the sake of objecting; and next are the 'Naturals', evidently inspired by Rousseau, who insist that mankind needs to return to a primitive state. Eighth are the 'Reasoners', anxious to prove everything by logic, always in defiance of common sense, and the category Lucas spends longest considering, partly because 'the leaders of the mob are very partial to them', but mostly because they evidently encompass many of his personal aversions. They have sought to prove observably Jacobin propositions – that the Hottentots possess the truest religion and most perfect society (Rousseau is half Reasoner and half Natural) – but they have also attempted the less political goals of rationalising speech patterns and proving that St Mark did not write the gospel whose name it bears.

Lastly, but most significant, come the 'Nothingers', people who believe nothing outwith what they themselves know, who have no principles emanating from any external code, temporal or spiritual. Thus the Nothingers may say and do what they like, for, detestably, they have no laws to obey and may alter their conduct by the moment according to nothing but their present exigency. Clearly, this is overtly Godwinian – and his doctrine of 'Necessity' is cited in his own words – but, in fact, Lucas' central contention is that to adopt such a position is to adhere to no philosophy at all. All ambassadors of the French Revolution are Nothingers, for instance, because they may argue anything they like according to their present advantage, their words having precisely no bearing on their future conduct, a point explicitly made by Elizabeth Hamilton too, whose villain, Vallaton, expounds a new philosophy which, she laments, is so constantly shifting that it can be neither prosecuted at law nor utterly refuted by even the most learned. As Lucas disgustedly puts it, citing the lifelong maxim of Lord James Marauder, the infernal quixote himself, a man belonging to all of these sects, 'ALL PRINCIPLE IS FOLLY.'[16]

Centrally, Lucas insists that every Jacobin, every new philosopher, will assuredly be a Nothinger, to whichever other sect he or she may also belong. All of Lucas' categorisations have been exercises in demonstrating that any new philosophical position is underlaid by either, or both, personal folly or vice sufficient to deny it the status of a legitimate political or metaphysical position. But it is the assertion that none of these doctrines has any basis in fixed principles that does most to undermine their validity, and thus their appeal. That new philosophy, however it is dressed, is simply the denial of principle is the conception underlying all anti-Jacobin treatment of it. Every new philosopher, George Walker wrote in the preface to *The Vagabond* (1799), 'has a system widely opposite to the other', but, he added, all these positions were 'agreeing only that every regular order and institution, religious, moral, and political, is worn out in this age of reason, and must be destroyed'.[17] Similarly, Mary Anne Burges exposed her 'Mr PHILOSOPHY' as a shadow with no fixed identity himself but meaning to any individual exactly what would be most likely to coax them into prostrating themselves at the altars of 'ATHEISM' and 'ANARCHY'. To 'Mr DISCONTENT' he promised that the present system would be destroyed; to 'Mr LOVE-CHANGE' he said that a new system would immediately appear; he assured 'Mr PARTY-SPIRIT' that everyone else had already succumbed; and he attempted to entice 'GOOD-INTENT' by appealing to his benevolence, pledging that 'the universal establishment of the rights and liberties of all mankind' was all he aimed for.[18] New philosophy was the ultimate nihilism, expressing itself simply as the absence of all constraint. For the author of *Massouf, or the Philosophy of the Day* (1802) all restraint was 'the most insolent presumption' on the part of anyone who sought to impose their values on another, and was 'the most contemptible folly' on the part of anyone who allowed this to happen. 'As to restraint from a Superior Being,' the author added, it was no more than 'an invention of subtle and crafty men, for the purpose of gaining a superiority over their fellow-creatures'.[19] Others, like Jane West, placed added emphasis on this attempt of new philosophy to overturn religious restraint, but the fundamental point remained the same.[20] The 'philosophy of the day' was to deprive mankind of both secular and spiritual statutes, so that each individual might be free to follow nothing but his or her own volition and interest.

Literary anti-Jacobinism, then, did not think of itself as waging a war against ideas, but against a more worrying menace still – the absence of any guiding principle whatsoever. And of course, once new philosophy had been exposed as, in Lucas' phrase, Nothingism, a set of non-principles cobbled together to give the most flimsy of theoretical bases to the desire of malicious individuals to act as they liked without restraint or compunction, a mortal blow was inflicted on each of the individuals cited by authors as part of the heritage of new philosophy, irrespective of what their philosophy might have been. Thus it was that to quote, or to refer to, or even merely to mention, any individual identified as a new philosopher in a novel was to exhibit them as a fraud, charlatan and, generally speaking, as a villain too. So although various anti-Jacobin novelists subpoena numerous new philosophers to stand before the primed and packed jury of their readers, quoting sometimes substantial passages from their works, it is never actually their thought or their works which come under scrutiny. This is a point that cannot be over-emphasised, especially since those few works of modern scholarship which have given some sustained consideration to the anti-Jacobin novel have tended to be taken in by the immediately evident citations of various Jacobin texts and thus driven to suggest that the novels were designed to counter some specific protagonists and tenets of the new philosophy. The two close examinations of George Walker's anti-Jacobin satire, by A. D. Harvey and Hugh H. MacMullen, for example, evaluate his *Vagabond* as primarily a counter-blast to Godwin's *Political Justice* and Rousseau's *Confessions*.[21] This is wholly understandable, since both texts are frequently alluded to in the novel, and indeed, it is no misrepresentation for MacMullen to devote most of his article to adducing the references Walker makes to Godwin and Rousseau. To find Peter Marshall, and other biographers of Godwin, alleging that the anti-Jacobin novels they have come across are all specifically 'anti-Godwinian' also comes as no surprise.[22] But it is an approach which misunderstands the underlying method of anti-Jacobin fiction. By looking at many anti-Jacobin novels together, as MacMullen and Harvey did not do, and by not analysing them purely from the perspective of one or more individual radicals, the tangential nature of these citations to the main campaign of anti-Jacobin polemic becomes apparent. Although numerous novels disparagingly quote *Political Justice*, to name just one text, conservative novelists principally aimed to forge an alloy of new philosophy which they then contorted to fit their own purposes.[23] It would be wise, in other words, to place more credence in the only *apparently* disingenuous claims made by even the most venomous anti-Jacobins that, as Robert Bisset put it in the preface to *Douglas* (1800), 'I here declare that it is VICE AND FOLLY IN GENERAL; *and not the vice of any individual person*, which I have in view' – a sentiment echoed by Elizabeth Hamilton when challenged by her *ci-devant* friend and correspondent Mary Hays about the subjects of the satire of her *Letters of a Hindoo Rajah*.[24]

In examining new philosophy in fiction, then, it would be rather tangential simply to list the occurrences of specific rebuttals of individual Jacobins, however much fun it might be to identify the characters that add such colour to the novels with specific radicals from 1790s Britain.[25] Rousseau and Voltaire, for instance, whose status and influence as philosophers could hardly be denied even by the most vociferous of anti-Jacobins, though often cropping up in the novels, featured as little more than fictional characters. Certainly, it was never any *philosophy* that earned them their place in their novels, but their image, their reputation, grafted on to them by propagandists who might just as well have never read their work, a tendency noticed by historians of the contemporary reception of both Rousseau and Voltaire. Bernard Schilling, in his inquest into *Conservative England and the Case Against Voltaire*, has rather irritably complained that his subject was regarded by British reactionaries as the prime mover of the Revolution in France and the chief inspiration behind all revolutionary activity in Britain, and yet Voltaire had never constructed a new theory of society or demanded the overthrow of the existing order. 'On the contrary,' Schilling protests, 'he was a well-known monarchist and himself distrustful of popular movements, of sudden and violent changes in a social scheme of things that had treated him so generously most of his life.'[26] Meanwhile, in his study of *Rousseau in England*, Edward Duffy has made much the same claims for his protagonist, concluding that it was Rousseau, not Voltaire, who 'became an eponym for revolutionary mischief'.[27] Both are equally correct, of course, in claiming for their subjects the status of arch-fiend, for according to the apprehension of most authors and readers of novels, the two philosophers were indistinguishable, and to all intents and purposes the same person, or rather the same demon.

Similar complaints about the abuse of Rousseau's good name are to be found in MacMullen's investigation into the satire of Walker's *Vagabond*. MacMullen seems genuinely surprised by his own conclusion that, 'In general, Walker misunderstands Rousseau; indeed, such misunderstanding seems wilful, based more on Rousseau's reputation than on his actual writings', and he points out that, in fact, Walker's opinions on, say, nature or the education of women, as he expresses them in the novel, are in exact conformity with Rousseau's.[28] This use of reputation not reality was a tactic universally used by the anti-Jacobin novelists, whether adopted by authors unconsciously, as seems to be the case with Walker, or deliberately, as was certainly the case with Edmund Burke. His construction of Rousseau was based not in the least on any close reading of Rousseau, nor even on the licentious and hypocritical vagabond that Rousseau himself had famously revealed in the *Confessions* (1782 and 1789), but was built on the single idea that the Revolutionaries worshipped him as an idol.

Burke even admitted that the real Rousseau would have had difficulty recognising what was being done in his name – 'I believe, that were Rousseau alive, and in one of his lucid intervals, he would be shocked at the practical phrenzy of his scholars.'[29] But this was precisely why such a straw-man was so useful, for he could be made to represent anything the polemicist wished. In Burke's work, the technique was most sustained in the *Letter to a Member of the National Assembly* of 1791. Having known Rousseau in England, Burke wrote, he was sure that 'he entertained no principle, either to influence his heart or to guide his understanding' – excepting, that is, the one characteristic that would form the basis of the whole of Burke's attack – '*vanity*'.[30] In fact, Burke's conception of vanity – which he defines as 'the worst of vices' leaving 'the whole man false' and 'nothing sincere or trustworthy about him' – is identical to Lucas' 'Nothingism'. But more significantly here, it was this strategy of attacking the man, not the philosophy, that underpinned all of Burke's offensive. As Duffy puts it, 'Once Burke has uncovered Rousseau's ruling passion, he needs address himself neither to the substance of Rousseau's thought nor to the quality and sincerity of his intentions.'[31]

Burke's strategy, then, was something of a paradox, though not inhibiting its potency in the least. His was an *ad hominem* attack on Rousseau, but not an attack on a real person, rather on a straw-man of his own creation, deliberately designed only as the perfect target for his contempt. In most anti-Jacobin novels we see the same technique in operation, attacks on new philosophers rather than new philosophy, but on artificially fabricated figures bearing little relation to their ostensible models. This was a perfect technique for novelists, greatly facilitating their attempts to attack new philosophy whilst never actually engaging in debate on its ideas and issues. They attacked, as satirical novelists had always done, individual characters, either as fools or knaves, and by creating their own new philosophers, they were free to construct new philosophy in its most vulnerable form. New philosophy was created as an amalgam of insidious ideas, separate strands of which could be apportioned by anti-Jacobins to individual characters selected to act as vehicles to drive a putative Jacobin principle before the guns of the novelists. This strategy meant that they could combine their central aim of showing new philosophy to be nothing but Nothingism, a non-philosophy, while simultaneously displaying and, by disproving, debunking some individual radical propositions as they were held by their phantom new philosophers.

Having now examined, at base, what new philosophy in the anti-Jacobin novel was *not*, for it was neither a genuine political philosophy nor, as some critics have suggested, the travestied ideas of any individual exponent of radicalism, we can now turn to the question of what it actually was that drew most of the anti-Jacobins' fire. In what follows, I shall be examining some of the specific arguments selected by anti-Jacobins to be extracted from the amalgam for attack, and then, how it was that they went about doing it.

Anti-Jacobins deplored any semblance of debate in fiction not simply because they felt it dangerous to open up the possibility of doubt and disputation amongst the innocents they imagined to be reading novels, nor only because the novelists themselves felt unwilling, on the grounds of either propriety or profitability, to interrupt their fiction with such stuff. Most of all, they felt that debate, questioning and ratiocination, were the very tools of the Jacobins and the hallmarks of their new philosophy. Just as new philosophy was invented, whereas its putative counterpart, the old philosophy, was inherited, so new philosophy was reasoned, whilst old philosophy was felt. Both points had been postulated most influentially by Burke, but the novel, and its picaresque variety in particular, might almost have been designed to elucidate the divide. *The History of Sir George Warrington; or the Political Quixote* (1797), for just one example, is fundamentally based on these simple premises – that Sir George is born into a world that functions perfectly and benefits everyone, but is driven by some mischievous impulse to attempt to overhaul it all and reconstruct it in some unworkable form – here according to the dictates of new philosophy – and that, from the beginning, he has instinctively known in his heart what is right, but that he is temporarily enslaved by the errors of false reasoning. The same pattern is repeated in *Dorothea; or, A Ray of the New Light*, Opie's *Adeline Mowbray*, Walker's *Vagabond* and, for that matter, Walker's *Theodore Cyphon* (1796), seemingly a novel inspired by Godwin's *Caleb Williams*, but still critical of any character who privileges reason over feeling.

In *Waldorf; or, the Dangers of Philosophy* (1798), Sophia King makes the distinction crystal clear as she shows us the fall of her protagonist from innocence, in which he 'never appealed to his reason' and 'at all times obeyed the impulses of his heart', to guilty compliance with the murderous schemes of the new philosopher Herdi Lok, resulting from Lok's remorseless and insidious instruction:

You should appeal to your own *reason* for approbation; the *heart* is but secondary, and ought to be in a state of subordination. Your judgement can never be wrong.

Reason is never erroneous, but *false* sentiment may be your destruction. You are influenced by a set of chimerical notions of probity and honour; but this is the effect of romance; you will soon discriminate *better*, and think differently.[32]

Of course, King was relying upon the understanding that Lok was entirely wrong, her point being that reasoning, in fact, could be, and almost always was, mistaken, whilst one's feelings were invariably right. Disastrous effects were bound to ensue if they were ignored. 'Waldorf,' says Helena, another victim of Lok, at the end of the novel, 'I expiate my crimes by sinking into an early grave . . . Oh! that philosophy . . . *betrayed* my heart, and *enslaved* my reason.'[33]

The other pre-understood contention behind King's irony was that for Lok to call that wisdom which is felt, and the equally Burkean notion of honour, 'chimerical', was the most glaring case possible of the pot calling the kettle black. It was certainly an awareness that King must have been able to presume existed in her readers, for the word almost belonged to the anti-Jacobins, so often were they to be found using it to describe new philosophy. It was their central contention that new philosophy was a process of systemisation which ran against the grain of real life, and yet, however utterly delusive it was in reality, it was something that was attractive enough to appeal to a picaresque character, and by extension to the posited readers who required the novelist's didacticism precisely because they were also tempted by the new doctrines. In Isaac D'Israeli's *Vaurien*, for example, our by-and-large sensible hero is beguiled by the circle of new philosophers gathered at Lord Belfield's house by their just conceivably noble attempt mathematically to systematise morality. His resistance is based on his love for the teachings of Christ in fact, but D'Israeli designs his *reductio ad absurdum* to excite our scorn for these philosophers by showing us the utter ludicrousness of such an attempt to impose from without a new system to explain a code of conduct which already exists and has worked so well for so long.[34] *Massouf, or the Philosophy of the Day* is even more explicit in depicting the prince, its hero and our representative, torn between his two counsellors, Ayoub (meant to stand for Pitt), who 'reasoned like a man who, to profound knowledge, added all that a long and most attentive observation of mankind could bestow', and Ibrahim (possibly Fox), who 'argued not so much from that which did, as that which ought to exist'. Being young, and idealistic (two characteristics generally associated with novel-readers), Massouf 'beheld in the speculations of Ibrahim a cure for those errors which

Ayoub acknowledged...and thus all that could be deduced from experience was exploded'. It takes the strange but edifying dream that fills the rest of the novel, a vision of a land where the new philosophy has taken root and brought nothing but confusion, misery and eventually revolution, to convince the prince of his error.[35]

As may be again seen from these instances, new philosophy was generally presented by novelists as some kind of chimerical programme, with few if any individual elements specified. It is possible, though, to dissect new philosophy, and isolate some of its main organising principles, although we should be wary when attempting this, since, as I have been stressing, new philosophy was an amalgam, seldom precise in the accusations it was levelling. Occasionally, some particular popinjays were very evidently brought forward, but they were always placed against this background of the ridiculous and unworkable system, always understood as impracticable, however iniquitous a specific tenet of the doctrine, once isolated, might be seen to be. And, of course, it should also be recognised that when specific articles of new philosophy were brought to the readers' attention, they were not to be reasoned against, but to be dismissed without recourse to debate.[36]

Edward Dubois, author of the somewhat blatant *St Godwin* (1800), provides a good starting point. His new philosophy was principally Godwin's doctrine of necessity, or at least this was what he chose to exhibit to his readers as the target for his satire.[37] But though named several times and supported with quotations and footnoted references to *Political Justice*, Godwin's doctrines do not feature as a coherent philosophical position, but only insofar as they sanction the abominable crimes perpetrated thus far in the novel both by and upon St Godwin. Locked in the Bastille, he muses thus:

Here it was that I first formed my notions, which I afterwards promulgated in England, of *absolute necessity* presiding over all the actions of men. Upon this ground, I cordially forgave his majesty [the King of France] for taking away my liberty, because I knew he could not avoid it; and I now, also, freely pardoned the mountaineers who had robbed and endeavoured to kill me, as I firmly believe that 'the assassin cannot help the murder he commits, any more than the dagger'. My marriage with Pandora [his son's fiancée] I ascribed to the *divinity of necessity*, or I should have been very much ashamed for having committed such a fraudulent act.[38]

In D'Israeli's *Vaurien*, *Political Justice* again forms the central text of new philosophy, featuring as Subtile's projected work 'Prejudices Destroyed, or Paradoxes Proved'.[39]

Illustrating another, also pivotal, anti-Jacobin conception of new philosophy, D'Israeli emphasises the wealthy Lord Belfield's objections to the new philosophy that he wishes to patronise. Belfield cannot brook the redistribution of property which his friends hold as a fundamental tenet of their doctrine – until, that is, they realise that they might lose a bountiful patron by clinging to their opinion on this matter, and, of course, conviction is not a word in their lexicon. D'Israeli's elevation of economic levelling as part of his definition of what constituted new philosophy was a focus shared by many authors. Although she later widened her sights, Elizabeth Hamilton in her *Letters of a Hindoo Rajah* (1796), for instance, clearly understood new philosophy as little more than 'levelling', that is to say the authorisation of theft by approval of the principle of equality. The episode which forms her central attack on the folly of Sir Caprice Ardent, Mr Axiom and Dr Sceptic, the accusation and charging of Timothy Trundle for theft, and his plea that he was simply putting into practice the principles he had heard his master express, convincingly distils new philosophy into levelling only, whilst still indicting any code of behaviour which privileges reasoned challenge to the *status quo* over felt acquiescence.[40]

Levelling was obviously a crucial part of anyone's conception of new philosophy. But if this was the threat of Paine's *Rights of Man* transliterated into fiction, then there were numerous authors who concentrated more on the menace of his *Age of Reason*. Levelling certainly appears less prominently than that other pillar of the new philosophy, atheism, in Thomas Skinner Surr's *George Barnwell*. What strikes the reader after a short acquaintance with a few new philosophers, though, is that the specific object of the attack is almost irrelevant, levelling or irreligion being virtually interchangeable. Compare the language of Hamilton's Axiom defending theft of property, say, who questions 'what is right? what is wrong? what is vice? what is virtue? but terms merely relative, and which are to be applied by the standards of man's own reason', with Surr's Mr Mental giving his different new philosophic credentials:

What is religion – but ceremony, or a set of ceremonies: – what are ceremonies, but superstition! For instance; how absurd, how degrading to a human being, with faculties so comprehensive that all nature bows before him, to which she unfolds her secrets and submits her laws – I say then it must be beneath the dignity of such a creature to bend his knees, to bow his head, and mumble syllables of absurdities strung together centuries ago, when, by the exercise of his own powers, he might be introduced into the arena of great Nature herself.[41]

Certainly all new philosophy shared this defining presumptuous arrogance, whatever its specific tenets might be. But, in the sphere of religion at least, we should not brush over the fact that there were actually observable gradations and variations from novel to novel.

Not all new philosophers, we find, adopted the atheism of Paine, but might come from the mould of a Price or Priestley, attempting to conciliate their politics with their faith. This usually received short-shrift from the novelists who introduced such characters. Mrs Nicknack, a character in Bisset's *Modern Literature*, for instance, is singled out amongst Bath society for being 'a most furious democrat' but still, we are told, 'says she is a Christian'. This cannot be, remarks our hero, for he cannot recollect any passages of sacred writ that inculcate the faults of which she is so manifestly guilty (only one of which seems political): 'greed, gossiping, disloyalty, lying, and slandering'.[42] On the other hand, in his *Douglas* of four years earlier, Bisset had taken pains to conjoin religion and new philosophy, presenting us with a preacher, variously called a Methodist and a 'seceder', who promulgates not only general licentiousness but also levelling, glorying in a mid-seventeenth century idyll when there was no king, no bishops and, as he tells it, no inequality of property.[43] These 'seceders' acknowledge no earthly head of the Church, reject the possibility of justification by works, and are firmly committed to predestination (and, curiously, 'the methodist doctrines of the new birth'), and we are left in no doubt that even this purely theological stance places them within the Jacobin ambit. 'Their political principles are as absurd as their religious,' our hero learns, 'and, if not well watched, would be very dangerous' – a conflation which supports Gary Kelly's contention that "Necessitarianism" was often seen as a secular version of Calvinist predestination'.[44] In fact, the metaphysical similarities between a political philosophy that contended that all actions and motives had their basis in external conditions, and a theology that insisted justification came through faith alone, may have passed most novelists by, but Kelly's suggestion is nevertheless supported by a number of novels, especially if Methodism is conjoined with Calvinism as it seems often to have been. Roger O'Rourke in *Modern Literature* passed himself off as a strict Methodist and new philosopher alternately, whereas Mr Myope, in *Modern Philosophers*, had been, Hamilton reveals, just as zealous an advocate for Quakerism, Anabaptism and Calvinism before acquiring his new philosophical enlightenment.[45]

Attempts to demonstrate the affinity of new philosophy and religious 'enthusiasm', a catch-all phrase that could mean anything from Calvinism to Methodism to Evangelicalism, anything that was not the conservative Arminianism of the Church of England, reached their apogee with Sarah Green's *The Reformist!!!* (1810), and secondly, 'Rattle's Double Oration', a sparkling section of Charles Lucas' *Infernal Quixote* (1801). Green's novel, echoing Robert Graves' *Spiritual Quixote* of 1773, charts the progress of another Methodist picaresque hero, censuring at first his religion and then, once the folly of that has been shown, and he switches enthusiasms, the campaign for political reform he takes up in London. He has, we are told at the beginning of the novel, 'a head crammed with wild and Utopian schemes for the future welfare and virtue of mankind', and it is a description that applies equally to both of his foolish fixations.[46] 'Rattle's Double Oration' crammed the same message into just three duodecimo pages. Supposedly a paper given to Mr Rattle, a member of a new philosophical coterie that Wilson, Lucas' hero, encounters in London, the 'oration' is a short speech apparently designed to rouse rabbles by igniting either their revolutionary or spiritual ardour. The orator may start either with 'Satan and his imps of darkness', or 'Tyrants and their ministers of tyranny', and thereafter, though most of the text is the same for the Methodist or Jacobin reading, every sentence or so, the reader must delete whichever phrase does not relate to his or her theme, and insert that which does. Thus, the orator addresses either his or her 'beloved Brethren' or 'beloved Citizens', encourages them to don the 'garments of Hope' and 'shield of Grace' or 'cap of Liberty' and 'shield of equality' and to pull down either the 'Temples of Satan and his Gang' or the 'Mansions of Kings and Nobles'.[47]

Although Rattle's Oration has something of the character of an authorial *jeu d'esprit*, of which Lucas was so proud that he engineered an opportunity to present it in his novel, its point is obvious. But if Lucas and others had been keen to show the similarities between political and religious enthusiasm in effect, in *George Barnwell*, more intriguingly, Surr shows their causes to be the same too. Mr Mental himself, telling his life story to George, revealed how he had fallen into new philosophy, demonstrating it to be the direct consequence of the harsh apprenticeship served under the ultra-Calvinist Mr Nutting. The Calvinist texts being the only spirited material in the libraries to which Mental had access, he quickly learned to espouse and profess their tenets, and from there it was but a short step to a debating club, scepticism and finally, atheism. Had Mental not been shown religion 'in so distorted a shape', George concludes, he would never have plunged into the rest of his errors.[48] Though we should not forget that Mental is to an extent modelled on Priestley, we should also remember that Godwin had had a zealously Calvinist upbringing, had been educated at a Calvinist academy and had been a Dissenting minister, and an itinerant one at that, for much of his early life, and that it is his example that underwrites these incarnations of a non-secular new philosophy.

But there was one angle on new philosophy than had a wider currency in anti-Jacobin fiction than any of even these few most prominent strands of new philosophy. If Jacobinism was distilled into new philosophy in the novels, then new philosophy was distilled into essentially an attack on the affectional relations between individuals in society, relations manifested in the institutions of marriage, parental duty and filial devotion, all areas, of course, which might immediately be identified as falling within the natural province of the novel. Closely examining Charles Lloyd's *Edmund Oliver* (1798), for instance, it is rather surprising how quickly his conception of new philosophy, at first given only very loosely, resolves itself into a revelation of its real target. 'The following pages,' his 'Advertisement' asserts in traditionally inexplicit, not to say meaningless, terms, 'were written with the design of counteracting that generalising spirit, which seems so much to have insinuated itself among modern philosophers'. But even before the novel proper has begun, he has explained that it is the 'introduction of concubinage' and 'rejection of cohabitation' to which he specifically objects, for, he says, these evils will lead to 'a callousness that spurns all affections' and can only destroy society.[49] When the narrative itself does get underway, it loses no time in exemplifying this distillation of new philosophy into nothing but a potentially catastrophic attack on the family. We soon meet Lady Sinclair bringing all the artillery of the new philosophy she has learned by rote to bear on winning Edmund as her lover, not her husband (although even that brazenness would be bad enough), and concurrently endeavouring to rid him of a second emotional scruple, his deference to his family's wishes. 'Let us not be swayed by prejudice!' she tells him,

You talk of the suffering of your parents, of the alienation of your connections; what are these parents, these connections to you? Are they more or less than human beings? surely not! Are their errors then, interfering with grand and general principles, which, unaccustomed to rank and station, respect all human beings alike, are these errors to be attended to? Are you to forget the indefinite and incalculable benefit that you will be of to society by trampling on the rubbish which fills the onward path of man, directing your eye singly to the distant horizon of human perfection?

When, just a few pages later, having broken up Edmund's family, Lady Sinclair uses more Godwinian new philosophy to justify her having switched her affections to another ('an irresistible necessity governs us'), even quoting chunks of new philosophical texts to support her case, Lloyd has underscored his point and proved that the central aim of the new philosophy as produced by Godwin and his cohorts was nothing more than this destruction of all lawful affectional relationships.[50]

We find the same contention in most other anti-Jacobin novels, generally very clearly, as in Jane West's *Infidel Father* (1802). There we see the eponymous new philosophical Lord Glanville bitterly regretting having educated his daughter Caroline 'to despise prescription, to think and act for herself', and to insist on what he had called her 'natural right to bestow herself on whom she pleased', for she now intends to use those spurious rights to marry, to Glanville's detestation, a 'knight of industry' who will, of course, prove her ruin. Only once they elope, and Caroline is driven to suicide, does Glanville realise the full implications of his own demolition of the principle of filial duty.[51] A few other examples will suffice. In *Douglas*, when Charles investigates the motive behind the new philosophy of a provincial barber, he finds it to be that he is bored with his wife and is partial to his friend's.[52] In Walker's *Vagabond*, the severest reprehension is reserved for a character called Mary, evidently drawing her arguments from Wollstonecraft, who strikes at the very roots of the family and the traditional rôle of women in society by earnestly wishing that women did not have to bear and rear children.[53] In *The Infernal Quixote*, we find Lucas once more tying together religious and political enthusiasm, this time by suggesting that they both aimed to dismantle the family. 'Enthusiasm is deaf to all the calls of nature,' he quotes from *The Spiritual Quixote*, before updating Graves' anxiety for the early 1800s with 'Did not the wretches of France boast the murder of fathers, brothers and sons? Does not Godwin renounce those ties?'[54]

What must be clear is that it was a substantial misrepresentation – not that any anti-Jacobin would have had any compunction about so doing – to distil Godwin's *Political Justice*, say, all eight books of its ramblings across hundreds of subjects, into nothing more than an assault on the family and its central institution, marriage. All Godwin had tentatively suggested, in the appendix to one chapter of one book, was that 'The abolition of the present system of marriage appears to involve no evils', but numerous novelists contrived to imbue this speculation with such significance that it could serve as the peg on which all their attacks on Jacobinism and new philosophy could hang, and Godwin continued to be cast as the murderer of any and all familial attachments.[55] In *Dorothea*, for instance, he is cited as the inspiration for the heroine's rejection of the 'prejudice' of filial duty and affection; in *Douglas* many lengthy notes quote *Political Justice* as the motivation for a Mr Sidney's desertion of his mistress once she has borne him a child and demanded that he fulfil his private promise and marry her; and in *Modern Literature* we hear the comments of the female circle of new philosophers who cannot believe anyone inducted as 'a disciple of Jemima [Wollstonecraft], and a votary of St Leon [Godwin]' would ever consider entering into the 'shameful aristocratic monopoly' of marriage, even with so charming a man as Bisset's hero, Charles.[56]

Of course, this remarkably propitious piece of casting was not wholly an achievement of writers of conservative fiction. Burke's *Reflections* appeared well before *Political Justice*. His apostrophe to Marie-Antoinette and treatment of Louis XVI as father to both his household and the nation, powerfully portrayed the Revolution as a threat to the family, and in particular to women within it or temporarily outside it.[57] And Burke's prophecies must have seemed justified when British radicalism in the 1790s, especially as expressed by those who incorporated it into their fiction, apparently began to assail the traditional structures of the family, and in particular the rôle of women in society. Both the lives and works of Hays and Wollstonecraft, for instance, appeared to refine new philosophy into attacks on marriage and the family, and to sabotage the domestic, private and generally submissive rôle of women so central to the conservative paradigm. It was anti-Jacobin novelists, though, who took it upon themselves to extract from new philosophy those parts which they could assert were demonstrably aimed at eradicating established patterns of female behaviour. They seized on Wollstonecraft's life-story, with her sensuality apparently getting its deserts in her death in childbirth, as a gift to their cause, although, as Kathryn Sutherland has pointed out, Godwin's posthumous memoirs of Wollstonecraft must take much of the responsibility for privileging her life over her writings. Her life was 'the obvious comment' on her doctrines, according to the author of *Dorothea*, who added, 'Oh, my countrywomen, be warned by her fate.' Helena Wells repeated the injunction in *Constantia Neville*: 'May all ... who contend that it [marriage] has been productive of more evil to society than good, read with attention the memoirs of her, whose conduct is now the subject of animadversion.'[58] They would have found more difficulty with her *Vindication of the Rights of Woman*, with its disarmingly orthodox views on women in society (at least in many of its concerns), but were spared having to read it, and admit its moderation, by Hays' *Emma Courtney* with its more obvious, and more vulnerable, demands for the sexual and political emancipation of women.[59] Both Wollstonecraft and Hays figure as Godwin's eminently proficient lieutenants in the campaign against the affectional bonds of society envisaged by the anti-Jacobins, many novelists indeed preferring to target them than him. Charles Lloyd, for one, although the 'Advertisement' to *Edmund Oliver* had referred the reader to Godwin's *Enquirer*, cited Mary Hays' *Emma Courtney*, rather than *Political Justice*, in support of his reading of new philosophy, and Elizabeth Hamilton's *Modern Philosophers* was a satire dedicated primarily to ridiculing Hays as Bridgetina Botherim. It was an unsurprising modulation since, whether Hays' novel was supporting or, as has been argued by Marilyn Brooks, to a certain extent challenging Godwin's political philosophy, it was she who imbued his principles with an emotional content and who brought much that remained identifiably Godwinian within the compass of the novelist's pen.[60]

The *Anti-Jacobin Review*, responding to *Emma Courtney*, got to the heart of the reworking of new philosophy that was taking place in the late 1790s. Its rhetorical question about whether 'women should be so brought up to make them dutiful daughters, affectionate wives, tender mothers, and good Christians, or by a corrupt and vicious system of education fit them for revolutionary agents' captured perfectly the antithetical relationship that was developing in the novels, making the worthy woman the diametrically opposed counterpart of the new philosopher.[61] Once it had been established that new philosophy targeted women as a vulnerable portal through which they could attack all of society, corroding the relations which bound it together, novelists were imperturbable in exposing the danger, defining new philosophy as a system which aimed first and foremost at deluding women out of their genuine duties and virtues. Hamilton's concise treatment of new philosophy in her *Letters of a Hindoo Rajah* was an early but still determined attempt to lay bare what new philosophy really meant. She presented her new philosophers as looking forward to the Age of Reason as a time when filial affection would be a crime of the deepest dye, indeed would not even be possible since 'no man, in the age of reason, shall be able to guess who his father is; nor any woman to say to her husband, behold your son!' Chastity, the philosophers predicted, would be a weakness and female virtue would be 'estimated according as she has had sufficient energy to break its mean restraints'.[62] A more sustained treatment was forthcoming nine years

later with Amelia Opie's *Adeline Mowbray* (1805), a novel which, however ambiguous the political stance of its author, could only have been
interpreted by the majority of her contemporaries as an inquest into
both the practicalities and morality of cohabitation and childbearing
without marriage. The novel itself returned a decisive verdict on both
counts, however tentative its author may have been about these conclusions. Such behaviour was iniquitous, Opie has Adeline reveal as part
of her lengthy recantation, because 'I am convinced that if the ties of
marriage were dissolved, or it were no longer to be judged infamous to
act in contempt of them, unbridled licentiousness would soon be general
practice.' And it was impracticable since 'What then, in such a state of
society, would be the fate of the children born in it?'[63]

But the campaign to expose what another novelist, Alethea Lewis,
referred to as 'the new philosophy of matrimony', which, she explained,
'as with everything else, is equality' – the campaign to unmask new
philosophy as an attack on the duties of women as guardians of the
family, and thus society, could not have had a clearer expression than in
the opening of *Dorothea; or, a Ray of the New Light*.[64] It is worth quoting at
length:

When our reformers of the present day set out in the career of destruction,
overturning all those barriers which experience and wisdom have been for ages
erecting and repairing; when through the breaches they make, a torrent of vice
and folly rushes in to overwhelm and destroy all those soft and gentle ties which
have hitherto surrounded the names of mother, wife, and daughter; when, not
content with annihilating the power of reason in the stronger sex, they undertake
to emancipate woman from the domination of religion, gentleness, and modesty:
is it not time to shew the deluded victims of modern philosophy, that whilst they
open the door to the *new light*, conjugal peace, filial affection, retiring grace, and
every feminine virtue shrinking from the blaze, take that moment to depart,
never more, alas! to return.[65]

And once new philosophy had been distilled into a debate which fell
within the boundaries of gender propriety so important to so many
women anti-Jacobins, a debate to which they might legitimately contribute (and the reading of which might also be authorised, since it
concerned women readers so especially), novelists were able not just
to caution their readers about the danger the radicals threatened, but
also to offer their remedies. Thus the author of *Dorothea*, typically, was
able to divide her prose between warnings – 'My fair friends! believe not
these declaimers; in themselves restless, disappointed, selfish, they seek
to make *you* their victims!' – and instructions about how new philosophy

was to be defeated, which of course took the form of a recommendation of traditional female virtues: 'No, let us be wives, glorying in the
performance of our duty: let us be mothers, ready to sacrifice all for the
dear helpless beings we produce.'[66] As it turned out, it was the former
technique that would predominate, for in the view of the anti-Jacobin
novelists, as well as being a plot to destroy the family by subverting
women, new philosophy was also a cover for wicked individuals to per-
petrate their predatory financial, sexual and also ideological campaign
against innocent women.

Following Burke, as he did in so many ways, with his depiction of the
Revolution as an assault on French family life, it was Edward Sayer who
first attempted to mould the new philosophy he presented in his novel
into the sort of sexual predation that constituted an attack on the family,
predation that had for so long been the mainstay of the novel form,
and which would continue to appear so often in anti-Jacobin fiction.
In his *Lindor and Adelaïde* (1791), the Jacobin Antoine persecutes the
innocent Adelaïde, an orphan, attacking the affectional structures she has
built for herself and disregarding his own marriage vows in the process.
When, ultimately, he attempts to rape her, the justification he attempts
is instructive in that, coming long before *Political Justice*, Wollstonecraft's
Vindication, or Hays' *Emma Courtney*, it would remain in constant currency
for the ensuing decade or so of anti-Jacobin novels:

What is the difference . . . between a woman who is one's wife and who is not?
Can a priest muttering a few words, supersede the call of passion or give a
higher zest to the affection of the heart? In the heart are the issues of love, and
where that leads, what institution of the church, what act of man, shall impede
its progress? The time is passed for such superstitious restraints, and we revel in
the full freedom of love, free in that as in all other respects.[67]

Familiar though they would become, Sayer was not wholly at ease with
these sentiments in 1791, and he added a substantial note voicing his
fears that it would be regarded as a breach of 'the strict rules of critical
propriety' for him to suppose that his character of Antoine, who had thus
far only been depicted as a political miscreant, would also be a sexual
degenerate. This seems rather quaint in the light of the artistic liberties
anti-Jacobin novelists would later be taking in the interests of their campaign, but, in fact, Sayer's candour provides a very clear expression of
why it was so useful for novelists to paint their new philosophers as sexual
predators and ravagers of the family. The excuse Sayer himself actually
gives for allowing this breach of critical propriety is rather doctrinal, for

he claims that once all curbs on action, save the dictates of pure reason, are removed, then no one will be able to curb their base passions. But this is unconvincing, and the fact that Sayer was prepared to break his own, and perhaps the critics', aesthetic rules suggests that he was willing to sacrifice them in return for the more severe reprehension he could arouse and bring down upon the Jacobins he was depicting. By making their new philosophers villains, the anti-Jacobins were smoothly and immediately incorporated into the traditions of the novel, no awkwardly artificial join rendering this new species of fiction conspicuously propagandistic.[68]

Certainly, had anti-Jacobin fiction contained only political strictures, without the personal incrimination of Jacobinism for which Sayer was apologising, it would have been rather two-dimensional. It would also have failed to capitalise on its potential, for the real success of the anti-Jacobin novel was to incorporate the attack on new philosophy within the traditional structures of the novel. It might not have been quite the case that, as A. D. Harvey has contended, the numerous citations of new philosophic texts in novels, and especially the *Vindication of the Rights of Woman*, were 'an indication of how far the novel tradition in which female virtue had a central rôle saw itself threatened by Mary Wollstonecraft's teachings'.[69] Such an interpretation would rely on novelists having actually read, and interpreted in a way that historians have not reached a consensus on, the works of Wollstonecraft. But the novel was evidently perfectly suited to *presuming* that new philosophy, Wollstonecraft included, would be merely a mask for traditional modes of sexual predation, the stock-in-trade, as Harvey rightly says, of the eighteenth-century novel.

The merging of what we might call the traditional, that is, non-political, villain, and the new philosopher of the anti-Jacobin novel, forming what I will designate the 'vaurien', is so central a technique as to demand separate consideration, and I shall be presenting this in the next chapter. Here, though, it might be useful to skip forward to some of those novels at the tail-end of the anti-Jacobin novel's lifespan which demonstrate how this vaurien character, the new philosopher as a reiteration of the traditional rake, took on such a pivotal rôle as to render obsolete the new philosophy which had originally defined him. In Charlotte Dacre's *Confessions of the Nun of St Omer* of 1805, for instance, the distinction between the two remains, but only just. Cazire, our heroine, is the prey of two men, the evidently new philosophical Fribourg, with his attempts to seduce her by drawing her into debates in which he talks openly of the 'prejudice' of marriage and the 'necessity' of following one's wishes, and the much more traditional Lindorf, who assails her with all the familiar eloquence of the rake, reciting poetry and throwing himself at her feet. Only after Lindorf, reiterating the proposition already made by Fribourg, attempts to entice her away from home to live with him without the benefit of matrimony, does Cazire realise their resemblance: 'The similarity of his arguments to those of Fribourg struck me instantaneously. I had often remarked their apparent resemblance, but the real difference between them consisted that Fribourg's were the offspring of reflexion, and Lindorf's of selfishness.'[70] Whether reflection or selfishness, the result was the same, and we see the new philosopher decoded as a libertine of the old school. But reading this recognition back into the novels of the high point of anti-Jacobinism *circa* 1800, we see how important the distillation of new philosophy into an attack on affectional relationships was. Centrally, it laid bare a potentially credible, if not quite feasible, system into something manifestly iniquitous, and, most ingeniously, brought out the irony invested in the term 'new philosophy', undermining the 'new' by the demonstration that it was nothing more than a cover for the oldest of vices. In the hands of the anti-Jacobins, new philosophy was therefore neither new nor a cogent philosophy. Perhaps the best expression of this may be left to the author of *The Citizen's Daughter* (1804). Victim of Charles Denham's attempts to cajole her into an unmarried relationship, Marianne Willoughby dissects his new philosophy with a scalpel-sharp insight which, though seldom expressed so clearly, underlies every anti-Jacobin novel. Her separation of arguments and intent, and her conflation of philosophy and licentiousness, are seminal:

the *plausibility* of your *arguments* cannot disguise the *baseness* of the *intention*; and I thank heaven, I am not *weak* enough to be subdued by *either*. I rely upon my own *exertions* to be *happy*, without seeking resources from *depravity* or *guile*; imitate me in this, and act only under the influence of those *virtues* nature has implanted in your heart, unprejudiced by the *sophistry* of *modern* philosophy or unbridled licentiousness.[71]

My analysis so far has emphasised that anti-Jacobin novelists, rather paradoxically, were above all keen to avoid debating what was perhaps the principal subject of their novels, the new philosophy. Reasoning was treacherous, to broadcast the doctrines of modern philosophy in a novel was irresponsible, and so strategies were developed, albeit intuitively, by which new philosophy could be countered without disclosing what it actually was, or even what the phrase was theoretically supposed to mean. Yet even if this strategy of constructing a putative new philosophy as they wished to see it, as nihilistic, selfish, conventionally wicked and therefore vulnerable to attack, even if this strategy represented the most outstanding achievement of the anti-Jacobins, their fiction is also to be found engaging in more customary forms of satirical attack. Anti-Jacobin fiction was, after all, fundamentally a satirical form, and perhaps in some of its better moments, deserves consideration alongside Peacock and Austen. Yet it is not my intention here to appraise from a literary point of view the satirical modes or forms employed by anti-Jacobins, whether sophisticated or blunt, innovative or archaic. It may, however, be of some historical pertinence to examine some of the techniques most frequently used in anti-Jacobin fiction, for their frequent repetition argues for a very close generic identity for the anti-Jacobin novel.

As mentioned earlier, however, there were some few anti-Jacobin novelists who proved exceptions to the almost ubiquitous policy of shunning any semblance of political debate in their fiction. Edward Sayer, writing very early in the Revolution crisis, is one, filling his *Lindor and Adelaïde* (1791) with long and intricate, not to say otiose, defences of the British *status quo*. Writing later, and with only his manifest idiosyncrasy to explain it, Sir Samuel Egerton Brydges was another to adopt the 'Jacobin' technique of having a protagonist or two engage in open, reasoned and ostensibly unconstrained disputation on the political points the author wished his or her fiction to make. Yet even in Brydges' novels, his *Arthur Fitz-Albini* (1798) for instance, our hero's long disquisitions contending against those who seek to challenge the importance of a rigid system of rank are very decidedly authorially contrived and controlled. When we examine his prose in detail, we find that there is no genuine debate, only the author's reports of debate, Brydges telling us that Arthur 'lamented boldly' this, or 'despised the fallacious, half-witted arguments' which others used to assert that. The novel becomes a very Hansard as the author records the progress of dinner-table debates such as one 'in which, I know not by what felicity, Fitz-Albini, taking the lead, fell easily into a long train of opinions happily expressed, without appearing to declaim or be tedious'.[72] If it was not a particularly sophisticated satirical technique for Brydges to display the semblance of debate whilst actually presenting just his side of it, he was being really quite cunning in not even vouchsafing his own side of the question.

Much more common than even this kind of semi-debated pseudo-ratiocination, was the statement of the arguments of new philosophy in travestied form, reduced to the absurd. In parading the folly of new philosophy thus, authors were spared the need for such obvious authorial intervention as Sayer and Brydges had required to safeguard the reception of the doctrines they presented for ridicule. A few examples of this common technique will suffice. When Halfaz, the new philosopher of *Memoirs of M. De Brinboc*, claims that he can overcome all the frailties of the body simply by acts of 'velleity', we know that this is ridiculous and are prepared for the authorial contrivance when it does come, the philosopher being unable to conquer the merest touch of sea-sickness.[73] Best of all perhaps is Elizabeth Hamilton's portrayal in her *Letters of a Hindoo Rajah* of the new philosophers gathered at Sir Caprice Ardent's house trying out their theoretical schemes in practice. External circumstances form character, they (with Godwin) are convinced, and to prove that there is no reason why, 'by a proper course of education, a monkey may not be a Minister of State, or a goose a Chancellor of England', they attempt to turn three hundred sparrows into so many bees by placing them in a giant hive. In accordance with a bee's habits, the sparrows leave the hive in the morning, but against the prognostications of the philosophers, do not return at dusk to commence manufacture of honey. More success is expected with some fledglings, and they are shut in the hive with some honey for inspiration for three days. When the hive is opened, far from flying away to find pollen, the sparrows, to the amazement of the metaphysicians, are found dead and rotting. Hamilton, recounting this through the letters of Zāārmilla, has not found herself obliged to comment at all on the arguments of the new philosophers.[74]

Again, though, this was very contrived satire. Hamilton, like the author of *De Brinboc*, was evidently misrepresenting Godwin, exaggerating some of his tenets to grotesque proportions, and diminishing the potency of her lampoon as a result. More efficient satire could be extracted from some few sections of what might be regarded as genuine new philosophy, arguments actually taken direct from the works of the radical philosophers, which were deemed absurd enough already to stand alone, undistorted by travesty, and authors such as Hamilton were obviously delighted to be able to introduce such episodes at every opportunity. Godwin's famous meditative walk through the streets of London, wholly unconscious of what was passing around him, was one such self-parodying spectacle, and it is with a certain insouciance that we see it in Hamilton's *Modern Philosophers*, when a Mr Sardon tells Bridgetina that he, like her, can now walk from Charing Cross to Hyde Park Corner without being distracted from his abstruse cogitations. In D'Israeli's *Vaurien* the episode is similarly satirised, first in unadulterated form, and then with a supplementary interpretation as Vaurien walks through London deep in thought about the ease with which fires, riots and explosions could be occasioned.[75]

More common still were free-standing pastiches of 'the famous fire cause', as Charles Lamb called it, the notorious passage of *Political Justice* in which Godwin imagined his valet, his father, brother or benefactor, and Fénelon, theologian and all-round ornament to society, all trapped in a burning building, there being the possibility of rescuing only one of them.[76] Charles Lloyd chose simply to have his hero recount the episode, and Godwin's debate on who should be rescued, as a self-evident proof of the new philosophy's vile heartlessness, requiring little or no authorial commentary.[77] Walker took the grim satire further, dramatising the debate, but still not allowing it to develop into a parody which misrepresented Godwin's own arguments to any significant extent. In *The Vagabond*, he presents Frederick with the choice of saving either his father or his childhood sweetheart. As Godwin had hypothetically counselled, instead of immediately using his ladder to effect a rescue, Frederick meditates on which of the two had more value to society. Both die as a result of his delay.[78] By 1800 and Sarah Wood's *Julia, and the Illuminated Baron* the episode had apparently become so well known, and so denotative of the new philosophy's iniquity, as to figure without any authorial notification of its provenance whatsoever. She presents Julia, Julia's benefactress and the young Maria trapped in a burning building, and sends a strange chevalier to their rescue. Though his instinct is to save Julia first, he hesitates, not because he is reasoning on utility, but because the women each suggest the others as more worthy of rescue than herself. Eventually Wood has her knight very pointedly insist that 'this is no time for argument', and he promptly saves them all.[79]

Such self-evidently invidious tenets of the new philosophy were the only occasions on which authentic radical principles could be afforded an unchaperoned place in conservative fiction. Doctrines were untrustworthy, and indeed, most often we recognise new philosophers in fiction not through their opinions but because we are somehow told they are new philosophers. Their names are frequently a giveaway – Messrs Newlight, Addlehead, Nincompoop, Mandred, Strongbrain, Swearwell, Subtlewould, Sourby, Rhodomontade, Ironfang, Reverberator, Bounce, Rant, Libel, Dragon, Allcraft, Myope, Glib, Axiom, Sceptic, Vapour, Marauder, Imphell, Rattle, Mortlock, Stupeo and Alogos all feature as new philosophers in the anti-Jacobin novel, as do a Mrs Egotist and Mrs Dupecull, a Sir Phelim O'Flimzy and a Jean Le Noir, and, each in separate novels, a Mr and Mrs Bounce, a Squire Ardent and Sir Caprice

Ardent, and two Mr Subtiles. The physiognomies with which authors endow them are also giveaways, working as both a hint as to what their opinions will be, and a physical manifestation of those ideas. Hamilton inserts a steady flow of information about Bridgetina Botherim's appearance in *Modern Philosophers*, for instance, so that by the end of the novel we know that she has a squint, a shrill voice, a twist in her shoulder, is short of stature, bald beneath her wig and so on. Charles Lucas prefers to provide all the information at our first meeting with his Marmaduke Pendragon, whose blond hair is cut short and dyed black, who rubs his face with onions to stimulate whiskers (which appear a 'dingy yellow'), who is fat and puerile of countenance, the combined effect of which is 'that no stranger of sensibility could look in his face without a smile'.[80] In *Vaurien* it is the grotesque deformities of the mind that D'Israeli points out to us. Each of his new philosophers has their own quirk: Rant rants, Subtile deduces, Reverberator recapitulates, Libel calumniates, Bounce controversialises and Dragon bays for massacre.[81] In *Berkeley Hall: or, the Pupil of Experience* (1796) Dr Sourby functions both as a representative modern philosopher and as a walking calamity who provides the comic relief. During the course of the novel he is tarred and feathered, shot in the leg, lynched by a mob, duped out of his life's savings, cuckolded, taken prisoner by the Iroquois and singled out by them as the only white man to be sentenced to death because they cannot see what service to society he performs.

Such personal invective, of course, was a significant front on which the satirical campaign of the anti-Jacobin novelists was fought. Beyond such rudimentary lampoons, though, the fundamental characteristic of any new philosopher was his or her hypocrisy, sometimes unwitting, sometimes deliberate. Worse, of course, was this second kind of hypocrite, those who acknowledged that they deliberately used doctrines they knew to be false simply to entangle their innocent prey in a web of casuistry. Such a one is Lady Appollonia Zulmer in Dacre's epistolary *The Passions* (1811), who candidly reveals to a correspondent that her corrupting letters to the naïve Julia have been filled with nothing but 'flimsy sophistry' designed to mislead. That this was an outstandingly straightforward method for an author to explain his or her attitude to new philosophy becomes obvious when Dacre makes Appollonia remorselessly divulge her machinations: 'How baseless, how false, the miserable doctrines and tenets I have broached to thee – false as hell itself!'[82]

I shall be dealing with these deliberate and calculating new philosophers at greater length in the next chapter, and, in any case, their

Jacobinism sheds little light on new philosophy as such, for they are opportunistic villains more than even counterfeit philosophers. More pertinent here are those dupes of new philosophy whose unconscious hypocrisy sheds illumination on its nature. One such is Frederick Fenton, very much the disciple of Stupeo in Walker's *Vagabond*, but more dupe than fraud, ingenuously confessing to what he at first thinks 'trifling' faults in the systems he professes, but which, as he acknowledges them, he realises puncture his vision. He even admits that he has never understood the subjects on which he holds forth.[83] This type of dupe, if not sacrificed to new philosophy, is often to be found moving on to some other equally foolish craze following their dalliance with Jacobinism. Sir Caprice Ardent, living up to his name, ends *Letters of a Hindoo Rajah* with his conversion to Methodism, and Mr Wilson, Jean Le Noir's associate in Britain in Pye's *Democrat* (1795), replaces his once ardent support for universal liberty on the French model with the equally ludicrous scheme for a plan to unite all the armies of Europe, according to their several qualities, in a grand alliance against France.[84]

The most popular device for exhibiting new philosophers' unconscious, but no less repugnant, hypocrisy, though, was to contrast their loud talk of levelling with their real love of privilege, submission and rank. In the quixote novels, it is a technique which features with almost monotonous regularity, the innate good sense and feeling of Sir George Warrington, for example, constantly discovering that, try as he might to share their principles, the behaviour of his new philosophical acquaintances runs contrary to all their professions of liberty, equality and fraternity. Sarah Green, in her *Reformist!!!* of 1810, brings the technique to the zenith of its sophistication perhaps, when her Percival Ellingford, a zealous champion of equality, threatens to beat his honest servant for, ironically, pointing out to him that such a levelled society could never function.[85] It is Brydges, though, with his usual crassness (something of a mixed blessing for a propagandist), who makes the point impossible to miss, his hero responding on our behalf to the obvious contradiction between a visitor's profession that 'I'm for equality, damme!' and his vow of vengeance against a servant who has accidentally run over his dog:

Here it was impossible for Le Forester to be quite silent – 'You are for equality, I think, Mr Simpson!' he said a little sarcastically? 'Yes, damme, if I ben't,' replied he; 'I think myself as good as any Lord in the land – but then for these blasted servants to behave insolent, damme if it is not intolerable; I'll kick 'em to hell, I say!'[86]

The sort of hypocrisy that Le Forester had easily identified as underlying Simpson's new philosophy, essentially an envy of those above him, but a fixed contempt for those below, was a constant theme of anti-Jacobin propagandists. Just as recurrent a theme in fiction, though, and perhaps amounting to an even worse sin, was the tendency of the anti-Jacobins' new philosophers to preach one thing to their inferiors, and then to condemn their resulting actions. It is a pattern seen most clearly in Hannah More's Cheap Repository Tract, *The History of Mr Fantom, the New Fashioned-Philosopher, and his Man William* (1795?), possibly the source for numerous reiterations of the fable in similarly motivated novels over the next few years. More's Fantom is a new philosopher, not malicious so much as hardhearted, selfish and unthinking, and his constant talk of Godwinian theories over the dinner table seems harmless enough, even if it deprives society of the real benefits he could, and ought to, contribute. Harmless, that is, until his valet William Wilson, having listened to his master's philosophism, decides to put some of his theories into practice, relying on his new knowledge that crime is no more than an empty term and that there is no hereafter, to sanction the theft of his master's spoons and wine. His fate comes quickly, as he proceeds from theft to murder, is caught, brought to trial, abjured by Fantom, made mindful of his folly and 'turned off', that is to say executed (though More's phrase is apparently a rare joke, punning on the term used for the dismissal of a servant). More later classed this tale as one of 'Stories for Persons of the Middle Rank', rather than one of her 'Tales for the Common People', a distinction that novelists seem to have recognised immediately, for in their many reiterations of the fable for a novel-reading audience, it is very definitely the Fantom character, rather than his servant, who takes centre-stage, and almost the entirety of the blame both as instigator of the crimes and heartless deserter of the eventual felon. Indeed, it is these criminals who turn, as it were, King's evidence for the jury of readers, and do most to indict their former masters and their philosophy.

Perhaps the earliest use of the Fantom motif in fiction is the story of Timothy Trundle in Hamilton's *Hindoo Rajah* who becomes the victim of the new philosophy of his master and his friends. He imbibes his principles, takes to crime as a result, and is then deserted by him. Hamilton's condemnation of the new philosophers here is much more severe than in the rest of her rather gently chiding novel: 'I did not think as how it would have been your honour, that would have had the heart to turn against me at the last', says Trundle to Axiom from the dock of the court in which he is being tried for theft. 'Many a time and oft have I heard you, and my master, Doctor Sceptic, say, that all mankind were equal, and that the poor had as good a right to property as the rich.' When, as Trundle is dragged off to the gallows, Axiom adds that the Age of Reason is approaching, when the 'fear of the gallows shall have as little influence as the fear of hell', Hamilton appears to have attempted to excite a real reprehension rather than the usual amused scorn.[87] An almost exact facsimile of the scene is to be found a year later in *The History of Sir George Warrington*, in which the butler actually did do it (burgle the house, that is), but only because he overheard the conversation of his master and Sir George regarding the virtues of equality and necessity.[88] Similar episodes appear frequently in other novels, servants always being corrupted by the carelessly disseminated 'flossophy' of their betters.[89]

Simply from the number of times it recurs, it seems safe to infer that this 'Fantom' motif was deemed particularly effective. Showing new philosophers as forsaking the victims of their own trifling with radicalism emphasised at once their folly and their disgraceful callousness. It emphasised the difference, the vital difference, between theory and practice, and by exposing this hypocrisy it proved itself a motif perfectly adapted for the novel. Authors aimed their novels (whether accurately or not) towards what More had called the 'middle rank', a class who might be supposed to include neither rogues who took up new philosophy because it suited their nefarious purposes, nor the credulous valets, butlers or maidservants whom the novelists showed to be so bewitched by the superficial doctrines of Godwinianism that they sincerely invoked them to justify their crimes. By targeting new philosophers who were imprudent, not vicious, who were irresponsible, not wicked, novelists were appealing to the section of society they thought most likely to benefit from their literary didacticism, designing their fiction for a particular purpose. Who could want to emulate these new philosophers – half fool, half knave – their novels demanded.

But if attacking new philosophers as a means of attacking new philosophy was one strong technique of the anti-Jacobins, and a strategy that obviated the need to address any specific tenets of that philosophy to boot, then a second method also inherent in the Fantom motif was to show the consequences of new philosophy once adopted in practice. The specific doctrines of new philosophy which the Fantom theme drew upon were particularly pertinent to novel-readers. Theft of property was the practical result, the novels repeated, of what might just conceivably, in theory, seem enlarged and liberal notions, and what consumer of novels could want that? Not even the asinine new philosophers who had been conjured up in the novels themselves could bring themselves to accept these consequences, as their willingness to prosecute the victims of their own precepts proved. Anti-Jacobin novelists showed quite straightforwardly that anyone with property, any one in the 'middle ranks', anyone who could afford to buy or borrow a novel, had a great deal to lose from new philosophy.

But it was not only the economic consequences of adopting new philosophy that the anti-Jacobin novelists elected to depict. A novel, with its eminently controllable narrative, was of all forms of propaganda the one most suited to showing effects springing out of causes, and this was a kind of lesson that had the further advantage of requiring the minimum of explicit didacticism. Who could miss, for instance, the lesson to be found in Halfaz's fate in *Memoirs of M. De Brinboc*, in which, having disappeared for a volume or two, he resurfaces as a dipsomaniac orator in an ale-house, the target for the mob's ridicule and missiles, toppling over with the wildness of his gesticulation, apparently imagining he is storming the Bastille, and demanding that the inn-keeper, who has denied him more drink, be hanged at a lamp-post? The surgeon soon has no alternative but to diagnose him as insane, and, despite their friendly efforts to prevent it, our heroes 'saw the unfortunate philosopher carried off to a mad-house; there, in all probability, to terminate the remainder of his singular and memorable life'.[90] Similarly self-evidently, in Hamilton's *Hindoo Rajah*, we are introduced to a young man whom Dr Sceptic is proud of having alienated from his clergyman father and of educating as an atheist, only for him to drop out of the novel until suddenly reappearing having ruined his beloved by insisting that marriage was an empty convention, having driven her to kill herself, and having himself been forced to suicide.[91] In her *Modern Philosophers* Hamilton was a little more insistent that her readers should not miss the consequences of the new philosophy practised by Vallaton, Myope and the rest. As well as the plot itself proving the disastrous results of their empty systems – the humiliation of Bridgetina and the death of Julia and her family being the most eloquent of comments – Hamilton periodically interspersed running tallies of the ruin so far wreaked by new philosophy. Mr Glib's children are in the workhouse, Mrs Botherim laments on one such occasion, Mrs Glib has gone off with a recruiting officer, Captain Delmond has died through grief at his daughter's behaviour and, the redoubtable Mrs Botherim concludes, even she will never be quite the same.[92]

Essentially, the comment that Charles Lloyd gives to his sagacious character Charles Maurice in *Edmund Oliver* might well have been placed at the end of almost every chapter of almost every anti-Jacobin novel: 'You evidently see in this case,' he says, 'the horrible effect of playing with human passions, and throwing down wantonly the barriers religion and morality have erected – and of adopting a method of cold and generalising calculation in conduct, which stands aloof from nature and human sympathies.'[93] Each chapter, each episode, attempted to provide a crucible in which the principles of new philosophy could be put into practice and, of course, found not merely wanting, but productive of the most conspicuous evils. This was the primary purpose, and the predominant method, of anti-Jacobin fiction, achievable with the minimum of authorial mediation. It was a technique that was merely made most obvious, was merely taken to its furthest extent, in the dystopias fabricated by a number of novelists to display the world promised, or rather threatened, by new philosophy. D'Israeli seems to have realised the efficacy of such a technique, for he added one such dystopian chapter to the second edition of his *Flim-Flams!*, depicting a town run on Godwinian lines, in which no one ever believed the word of another, for 'CACO-NOUS', that is to say Godwin, had spoken against promises, no one ever performed favours for another, since gratitude was a thing of the past, in which each man had to act as constable himself, for no one respected private property, and each woman refused to keep house, 'in consequence of what CACO-NOUS had written against cohabitation'.[94] In effect, though, both *Flim-Flams!* and *Vaurien* had been constructed in their entirety as literary laboratories for the refutation of the new philosophical hypothesis. Likewise, *Massouf*, with most of its narrative couched as the elaborate dream of its hero, as well as the novel being in the allegorical form of an Oriental tale, was wholly an attempt to disprove the new philosophy with which the ardent, young prince had been tempted. But it also included a miniature dystopia, inset into the narrative, Massouf visiting a colony of 'the enlightened' where he sees not enlightenment, but savagery, children playing with the severed limbs of their grandparents, incest and bigamy commonplace, and the strong and the talented executed for encroaching on equality.[95] The dystopia, the dream, the Oriental setting are all distancing layers for the didacticism, but once they have been peeled away, the analogy with Britain in danger in 1802 is evident.

Similarly multi-layered are the tours on which the protagonists of *Berkeley Hall* and *The Vagabond* are conducted. Their quests for pantisocratic utopias in the interior of America are detailed as both fail utterly, the new philosophy they bring with them wholly unsuited – as ever – to the realities of their situations. Both authors systematically demonstrate new philosophy to be incapable of dealing with everything from the storms of the Atlantic voyage to the need to defend the new philosophers from the depredations of the Native Americans, from the tricks of Philadelphia lawyers to the barrenness of the land and their realisation that slaves are apparently necessary to make it productive. In both novels, the civilisations of the Amerindians, which the protagonists, in accordance with so much Jacobin thought, suppose will be natural and noble, are exposed as just as corrupt as the new philosophers themselves.[96] Only in *The Vagabond* do the new philosophers discover their promised land, a beautiful country that seems to be brimming with all good things and crowded with spires and domes, a nation, in other words, which resembles the Britain that the vagabonds have left. But it is a country that has undergone a revolution, a 'Perfect Republic', as Walker's chapter title calls it, founded on 'the Principles of Equality and Political Justice', a country in which all manner of new philosophical doctrines are played out and which, as we quickly discover, will shortly have achieved its own ruin. Walker makes no secret of what his novel is really addressing. 'It is astonishing,' he informs us in a note, 'how ridiculous and even irrational the new doctrines appear, when taken from the page of metaphysics, and contrasted with practice', and we are shown how under the new regime no work can ever be completed, due to Godwin's conviction that each man need work only half an hour a day; how the government, such as it is, is filled with rabble-rousers and drunkards since each citizen had been given the vote; and how women had determined that they should be equal with the men – until, that is, the men began to use force to make the women undertake all the labour necessary for providing food, raiment and shelter, when they soon found it advisable to entreat 'to be reinstated in the ancient slavery'.[97]

Walker often interrupts his fictional dystopia with notes drawing attention to the parallels with the genuine one to be found in Revolutionary France, or at least to be found in the anti-Jacobin historians whom he quotes in support of the analogy. This nicely links the sort of 'theoretical' anti-Jacobin fiction Walker was writing with the type of conservative novel which concentrated on representing the real Revolution, as detailed in the preceding chapter. But it also emphasises Walker's central purpose – to use his fiction to exhibit the fate of Great Britain should she be allowed to become victim to the new philosophy. Portraying all his new philosophers recant their idiocy one by one, he even dramatises the conversion he hopes to effect in his readers, or which, at least, his anti-Jacobin propaganda has as its theoretical *raison d'être*. 'I will return,' cries

Dr Alogos, once the most convinced pantisocrat but now determined to get home to Britain, 'I will return . . . that I may at least set my example to them, and would to God they could see the precipice to which they are blindly straying.' Just as significant, though, was his afterthought that he would also endeavour to 'open their eyes to the private views and interests of those miscreants who are shaking the torch of sedition in their face, while they seek only an opportunity of picking their pockets', for in drawing this distinction between himself, whom he evidently thought of as a victim, and others, whom he arraigned as villains, he was hitting upon what was a subtle but important distinction between new *philosophy* and new *philosophers*.[98] New philosophy was a flimsy chimera, perhaps in itself even harmless, and Alogos, though certainly a new philosopher, was a dupe more than anything else, a fool foolish enough actually to believe in it. The new philosophers from whom he and his kind imbibed their folly were no dupes though, but knaves whose conviction of, or even connection with, any form of ideological radicalism was slender to say the least. They were the 'vauriens', men and women who adopted new philosophy as a means to an end, and they form the subject of the next chapter.

CHAPTER 4

The vaurien and the hierarchy of Jacobinism

> I must, however, acknowledge that we have some restless Spirits
> amongst us, who by their seditious Writings have contributed not
> a little to the Work of Destruction ... I thank Heaven the number
> of such Miscreants is but small, when compared to the Spirit of the
> whole Nation!
>
> Ann Thomas, *Adolphus de Biron* (1795?)

In the partly mimetic, partly dystopian, world envisaged by the anti-
Jacobin novelists, 'new philosophy' was the language in which
Jacobinism was conveyed and understood, the currency in which it circulated. The new philosophers, however, were not so much Jacobinism's
perpetrators, as just the first in the long line of its victims. There were two
kinds of miscreants populating the anti-Jacobin novel – those who had
been somehow convinced of the virtues of new philosophy, had really
believed in all that it seemed to offer for the good of mankind; and those
who had been responsible for instilling this conviction, this delusion, who
had made dupes of the new philosophers. This second sort of character
used new philosophy without ever being quite so naïve as to believe a
word of it themselves.

Such men, and in some cases women, I shall rather arbitrarily be referring to as 'vauriens', a term imported from the French (from which it
translates as a good-for-nothing) by Isaac D'Israeli for the protagonist of
his novel of 1797, *Vaurien: or, Sketches of the Times*. As we shall see, D'Israeli
by no means invented the concept of the vaurien, nor was he the first
to distinguish between the Jacobin who was a fool and the Jacobin who
was a knave. Indeed, the distinction was central to anti-Jacobin ideology,
and certainly to its fiction, for if every admirer of the French Revolution
and its principles was to be thought a designing villain, a vaurien, then
this would force the indictment of a vast section of the British population, certainly in the first years of the Revolutionary decade, on the
same charges as might be levelled against a Thomas Paine or Mary

Wollstonecraft. In themselves, the retractions of support for Revolution that were so characteristic of the British response to events in France by 1792–4 suggest that British radicals had been dupes, rather than the sort of villain who alone could be committed to a such a savage, bellicose and atheistic cause.

This simple discrimination between vaurien and new philosopher, however, is not sufficient to comprehend the Jacobinism envisaged by the anti-Jacobin novelists, and indeed individual novelists seldom overtly make such a clear-cut distinction. Any two individual characters of these types were merely two points on a finely graduated scale of villainy, a 'hierarchy of Jacobinism' it might reasonably be called. Before moving on to a discussion of the vaurien, then, this hierarchy of Jacobinism, and the ways in which it was imagined to operate, demands examination. It was the means by which, to borrow Edmund Burke's famous analogy, the few noisy and irritating Jacobin grasshoppers in the field could possibly incite to rebellion the docile cattle whose innate desire was to continue to repose beneath the shadow of the sturdy British oak.[1]

In the previous chapter I examined Hannah More's *History of Mr Fantom, the New-Fashioned Philosopher, and his Man William,* and some of its many reiterations in novels over the following few years. This was a fable of a fool's new philosophy overheard, and acted upon, by a servant, who would speedily pay the penalty with his trial and execution. Its basic import was clearly that new philosophy, and the Jacobinism it represented, was a contagious disease which, though its symptoms might seem minor in the first instance when educated and affluent men like Fantom were contaminated, was much more virulent among certain more susceptible sections of society in which the infection could all too easily prove fatal. In More's terms, new philosophy trickled down the social order, servants being most vulnerable to its assaults on their civil and religious virtues, or rather it was they who were most likely actually to act upon these new principles, and thereby incur the just retribution of both the temporal and, we are generally told to assume, spiritual authorities. Certainly, this was also the case in a great many of the 'Fantom' episodes which followed, in all of which, of course, the law worked perfectly, quickly apprehending the lawbreakers so that they might accuse their new philosophical masters and mistresses of encouraging the crime. Timothy Trundle in Hamilton's *Hindoo Rajah* (1796) had been servant to Dr Sceptic before robbing him, the thieves of all Dr Alogos' property in Walker's *Vagabond* (1799) had been servants, David Turner had been butler to Mr Goldney before stealing from him in *The History of*

Sir George Warrington (1797), the heroine of _Dorothea_ (1801) had brought upon herself the burglary and beating perpetrated by her once obedient and chaste servant and the girl's illicit lover, whilst Adeline Mowbray, in the midst of her own despair, had 'feelings of a most overwhelming nature' when she recollected that she had been the cause of plunging a servant into new philosophy-inspired vice.[2] For that matter, it was generally servants who were induced by their wicked, Jacobin masters to carry out attacks on our heroes and heroines in the more gothic of the anti-Jacobin novels, the servant of De Verney, for instance, acting as accomplice to his master and Marat in their plan to assassinate the noble St Cyprian in Craik's _Adelaide de Narbonne_, or Jacquetta and Basili assisting the infamous schemes of their pro-Revolutionary master, Revillon, in Robinson's _Hubert de Sevrac_.[3]

These servants were ensnared by new philosophy, we are often made aware, because they were poor and had nothing to lose by adopting the new system, because they were ignorant, their critical faculties not sufficiently sophisticated to expose the sophistry of new philosophy and because they were fanciful enough to imagine that the chimerical ideals that new philosophy offered could ever actually exist. Servants were not alone at the bottom of this hierarchy of opinions, for at least two of the same characteristics that had rendered them prone to the new philosophical poison – their willingness to believe new philosophy's empty promises and their inability to contest and rebut its fallacies – were supposedly shared by another group apparently particularly susceptible to its allurements – women. Adeline Mowbray is a prime example of a woman meant to appear too ardent, or perhaps too credulous, for her own good, a woman who takes up the new philosophy of Glenmurray to a much greater extent than he knows to be either practical or fitting. She pays the penalty when her disavowal of society's 'prejudices' leads to her ruination and a contrite death. The same impassioned and doomed endorsement of new philosophy is exhibited by Dorothea in the novel that bears her name, although she is allowed to survive her folly and to live happily the traditional life her mother and husband had long recommended. Elsewhere, there were some much less sympathetic treatments of women made victims to new philosophy, more misogynistically suggesting that an innate female licentiousness was the reason for their vulnerability to Jacobin doctrines. But just as frequent, and more significant here, it was the inability of women to refute new philosophy which made them vulnerable to its fascinations. In Elizabeth Helme's _Farmer of Inglewood Forest_ (1796), for instance, the penitent Emma leaves a manuscript to be read after her death explaining how it was that she was drawn into her immorality, atheism and licentiousness. By degrees, she says, she imbibed the tenets of her new philosophical seducer, Whitmore, 'and became a professed free-thinker,' 'for he used to engage me in controversies that I was not able to defend; and to bear down my reason with his volubility, and erroneous maxims dressed in flowery language, until I was forced to yield the point, though at the same time my heart bore testimony of their fallacy'.[4] The aristocratic young women of Vienna who people Sophia King's *Waldorf; or, the Dangers of Philosophy* (1798) are even less capable of coping with the dissipated principles that Waldorf so sedulously strives to disseminate. Herdi Lok, Waldorf's mentor, knows full well these dangers of exporting new philosophy to those unfitted to receive it. Of one of Waldorf's victims he comments, 'How could you expect to make Sophia a philosopher, or a determined atheist of a confirmed bigot? A weak mind must not be tampered with, nor dangerous doubts infused onto a flimsy understanding: you might as well put a loaded pistol into the hands of a baby; for destruction is sure to follow...' Being female, being creatures of sensibility, being Catholic 'bigots' and having the propensity to fall in love with a handsome and mysterious new philosopher, a substantial section of society is vulnerable, according to King. Waldorf cuts a swathe through them, leading whole families to their death as daughter after daughter dies 'a victim of the tenets of Waldorf', tormented by 'the reproaches of her conscience'.[5]

The real crime of the new philosopher, we find, was not the possession of new philosophical doctrines, but the spread of such dangerous opinions to sections of society unfitted for their reception. Thus it is that Mr Cameron, a magistrate in *The History of Sir George Warrington*, reprimands the eponymous political quixote at the trial of his friend's butler for robbery, not for his new philosophy *per se*, but for 'speaking in terms which an ignorant mind or a base heart may easily wrest to their own purposes'.[6] And throughout anti-Jacobin fiction, we find this specific censure of transmission rather than belief reiterated, just as Price and Paine had been deemed most culpable for propagating, not simply holding, their opinions. One thinks of the trial of Paine for seditious libel, when the Attorney General had asked the jury to 'be pleased to take into [their] consideration the phrase and manner as well as the matter'.[7]

For the learned themselves, new philosophy was most often a well intended, but mistaken, attempt to ameliorate the condition of mankind, a 'species of moral chemistry,' as Jane West put it, 'which rarefies, distils, evaporates, and compounds virtues, till they change their natures and become vices'.[8] And for those equipped to control the potent forces unleashed by such experimentation with the civil and moral laws of society, it was foolish perhaps, but just about permissible to delve into new philosophies. Burke had admitted as much in his *Reflections* (although he was to harden his line in *A Letter to a Noble Lord*), lamenting that those who had been given the opportunity to explore the nature of society and comment on its few regrettable faults now proved refractory and thought themselves free to use their learning for whatever purpose they chose, however dangerous to that good order which had allowed them their privilege. 'Happy if learning, not debauched by ambition,' he said, 'had been satisfied to continue the instructor, and not aspired to be the master!' Once the new doctrines had been spread to those completely unfitted to receive them, 'learning will be cast down into the mire and trodden down under the hoofs of a swinish multitude' as also, he pointedly warned, would be 'its natural protectors and guardians'.[9] Thus the quiet philosophical researches of, say, Mr Mental in *George Barnwell*, we recognise as innocuous if kept to himself, but highly reprehensible as soon as he begins to communicate them to the ingenuous George. Then, like Priestley, whose lifestyle Mental parallels, he deserves the mob that gathers at his house intent on destroying his scientific apparatus, the symbol of his iconoclastic theorising.[10]

And of course it is the mob, the swinish multitude, the *sans-culottes* who could actually make revolution a reality, that underlie this hierarchical conception of Jacobinism's dissemination, that are signified by the ignorant and indigent dupes of new philosophy's sophistry. When Fantom, or one of his many reiterations, carelessly ignites the flame of new philosophy in a servant or other figure ill-fitted for the reception of such doctrines, he, the Fantom figure, stands symbolically for the rabble-rouser of old repute, but endowed with new terror by the recent events in France. It is imperative, therefore, that every good citizen keep those below him or her in the hierarchy in ignorance of their distress and the possibility of alleviating it. It is a concern spelled out in *Massouf, or the Philosophy of the Day* (1802). There we are shown the would-be reforming prince learning that 'Where nothing is discussed, every thing is patiently endured.' Coming to the crux of the matter, and addressing the particular iniquity of a Mr Fantom, Massouf's counsellor adds that

where, from the spirit of discussion artfully promoted, the poor are industriously excited to draw a comparison between their own wants and the superfluidities of their fellow subjects – where an existing evil is sedulously pointed out to them, to which it is not in the power of men to provide a remedy, the happiness of each individual must sink in the general wreck of society, and those who cannot escape from famine and from slaughter, must become its helpless victims.

And lest either Massouf or the reader should somehow miss this stark warning, just such an event is dramatised at the close of the novel. The population set fire to the tower in which Zemedin, the philosopher who had goaded them to revolt, continues to pursue his incendiary, and all too flammable, speculations.[11]

It is the inability of the mob to realise that new philosophy was never meant to be put into practice that makes them so dangerous, but it is a characteristic shared by those new philosophers who impart it to them too. Only those at the top of this hierarchy down which new philosophy percolates realise its fraudulent and chimerical nature, their victims investing progressively greater and greater faith in principles which had never been meant to be believed. Herdi Lok, for instance, the originator of the licentious philosophy that corrodes morals, religion and loyalty in Sophia King's *Waldorf*, believes that the doctrines he preaches will be perfectly possible to institute only as Mephistopheles believed that Faust would have no regrets about his bargain. Waldorf, on the other hand, Lok's first gull and the character in whom the reader's sympathy is invested, is easily beguiled by the promises of new philosophy, but still consistently exhibits a conscience that is anathema to Lok's system, and soon – although too late – begins to doubt its practicality and probity. An orphan with no means of subsistence in a strange city, Waldorf is ripe for cozening, and, for precisely the same reasons, unfit for the seductive doctrines of Lok. But if Waldorf is unsuited for new philosophy, his mistress, Helena, to whom he passes on his principles, is even less able to see that its consequences could only be destructive, and even less able to cope with the freedom it permitted and encouraged. Ruin is sure to follow, and her innate depravity quickly comes to the surface, as she makes 'her principles subservient to her pleasures' until her inevitable suicide ends a pan-European career of promiscuity, and worse still, proselytisation of others.[12]

Frederick Fenton, hero of George Walker's *The Vagabond* provides another good example. Sent from home to continue his education, he imbibes his Jacobin principles from Stupeo, a wily new philosopher who obliterates any residual feelings of filial duty in Frederick by promising him the company of any number of sexually available women. But worse, *ingénus* like him actually believe and therefore evangelise the tenets of their own seducers. Frederick is even foolish enough, on his peregrinations around British Jacobin circles, to accuse other new philosophers of insincerity and betrayal of their great cause. 'Hypocrites!' he reprimands two founder members of a London debating society as they plot to fabricate evidence of new governmental atrocities, 'will you sully the beauty of truth by such actions?' And as they escape, fearing him to be a government agent, so uncommon is it for them to consort with genuine radicals, they leave Frederick to put the case for reform to those who remain to listen, something which he does with more conviction, but far less success.[13]

We cannot help but feel a certain sympathy for Frederick, just as we do for the political quixote, Sir George Warrington, who, when he encounters other disciples of new philosophy, never finds that they live up to his naïve expectations. Benjamin Potter, for instance, disappoints the early opinion Sir George has formed of him by admitting that 'This liberty and equality is glorious work for me', explaining that until a few days ago he was merely a footman, but now he has become a gentleman and eloped with his master's daughter and her £10,000. 'And it is villains like these,' Sir George is forced to concede, having been given an insight into the true motives of this new philosophical footman, 'who disgrace a cause that is so noble in itself!' – to which the author cannot resist adding, perfectly expressing his or her intentions in filling the novel with this sort of episode, 'Alas! he was yet to learn, that, among many who adopted his favourite system, there were but few who, like himself, thought only of the general good that might spring from it.'[14]

This Benjamin Potter, another servant, is victim of another Fantom-figure. 'My master was always preaching about the rights of man, and such like', he explains, 'so I have taken the liberty to run away with his eldest daughter, and consider myself quite on a footing with him.' Yet unlike Fantom's servant, Potter's deliberate felonies, as well as the conventionality of the offences, set him up as more than merely an innocent victim of another's careless talk. He is, to a certain extent, a villain in his own right, for, as the author very deliberately points out, he is like by far the greater part of new philosophy's adherents who 'entertained no hopes, but of raising themselves by the destruction of others'.[15] Nevertheless, for all that his own position is more complicated than many other servants corrupted by their masters, Potter's crimes are still less condemnable than those of his master, Squire Thornton, and his quixotic friend, Sir George, who provide the opportunity, and the justification, for his villainy. Yet they too have been dupes of new philosophy in their turn every bit as much as Potter. Like him, they combine the rôles of victim and victimiser, being merely links in the chain of new philosophy, something made very clear in *The History of Sir George Warrington*, with its sympathetic treatment of the quixote figure. Elsewhere too, even the most abandoned new philosophers often command pity more than censure. Mr Glib, for instance, in Hamilton's *Modern Philosophers* (1800), though partly responsible for the ruination of Bridgetina, we find to be a sacrifice to other new philosophers, made victim by his folly not his wickedness. It is Maria Sydney who identifies that he 'seems to make use of some author, who probably little imagined that his theory would ever meet with such a practical advocate', and since the notes cite Godwin as the culprit, we have no difficulty recognising the figure above Glib in the Jacobin hierarchy.[16] This question of how new philosophy was transmitted to the likes of Sceptic, Axiom and Waldorf, to Glenmurray, Dorothea and George Warrington, from whom it would pass on to others, was almost always a central consideration for literary anti-Jacobinism, for these Fantom-figures were the representatives of the reader in the novel, members of the middling ranks, who needed to be told not only to avoid infecting their inferiors, but also how to protect themselves from the contagion.

It might be supposed that within the class structure inherent in the Fantom motif, with philosophers of the middle ranks corrupting domestic servants lacking in the economic security and critical faculties to render them immune to its lure, the most likely source of the Jacobinism taken up by the new philosophers might have been from *their* economic and social superiors. For many of the more Evangelically inclined anti-Jacobins who aimed to amend the manners of the great this was, to an extent, true. Yet to extrapolate from the descent of the new philosophy from masters to servants that these pestilential doctrines generally percolated down a socio-economic hierarchy, or one constructed according to the level of education available, would be mistaken. Those in society's élite, those in the ranks above Fantom and his peers, feature in anti-Jacobin literature as dupes to the same, if not a greater, extent as those at the bottom of the scale. They are presented as just as vulnerable to the allure of new philosophy, for it is their vanity, and their desire to conform with the *ton*, that attract them to voguish, that is to say *new*, philosophy, and by inviting new philosophers into their houses, they are being just as credulous as the servants attracted to their principles for more material reasons.

The distance between aristocratic pride and new philosophy's strictures was often shown to be virtually negligible. When Lord Belfield,

Vaurien's host in London, insists that his ducal insignia be affixed even to every lowly cart in his possession, for instance, it giving him great pleasure to single out his carts from the commonality, the new philosophers he has gathered around him applaud it as a deliberate effort to degrade every appendage of nobility.[17] The philosophers are wrong, of course, it being Belfield's constant endeavour to exalt aristocracy in every possible way, the very preoccupation, indeed, to which they owe their welcome in his house. Indeed, from the number of novels that show us these degenerate aristocrats dabbling in philosophy, we might conclude that it actually *was* supremely chic to sponsor such new philosophers. Jean Le Noir, for example, in Pye's *Democrat* (1795), visits a lord who, not content with his great wealth and status, desires to be 'a fomenter of discord, and the head of an unprincipled faction', whilst Sir Caprice Ardent, in Hamilton's *Letters of a Hindoo Rajah*, gathers around him Messrs Axiom and Sceptic, Puzzledorf and Ergo, before growing tired of that pastime and switching his enthusiasm to Methodism.[18] These attacks on the sponsorship of radicalism by the British élite had their most vituperative expression in *A Letter to a Noble Lord* (1796) in which Burke mauled the Duke of Bedford for his supposed support for Jacobinism. Yet for all that the Duke and his like were to be condemned because they were doing more than anyone to bring the revolution to Britain, they were also to be pitied as deluded dolts. '[P]oor innocent!', Burke calls him: when the revolution comes it will make such aristocrats its first target irrespective of 'the services they render to this Gallick cause'. Jacobins are 'the Duke of Bedford's natural hunters; and he is their natural game'. And while they smile on the Duke for the present, they are secretly planning the butchery to come.[19] It was a point made over and over again by anti-Jacobin fiction, although seldom with quite the level of savagery predicted by Burke in his final, paranoid years.

But if the hierarchy that existed for the transmission of new philosophy through society was not class-based, who was it who so nefariously planted the seeds of new philosophy amongst the loyal and contented population of Britain? If we consult More's *History of Mr Fantom*, we see that she cites as the principal motivation for Fantom's new philosophy 'a famous little book, written by the NEW PHILOSOPHER, whose pestilent doctrines have gone about seeking whom they may destroy', by whom she certainly meant Thomas Paine (as later editions of her works make plain with their footnotes).[20] Paine was a marvellously convenient common ancestor for all new philosophy in Britain, the double-barrelled attack of his *Rights of Man* and *Age of Reason* giving Jacobinism an all-encompassing breadth united in one man which might have had to be invented had it not already existed. Certainly we can see More's lead being taken up if we return to *The History of Sir George Warrington*. The new philosophy of both Squire Thornton and the political quixote himself, joint corrupters of Benjamin Potter, are attributed to Paine, Sir George's contamination precisely traceable to the parcel of books which contained *Rights of Man*. Indeed, Potter recalls that Thornton has been always talking of Paine and repeating that he is the first man in the kingdom, even if only a staymaker.[21]

However, the author of *George Warrington* presents another figure in the hierarchy of new philosophers, an intermediate link in the chain that attaches Paine and Sir George, responsible for leading the political quixote into the most idiotic, and dangerous, of his errors. This is a Mr Davenport, himself a victim of the opinions of the Fantom-like new philosopher Mr Wilmot, but a willing victim and one whose republican and atheistic sympathies are sustained by no genuine belief, save the conviction that they might be profitable to him. All this is exhibited in his introduction: 'Having nothing to lose, and depending solely on his patrons for subsistence, he of course followed them in their adherence to the party formed in favour of the French Revolution and was by them deputed to gain as many votaries as possible to their side.'[22] Davenport selects Sir George as his prey, and draws him into avowing such republican sentiments as will lay him open to the charge of treason, and to withdrawing money from his bankers, ostensibly for the nation's defence but really pocketed by Davenport. Worse still, he encourages Sir George to export further his spirit of mutiny to others, enlisting him, under false pretences, as the leader of a campaign against Mr Annesley, a supposedly exploitative employer. Sir George leads a demonstration, but the mob turns unruly, then insurrectionary. Eventually, the scales having fallen from his eyes, Sir George is obliged to resist them by force. But the process by which the principle of rebellion against the *status quo*, in theory in the new philosopher's case, and then in practice at the hands of the mob, has trickled down from Davenport to the multitude, using Sir George as a conduit, is what remains the most conspicuous theme of the episode. And these are the three essential components of the hierarchy of Jacobinism – the villainous vaurien, the foolish new philosopher and the mob that, knowing no better, put their schemes into shocking practice.[23]

In fact, as the reader is made continually aware, Davenport's scheme is designed neither to address the grievances of the workers, nor to further the aims of the 'party', as he calls the Jacobin interest for which he is theoretically an agent. We soon discover he has a private grievance against Annesley, and sees Sir George as the weapon with which to gain revenge. This is significant, for such selfishness and, indeed, such a-politicalness, is the hallmark of the vaurien, the rôle which Davenport plays with aplomb. It is this characterisation that explains why anti-Jacobins filled their novels with vaurien figures. The Fantom motif was explicitly designed to convince a middling-rank readership, largely supposed by authors to be reading their novels, of the dangers in even trifling with new philosophy, but they wished to do this without the necessity of actually debating points of doctrine, for such politicisation of fiction would have been both a literary and ideological transgression. New philosophy's principal fault, the novelists implied, was simply that it was such an eminently exportable commodity, and would be transmitted to parts of the community entirely unable to see through its lures and all too willing to endeavour to make its idle dreams real. The vaurien was another technique which, without having to address new philosophy head on and in its own terms, without having to engage in political controversy, perfectly demonstrated new philosophy's hollowness, exhibiting the supposed truth that, from its source onwards, Jacobinism had nothing to do with any genuine concern for the nation or its population, or for anything so pure as truth, political justice or the rights of man, but was merely a subterfuge for the age-old vices of an number of mischievous individuals. Such persons were the vauriens, figures who were always at the head of the hierarchy of Jacobinism, no matter what their social or economic status, their mental capabilities, nationality or gender. Whether they were members of the aristocracy, such as Lord James Marauder the Infernal Quixote, members of the gentry or middle class, like Glenmurray in *Adeline Mowbray*, or from the most obscure of origins, like Davenport and innumerable others – whether they were French agents or indigenously reared rogues – whether they were coquettes or rakes – the one thing that remained constant was their regard not for what they could do for Jacobinism, but what Jacobinism could do for them and them alone.

Vaurien himself, the anti-hero of D'Israeli's novel, as well as being rather atypical in certain respects, does not provide the earliest example of this most common of figures in the anti-Jacobin novel. The motif gradually evolved in the hands of the numerous writers who used it in the 1790s and beyond. It was to receive its most forceful theoretical exposition in Burke's 1796 *Letter to a Noble Lord* in which he warned, very much in the language of novels, that 'a den of bravoes and banditti' had assumed 'the garb and tone of an academy of philosophers'.[24] But it was in frequent use before that, for example in an anonymous pamphlet of 1792 called *Liberty and Equality*, in which the real motive of the unequivocally named 'new philosopher' Judas Mac'Serpent is exposed as nothing more than greed. He was paid four livres a day by the National Convention for doing all in his power 'to create disturbances in different parts of England, so as to promote the views of France, which are,' the letter helpfully explains, 'first to ruin, and then to subdue your island'. 'To affect this,' the letter continues, 'you must mix, as much as possible, with the lower orders of the people, and endeavour to make them discontented with their present situation, and jealous of those above them.'[25]

Although much of this would be carried over into numerous anti-Jacobin novels, the continuities are perhaps less significant than that which would be altered. Most apparently, the tenor of such narratives would be changed for the novel form, which, however great appeared the fears that the novel had recently found a new audience among the lower orders of society, was still not directed by 'A Poor Man to His Equals' as this tract purported to be. If we compare D'Israeli's *Vaurien*, for instance, we find that the Jacobin villain is aiming to seduce not the sort of countryfolk attracted to the ale-house at which Mac'Serpent held sway, but that section of the British public who felt better represented by the novel's protagonists, Charles, a parson's son just arrived in London from the country, cousin to Lord and Lady Belfield, and Emily, daughter of a Lieutenant in the navy, only recently descended into straitened circumstances. And a second difference was that in novels the vaurien figure would on the whole be endowed with a slightly altered motivation, just as self-serving in principle perhaps, but without the salary from France to formalise the treachery, and without the same degree of personal spite against England possessed by Mac'Serpent.

In D'Israeli's *Vaurien*, however, these distinctions are rather blurred. Vaurien himself is a Frenchman, well practised at spreading the new philosophy so as to foment revolt, already having a long career of insurgency behind him in more or less every European nation, as well as America and the Ottoman Empire, and who at last has turned his attention to Britain. Once there, indeed, we see him walking the streets of London, meditating on the ease with which riots could be induced, fires started and bombs planted, and he is anxious, for obvious and sinister reasons, to examine the armoury at the Tower of London and the dock-yards at Plymouth. Additionally, Vaurien's principal aim, once in Britain, is ostensibly to enlist the forces of discontent – Scottish philosophers, Dissenting preachers, Jews, clergymen wanting prefer- ment as well as political radicals – into a phalanx of sedition that could deliver the Revolution. Such malcontents, Vaurien identifies, have long nursed their grievances, but have never attempted to redress them by any of the inflammatory means he now suggests, and Rant, Dragon, Subtile and the other new philosophers he meets, for all their rhetoric, have failed to mobilise the fools and knaves of Britain. Yet, if Vaurien is a French *agent provocateur*, it is only on a freelance basis, and he is not being paid from the coffers of the Revolutionary government. Indeed, he lives off the patronage of the credulous Belfields, and is at all times anxious to maintain their interest in new philosophy because his livelihood depends upon it.

Similarly, although Vaurien claims that the ruin of a young woman was a diversion from his real aims and that 'It is only national treasons which I feel as my genius', not only does he apply the same skills to both his public and private intrigues, but the campaigns he wages to subvert the nation and to seduce Emily progress in tandem. In fact, much more of the novel is devoted to Vaurien's assault on the virtue of Emily than is to his grand revolutionary project. In both these spheres, D'Israeli forces us to conclude, with Vaurien, that 'The French. . . have very inventive heads, and the English very unsuspicious hearts.' Unlike Mac'Serpent, Vaurien's motives are always two-fold, half personal and half political.[26]

This is a pattern one might expect in the novel, always written to some extent as a work of entertainment however much of the political pamphlet's didactic intent remained. In fact, in some pamphlets Thomas Paine himself was being refashioned in the vaurien mould. His portrayal by John Gifford, for one, concentrated on his stay-making, debt, theft, Sabbath-breaking, wife-beating, perjury, bigamy, impotence and possible sexual deviance, before addressing the errors of his political thought.[27] In other anti-Jacobin novels, although it was important that this blend of personal debauchery and political corruption was maintained, the balance between the two tilted so that Mac'Serpent's public, political motives, as symbolised by his payment from France, became less and less significant. This progression from public to private villain becomes remarkably conspicuous in the comparison of other early conservative novels with those that would come later, but is also sometimes evident within individual novels. Pye's *Democrat* of 1795, for instance, one of the first anti-Jacobin novels, presents the balance tilted still more towards public villainy. Like his fellow Frenchman Vaurien, Jean Le Noir has always been found wherever there is mischief afoot. With the sort of internationalism we recognise from the peroration to Richard Price's *Discourse on the Love of our Country* (1789), Le Noir carries the germ of republicanism along a well-travelled trail. From America, where he has fought for independence from the British, to France, where he soon becomes friends with Robespierre, Marat and Paine, he naturally 'turned his thoughts anxiously to the idea of introducing a system of equalisation and fraternity between the *degenerate* Britons, and his own regenerated countrymen'.[28] Once there he occupies the same rôle of freelance French agent as Vaurien had done, constantly intent on inciting rebellion, and the novel becomes a fairly conventional picaresque journey around Britain, remarkable only because Pye shows Le Noir's continual disappointment that there exists so little genuine revolutionary sentiment wherever he looks. He seems to fit into the mould of a Mac'Serpent, but Le Noir is not wholly the political reprobate, even if it is only before his hero arrives in Britain that Pye shows the personal side to Le Noir's machinations. Pye presents the genesis of his avowal of new philosophy as being sited wholly in the attempt to satisfy his appetites, material, social and sexual. His desire for equality we find to have been motivated by the fact that other boys in his village had managed to accumulate more nuts, apples or grapes than him. His adoption of radical ideas on the union between the sexes we find to have been based on his desire for the beautiful Adelaide de Tourelles, whom he abducts in an episode reminiscent of the Marquis de Montalt's abduction of Adeline in Ann Radcliffe's *Romance of the Forest* (1791).[29] This established, it underlies our understanding of his campaign to foment revolution throughout the novel. But Pye's somewhat crude attempt to fuse the public and private vices of Le Noir merely emphasises the success with which later novelists would incorporate a much greater degree of personal motivation, at the expense of the more public impetus for their villainy, to indict their Jacobins.

Certainly by the turn of the century, it becomes rather difficult to isolate the political drive of the vauriens, so submerged is it in their private designs. *Dorothea* offers a relatively good view of the discernibly political strategy of its vaurien, Thomas Williams, but even here, with his overtly political involvement with the United Irishmen and his successful attempt to incite the mob to attack Kilkenny gaol (bringing to mind such political realities as the Gordon Riots and the Fall of the Bastille), all is not as it seems. Though Williams goads the mob to action by enraging them against the 'tyrannical' arrest of the leaders of the attempted rebellion just put down, his real aim, we find, is to engineer the release of a rich Dublin boy, who has been led away from the straight and narrow at his college by the high-flown orations of a set of reformers, and to return him to his father and collect the reward which the father would no doubt provide. And this personal agenda is exactly in keeping with all we have learned of Williams so far, for remembering his introduction into the narrative, as a young student at Oxford, resentful of those who succeeded there with less ability but more money, we know that he adopted the Jacobinism that would bring him to Kilkenny only for personal gain. Indeed, he evidently does not believe a word of the new philosophy peddled by his Jacobinical associates, but resolves not to let that stand in the way of the opportunities it seemed to offer:

The absurdity and impossibility of their plans Williams had early detected; but, said he, I already know that not all men are equally clear-sighted. If these specious reasoners get the ear of the multitude, who knows what consequences may arise? An epoch of confusion is, perhaps, the only one in which, circumstanced as I am, I can expect to reach my proper sphere: to me then it is most desirable, and it is a *duty* I owe myself, to lend a hand to the cause which alone is likely to place me where I ought to be.[30]

In fact, as the novel progresses, we find that Williams' new philosophical acquaintances at Oxford, men who (perfectly illustrating the hierarchy of Jacobinism) adopted new philosophy only because it seemed fashionable and quickly dropped it without realising the damage done to their social inferiors, are the exception, and that Williams himself, with his personally motivated Jacobinism, is the rule. The United Irishmen, to whom Williams soon becomes secretary and treasurer, are certainly of the same stamp as him: they have nothing to lose and 'were willing to take the chance of a scene of confusion; in the belief, that where property is exposed to the scramble, the most agile will be the greatest gainers'.[31] This is a nest of vauriens, in other words, with their own interest their only aim. Moreover, this insight into Jacobinism's motives exhibits the full horror of such a system to anyone who has even the least stake in the *status quo*, who has anything at all to lose in the 'scramble' which they aim to induce.

The deceitful attempts of vauriens to enlist the support of the lower orders with a populist plan for the redistribution of wealth which they never intended to implement was one of the prongs which Burke had taken up in his attempt to deflate the Revolution and all it stood for. He had warned in the *Reflections* that the plunder of the rich would 'give but a share inconceivably small to the many', and portended that 'those who

lead them to repine, never intend this distribution' in any case.[32] Pye's
Le Noir, on his tour of Britain, disconsolately confirms this, discovering that any 'persons possessing even a moderate share of property...
however fond they might be of theoretical equality, they were not fond of
hazarding any step towards the practical part'.[33] Others found the same.
At one end of the financial scale, Lord Belfield, in *Vaurien*, refuses to stand
any talk of economic levelling in his house. And at the other (the end, in
fact, at which most Jacobins were to be found, as evinced by Frederick's
surprise on discovering Dr Alogos to be a rich man, 'for he had found
the pupils of the new school, in general, a little short in financial affairs'),
Citizen Ego, an itinerant orator in the Jacobin cause, evidently regards
new philosophy as nothing but a money-making scheme. He charges
admission to his lectures, urges his auditors at every opportunity to give
generously, does not fail to remind them where they can purchase copies
of his speeches. Lest his debating society should lose fee-paying members,
he forges letters from various parts of the country recounting atrocities
committed by government agents and urging the club to continue in
its good works.[34] Even more audacious is the scheme of the duplicitous
Chauncey to establish a pantisocratic utopia run on Godwinian lines in
Berkeley Hall: or, the Pupil of Experience (1796). Once he has found some
naïve investors he absconds with their money, leaving the community to
collapse under the weight of its own folly.[35]

This self-interest was most evident when it was contrasted with the
altruism of the true patriot. Sir Samuel Egerton Brydges, with his customary crassness, was continually reminding his readers that his hero,
Arthur Fitz-Albini, 'felt no satisfaction in employing his thoughts upon
himself or his own affairs' and thought it 'of little consequence...what
may be the state of [his] private circumstances' – all of which was by way
of contrast with the 'adherents of a certain party ... who console the
envy and malignity of their hearts at the inferior situations in which it is
their lot to be placed, with hopes of an early change, when it will be their
turn to triumph, and trample on the necks of those, who now, according
to their ideas, oppress them'.[36] Sarah Green made this distinction the
central lesson of her *Reformist!!!* of 1810, the preface of which spelled out
that 'Self-interest governs, in a great measure, the whole world; and the
political reformist is only eager to get into place...'[37] Even if Green was
talking of those seeking parliamentary reform rather than any more revolutionary goal, this merely emphasises the point, for, as other novelists
made clear, the vaurien found the parliamentary opposition his natural
habitat – not because a vaurien would have any particular principles in

common with Fox, the Duke of Bedford, or Burdett, say, but because they would, in the view of many a Pittite novelist, both share the same absence of integrity. In Wildman's *Force of Prejudice* (1799), for instance, we see Sir William Clementson, 'all that we can possibly suppose of moral depravity', supporting the opposition in the Regency Crisis of 1788–9, hoping – as was Fox, we are given to understand – for great personal gains from the installation of the Prince of Wales as Regent, and having no concern for the effect of such a move on the nation as a whole.[38]

Clearly, new philosophy could be used as an infinitely malleable means to make some personal profit in the pursuit of money or status, or as an entirely ductile screen for some obscure personal resentment, but for most of those vauriens who employed its rhetoric its purpose was clear: lust. This is not to say that the vaurien's desire for property and power, and his or her licentiousness, were not eminently compatible. As in *Vaurien* and so many other anti-Jacobin novels, the anti-hero of *Dorothea* manages to combine his licentiousness (and avarice) with his public Jacobinical activities. Having arrived in Dublin to find that Ireland is not quite ready for revolt, Williams 'took advantage of this breathing time, to consider how his private interest might be furthered in another way' – that is, how he might get his hands on the £5,000 of the orphaned Catherine O'Neale. It proves an easy matter to accomplish, and when he has married her, without her guardian's consent, appropriated her fortune, fathered a son and run off leaving her with only self-absolving sections of *Political Justice* for comfort, he is open to our condemnation for his rakishness and rapaciousness as much as his radicalism.[39]

The conservative campaign to reveal Jacobinism as primarily an attack on affectional relationships was explored in the last chapter. The vaurien was the vehicle for this exposé. He or she was the libertine who simply appropriated new philosophical discourse to assist in their campaigns of carnality. So fundamental is this to anti-Jacobin fiction, that for Laura, in *The Vagabond*, to opine that 'I do sincerely believe that those men who preach up promiscuous intercourse of sex do it merely to cover their own depraved desires', is little more than a truism. She herself has been a victim of one such rake-cum-radical. Frederick Fenton has endeavoured to seduce her with the logic of *Political Justice*. Her refusal to comply has convinced him that, despite what Godwin and Wollstonecraft held, women must after all lack the capacity to understand new philosophy. His theorising evolving in tandem with his libido, he talks himself round to ignoring her arguments and browbeating her into submission. Ultimately all his faith in the power of reason evaporates in the heat of his lust. Still unable to prevail, his philosophy finally vanishes to reveal only that which animates it, and he 'resolved to supply his want of persuasion by violence' and 'he exerted that prowess which men are endowed with for other purposes'.[40]

Those novels set in the French Revolution itself, from *Lindor and Adelaïde* in 1791 to *The Nun of Santa Maria di Tindaro* in 1818, seem to specialise in depicting their vauriens using the Revolution and Jacobin doctrine merely to gratify their own depraved desires. In Sayer's novel, it is Antoine who persecutes Adelaïde when Lindor has died at the hands of the Jacobin mob, pressing his suit with questions about what difference the blessing of a priest or the empty ceremony of marriage could possibly make to a lover, such as he plans to force Adelaïde to become.[41] In Stanhope's, it is Charles Angerville who 'leagued himself with the assassins of his king' just so that he might gain possession of Helena, the wife of a friend who has taken up arms against the Revolution.[42] In *Memoirs of M. De Brinboc* (1805) the pattern is even more pronounced, the author continually reiterating that the Marquis de Chevreville has been a villain of the deepest dye under the *ancien régime*, and would continue to be so under any administration, and that he looks upon the Revolution, which has allowed him to return to France from the exile imposed after the violation of his sister-in-law, merely as the perfect opportunity to pursue the beautiful Eugenie. It is a project all too easily accomplished too, since her 'disaffection to the present order of things' (which, of course, was to be expected of any self-respecting heroine) means that a word in the ear of his Revolutionary friends, Marat amongst them, would be sufficient to force her to submit to him or face the guillotine.[43]

Naturally, the architects of the Revolution were the very worst of vauriens themselves, men who had engineered the Revolution, if the opinion of several British novelists is to be believed, purely to gratify their desire for innocent heroines. In *Adelaide de Narbonne* (1800), Craik shows Marat designing legislation purely to gain Adelaide as his wife, a plan he reinforces by immuring her until she agrees.[44] It is a tactic echoed by the mysterious 'Count' in Moore's *Mordaunt* (1800), who, with the assistance of his friends the Revolutionary commissioners Collot d'Herbois and Couthon, has arranged for the imprisonment of the object of his desire, the Marquise, so that he may offer her freedom in return for her acquiescence to his proposal of marriage.[45] In Robinson's *Natural Daughter* (1799), Mrs Sedgeley finds herself incarcerated in the Abbaye gaol and is visited by a disguised man who offers to set her free if she will give herself to him. When she refuses, he promises to add her name to the list of victims of the guillotine, for, she recalls, 'I now discovered that the barbarian inquisitor was the despot Marat', whose assassination the following day is all that allows her to live to tell the tale. Along with Robespierre's passion for the heroine's sister, Robinson appears to suggest that the leading Jacobins were united in nothing so much as their weakness for British gentlewomen foolish enough to visit Revolutionary France.[46]

The Marquis de Chevreville, 'the Count', Marat and Robespierre – these were all essentially villains straight out of a gothic novel, a portrayal made possible by a combination of the truly barbarous events of the Terror and the anti-Jacobins' deliberate envisioning, from Burke onwards, of Revolutionary France in highly gothic terms. Marat, persecuting innocent and defenceless heroines whom he had incarcerated in gaols under his personal control, and in which he might visit them in disguise bearing threats or promises of freedom, reminds us of no one so much as Ann Radcliffe's Montoni, endeavouring to cajole or compel Emily to marry him as she is imprisoned in the Castle of Udolpho. In those anti-Jacobin novels set in a contemporary Britain, where it was an article of ideology that this kind of gothic persecution was inconceivable, a similar licentiousness remained the defining characteristic of the vaurien, but he or she appeared in the traditional guise of the rake, or his female equivalent, the coquette. They used new philosophy as Marat used the Revolution, appropriating its rhetoric and its devious and delusive tenets to co-opt their proposed victims into compliance with their nefarious schemes. To take just a handful of examples, we have seen Whitmore drag Emma into debauchery by attacking the 'formalities of the law' and 'the jargon of priestcraft' as utterly meaningless in *The Farmer of Inglewood Forest*; we have seen Lady Gertrude Sinclair attempting to inveigle Edmund Oliver into vice by revealing that the normal bonds of society were mere 'prejudices'; and we have seen Sir William Clementson, in Wildman's *Force of Prejudice*, assailing the virtue of Augusta with talk of marriage being 'only a civil institution for the more legal protection of property, and never solemnized at the altar until a very late period'.[47] We have witnessed Charles Denham in *The Citizen's Daughter* pursue his quarry with 'I know my adored Marianne, you are above the weak prejudice of an uninformed mind' (which he later translates as, 'I could place you in some little cottage, where, unshackled by the restraints of tyrant custom, and unknown to my family, I could visit you'), and we have seen Marianne reject and expose his scheme, since 'contrary to all the enlightened doctrines of the new school', she determines to persevere 'in the weak prejudices of conjugal felicity in preference to the philanthropic principles of nature and equality'.[48] Perhaps most blatant of all are the attempts of Sidney to draw the naïve Eliza into licentiousness with 'Mrs Wollstonecroft's [*sic*] divine work' in *Douglas*, and the Infernal Quixote's use of 'the wonderful arguments of William Godwin', as well as certain passages of Wollstonecraft, to undermine the morals of Emily, the object of his desire.[49]

In all these vauriens, whether French or British, we can hardly detect a political side to their machinations at all, save only that their rhetoric, the tool that they use, retains the outlined impression of its original intent. In fact, by the later 1790s, so transparent had the actual intentions of the vaurien become, and so distinct from the nominal aims of the rhetoric which they used, that Jacobinism and new philosophy began to lose any identity of their own, and feature as nothing more than empty bombast, phrases no longer anchored to the demonised ideas, texts or individuals which the anti-Jacobins had originally picked out for obloquy. Thus, in *George Barnwell* it is not Mental, the new philosopher, who takes centre stage as the real villain, the real vaurien, but Miss Milwood, who, though never exhibiting any sustained Jacobinism, and without any real radical credentials, becomes the focus of our contempt. When she does use the language of Jacobinism it is without conviction and almost as an afterthought, these passages seemingly inserted artificially by the author just as he had inserted the whole character of Mental into his adaptation of the Lillo play on which the novel was based. George, whom she has seduced into an illicit liaison and sundry criminal activities, demands that they must marry, to which she artfully replies, playing on his scepticism: 'Do you allude to the mummery invented for the use of those, who have not faculties of their own to define the laws of nature? Am I the less yours – are you the less your Milwood's, because a ceremony is omitted?' And when George finally discovers that his lover is already married, she, being a practised coquette, can instantly summon up some of the rhetoric of new philosophy to excuse her adultery, beginning 'I know the jaundiced eye of prejudice, views it in all the hideous colourings of vice', before masked men, in her pay we later discover, burst in and 'kidnap' her.[50]

In the same year, and in more or less exactly the same terms, Gertrude Sinclair in Lloyd's *Edmund Oliver* uncovers the reality of her seducer's new philosophy, discovering that he is married:

Great God! D'Oyley, and is it for this that we spurned at prejudice? – laughed at the forms of men? – Is it for this that we abandoned all institutions, and positive rules, and have thrown ourselves into the amazing depths of intellectual calculation, unbiased save by the character of the passing moment? ... I now understand too well your objections to marriage – your well feigned aversion to all the barriers in the generous impulses of an independent mind.[51]

Neither Milwood nor D'Oyley were Jacobins, if a Jacobin had actually to believe in Jacobinism, but at least they had been endowed with a consciousness of what new philosophy was. But there were numerous other novelists, writing after the Revolution crisis had subsided, who, though they retained the vestige of Jacobin oratory, accompanied it with no acknowledgement of the provenance or implications of such sentiments. In the anonymous *Leonard and Gertrude* (1800) for instance, Collins, who aims to settle personal scores by chasing off the local squire, attempts to incite the villagers to riot with talk of their 'rights' having been violated. Yet though this word forms the constant refrain of his rabble-rousing, he never enunciates a more distinct Jacobinism, nor any greater advocacy of new philosophy, and both the derivation and the potentially calamitous ramifications of his opinions remain unstated.[52] Other vauriens use distinctly Godwinian words like 'prejudice' or 'necessity' just as promiscuously, demonstrating that though they are still being defined as villains by this vocabulary, they have entirely come away from their ideological moorings.[53] We see, in other words, the villain having taken on all the characteristics of the vaurien, but having lost the very *raison d'être* of the rôle; we see men and women who are new philosophers according to their language but not in the least according to their objectives. The Jacobinism of D'Israeli's Vaurien, Pye's Le Noir, Walker's Stupeo or even Hamilton's Vallaton, however superficial this had been in itself, had evaporated to leave only a rhetorical residue.

What had been retained, though, in all the examples we have just been examining, were the signifiers of Jacobinism, its vocabulary, its cant phrases and, indeed, its tendency to spread its poison to others (for the essence of the rake and coquette was that, like Jacobinism, they dragged others into their depravity too). What the vaurien's rhetoric and actions had originally signified in the context of the debate on the Revolution had been left behind by later novelists, but without losing any of the contempt for Jacobinism which was inherent in the portrayal of the vaurien. Through the vaurien, a technique employed from the early 1790s onwards, we find that Jacobinism had no identity of its own, but was always only a cover for something else. This might be personal libertinism, the desire to grow rich at the expense of others, or sometimes merely personal spite. New philosophy was nothing but empty words, had no shape or substance independent of the debauched will that directed it. Its apparent adherents merely used such cant as would achieve their corrupt ends, a fact that Stupeo, in Walker's *Vagabond*, perfectly demonstrates. 'What is the use of words,' he challenges, speaking on behalf of all vauriens, 'if we are not to turn them to our advantage?'[54] The vaurien obviated the need for any actual debate of Jacobinism in the novels. Authors were able to incite the reader's reprehension without the need to resort to any actual explanation of why Jacobin principles were so iniquitous. Despite what we might at first assume, they neither aimed, nor actually attempted to counter any authentic radical principles in their work, but invented new philosophy, and provided their own definition of Jacobinism, to act as the targets for their attacks. The vaurien represents the apogee of this technique, their principal popinjay, meant to personify Jacobinism, but only the Jacobinism which they themselves had invented. It enabled them to deny Jacobinism the status of a coherent and legitimate political or moral philosophy. It conclusively demonstrated that Jacobinism and new philosophy offered nothing which anyone might genuinely want. It was a perfect technique, for such a figure already had a rôle ascribed to him or her in the novel, as rake or coquette, gothic villain or even a demon in disguise, as was the case in Sophia King's supernatural tale, *The Fatal Secret*. Having ensured that the individual they had created stood for the Jacobinism they strove to combat simply by the attribution to him or her of a few key signifying phrases, nothing could be simpler for the novelist than to indict radical principles as they proceeded with the unravelling of their plot.

CHAPTER 5

Levellers, nabobs and the manners of the great: the novel's defence of hierarchy

'It is so,' said Edward, 'the happiness, nay the very existence of society, depends upon the due subordination of its members, and the contentment with that station assigned to us by Providence.'

Men who are born to fortune are appointed by Providence to the administration of a certain portion of the interests of the world: they are the helmsmen of happiness; and if they desert the wheel, is there any wonder that the even course should be lost?

Robert Dallas, *Percival, or Nature Vindicated. A Novel* (1801)

One of the principal reasons for the attack on the novel in the late eighteenth century was that it was said to encourage equality. It is a proposition with which numerous twentieth-century scholars have agreed, contending that the eighteenth-century novel was somehow an intrinsically 'bourgeois', or at least 'democratic', form, insisting that it stressed the equality of man because every character possessed an equal capacity to feel, to fall prey to adventures, to become a protagonist.[1] Contemporary critics of the novel, though, were worried less about the sudden elevation of a protagonist out of his or her social station, and more about the effect these texts were having on their readers, men and women who were, they feared, increasingly being recruited from the lower reaches of society. Such new readers were having aspirations implanted in their giddy heads, wholly out of keeping with their real stations in life. Reading of masquerades and fainting fits, of midnight trysts and elopements, of the likelihood of being a mysteriously displaced aristocrat, could only militate against good order, it was said, by encouraging an equality of ambition and even of behaviour. Such criticisms of the novel as these had been vociferously current for several decades before the French Revolution induced a new sense of crisis in Britain. So also had been the primacy in conservative political and social thought of the concept of a Providentially ordained inequality in society, and the necessity for every

126

member of society to submit to it, a dictum succinctly outlined by Edward Tatham:

In the subordination and gradation of persons and rights, consists the very life and health of every well constructed state. In this political arrangement, made not by the wisdom or the will of man, but by the invisible hand of Providence, every man moves in that sphere of life, whether higher or lower, in which that Providence, not his own choice, has placed him at birth.[2]

Though neither notion was new, anti-Jacobinism, as was so often the case, took up both arguments with increased vigour in the 1790s and 1800s, restating the fundamental importance of hierarchy to the well-being of the commonwealth, and pointing to novels as one of the chief threats to this necessary submission. As I have already suggested, it was partly as a result of this reinvigorated condemnation of fiction that the anti-Jacobin novel came into existence. It was only natural, therefore, that these novelists should take particular care to demonstrate their conviction of, and commitment to, the sort of hierarchical society, with each member of the community occupying an unalterably defined position within it, that the novel had been accused of undermining. It is these constant endorsements of inequality, of unalterable rank and of submission, that will be explored in this chapter.

The centrality of the social and political theory of hierarchy and inequality to the conservative paradigm would be difficult to overestimate, but this is not to say that every advocate of this kind of social organisation attempted to prove its rectitude with the same arguments. Without in the least falling short of a standard degree of vehemence with which these opinions were upheld, there were writers who variously contended that society's division into separate ranks was divinely ordained, that it was a state of affairs that could be proved merely by means of theory and reason, or that this configuration of society could be endorsed simply on practical grounds alone. This array of arguments has been authoritatively analysed, in both their elevated and popular manifestations, by Robert Hole and H. T. Dickinson.[3] But there remains a danger in unquestioningly accepting contemporary assertions of this theory of separate spheres of activity for separate sections of society. Just as historians have begun to question whether separate *gender* spheres were a reality for most, or even for many, women and men in Britain during the Revolutionary and Napoleonic wars, or whether these concepts were merely a rhetorical construction imposed by writers and speakers whose opinions generally went unheeded, so the same sceptical scrutiny might profitably be adopted when considering the rhetoric of social hierarchies. This is perhaps not the place to undertake such a complex task, yet two related points are worth making. First, we should remember to be at least suspicious of any effect the ideology of hierarchy and inequality actually had on those to whom it was preached. This will become relevant when we see just how stringently and infeasibly some novelists preached their doctrines of social immobility. And second, even if this ideology was more rhetorical than real, it was certainly disseminated at least as far down a chain of reception as the authors of novels, who faithfully filled their fiction with it. By the mid 1790s, Hole has found, arguments stressing the inevitability, probity and wisdom of inequality, more than any other aspect of the conservative ideology, 'dominated debate and were a constant theme from establishment pulpits'. Exactly the same was true of novels, save that in fiction, this dominance continued for many years beyond the zenith of the Revolution crisis.[4]

Anti-Jacobin novelists made it their constant endeavour to show Britain to be possessed of a social hierarchy running up and down it like a backbone, with a pronounced top and bottom, and any number of intervening grades. But crucially, and as with gender spheres, each step on the ladder was entirely equal in importance. It was consequently equally dangerous to attempt to step off any one of them. All individuals in Britain, they insisted, had their own preordained and unalterable position in society, a position in which their own personal characteristics and qualities were submerged in the characteristics and qualities of the particular caste into which they had been born. It was not merely degrading to attempt to escape one's station, but ridiculous, and dangerous. Aristocrats were meant to remain aristocrats and to act like them, farmers were meant to remain farmers and milliners' apprentices were expected to remain milliners' apprentices. Just as it was a clear transgression for women to enter the sphere of the public and political and for men to meddle in the running of the household, so clergymen were not meant to be fashionable, and (with particular relevance to the authors of anti-Jacobin fiction) the unlearned were not meant to be philosophers.

To an extent, anti-Jacobin novelists were happy to assume that their readers agreed with them that this concept of a great chain of being which stretched throughout society was divinely ordained, and that it was inherently sinful to seek to resist it. Edmund Burke had done much the same in both his *Reflections on the Revolution in France* (1790) and the *Appeal from the New to the Old Whigs* (1791), in which he set out his ideas most forcefully. Yet other, more reasoned, vindications of inequality were also appropriated from the wider debate by novelists, often with little or no concession to the different readership that might be expected. It is necessary to be wary, of course, of attributing every apparent fictional recital of some specific piece of conservative dogma to a specific source amongst the welter of anti-Jacobin tracts and treatises. The various strands and arguments of conservative thought in the 1790s were general property in most cases, and novelists might have appropriated any position from any number of pamphlets or sermons, or simply have developed the argument for themselves. There are, however, some general similarities to be elicited, similarities which demonstrate the way in which novels did shadow, as it were, the major strands of the conservative ideology of the Revolution crisis.

One thread of late eighteenth-century conservative thought, for instance, sought to base inequality on an almost scientific, or at least reasoned, foundation. William Paley's *Reasons for Contentment* (1793) and *Natural Theology* (1802) were perhaps the most popular examples of this sort of strategy in action, but a more compelling, but similarly rational, argument was put up by Adam Ferguson in his *Principles of Moral and Political Science* (1792). Ferguson's arguments on equality were convoluted and diffuse, but they may be distilled into two contentions which were representative of the arguments used by a large section of inequality's apologists. His first principle argued that because each individual had a different disposition, some being covetous and frugal, say, and others neglectful and dissipated, and because each individual was of unequal ability and application, there would always be distinctions in the fortunes of mankind, and from a difference of fortune, Ferguson argued, there must always result 'a distinction of estimation and rank'.[5] This was a point so central to any defence of inequality that it is unsurprising to find it often reiterated in fiction. It was the line of argument John Moore opted for, for example, in his *Mordaunt* of 1800 when he sought to denigrate the attempt of the Revolutionaries to introduce what they called 'egality' into France. Moore's protagonist might well have been reading Ferguson when he wrote to a correspondent in Britain that what he had seen perfectly showed that 'there can no more be an equality of fortune, than there is of stature, of strength, of understanding, of activity or industry'.[6]

The second element of Ferguson's rationalisation of inequality was a little more abstruse, drawing upon a distinctively Scottish theory of political economy and paying homage to the work of Adam Smith. Not only were inequality and hierarchy natural, Ferguson argued, but they were positively useful too, which is to say that they were profitable both to the individual and the nation since they provided an incentive for ingenuity and industry. To an extent, Ferguson was taking a dangerously radical line here, for he contended that it was partly the ambition of those in the lower orders of society which conduced to this profitability. But he was careful to temper this with more conventional arguments, seeming never to have imagined that the ambition of which he spoke as 'a spur to their industry and an incentive to labour' would actually ever be successful in raising any individual out of their station relative to their superiors, but would serve only to enrich the nation as a whole. This is apparent from the metaphor with which he attempted to clinch his argument. He envisaged a nation labouring under the burdens of equality as analogous to a number of individuals all attempting to complete a manufacturing process from start to finish on their own, whilst a society organised into distinct ranks was comparable to an association of individuals gathered to work on the process together, each carrying out a small part of the operation numerous times according to their own particular talent. There could be no question, he concluded, which method would be more efficient.[7]

Even in as unlikely a place as Clara Reeve's unrepentantly gothic novel *Memoirs of Sir Roger de Clarendon* (1793), there are unmistakable hints of this economically based vindication of inequality. Reeve ends her novel by running down a list of those classes of readers she hoped her message would reach, and what it would teach them. The summit of her ambition is to teach princes to beware evil counsellors, but she has special lessons for every degree of society right down to 'the people at large', whom she wishes to teach 'submission to their lawful prince, to the laws, and to the Magistrates', as well as 'to shun all those who would seduce them to worship the idol *Equality*, which, if it could be introduced, would reduce them to indolence and despondency'.[8] This was a fairly standard moral lesson couched in fairly standard moral language, but when we add it to her stated wish to instruct those engaged in arts and trades in the importance of avoiding imitation of luxury and of being honest and frugal, and the lesson she reserved for those in public office, in whom she hoped to inculcate an utter aversion to embezzlement, a more economic defence can be seen to accompany what remained a theory of inequality largely premised on an only vaguely explored concept of Providence. Her concluding remarks emphasise the economic dimension still further. She ends her novel, she says, with the hope that it will have taught 'that a true and regular subordination is what makes all order and degrees of men stand in need of each other, and stimulates them to exercise their courage, industry, activity, and every generous quality, that supports a state and government'.[9] There are certainly shades of a Fergusonian apology for inequality here, even if Reeve did not trouble herself to explain exactly how inequality stimulated industry, and even if the economic arguments were simply grafted on to a more traditionally religious explanation.

However, some strands of Christian social theology did manage to devise other means by which to justify social inequality without having recourse to these materialist arguments, and again it was a defence that was reproduced in fiction. As Hole has noted, William Wilberforce and a number of other similarly inclined Evangelical apologists for the *status quo* added an element of moral paternalism to the usual formulas, arguing that Christianity made inequality less of a burden, but above all, that it rendered any trifling difference of rank entirely inconsequential, for the only state of existence that mattered was yet to come.[10] Elizabeth Hamilton's novel *The Cottagers of Glenburnie* (1808) strove to show this and thus to strip the 'doctrine of Liberty and Equality . . . of all seditious import', as one of its chapter titles put it. The proof she offers that only one's rank in the eternal hierarchy of souls is significant comes in the form of two funerals, occasions that interface between transitory earthly distinctions and the lasting ranks of the afterlife. One is Lord Longland's, a lavish spectacle with herds of plumed horses and troops of hired mourners, none of whom is interested in remembering the supposed object of their lamentations; the other is that of the humble Mrs MacClarty which, though unadorned with such trappings of grief, is an occasion for all those who had known the deceased and her virtues to mourn truly. Mrs Mason loses no time in drawing the necessary conclusions:

'Where now,' thought she, 'are the distinctions of rank? Where those barriers, which in this world separate man from man? Even here sorrow only embalms the memory of the righteous . . . Why then should those of lowly station envy the trappings of vanity, that are but the boast of a moment, when, by piety and virtue, they may attain a distinction so much more lasting and glorious?'

Real contentment, Hamilton elicits, is to be found only in that peace of mind which 'is distributed by Providence with an equal hand among all the various classes of society'.[11] Wilberforce and others had even argued that the lowly path in life was a positive advantage, not so much because it pleaded one's cause at the final judgement, but because a simple life put temptation out of one's way. Francis Lathom was one novelist who conscientiously took it upon himself to support this claim, his otherwise rather blithe *Men and Manners* (1799) including some lengthy passages on the subject. 'The poor man soon finds how little he has to expect in this world,' explains Jacob, a man of vast experience in these matters as his life-story has revealed, 'and his conscience then points out to him the way to expect it in another.' The rich man, on the other hand, 'has so much to think about here, that I should fear he often forgets there is an hereafter!' When he does remember, Jacob asks, who will be the happier, he, or the poor man who can never forget that to which he has to look forward? Lathom goes so far as to dramatise the effect of such arguments on a poor old woman who has the good fortune to be sitting outside her humble cottage as Jacob and his interlocutor pass by: ' "Oh Sir," cried Dame Bridge, 'how comfortable and pleasant it makes me feel to hear you talk; it becomes a gentleman like you, that have had the opportunity of learning, to tell the poor people these things for their comfort." '[12]

That the wealth and power of those in the higher ranks of society could only work to their disadvantage was a strain of anti-equality social theory that did not have to be based on the theological argument of the difficulty a rich man faced getting into heaven. As it became more secular, however, the argument became more unconvincing, the trick of contending that affluence was onerous and privilege a burden becoming increasingly difficult to pull off. Such defences of inequality in the novels could often be breath-taking in their audacity, but also began to look ridiculous. A passage from Charles Lucas' *Castle of St Donats* (1798), for instance, seems almost a parody of itself as the *ci-devant* Duke de Meritè explains his wish to be known only as Mr Smith from then on:

The poor think the rich are most happy: the rich indeed have the outward appearance of it, and the poor of misery: but look within, – a superb dwelling, fine clothes, and delicate viands are no longer the means of happiness to a great man; custom makes them common, and often loathsome, while discontent, ill health, and the greatest of all evils, idleness, make him far more wretched than the poor fellow, whose simple labour, natural to man, gives him health, spirits, and expels that dreadful lassitude of thought.[13]

And in fact, Lucas was treading a dangerous path here, for in claiming that any one rank was somehow better off than any other he was inviting comparisons which could only be dangerous. Much more often it was the endeavour of the anti-Jacobin novelists to demonstrate that each rank in society was an equally good place to be. Thus the aristocratic hero of Sir Samuel Egerton Brydges' *Arthur Fitz-Albini* (1798), meditating upon a humble ploughman, finds the same reasons for him to be cheerful as the

Duke de Meritè had identified ('Does not his employment innocently and usefully occupy his time and thoughts? . . . Does not health brace his nerves; and labour exclude uneasy thoughts?'), but also realises that the ploughman's good fortune in no way affects his own, and that his nobility and the ploughman's vocation should demand the same respect because they are the exact counterparts of each other, unsustainable if they are forced to stand alone.[14] It was as much a sin for a noble to be envious of another rank of society, in other words, as it was for a peasant or a labourer, though, as could only be expected, it was those towards the bottom of the great chain of being whom novelists seemed most anxious to assure of the iniquity of seeking to alter their appointed station.

Thus, in *Solyman and Fatima; or, the Sceptic Convinced*, an Oriental tale of 1791 by T. Wright, the protagonist is born to be a shepherd, but, ardent for knowledge and riches, wishes, with a degree of quasi-biblical symbolism, to desert his flock and to leave his native plains of Cassimere. Wright's ruling on his protagonist is severe: 'he knew not that ambition prompted the restless wish, nor considered that the sphere of life allotted by Providence to every individual, is productive of pleasures adapted to the capacity, and affords the proper scope for the execution of moral duties'.[15] By contrast, we are shown Zadah, his father, a man who has always been an unassuming shepherd who enjoys the gifts of Providence with thankfulness and a man whose days, therefore, have been irradiated by 'one clear beam of social bliss'. He knows that any reasoning 'which would affix the idea of happiness to any particular station of human life' is erroneous, the secret of contentment being that humility 'which, by leading to a just distrust of our own wisdom, impels the mind to rest implicitly in the unerring ordinations of Providence'. The unravelling of the quixote-style plot soon proves him right. When he finds a huge jewel Solyman can live the sort of life he has always dreamt of, but since he is not to the manner born, he quickly becomes indolent and unhappy, and moreover, is unable to run his household, so that it soon descends into disorganisation and becomes a burden rather than a pleasure to him. Needless to say, it is precisely at this point that he 'began at length to conclude, that the wisdom of Providence has proportioned the several stations of mankind to the measure of intellectual capacity', and that 'the happiness of individuals is properly found in that walk of life which a power infinitely more wise hath allotted'. In fact, Wright's persistence in teaching this lesson soon becomes rather daunting for he reiterates his point at every opportunity, and, as if his own authority was not enough, closes the novel with a celestial endorsement of the moral Solyman has drawn, a messenger of Allah descending to pronounce that 'the station assigned to each individual is that wherein his happiness is to be found'.[16]

The Oriental tale was a form marvellously well adapted to showing the practical arguments that Tatham and others had raised against any attempt at equality. In another, *Massouf, or the Philosophy of the Day* (1802), the author used a similar technique to Wright's, for the same purpose, by describing the dystopian dream of his Prince Massouf of a land in which equality had been tried, and had led to bloody anarchy. The prince's wise counsellor, Ayoub, brings the novel to a close with an interpretation of his dream, although his oneiromancy must be superfluous to anyone who has read through the dream themselves. 'Proceed, then, Oh Massouf!' he says, 'to an unwearied performance of the awful duties of thy station; urge and enforce, as much as is in thy power, the same conduct in others. A community, where each individual is virtuously employed in the duties of his station, has attained the summit of human prosperity.'[17] Actually, there is one final episode to follow this lesson in *Massouf*, for the prince has yet to fulfil his own appointed rôle as hero of a novel by marrying Fetnah, Ayoub's daughter, to whom we were introduced as a likely bride at the very beginning of the novel. When the marriage does take place, Massouf can be said to have reached that 'summit of human prosperity' of which Ayoub had spoken, partly because marriages in novels are conventionally productive of just this kind of absolute felicity, and partly because, as a novel's hero, he has now duly performed the duties of his station.

The elision of a hero's fulfilment of his literary duty (to get married) and his social duty, which in Massouf's case is to rule wisely and benignly, was a technique perfectly suited to novels, and one that was hardly an option for the authors of sermons and tracts. If, though, it was rather an oblique way of making the point, probably too subtle for effective propaganda, there were other techniques similarly well adapted for fiction which novelists were quick to take up. They present their readers with vast numbers of happy servants and labourers, for example, men and women who would not wish to change their social position for anything in the world even though they derive from what we might have considered, before we had learned the doctrine of propriety of rank, the lowest classes of society. Generous masters and mistresses that they are, French aristocrats forced to emigrate from their native land in novels such as *Adolphus de Biron* and *The Parisian* generally offer their servants the chance to remain under the Revolutionary regime that will grant them their freedom. The offers are always indignantly refused.[18] Those who are forced to stay in France lament the loss of the aristocrats: 'Folks may say what they will,' says one wretched woman when the local grandees are forced to flee from the approaching Revolutionary army, 'but I am sure that one such good house as our castle above was, is a thousand times better for the poor than all these new notions that have brought us no good yet.'[19]

Even if this was fiction, it was tangible 'proof' of the wisdom of hierarchical society, not the mere speculation (however confident) that necessarily emanated from the pulpit and filled the disquisition. When it came from the mouths of the poor and needy, as a novelist could easily contrive it to do, the theoretical economic justification of inequality gathered authority, as Massouf discovered when, still dallying with the youthful ambition to put the world to rights, he asks an indigent bag-maker whether he is not jealous of one of the nation's principle merchants and all his opulence. 'By no means,' says the man, displaying an admirable grasp of political economy,

such immense and prodigious capitals as his are necessary to give energy to trade, which without them would stagnate, and in a country so populous as ours, thousands, who, like myself, owe their bread to it, must starve: besides, I am not poor; thanks to the flourishing state of commerce, wages are high, and few men need be poor in town. Poverty will, it is true, in some degree always exist: it is often the consequence of natural infirmity, of sickness, of unavoidable calamity; but oftener of indolence and profligacy.[20]

The bag-maker's communitarian theory, just like that of Ferguson or Tatham, rested upon the idea of a pyramidal society uncompromisingly divided horizontally into distinct ranks but with vertical connections cutting across the strata so strong that, although they did not infract on the sacred configuration of classes, they did bind together those ranks in a web of mutually beneficial relations. Everyone, in every station in life, benefited from a rigidly hierarchical society, not just compared with its notional opposite, the sort of equal society which could only lead to anarchy, but in absolute terms too. For Robert Dallas, in his *Percival, or Nature Vindicated* (1801), it was something best expressed with a pleasant metaphor. Equality, one of his characters equates with 'the level of the ocean which is at the mercy of the winds, whereas,' she goes on, 'the distinction of ranks is the firm earth of which the acclivities and declivities, the hills and the valleys, ensure the verdure, fertility, and beauty'.[21]

The principal duty of the lower orders of society could be fulfilled simply by their submission to the hierarchy, something perfectly dramatised in Mary Meeke's *Count St Blancard* (1795) in which the plot somehow places a provincial woman of little status and few parts in the way of the true Count inheriting his usurped fortune and title. Since the Count has always proved himself the perfect aristocrat-in-waiting, donating alms right, left and centre (including to this woman), whilst she knows that she has none of these qualities, it is only natural that she should abdicate in his favour. Nevertheless, it still seems rather blatant that Meeke has her defer to the Count by signing a blank piece of paper on which he may write out whatever settlement he thinks fit, awarding himself the title, and his kinswoman some small recompense for her obedience to Providence, but certainly not enough to elevate her out of her station in life.[22] Members of the lower orders often played a more active rôle in fiction, dramatising, as it were, their loyal submission. Trusty servants are always to be found getting their social superiors out of danger, for example, as in *Adolphus de Biron*, in which Miss MacIntosh has no sooner fallen from her horse than the faithful old sea-dog, Archie, has saved her from serious injury. Captain M.'s extempore meditation of 'the necessity of Order both on sea and shore' is deemed so edifying by Mr Bruce as to deserve full transcription in his letter to Adolphus:

Protection claims our Gratitude, and many other good Effects which cannot come within the Scheme of Equality. – I regard Archie for his honest and good Disposition, and he is sensible of my good Offices and Protection. The Wise Disposer of all Things has assigned to every one his Station and the Whole Chain of Beings are dependant on each other.[23]

Just in case any readers had unaccountably persisted in missing the point that the existing hierarchies were responsible for all the beauties and benefits of British society and were reciprocally beneficial to all groups of society, Thomas has one of her characters, the worthy Mr Stanley, trot out the familiar tale of the 'Schism in the Body Natural'. He argues that 'this beautiful Fable', in which the body's limbs refuse to pander to the desires of the belly, and are surprised to find themselves languishing as well, 'is perhaps a better Answer to Mr Paine's Rights of Man, than a laboured Confutation'.[24] Indeed, why hazard a laboured confutation, why encourage any sense of debate at all, when the novel was such a well-adapted medium for exhibiting the reciprocal benefits of ranked society in a manner that would brook no dissension? Who could argue, for instance, with *The Brothers*, a 'Novel for Children' of 1794, in which we follow the education of Henry, the son of a prosperous gentry family, taught all the duties of his station, and Tom Jenkins, a 'peasant' instructed at the local Sunday school to serve and obey? Both of them precocious, Henry and Tom anticipate the rôles they, as master and servant, will play in later life. Henry donates his old clothes to Tom, whilst Tom, always anxious for Henry's well-being, rescues him from a potentially disastrous bird-nesting accident.[25]

But the conception of a mutually beneficial bargain inherent in civil society was most obvious when novelists sought to stress the economic justifications for inequality, their desultory attempts at political economy really acting not so much as reasoned arguments designed to convert, but as a large-scale metaphor for the necessity of hierarchy. In George Walker's *Vagabond* (1799), for instance, the point is proved with the help of a pineapple. Only the rich can afford to buy such a luxury, complains the would-be new philosopher, Frederick, and while they spend a guinea on it, the poor starve for want of a half-penny's worth of bread. Fortunately, there is a man of sense on hand to expose this fallacy. Were it not for the rich to buy each pineapple, he explains, shares of the guinea with which they are bought would not descend to the many people who thus derive their livelihood. Would Frederick want the fruiterer, the gardener, the glazier, all to starve, not to mention all those others who produce the materials for these trades? And, he must surely realise, it is obvious that only this kind of integrated and inter-reliant society could produce an exotic fruit like a pineapple, and, by extension, anything of any value.[26] Manifestly, it was actually the duty of the rich to indulge themselves. Indeed, an upright servant in Sarah Green's *The Reformist!!!* (1810) calls it 'no better *nor* a downright sin' that his new philosophising master wishes to walk to London and to sleep under hedgerows on the way, for it deprives all those inn-keepers and coach-drivers who ought to have benefited from his spending.[27] It is a sign of how far this trickle-down principle had been absorbed into the fabric of the novel that it could even displace that most conventional duty of the rich, charity. The fortune that accrues to Edward, a central character in Dallas' *Percival*, he proposes to manage with thrift so that he will have all the more to give away to the deserving poor. Luckily, the wise Mr Bevil is there to correct him by pointing out this is not the approved way of managing a fortune, it being the duty of 'men of fortune' to support *commerce* by spending their wealth, for 'every man who spent his income added to the general welfare'.[28]

Novelists were keen to demonstrate that in certain respects there was a distinctly onerous side to being at the head of the social scale. In fiction, aristocratic heroes and heroines were often to be found lamenting that their status imposed more limitations than freedoms, a socio-political comment generally mediated through the refusal of their proud parents, representing the strictly but necessarily ordered society, to sanction their union with the partner of their choice. More than one hero found, like Henry Villiers in *Plain Sense* (1796), who even wished to pass on his title to his brother so that he might marry the indigent Ellen, that 'his detested title, like Dejenira's fatal gift, stuck close and filled him with torment and despair'.[29] But the fact that, as in all the most popular novels of the 1790s, it was a problem which could be quickly resolved by revelations of true pedigrees and bequests of large fortunes merely emphasised the error of attempting to abdicate one's social responsibilities, as Henry had wanted to do, or, worse, of violating its edicts, by an elopement perhaps. In novels, both those of high and low estate had to wait patiently for the workings of the plot to secure their felicity, the rich and powerful having to submit to the dictates of their rank just as did the poor. Indeed, it was often pointed out that the élite could learn a thing or two about submission from their social inferiors: 'look at the lower ranks of people, who earn with difficulty a scanty meal with hard labour', says the pious Mrs Allwyne to the hero of Charles Lloyd's *Edmund Oliver* (1798), '– they are cheerful, and perhaps thankful – and will you, in the enjoyment of plenty and many accommodations, give way to a restless and dissatisfied mind . . . ?'[30] At least one aristocrat, Lord Bendham in Meeke's *Conscience* (1814), takes her advice and submits to the rules of his class. Unhappy in his station, he draws solace from his duty, just as so many faithful servants have done: 'we must console ourselves,' he says, 'by the cheerful enjoyment of those blessings within our reach, *and* by dispensing our superfluities among those who are less amply provided with the goods of this world'.[31]

Stressing that rank could be onerous, equating the different but similarly demanding lots of the rich and the poor, the powerful and the submissive, novelists were stressing the social bargain in which each rank had their prescribed duty which contributed to the welfare of the whole. Charity, the chief duty of the élite, obviously illustrated this well, for it benefited society in material terms that were actually fairly demonstrable, or at least easily imaginable. An active philanthropy was the novelist's shorthand for virtue, for sensibility and thus for fitness to be a hero or heroine. If an author wished to urge a protagonist or a reader to favour a particular character, then it would be done by showing that character in the act of dispensing alms to the needy. But charity also became the symbol of all that justified rank and held society together, the chief duty of the rich and powerful and the principal vindication of their elevated status. Just as we recognise good individual aristocrats by their philanthropy, so we recognise the virtues of the institution of aristocracy by the same sign. True patricians were proud of their rank only because of their consequent usefulness to society. Thus, in Jane West's *Tale of the Times* (1799), we know that Sir William Powerscourt's 'strong attachment to the seat of his ancestors was more the result of generous philanthropy than any lucrative consideration' and 'as he rode around his estate, his feelings resembled those of a conscientious guardian rather than a self-accountable owner'.[32] Such benevolence was the only reason to value nobility, genuine aristocrats knew. They would not care if they were somehow deprived of their rank, as seemed to happen all too often in novels save that, as Arthur Fitz-Albini put it, 'I cannot bear that the hereditary hospitality of this place, so useful to a poor and numerous neighbourhood, should end in me!'[33] What Fitz-Albini obviously did not realise was that even if he did end up being stripped of his rightful wealth, as his father's dissipation was constantly threatening, any rightful aristocrat who was somehow usurped in a novel could, and always would, exhibit their nobility in whatever circumstances they found themselves, gathering about themselves a 'solitary pensioner' or two, and perhaps 'a little humble circle' to whom they might render a thousand kind offices however poor they were themselves – as did Althea Dacre in Smith's *Marchmont* (1796).[34]

If charity represented the primary duty of the élite, their part in the grand social bargain, it was not as unproblematic a function as might be thought. As we have already seen, they had a duty not to be recklessly munificent, being required conspicuously to consume the luxuries that would indirectly conduce to the benefit of all, to eat their fair share of pineapples as it were. Secondly, they had a responsibility to ensure that, in the joy of their benevolence, they did not disrupt society's hierarchies by propelling any individual out of his or her allotted station with inappropriate beneficence. Eliza Parsons was one to warn of exactly this danger. 'To assist the unfortunate in the line they have been accustomed to, and procure them comforts in the sphere Providence has placed them, is the most essential mode to procure ease and happiness,' she said, but this was to be contrasted with the sort of improper benevolence which simply lavished money on those thought deserving, 'for we may observe, in a thousand instances, that, when interest or fortunate occurrences raise a man beyond what birth and education fitted him for, he is, generally speaking, awkward and unhappy in himself, envied and ridiculed by his equals, and despised by his superiors'.[35] Edward Percival, eponymous

hero of Robert Dallas' novel, had made just this mistake, rewarding the
industrious and honest shoemaker who had handed back his lost pocket-
book with the £20 note that it still contained. This was utter folly, it soon
transpired, for such wealth was dangerous to the shoemaker, who proceeded to spend his 'God-send' on drink, nearly destroying his family
by his extended intoxication – something his modest profits had never
allowed before.[36]

In fact, this parable forms part of a protracted discussion of the duties
and dangers of charity, a 'congress of benevolence' as one character calls
the collected debates Dallas depicts when his hero suddenly inherits a
fortune. The congress attempted to resolve some of the finer problems of
philanthropy's propriety, quantifying, for the benefit of any reader who
had just inherited £12,000 per annum perhaps, the right way to spend
a fortune (answer: retain £4,000 for living expenses, £2,000 to cover
any unexpected outlay, put £2,000 in bonds, so that good dowries can
accumulate, and set aside the other £4,000 for 'making others happy').[37]
Such considerations in his fiction make it obvious that Dallas' didacticism
was aimed not so much at any would-be levellers amongst his readers, as
at those who were in possession of rank, wealth and power, and who, in his
opinion, were in danger of misusing them. This is why Dallas took pains
to admit that for every good and benevolent aristocrat, there were many
who, lamentably, were as corrupt as his heroes were upright. 'Men who
are born to fortune are,' he said, the 'helmsmen of happiness' and if they
deserted the wheel, anarchy could be the only result.[38] Such an argument,
endorsing the idea of corrupt authority, was not needed to dissuade
potential levellers, nor to counter any perceived Jacobin threat, but rather
would tend to support their cause. But it was nevertheless a central part
of the anti-Jacobin campaign in fiction. Novelists sought to demonstrate
that it was just as dangerous for the élite to neglect, or repudiate, their
duty, as it was for the lower orders of society to eschew theirs; that, in
fact, any challenge to the current social order, from wheresoever it came,
would be equally disastrous and must lead to the triumph of anarchy
which France had just witnessed. It is these separate, but analogous,
dangers – of levellers, of ambition and of the corrupt aristocracy – that
I shall be exploring in the following sections.

The concept of the forced equalisation of rights, ranks and property had
been a bugbear of all those who supported the *status quo* for many generations past. It was as easy matter to fit the Jacobins into this tradition.
Levelling was not comprehended as a legitimate social or political theory,

worthy of serious consideration, but rather as crime. It was supported only by those who had nothing to lose. Thus it was self-evidently an evil. So, for instance, in Mary Anne Burges' topographically allegorical *Progress of the Pilgrim Good-Intent, in Jacobinical Times* (1800), the descent into the 'valley of Equality' was such a dangerous path that any who ventured it had to disencumber themselves of all their possessions, throwing off provisions, money, robes and crowns alike, only to see them picked up by others, usually the 'BLOOD-MEN', for whom Burges means us to understand the cunning Jacobins who had led their unsuspecting adherents into the valley in the first place.[39] Levelling meant disorder, in the literal sense of an disruption of the proper order, as Clara Reeve made plain in the preface to her *Memoirs of Sir Roger de Clarendon* in 1793. 'The new philosophy of the present day avows a levelling principle,' she told her readers, which meant, she precisely explained, that it 'declares that a state of anarchy is more beautiful than that of order and regularity' – a manifest absurdity.[40] Likewise, the author of *The History of Sir George Warrington* (1797) peremptorily concluded that 'a state of equality is a state of envy, anarchy, and confusion', a statement that brooked no debate, nor, most authors apparently thought, needed one.[41]

But this fairly crude dismissal of levelling was not a strategy that enabled anti-Jacobin fiction to reach its full potential. Certainly Reeve seemed to recognise this. As well as founding her attack on levelling on the premise that it was intrinsically iniquitous, she stated quite explicitly how she would impart this lesson. On the one hand, she said, her aim in *Memoirs of Sir Roger de Clarendon* was 'to give a faithful picture of a well-governed kingdom, wherein a true subordination of ranks and degrees was observed', since, she added, 'there is nothing more likely to convince mankind of the errors of these men' – the levellers – 'than to set before them examples of good government'. Additionally, though, she told her readers that she would also seek to display the 'mischievous consequences of their own principles', that is to say the results of levelling.[42] This would prove to be a much more common, and effective, tactic for novelists, for as writers of fiction, they were in the unique position of being able to 'prove' the errors of levelling by exhibiting their consequences. In order to pursue this approach, however, novelists were obliged to confront the fact that levelling was a term that, though it had an immense emotional resonance and manifold connotations, had no precise definition, nor any genuine proponents. 'There were no levellers,' Robert Hole has concluded.[43] Any levelling that did exist in 1790s Britain was comprised almost entirely of a belief in an equality of men based on the grounds of religion or natural rights. Very few radicals, and certainly not influential figures such as Price, Priestley or Paine, were prepared to go any further than the demands for political reform that the previous generation of radicals had made. Indeed, the major theoretical innovation of the Revolutionary decade was probably the conception of an equality of generations, as postulated by Paine and attacked by Burke, so that each man had as much right to be free as his forebears. But this was hardly levelling, for not only was it highly theoretical, but it refrained even from contrasting the material condition of one current inhabitant of the planet with another. Indeed, many radicals were themselves extremely anxious to acknowledge the distinctly limited aims of their own manifestos. Anti-Jacobins, though, were careful not to let petty objections like these very clear statements of moderation interfere with their campaign to smear radicalism by inventing a radical agenda, and then accusing it of the very worst crimes they could imagine. Particularly active in this endeavour were the novelists. They added flesh, as it were, to the monster that anti-Jacobinism as a whole had manufactured. Their genius was to use the freedom that their fictional form gave them to portray radicals in exactly those lights which the radicals were most anxious, and for good reason, to avoid.

In 1795, for example, the London Corresponding Society insisted that whatever ideas of equality it had ever dabbled with, it had never included the levelling of property amongst them, and that the Society could never 'have conceived that so wild and detestable a sentiment could have entered the brain of man'.[44] And yet in the same year, as distinguished an author as the Poet Laureate had produced a novel depicting the career of a vaurien, the eponymous *Democrat*, who was perpetually intent on furthering the levelling cause in Britain and was himself 'particularly attentive to the equalization of property'.[45] This same strategy of inventing levelling in exactly those terms that would be most terrifying to the majority of society, regardless of whether or not their fabrication afforded a genuine reflection of the radical programme, is also apparent in novelists' attempts to exhibit the putative levelling of all distinctions between the sexes. Excepting Wollstonecraft and her circle, and perhaps one or two other individuals, very few if any radicals were demanding rights for women in the 1790s, and certainly not that women 'exert the divine privilege of resistance, and throw off the shackles of domination', as Dr Alogos, in Walker's *Vagabond*, demands of his daughter. His daughter's righteous indignation and persistence in thinking 'that the very difference of sexes should teach us that they are designed for different pursuits' argues against Alogos, but the smear that has already been successful is far more effective as anti-Jacobin propaganda, with levelling tarred as a system which would hit Britain with the double horror of gender, as well as economic, equality.[46]

Even when novelists did turn their attention to political radicalism, the one area in which they could justly have accused British Jacobins of seeking some degree of equalisation, their chief tactic was simply to present the aims of radicalism in the most frightening manner possible. Constitutional reform, according to the anti-Jacobin novels, did not mean the elevation of each adult man to the dignity of enfranchisement, but the diminution of those who already, and rightly, possessed political power to the level of the rest. It meant also the inevitable ruin of the nation as a result of men not qualified to govern taking over the reins of power. Certainly Pye was unequivocal about the consequences of allowing the lower orders of society to play a political rôle. His Lord Montgomery tells us what to expect, for he knows 'both from reason and experience' that 'government cannot be well administered by ignorance and indigence', which is what political reform must inevitably mean, and therefore 'he detested democracy'. By contrast, he is 'strictly an *Aristocrat*', by which Pye meant us to understand that 'he was taking aristocracy in its true sense, of power in the hands of the wealthy, the noble, and above all the virtuous', all of which qualities would be exiled from government if, heaven forbid, political power was extended even wider than it was at present.[47]

Such an extension had been tried in France, of course, and the consequences were there for all to see, although this did not stop a Frenchman in Susanna Pearson's *The Medallion* (1794) from descanting on what a reviewer identified as the theme of 'universal equality', his speech confuting political radicalism with social, and even economic levelling so that, cleverly on the part of the author, the one appeared the natural corollary of the others. The Frenchman advocates 'a constitution on a much more sublime plan' than that currently enjoyed by Britain, and he projects, he tells us, 'a system that disdains to be set in motion by any particular rank of men; a system by which the peer is levelled with the shepherd, and the servant seated on the bench with his master; a scheme which strips off the distinctions invented by pride and supported by tyranny . . . ' What is immediately evident is that the Frenchman is demanding constitutional reform purely because it would level society, and it is for this same reason that the upright Britons who hear him oppose the plan. The social divisions of society are what form the basis for good government, they say, do away with one and you do away with the other. 'I don't see any reason why,' says one, 'a baker, for instance, who has been up to the elbows in dough all his life-time, should make bold to open the state-oven, and pop his impudent fingers into every pie, and lick, and smack, and spit, and turn up his nose at everything that does not suit his taste. Indeed, I don't think he has any business there at all.' No one, he continues, can be in the cellar and the garret at the same time, and the baker,

with no other knowledge that what he has picked up at his kneading trough, looks just as silly as a nobleman would do, who should tuck up his shirt-sleeves, pin a white apron before him, and flourish his dredging box. Because why? the nobleman knows no more than a sucking child of the baking-business, that the baker is just as wise in state-affairs.[48]

To institute political reform, however mild, we find, is tantamount to levelling society, putting the baker and the aristocrat on a level. In the process both figures would lose the purpose of their ranks and fail in their duties. There would be no good government and no bread.

Most novelists, however, preferred to dramatise levelling's effects, the plan which, after all, was best adapted for their medium. A fine example is to be found in Helen Craik's *Adelaide de Narbonne* (1800), in which a maid, Jacqueline, attends a ball dressed as Adelaide, her mistress, for, as she later explains, she imagined that her master, the Jacobin De la Ville, 'would not be displeased at the fancy, since it was agreeable to the system of equality he is continually expatiating on to all around him'. Of course, her master is displeased, exhibiting just the sort of hypocrisy we have come to expect from all Jacobins, but he is especially irritated because Jacqueline's imposture is discovered only when she is set upon by the band of brigands whom he had engaged to abduct his wife, and who understandably have mistaken Jacqueline for her mistress. Jacqueline's frightened response to the episode is clearly meant to be edifying. The Jacobinical brigands sneer at her protestations of innocence, she reports, and 'the jargon they talked about equality, will make me hate the word, I am sure, as long as I live, and has cured me of every wish for putting myself on a footing with my superiors in fortune'. Even a Girondin like Charlotte Cordet could draw the obvious moral, and she tells Jacqueline 'to reflect on the folly and danger of stepping aside from the path Providence has assigned as your proper station'. Such, of course, were the dangers of equality, or at least that sort of equality which demolished the barriers between ranks, for the hero who naturally comes to Jacqueline's rescue displays a different sort of levelling, paying her 'as much respect and attention' as if her mistress had been the victim of the ambush, even though 'he knew I was not My Lady'.[49] Craik had made the lesson unmistakable. Everyone, no matter what their station in life, deserved the same respect, but not only did they forfeit it when they stepped out of their allotted place, but they brought danger to themselves and the entire community.

A second means of dramatising the perils of levelling was for novelists to depict an imaginary society in which all distinctions of ranks had, somehow, been abolished. It must have been a particularly satisfying technique for anti-Jacobins to employ, for it lampooned the utopias projected by many post-Rousseauean radicals towards the end of the eighteenth century. Prince Massouf witnesses such a community in the novel that bore his name, and though he makes no comment, his descriptions are enough to enforce the lesson. Inequality, we find, is not only natural and necessary, but can only be eradicated, if at all, with ruthless and inhuman force. There is no doctor amongst the 'colony of the enlightened', for instance, for this would destroy equality. And this absence of anyone prepared to learn medical skills has not helped a community that is dwindling in numbers anyway, although the main reasons for this decline are rather more appalling, as Massouf soon discovers:

In the infancy of the colony some of the strongest men had been put to death, by public consent, for encroaching on the weak, and some of the crafty for the same encroachment on the simple. All the persons of weak constitutions had perished through the excess of their labour in tilling the portion of ground allotted to them – all employment but tillage, to which the soil was not grateful, being useless; for barter was forbidden, as sure ground of inequality, which might attain to the most destructive height.[50]

The correct interpretation of Massouf's dream was clear. Levelling could not work, for men differed from one another, a fact which, in itself, provided the proof of inequality's righteousness and its efficacy. But just to attempt such levelling, let alone to achieve it, was a violation of the real rights of men, rights which pertained to their very existence. Did not men have a right to the possession of property, perhaps accumulated through their own exertions and talents? And who could possibly suggest that men did not have a right to their lives, the very thing that the levellers wished to deprive them of, simply because they were that much more muscular or intelligent than their neighbours? 'There can be no kind of equality for men in society but that of rights,' affirmed Moore, talking of the rights of all to property and liberty under law, not the sort of natural rights that justified a political rôle.[51] It was the same lesson that George Walker had wanted his readers to take from the dystopia of his *Vagabond*, the 'Perfect Republic' founded on the 'Principles of Equality and Political Justice' which makes even Dr Alogos realise his errors. His conclusion that '*an equality*, the most exact and perfect in respect of every moral and social obligation, springs from *inequality* itself' lay at the heart of all anti-Jacobin fiction.[52] True equality emanated from the equality of responsibilities incumbent on each member of society, equally important for each degree, whilst 'those who attempt to level, never equalise,' as Burke had insisted, but 'only change and pervert the natural order of things'.[53]

The attack on social mobility, the attack on – as Elizabeth Hamilton put it – the 'epidemical frenzy, which has of late spread through our country, the desire of shining in a sphere above our own', was the second prong of the anti-Jacobin defence of hierarchy. Like levelling, ambition was not a new danger in the 1790s, but it did become, in the eyes of many, a more urgent threat. Indeed, the fear of the middle rank of society seeking to rise above their station – what Hamilton called the 'accursed passion for gentility' – was, if anything, more often and more anxiously treated in the novels of the 1790s and 1800s than had been the danger of the more overtly Jacobin political or economic levelling.[54] The difference was that these 'social levellers' were men and women who sought to elevate themselves alone, not to apply a general theory of equality to society, for, as their words and actions proved, they were as jealous of society's divisions as anyone. Yet their individual challenge to society's ordered ranks represented a glaring dereliction of the duty incumbent on them as a result of their place in society, just as it had been a crime for those in the lower orders to seek to destroy all rank. They were frequently shown to be tantamount to the same thing, for, as we have seen, levelling was customarily exposed as being based only on covetousness, and it was this same envy that motivated any individual seeking to better his or her station. Certainly, it is this that the reader is meant to understand from Ann Thomas' *Adolphus de Biron*, in which she exhibits a mutinous sailor who speaks against rank and discipline, until, that is, he is promoted himself, at which point he becomes a hateful tyrant. His levelling talk, we realise, was purely a cover for his personal ambition, an ambition which might equally have had its expression in an urge for his own promotion.[55] It is an association that is made linguistically, but no less pointedly, in Sayer's *Lindor and Adelaïde*, in which the real rôle of the ambitious, *nouveau riche* banker who arrives to upset the consecrated, aristocratic order of the village is suggested by his name – Monsieur Levilles, an appellation requiring no English translation to be understood.[56]

What we also see in Thomas' story of the mutinous sailor promoted to become a tyrant was that he is completely unsuited to his elevated post, his petty dictatorship being the proof that he belongs in his original lowly station. Both his original insubordination and his later inadequacy are threats of equal magnitude to the smooth operation of the ship. Wishing to raise oneself was not a crime in itself, but would always become one simply because one would not be able to fulfil the duties of one's new position. In general, though, in novels this crime was one shown to be committed not by members of the lower orders, but by members of the middle classes, for it was they, we are continually assured, who aspired to join the ranks of gentry and nobility. What they did not realise, seeing only the splendour of the aristocracy and jealous of their lives of opulence and ease, was that under the terms of the bargain of rank, the élite had the most onerous and necessary responsibilities of any in society. It was exactly because those who were not born to high rank could not fulfil these responsibilities when they found themselves elevated to the height of their aspirations, that they were such a danger to the peace and security of the nation.

In addition to the gravity of this encroachment, novelists doubtlessly tended to concentrate on the incursions of the middling ranks into the province of the élite because this middling section of society represented their natural constituency. But perhaps the most compelling reason for the ubiquity of their fictional assault was that by the 1790s novelists possessed a ready-made vocabulary, or demonology, to describe and dramatise the careers of those members of the middling orders who sought to level the wise social barriers set up for the good of the community. The East Indian nabobs, the boarding-school educated, novel-reading misses, the upwardly mobile *nouveau riche*, and numerous other assorted impostors all trying to be that which they were not and were not meant to be, had all been traditional butts of fiction's satire. In particular, the idea of the nabob, the lowly man who had gone away to India or some other equally foreign destination, only to return with a fortune, possibly got by means the most nefarious, was a very serviceable figure for novelists wishing to show the dangers of new and unmerited social standing. The nabob was also a figure who had been given a new, or at least more contemporary, signification by the trial of Warren Hastings (1788–95), another of Burke's impassioned causes, and a protracted case which tarnished the image of British activity in India for many (although Hastings, the East India Company and even, in some few aberrations against sensibility, the slave trade, had some capable novel-writing apologists).[57]

Certainly by the turn of the century, nabobs were being widely censured. The almost universal opinion was given by Eliza Parsons in *Woman As She Should Be*, whose Mr Menville, having forced our heroine to marry him instead of her true love, added to this conventionally villainous behaviour all the faults of the nabob, as described by Mrs Colemore:

> Do you know that I hate your nabobs, accustomed to eastern indulgences, a multiplicity of women, a world of splendour, their whole attention taken up by accumulating riches, at the expense, too often, of justice, mercy, or compassion: all the finer feelings of the soul are subdued. By peculation, by distressing the unhappy, they acquire the greatest part of their fortunes; and, with every humane sentiment expunged, they return with callous hearts to their native country, to dazzle the multitude with their magnificence, and triumph over those who have ten thousand times more merit, but are less beholden to chance or good fortune than themselves.[58]

It is in this last sentence that the real purpose of nabobs in fiction reveals itself, for they were primarily of symbolic value. They return to Britain purely to upset the *status quo*, possibly in a useful way, providing a timely dowry to a penurious heroine perhaps, but more often as a demonstration of the lamentable consequences of capsising the social order, as a warning to others not let their good fortune trick them into thinking they are better than they are, and as a lesson to others not to let ambition get the better of them. How much happier would the nabob have been, muses Alethea in Smith's *Marchmont* (1796), had he only been 'contented with the humble lot to which he was probably born' and not 'in search of a higher fortune', gone off 'to those climates where the soil, manured with blood, seems to produce only disease and death'.[59] Novelists frequently demonstrated the folly and vice of seeking to raise oneself above one's allotted station by turning their nabobs into sadder, wiser men after they have been dragged into ruin and disgrace by their desire to better themselves. The conclusion to *Douglas* (1800) is typical, Robert Bisset telling us that one of his characters, having been bankrupted by the ludicrous extravagance he thought it meet to display, 'heartily regrets the time he left off business and commenced gentleman'.[60]

As these examples illustrate, the nabob did not have to be an East Indian adventurer, for the same rôle could be taken just as well by any social upstart. Clara Reeve located her nabobs in the fourteenth century, where, she made it abundantly clear, they were worthy of just as much contempt. 'In the times of our Gothic ancestors,' she informed the reader of her *Memoirs of Sir Roger de Clarendon*, 'the man who lived, or dressed beyond his degree in life, would have been scorned, shunned, and despised by all his neighbourhood.'[61] A more common target amongst novelists, though, was the contemporary bourgeoisie, although no author saw fit to provide a specific definition of exactly who fell within this class. A general pattern of attack is evident, but lacking a precise focus. Charles Lloyd put a figure on his nabob's new eminence – he was 'a person who, from the lowest situation in life, has raised himself … to the important rank of a man possessing 100,000l.', but Francis Lathom established his Sir Gilbert Oxmondeley in the vaguest of terms as an humble tradesman in the City, before suddenly elevating him to a baronetcy and a fortune (so much of a shock that his wife had instantly died in exultation). Mary Robinson's Alderman Bradford was simply 'a rich citizen' who wanted to show all mankind that he was 'as great a man as the first lord in the land' – an ambition that would plunge his family into the standard dire consequences.[62]

Like the nabob, and like the 'stock-jobbers' from Burke's *Reflections*, these tradesmen were simply metaphors for social mobility. Their rôle was really as a social, not economic, challenge to the feudal order. They had to share that rôle with a wide variety of other upstarts, all of whom challenged the hierarchies of society, but, on the surface, presented a much less revolutionary threat than has been traditionally ascribed to the continually rising bourgeoisie. In fact, nabobism was the primary characteristic of a whole mesh of intertwined groups appearing in novels as challenges to proper hierarchy. A boarding-school education, for example, came under repeated attack in novels for providing young women with an education totally unfitted for their real expectations and duties, for encouraging 'nabobish' tendencies as one might say. It was the same fault of which novels were guilty. They too encouraged expectations and ambition. Indeed, many novelists were quick to show their own awareness of the supposed propensity of their chosen form to incite in their readers aspirations above their station, and they doubtlessly hoped to exculpate themselves of the charge by detailing the process in their fiction.[63] On its own, such folly was not possessed of much revolutionary potential, but as part of the overall pattern of nabobism, it became far more dangerous.

The revolutionary threat becomes more evident when we appreciate that nabobism was the specific crime for which new philosophy was often indicted, for it too corroded all social distinctions, encouraging its adherents to be dissatisfied with their station by telling them that social and political distinctions were mere prejudices that ought to be levelled.

It is an association that becomes manifest when we compare Eliza Oxmondeley, the daughter of the nabob of Lathom's *Men and Manners*, with Bridgetina Botherim, the budding new philosopher of Elizabeth Hamilton's *Modern Philosophers*. Whilst Eliza's errors are not more serious than her desire to transform the Oxmondeley estate into the sort of place she has read about in innumerable novels, full of eerie woods and decaying chambers, Bridgetina has adopted all the delusive principles of Godwin, Wollstonecraft and Hays. Both these patterns of transgressive behaviour, though, may be directly traced back to the social ambition of their widowed parents, especially the encouragement the two daughters were given to read novels. Mrs Botherim, Hamilton stresses right at the beginning of *Modern Philosophers*, is ill-educated and vulgar, but designs her daughter to move in a sphere much more elevated than her own, and praises her supposed erudition: 'You have no ideer [*sic*] what a scholar she is,' she tells one of her friends, 'she has read every book in the circulating library.' But since her background has not provided her with the discernment to sift and understand the books she reads, Bridgetina's education has been her ruin, for she has been drawn only to novels and metaphysics, been caught in the snares of the designing new philosophers who frequent the library. Exactly the same is true of Eliza, save only that since Lathom was not concerned to write an explicitly anti-Jacobin novel, her sins are less obviously ideological. Their rootedness in her vulgar father's ambition, though, remains evident: 'The reading of novels, without sufficient discrimination to choose characters worthy of imitation,' writes Lathom, had given Eliza 'a language and manners, whose flippancy and ill-managed gaiety her father, *unlettered in the qualities for which he mistook them*, conceived to be elegance and wit'. Both her father and Mrs Botherim relish the impertinence with which their daughters treat them. In doing so they only emphasise the grotesque inversion of the traditional hierarchy, at the head of which they ought to be.[64]

In Charlotte Smith's *Banished Man* (1794) a whole series of upstarts fills the neighbouring house to the old-established Ellesmere family. Only one is an overt Jacobin, a Presbyterian businessman who has the audacity to display busts of Benjamin Franklin, Richard Price and Thomas Paine, but all fulfil the same function. Whatever their politics, they have the same potential to wreak ruin on society, for all are usurpers of the prestige and, more worryingly, the function of the traditional, age-sanctioned grandee. Moreover, all have expropriated the rightful inheritance of others, doubtlessly more fit for that rôle, and have done so in exactly the same way as had the Manfreds and Montonis of the conventional gothic novel, adding another layer of resonance to these portraits. It is no coincidence that the favourite book of Mary, the heroine of Brydges' *Mary de Clifford* (1792), is 'the inimitable *Castle of Otranto*', with its tale of the true heir dispossessed by a repugnant usurper, for its plot mirrors her own predicament. She loves the melancholy Woodvile, of 'the most illustrious descent' but whose natural benevolence and talents are going to waste because of his family's poverty. But she is being persecuted by Sir Peter Lumm, whose father had built up his fortune from nothing in a woollen-draper's shop, and who, 'perhaps through villainy', had been created a baronet and bought his estate.[65] This was the sort of usurpation that, according to Brydges, was happening daily in modern Britain, and it had to be stopped. All patriots must make a stand against 'the incalculable evils of which the manner of such men are the prognostications,' wrote Brydges, telling us that he meant specifically 'stock-jobbers, loan-contractors, army and navy-contractors, and East-Indians', and that the evils he feared were 'either despotism, or anarchy!'[66] That usurpation brought despotism was to be seen in *The Castle of Otranto*; that it brought anarchy could be seen in the ill-advised attempts of the French to meddle with the rightful order of society.

Brydges, genealogist and long-term litigant at law (in the not unconnected, and not surprisingly unsuccessful, attempt to have himself recognised as the Earl of Chandos), was to take the anti-nabob campaign to its furthest extent in his three novels, and in doing so, turned it into something fairly ludicrous to the modern reader. He parroted Burke's arguments, but nevertheless seemed to be exactly one of those 'creeping sycophants ... the blind abject admirers of power' who, Burke himself regretted, always idolised hereditary wealth. Burke had made it clear that ability had its place in the governance of the nation – 'You do not imagine that I wish to confine power, authority, and distinction to blood, and names, and titles' – but had insisted that it needed a probationary period, as it were, to prove itself, and that, since ability was so active and vigorous whilst property was always so 'sluggish, inert and timid', hereditary property needed special support.[67] To a certain extent Brydges had to agree that ability should be somehow recognised, but although he conceded this in his third novel, *Le Forester*, startlingly, it did not stop him arraigning most of Pitt's government for their lowly origins.[68] Brydges was livid that recent years had seen a sustained endeavour 'to overturn all the antient [*sic*] principles of society, to treat the pretensions of birth, not only with contempt, but abhorrence, and to give a daily increasing influence to new-got wealth, however acquired and whencesoever sprung'. His novels he produced as warnings to the nation, echoing Burke's language and his deep concern about the proximity of revolution: 'new-got wealth is active and intriguing; antient property is sluggish,' he insisted. 'If the barrier of birth is thrown down, a restless and wicked ambition will never cease to disturb the quiet of society.'[69] Where Brydges was unusual amongst novelists was that he endeavoured to explain what was implicit, but seldom explained, in other attacks on nabobism – just why it was that nabobs threatened revolution.

One strand of orthodox conservative eighteenth-century political theory, which Burke both followed and shaped, held that it was proper that property should form the basis of political influence for a variety of practical and moral reasons. Men of considerable property, conservative ideologists generally agreed, as well as having such a substantial stake in the nation that they would be particularly zealous for its well-being, were more likely to possess the intelligence, abilities and discernment to govern the nation well, either themselves or by proxy through limited democracy. Moreover, their wealth made them impartial, unprejudiced and unlikely to implement mercenary measures, whether to enrich themselves or to sell out the nation, and their resources endowed them with the leisure necessary to perform such an important rôle on behalf of the whole country. For evident reasons, this theory partially explains the concern about new-got wealth, for those suddenly elevated to a status which entitled them to political power might well be deficient in one or more of these qualities. Some novelists besides Brydges echoed this pragmatic anxiety: 'where the nobles can trace their descent from a long chain of legislators, orators, and heroes,' wrote the author of *Berkeley Hall* (1796), 'there is an innate spirit of honour, which disposes them to great and glorious deeds; and an education which secures them from low and narrow views, and enables them to be of the most benefit to mankind'.[70] But these supposedly practical arguments did not really stand up to reasoned scrutiny, either on theoretical grounds – for property was the sole index of fitness for political influence that theoreticians had thought fit to postulate and nabobs clearly met this qualification – or on practical grounds – for the mere *newness* of wealth could hardly have been institutionalised as a bar to a political rôle in real life. Both Pitt and Fox, after all, came from newly wealthy families. Nor, for that matter, was the newness of wealth an objection that could be taken into consideration in the franchise. It was for these reasons that, as Dickinson has found, although many in the political establishment were fearful of new wealth, not all conservatives shared their anxiety.[71]

Novelists, though, were much more united and severe in their campaign against nabobs than those anti-Jacobins who used other mediums. Partly this was because, as we have seen, it was a campaign which conventional fictional modes naturally supported, but their fervent solidarity also stemmed from the fact that they took a different line from the exclusively political anti-Jacobins. Novelists constructed nabobism as primarily a threat to the social, rather than the political, order. It soon becomes apparent that their condemnations of nabobs and their ilk were fundamentally based on the inability of such figures to carry out the basic social duties of the class to which they had so recently been elevated, irrespective of their political competence. Principally, nabobs, we are told, did not ameliorate the lot of those less fortunate than themselves, whether by dispensing charity or by kind words, and as a result the bonds which held society together in harmony began to dissolve. It was a failing to which servants especially were intuitively attuned, for they were the losers when the élite did not fulfil their side of the social bargain. The complaint of Mrs Moseley, a housekeeper in Smith's *Marchmont*, for example, could stand for innumerable others. 'But so it is!' she says, whilst conducting our heroine around the almost ruined mansion of which she has the care, a building now decaying because the real, hereditary owners have been forced out by a coalition of parvenus and lawyers, 'such upstart creatures may be rich, but they are never gentlemen – nor know how to behave as such' – a sentiment, we are told, to which Alethea 'very heartily assented'.[72]

However, the real danger threatened by nabobs, it was held, was that this failure to fulfil the socially conciliating duties incumbent upon the élite led inexorably to a dissatisfaction with the hierarchical structure of society among the lower orders, a discontent that was not appeased – as it would be by the rightful social order – by any of the benefits of hierarchy that make subservience bearable. Those who have had 'no time to defecate and purge away their base-born grovelling principles and humours,' as one novelist put it, 'render power and eminence odious, oppressive and ridiculous'.[73] The nabob did not fulfil his or her side of the social bargain, and consequently inequality lost its principal justification. Thomas Skinner Surr's description of the Emerys, a *nouveau riche* family whose fortune has derived from business, in *George Barnwell*, is particularly revealing in this respect: 'Instead ... of alleviating the consequences of that inequality of society (*which experience seems to pronounce inevitable*), the occupation of their lives was to increase that splendour, which dazzled – but never cheered the poor! The feelings of benevolence, the impulse of charity, the glow of sensibility, are words they may have heard, but emotions they had never felt.'[74] Benevolence, charity, sensibility – these were the links in the great chain of being, and once they had been cut, a restless populace was left not just with a harder existence, but, more worryingly, with no reason to respect or submit to their social betters. The implication was clear. Nabobism provoked social unrest which in the 1790s and 1800s could mean only revolution.

And if Surr had merely implied the peril, Brydges spelt it out. 'If aristocracy be wise, let these things be heeded', he wrote in the preface to *Arthur Fitz-Albini*, before setting down the reasons for his hatred of nabobs which proved deducible into three basic maxims. The first and second of these are fairly self-explanatory, and not at all new. 'The man who inherits an honour is generally more virtuous, if not more able, than its first acquirer,' he asserted, omitting any justification of his opinion since he evidently felt so strong a conviction that he could not conceive of any objection. His second maxim advanced his argument that fixed and unalterable hierarchies were what kept the peace amongst the lower orders, as became apparent when he insisted that among 'the principal advantages of hereditary rank, is its tendency to soften the heart-burnings of inequality, by counteracting the operations of intrigue, violence, extortion, and dishonourable riches'. But it was his third maxim that formed the crux of his argument. To bestow respect and pre-eminence on new-got wealth, he warned, 'will establish an inequality which, as neither *prejudice* nor *philosophy* can defend [it], must involve in its downfall the system with which it is connected'.[75] In other words, these social parvenus corroded the *prejudice*, by which he meant the habits of ages which accustomed mankind to subordination, which maintained the peace of society. They did away with the 'sort of magic sound in a superior title, which induces the multitude . . . to exalt the thus-gifted mortal into a phoenix', as Mary Meeke put it, and which would thus effectually counter those who 'talk of the levelling system, and of mankind being equal'.[76] And second, nabobs undermined that philosophy which convinced all citizens of every degree that inequality was right, by which Brydges meant the arguments for the intrinsic, practical benefits of hierarchical society which we have seen to have been so generally posited as a defence of inequality. Because their new status had not been sanctioned by generations of power and influence wielded wisely and well, and because they did not carry out their side of the social bargain, nabobs put inequality and those who defended it in an embarrassed position. Violence must be the result:

> If once the respect that has in all ages and nations been paid to birth, be totally abandoned; if hereditary riches, education, and those habits of early life, which give exalted sentiments, and expanded powers of thinking, be not considered as generally necessary to qualify man for the superior orders of society – it will soon appear that all the principles upon which subordination of ranks can be defended by the philosopher, are subverted; that all the evils without the advantages of inequality of conditions are imposed upon mankind. . .

The result must be 'that every order is excited to a restless and dangerous fermentation; while the meanest and the worst of mankind, trample in bloated wealth and honours, on the necks of the people'.[77] There is no doubt that Brydges was more extreme in his detestation of nabobs and the *nouveau riche* than most of his fellow anti-Jacobins, and was far more panic-stricken about the likely consequences. Nevertheless, nabobism was almost universally condemned by novelists, and whatever the exact balance each author was seeking to strike between comic effect and a serious political lesson by such satire, it was always an attack that was based on the threat such characters posed to the harmonious and stable society for so long enjoyed in Britain.

If we are to believe the frightened assertions of anti-Jacobin fiction, the third great threat to Britain's well-being was posed by the corruption of her own élite, even those who, unlike the nabobs, had an unimpeachable pedigree and thus an incontrovertible right to sit at the head of society. Such corruption was figured as every bit as dangerous as levelling, for it generated and encouraged it. And it was every bit as injurious to the nation's health as nabobism, for corrupt aristocrats, no less than nabobs, had no idea of how they ought to fulfil the conciliating duties incumbent upon them. They therefore destabilised the nation from the top every bit as surely as a leveller's attempts to do so from the bottom.

Criticism of the élite in fiction was not a new phenomenon that developed only in response to the Revolution. Novelists had long peopled their works with a vaguely defined but still homogenous patrician class. When this *dramatis personae* and the demands of plots which required a villain or two collided, novels necessarily involved some depiction of élite corruption. Moreover, it was a simple matter for novelists to turn their novels of fashionable life into satirical attacks on the debauchery of the aristocracy. The much more coherent and evangelical, and indeed Evangelical, assault on élite immorality relaunched in the wake of the

American War of Independence (according to Joanna Innes' appraisal), was likewise not a new phenomenon, even if it did get invested with a new sense of urgency in the 1790s.[78] The King's *Proclamation Against Vice and Immorality*, the culmination of a short campaign by Evangelical groups, had appeared in 1787, and Hannah More's *Thoughts on the Importance of the Manners of the Great to General Society* was published a year later, going through seven editions before the fall of the Bastille. Indeed, Gerald Newman has gone so far as to assert that the Evangelicals deliberately hijacked anti-Jacobinism, so that they might use it as a screen behind which to attack the aristocracy.[79] The question naturally arises, therefore, of whether the attacks on the dissolute manners of the great in the novels of the 1790s represented anything new, and fitted to their immediate political context, or whether they represented simply the continuation of an existing campaign.

This is not an easy question to answer immediately, even if there were a number of major novelists, such as Jane West for one, who were eager to blame the coming 'annihilation of thrones and altars' not on 'the successful arms of France', but on those corrupt and corrupting principles emanating from the fashionable élite which 'by dissolving domestic confidence and undermining private worth, paved the way for universal confusion'.[80] Much of the literature of the would-be reformers of manners in the 1780s – their tracts and treatises, their earnest letters to editors – made much of the particularly alarming 'temper of the times', so when we find that those who sought to pressure the élite into reforming their behaviour in the 1790s used similar phrases, warning the élite that it was more important than ever that they reform during such a grave crisis in human existence, we cannot be certain that they had been prompted to do so only by the advent of a new revolutionary danger coming from France. West, and others, even pointedly insisted that they cared little for religion as a means of maintaining the stability and harmony of society in the 1790s if its beliefs were not actually inscribed on the hearts of those who saw fit to profess it.[81] Additionally, many of those novels written in the midst of the Revolution crisis which urge a reformation of the manners of the great do so by insisting that the aristocracy stop duelling, or gambling, or profaning the Sabbath, the same set-piece battles, in other words, that Wilberforce and More had been fighting in the 1780s.[82]

On the other hand, much anti-Jacobin fiction did criticise the behaviour of the élite in terms which pertained directly to the concerns of the Revolution crisis. On a rather frivolous level, Thomas Skinner Surr, a man who would go on to make a very successful career out of the novel of fashionable life, delighted in showing the reader how aristocratic corruption could militate against the patriotism which ought to have been mandatory during the conflict with France. He describes how Lord Morley, a fop, bursts into the room with what he calls news of the first consequence – that a man worth a whole corps of soldiers has escaped from the French. Mr Freeman, a Yorkshireman of good sense, naturally supposes that Sir Sidney Smith, the admiral, is meant, but after the usual confusion we find that it is Monsieur Caperonis, 'the first dancer in Europe' to whom Morley is referring.[83] Far more explicit in linking aristocratic corruption and Jacobinism is Charles Lucas' *Infernal Quixote* (1801). Here the intertwined fates of two boys born at exactly the same time and in the same village – one Lord James Marauder, the aristocratical *and* Jacobinical quixote of the title, the other the curiously named Wilson Wilson, our humble yet loyal and heroic protagonist – perfectly exhibit the standard maxim soon gleaned by Wilson that 'it required something more than high birth, education, or abilities to make a gentleman'. Yet Lord Marauder's depravity is figured not as excessive gambling or even inveterate promiscuity, but as an incendiary career amongst the United Irishmen, a clear and decidedly contemporary case for the corruption of the élite.[84] Other authors similarly suggested that aristocratic corruption was indeed the exact counterpart of new philosophy, although they generally exhibited their corrupt aristocrats operating according to Jacobin patterns in the domestic sphere, not the public life in which Marauder had operated. It was no trouble to demonstrate, for instance, that the sexual predation of a libertine aristocrat was the exact equivalent of the licentiousness of the new philosopher – a parallel reproachfully drawn out by Charlotte Smith in a footnote in her *Young Philosopher* (1798) which noted the ease with which the libidinous sentiments regarding the folly of matrimony of 'a man of the world' could be confused with those of a new philosopher who would also see flaws in matrimony.[85] And it was equally easy to contend, as Jane West did in her *Tale of the Times* (1799), that a dissolute aristocrat's obliviousness to the plight of the deserving poor was simply the counterpart of the new philosopher's equally contemptible contention that the poor were always much better off than the rich since they were so much closer to the noble savagery and arcadian perfection in which all men and women ought to aspire to live.[86]

The most explicit linkage of élite corruption to new philosophy may be seen in the depictions of the imprudent and often fatal attempt of the upper classes to introduce the lower orders to 'enlightened' political thought (see chapters three and four for a discussion of this 'Mr Fantom' motif). But this was only one means of explaining how élite corruption could drag Britain towards discord or even rebellion. Indeed, it may have been the most direct technique available, but it remained rather abnormal, for attacks on the corruption of the élite more typically focused on their dereliction, rather than their direct contravention, of their duty. Exactly as nabobs were guilty because they could not fulfil the requisite functions of their new station, so corrupt aristocrats also threatened unrest, and ultimately revolution, because of their failure to perform all those conciliating tasks which made hierarchy bearable to those at the base of the social order and provided its intrinsic justification. In Charlotte Smith's *Marchmont* (1796), for instance, whilst wandering about the lands formerly owned by the Marchmonts, Althea comes across a scene of such utter poverty that she cannot 'wonder that any man should quit his paternal cottage' and desert the quiet acquiescence of the social order which his habitation of that cottage represents. She knows that while the Marchmonts had lived on their ancestral estates, 'the voice of sorrow, that they could relieve, was never heard', whilst under the new and unfeeling landlords the poor cannot obtain even 'the absolute necessities of life . . . even by the most unremitting labour'. Since it is the task of the local gentry to make up the gap between what a labourer can earn by industry and what his family needs to live, she concludes, so it must be the crime of the new landlords that these labourers are deserting their cottages and the old order which they symbolise.[87]

Moreover, this aristocratic negligence was so much the worse because, unlike nabobs who knew no better, genuine aristocrats deliberately withdrew from the duties which they were well aware were their burden. Certainly this is a lesson that Percival, in the epistolary novel that bears his name, is forever trying to instil in the restless aristocrats with whom he corresponds. Thus Miss Emma Coverley's longing for a life without the rank and fortune which plagues her with troublesome suitors is given short shrift. 'For shame!' he writes, 'you have a brilliant post assigned you' – it would be an outright sin to let any temporary 'mortification' persuade her to relinquish it.[88] More often the remissness of the nobility had an even less worthy motivation, and would prove more destructive. Mr Mortlock, in Pye's *Aristocrat* (1799), for example, having received a French education, has developed an unhealthy regard for all the debaucheries of the French style of aristocracy, that is to say a nobility that was all status, power and extravagance. Mortlock never considers, Pye tells us (taking the opportunity to specify what the responsibilities of rank actually were), 'the different part an English gentleman, who has the important duties of legislator and magistrate to fill, must act on the theatre of life, compared with the splendid insignificance of the foreign nobility, whose sole view must be directed to shine in a court or camp'.[89] It was a most instructive comparison, for it revealed exactly why a decadent aristocracy posed such a threat. The stark *donnée* that lay behind Mortlock's foolish admiration for the aristocrats of France was that by the mid 1790s, when the novel was set, and 1799, when the novel was published, the majority of his quondam rôle models would no longer be alive. Either the guillotine or forced emigration had been the reward of their supercilious and selfish nobility. Moreover, the Revolution could be directly attributable to their corruption of the institution of nobility.

Certainly, much of the first wave of British responses to the Revolution, including those responses registered in fiction, had indicted the tyranny of the French *ancien régime*, and especially the despotism of its nobles, as the primary cause of the great rebellion of 1789–94. The French King had been misled, and his people misruled, by the corruption of the nobility, misrule which had caused such resentment that rebellion had seemed an attractive, and even understandable, option. Thus Mary Robinson's acute but naïve heroine in *Hubert de Sevrac* (1796), though herself an aristocrat forced to flee Paris, could sympathise with the Revolution because it was an attempt to end the evils of the *ancien régime* 'when the few were happy, and the million wretched! when virtue, valour, genius, and humanity, bowed at the foot-stool of ignorance and pride', when 'palaces rang with festivity, and dungeons groaned with victims', and when 'malice or caprice . . . had the power to scourge the suffering multitude, or awe them into silence'.[90] It was the disquieting recognition that corrupt aristocracy lay behind the Revolution which underlay the new urgency added to the campaign for the reform of the corruption of the élite in the 1790s.

In the anti-Jacobin imagination the public tyranny of the French élite had its corollary in their private vice, notably in the case of Marie-Antoinette. Both led to Revolution. The same was true for Britain. The grim warning that the moral vices of the élite could push Britain into revolution was given in as sprightly a novel as Mary Charlton's *Rosella, or Modern Occurrences* (1799). The reader is presented with a typically dissipated aristocrat, Lady –, who is guilty of a fairly conventional array of profligate crimes – coquetry, gambling, ordering goods for which she is unable to pay and inveigling her lover into forging banknotes to extricate her from her dilemma, for all of which she excuses herself,

Charlton tells us, 'because the virtues or merits of her ancestors have transmitted to her . . . she claims, a right to become degraded and vicious, without feeling the keenness of that stigma which the world affixes to the humbler offender'. Somewhat unusually, Charlton opens the case up to discussion amongst her more sensible characters, and the political danger of such an attitude is slowly revealed. First, one character, Delamare, points out that good behaviour amongst the lower orders of society can hardly be expected when the élite provide such a bad example. 'Good God!' he says, 'that we should dare arraign the prevalence of licentious opinions amongst the multitude, when they must be voluntarily blind, or else behold the general licentious conduct of the titled and rich.' But he goes on to elucidate the full, shocking implication of such double standards, for must not disgust give way to something far more dangerous? 'If the anecdotes of the great do not always redound to their credit, if the daily prints will record their follies and their vices, and if the pious promoters of learning amongst the labouring poor will enable them to prose over 'those pictures of our times', why do we stand astonished at the diffusion of levelling principles?'[91] No longer were the private vices of the élite merely symbolic of their political shortcomings, and no longer did their vices simply represent their dereliction of duty. Charlton had actually charted the process by which the personal corruption of the aristocracy led directly to the swelling of contempt for the higher ranks of society, and then, possibly, the determination to overthrow them. Anti-Jacobinism had its own very pressing reasons for attacking the corruption of the élite, then. The conservative campaign to reform the manners of the great in the 1790s and early 1800s was neither the mere puppet of the Evangelical movement, used to add respectability to their attack on the aristocracy, nor was it simply the continuation of a reform movement well under way for several years before the French Revolution broke. It was instead a cogent and vital part of the conservative campaign to protect Britain from the danger of Revolution.

The anti-Jacobin campaign to expose the corruption of the élite was not a remedy for rebellion as it already existed in the country, but rather a course of preventative medicine. It was, though, a treatment that was not without risk to the patient – the nation and its social hierarchies – since in pointing out the degeneracy of the aristocracy, those who campaigned for the reform of the élite, and especially the novelists with their supposedly large and unsophisticated readership, could well be accused of simply providing ammunition for those who condemned the *status quo*, of adding grist to the levellers' mills. The scathing attacks launched on the behaviour of the aristocracy in the most orthodox of conservative fiction, in the novels of Jane West or Elizabeth Hamilton say, were, on the surface at least, as subversive as the depictions of ignorant peers, foolishly and weakly attacking the Revolution in a radical novel like Charlotte Smith's *Desmond* (1792). Did these literary 'Saints', in other words, and as Gerald Newman has suggested, do 'much more to subvert the established order than to uphold it'?[92]

Certainly, authors such as West were not unaware of the tightrope they were walking, and took care to avoid any imputation that they were compromising their political orthodoxy, and propelling the nation into jeopardy, by pursuing too vigorously their Evangelical agenda. It was West herself who included a 'Legendary Tale' in her *Gossip's Story* (1796) with a moral that, she pointedly submitted, 'may recommend it to the few, who still love to see nobility clad in the respectable robe of virtue; and eminent rank described in unison with dignified sentiments and generous actions'.[93] And it is in this same cause, that, this time without regressing to some former mystical age when nobles were truly noble, she explains her theory of aristocracy to our heroine, who has clearly been reading some Evangelical attack on the corruption of the élite:

But remember, Sophia, the rich soil that gives birth to these *fungi* also brings forth the most choice productions. If you are often annoyed by knaves and fools in ermine, you will frequently find more polished manners, more enlightened views, and, let me add, superior dignity of character, and sterling worth . . . No object is more grateful to the reflecting mind, than a good man irradiating the ample sphere of greatness.[94]

This last phrase, of course, points at the conventional justifications of rank with which we are already familiar, but the question that West is forcing herself to confront is that of how the acknowledged utility, and abstract moral rectitude, of the aristocracy, and the *status quo* which they represent, is to be reconciled with the lapses, not to say outright wickedness, of many of its members.

West's attempt to resolve the paradox simply by pointing out that some individual aristocrats might be corrupt, but the majority were not, was not a wholly satisfactory solution for all authors. Charles Douglas, hero of Robert Bisset's first novel, for example, came up with the following formula when his animadversions against two manifestly iniquitous aristocrats, Sir Duncan Dismal and the Earl of Rackrent, provoked the former to question 'Are you *a leveller*?' Bisset evidently deemed Charles' answer important enough to merit all the emphasis the printer could muster:

Far from it; I respect the peerage as AN ORDER INDISPENSABLY NECESSARY FOR THE BALANCE OF THE CONSTITUTION, but that is in their corporate, not their individual capacity. *Individuals whether peers or commons*, I respect in proportion to THEIR WISDOM AND THEIR VIRTUES, and wish to associate with them, or not, according as I find their manners, habits, situations. . .

A practical illustration is soon forthcoming, Bisset inviting his readers to make the acquaintance of a repugnant Duke whom Charles' once radical friend Wilson introduces as 'one of the instances from which I used to infer the inefficacy of the peerage to legislative and judicative purposes'. Charles patiently explains the folly of such a conclusion:

I will grant that there are others of the peerage besides old Quondam, whose pursuits are frivolous and despicable, and whose character is insignificant, and, not-withstanding their rank, ridiculous, and even contemptible; but peers, as an ORDER, are of the highest consequence to the balance of the constitution, and are aggregately good lawgivers, because the laws which they propose, or adopt, are aggregately beneficial; and are good judges, as their sentences are aggregately just. The nature of the institution renders it impossible that there should not be fools or fribbles among them, but, as a body, they act wisely and equitably.[95]

But even this did not represent the full resolution of the question, for something approaching a hard and fast rule is deducible not only from Bisset's, but from the entire anti-Jacobin canon's attempts to reconcile individual aristocratic corruption with the absolute necessity and positive virtue of the élite as a whole. This rule was founded on the division of all questions of the competency of governors or the rectitude of the *status quo* into institutions and manners. This is not to say that all novelists consciously or explicitly made such a distinction, but the fundamental differentiation between the structures upon which society was based, those infrastructural organisations such as the Church, the constitution or the law, all neutral in themselves, and the individuals whose manners, whose behaviour, dictated the operation of those institutions, did underlay their work and is frequently very visible. Certainly in the case of the degeneracy of the élite it is a distinction that is always very apparent, the institution of aristocracy being sacrosanct, pure and uncorrupted in itself, but the manners of the individuals who together composed that order being often the most corrupt. Crucially, this criticism of manners was not allowed to depreciate the intrinsic value of the institution of hierarchy and thus persuade the foolish and the rash that the order of aristocracy itself warranted amendment or even annulment. Such a move could only end in disaster, as, manifestly, had been the case in France.

Bisset's analysis of the élite's corruption had already come close to proposing such a division between institutions and manners, but he too could be more lucid on the subject when giving his consideration to the causes of the French Revolution. Charles Douglas 'allowed that the old government of France had been very deficient in many of the constituents of just and beneficial polity', but he absolutely refused to accept that this had been due to the institutions of the *ancien régime* and doubted whether 'the evils ascribed to the government were not owing to the manners of the people'.[96] To most, the French Revolution was an attack on all the old institutions of state and society, and an attack that, by destroying those institutions, had unleashed the personal depravities of the people. Anti-Jacobin novelists were therefore intent on demonstrating that only Jacobins would propose changes – the dangerous innovations about which Burke was so concerned – to the institutions of Britain. West, for instance, presented the Jacobin Fitzosbourne frequently giving voice to the most extreme folly, or perhaps iniquity, by 'expatiating upon the folly of legislators, in not accommodating institutions to the varying humours of the people whom they meant to control'.[97] Not only was he suggesting that institutions should be tailored to manners, but, since it was a relaxation of the divorce laws he had in mind, it was the corruptest of manners which he thought should form the basis of the constitution. It is really Fitzosbourne's failure to appreciate the inviolate nature of all institutions that fits the pattern of anti-Jacobin fiction.

This is not to say, of course, that anti-Jacobin novelists presented Britain as a perfect society suffering from no ills. Even some of the most reactionary authors contemned press-ganging, slavery, the game laws and various other afflictions. But whatever the specific grievance, the essential point which the anti-Jacobins hoped to impart was that these were abuses, not institutional, but the product of corrupt individuals. West, for example, regretted the decadence of the Church administration, but exhorted her readers not to 'confound the mistakes of her governors, or the faults of her officials, with the essentials of her institutions'. Likewise, the author of *Such Follies Are* regretted the corruption of the electoral system, but insisted that 'were the whole body of Electors' as 'conscientiously scrupulous' as the hero of the novel, 'we should have no cause to ask for a Parliamentary Reform'.[98]

Authors' acknowledgements of the absolute probity and necessity of these institutions was a concession to orthodoxy, a statement of an overt anti-Jacobin rectitude which they hoped might protect them from any accusations of radicalism. It is a technique quite flagrantly adopted in *Such Follies Are*, which kicks off with the rather seditious allegation that Britain's Poor Laws ensure that 'the condition of vassalage seems not utterly extinct among us' since the revenue set aside for the support of the poor was often subject to the depredations of those charged with distributing it. But the novel goes on to chart the reform of this abuse by the goodly Mr Hanbury who, without attempting to alter the operation of the Poor Laws themselves, 'soon placed matters on a more eligible footing, and rendered the condition of many poor families more worthy of the ample provision which the humanity of our laws provides for them'. The novel insisted that the legislation in itself was good, but only its former operation corrupt.[99] It was a technique adopted even more brazenly, and probably needfully, by Charlotte Smith, whose habitual attacks on the law, motivated (as she frequently admitted) by her personal circumstances, coupled with her reputation as a Jacobin, would surely have turned a taint of democracy into an indelible stain had it not been for the propitiating riders with which she always accompanied them. The legal villainy that she detailed in *Marchmont* (1796), for instance, took place in 'a country celebrated for its equal laws', was clearly 'the abuse of those laws' and 'entirely illegal', was 'the abuse of the laws of the best governed of all possible communities' and left her wondering 'why the best of all possible laws are often abused'.[100]

If certain authors were using their endorsement of the inviolability of institutions to surround themselves with a cloak of political propriety, others were attempting to expose the gap between institutions and manners not as a defensive mechanism, but in order to suggest a means of bridging it. Such an author was Elizabeth Hamilton, whose *Translation of the Letters of a Hindoo Rajah* (1796) constitutes probably the fullest and most sophisticated treatment of the divide between institutions and manners as well as containing suggestions for the emendation of the abuses to which British society was prone without in any way eroding the vital institutional pillars of that society. Hamilton's novel is in two parts, and although its engaging prose seldom gives the impression of being rigidly schematised, it is not an over-simplification to distinguish between the first volume as a survey of the theoretically perfect institutions of Britain, and the second, as an investigation into the manners which are, in reality, to be found there. The eponymous Rajah Zāārmilla acts as linchpin, for it is he who, in volume one, receives information about Britain from Captain Percy, an idealist who describes his native land's theoretical perfections, and then from the Brahmin Sheermaal, who has already visited Britain and can consequently add a more sceptical gloss to Percy's optimism. His cynicism paves the way for the events of volume two, in which Zāārmilla journeys to Britain only to discover for himself the deplorable corruption of all the institutions which he has been taught to venerate whilst still in India.

To start with Percy teaches Zāārmilla that all Members of Parliament are uninfluenced by the fervour of party, and act without avarice or ambition, that all Christians are free to attach themselves to whichever sect they wish, without having their liberties infringed, that women are treated as rational beings and that there are no castes in Britain, with honours being bestowed according to merit. Learning of all these perfections makes him congratulate the British on their virtue and welcome their attempts to spread these blessings to other parts of the globe. Such utopianism makes for potent and chastening irony, even if it stands alone. But it is an effect that Hamilton remorselessly cultivates as she has the Rajah discover for himself the error of his convictions. Nothing is as it pretends to be, Zāārmilla finds, because the British ignore the rules by which they claim to live. Though the élite professes itself Christians, for example, 'the only devotion known to the majority of the community is the Poojah of cards and partridges'.[101]

It is in this use of her comparative technique that we find the real aim and achievement of Hamilton's satire, for she aspires not merely to demonstrate the breadth of the gap that had developed between Britain as she ought to be and Britain as she was, but attempts to point out the means, in the individual cases which she details, for the rectification of these abuses by a return to the institutions which Zāārmilla has already had explained to him. The Rajah, in other words, perhaps somewhat naïvely continuing to abide by his pre-existing respect for British institutions, is not the typical *ingénu* of the Lesage-inspired picaresque satirical novel, but is a walking reproof to British corruption and an appeal, in human shape, to the corrupt to return to the original principles enshrined in those institutions. He recognises that the signifiers of virtue have become dislocated from that which they were meant to signify, but such is his admiration for the original institutions that he cannot conceive of a society which would be so foolish as to have deserted them. This inability to imagine why anyone would wantonly depart from the perfect institutions of British society, can only chasten those who are reading his letters and who, being better versed in the sad corruption of the day, can recognise this divergence from first principles only too well.

Clearly, what Hamilton was demanding, a demand that was actually implicit in the structure of her novel, was a reform of manners which would allow society to return to the perfect and pure institutions upon which it ought to be based. It was a lesson which Hamilton applied to all British institutions, and to all those whose manners had perverted them, whether in a spiritual or temporal sphere, for just as the manners of those who attended Church had corrupted the original principles of religion, so the Jacobin behaviour of Sir Caprice Ardent or Dr Sceptic had degraded the true purpose of the squirearchy and gentry. To a certain extent, Hamilton's campaign ran parallel with that of the Evangelical reform of manners movement, and that Hamilton herself clearly had some sympathy, if not direct connections, with the 'Saints' is evident from her attacks on those members of the élite who possess merely the outward show of religion or allow their own folly to corrupt their social inferiors. Yet to suggest, as Gerald Newman has done, that the reform of manners campaign, to which Hamilton was clearly contributing, was *'an extremely radical process'* which was merely *'working under cover of an extremely conservative one'* is, at least as far as these novels were concerned, inaccurate.[102] In Hamilton's fiction, and in the rest of the novels under discussion here, both anti-Jacobin and Evangelical aims were inextricably bound up together.

In fact, Hamilton's notion of the necessity of the reform of manners, but without any meddling with institutions, relied just as much on Burke as on any more spiritual programme. His retrospective consideration of the correct procedure for removing a tyrannical monarch, as had been necessary in 1688, might have served as a pattern for the solution to the anti-Jacobins' problem of how to confront the corruption endemic in British society without undermining its sacrosanct fabric. Those who had constructed the 1688 Revolution, according to him, might have deviated a little from the straight line of succession, but had 'kept the principle' and 'shewed that they held it inviolable'.[103] It was a lesson that was painfully obvious to a French aristocrat such as Pye's Count De Tourelles, who admitted, too late, to his British friends that 'By returning to the original principles of our constitution, we should have found materials to form, and foundations to bear, a fabrick as beautiful and as permanent as your own.'[104] In contradistinction to the French experience, anti-Jacobinism shared with Evangelicalism the certainty that any attempt to amend society must rely on individual and private reformation rather than any general and public programme. Only Jacobins, French and British, believed in the perfectibility of man and the possibility of achieving, as a species, a new and better society. This was, of course, a contention which could be effortlessly covered in fiction, which almost always dealt with the histories of individuals.

The clearest statement of the anti-Jacobin novelists' faith in a quasi-Evangelical campaign of personal reform, and its contrast with the Jacobin strategy of institutional innovation, is to be found in Charles Lloyd's *Edmund Oliver* (1798). Lloyd was no Evangelical, but nevertheless had his mouthpiece character, Charles Maurice, react to the Jacobin D'Oyley's 'very sanguinary wishes with regard to the present ministers and governors of this country' not with anti-Jacobin bombast, but with the opinion 'that the evil lies deeper than you imagine', adding that the 'whole mass is tainted with corruption', and 'with corruption it ever will be tainted while each man has a selfish and individual aim in society'. The solution, as we would expect, is the reform, by individuals, of their manners, as Charles explains: 'I would exactly reverse the method of our modern democrats, who (neglecting the vineyard of their own hearts) are always attacking bodies of men, yet even avoid wrestling with human nature itself; who are perpetually declaiming for reform, yet indulge in their own persons all those vices and passions which make aristocratical institutions so eminently necessary.' His doctrine of private amendment and political non-resistance sums up the anti-Jacobin position. 'I would recommend to each man in his particular sphere (first disciplining his own habits) to introduce moral reform,' he concludes, adding 'I would desist from meddling with political bodies' and conform 'to a system of complete passiveness'.[105] Thus if a county constituency needed rescuing from 'the indignity of becoming a mere ministerial borough', as it did in Edmund Marshall's *Edmund and Eleonora* (1797), it would be achieved not by an alteration to the constitution which permitted bribery and coercion, but by the personal reformation of the Member of Parliament who had been tempted by the lures of the Ministry.[106] Thus, only the personal emendation of a tyrannical husband could save his wife from his cruelty, not any revision of the marriage laws which permitted such persecution.[107] And thus, most importantly of all, if revolution was not to strike Britain, then it would be personal virtue which would protect the nation. Just as personal vice both equated with and actually precipitated public profligacy, and perhaps rebellion, so personal virtue equated with, and would ensure, public morality and subordination. 'Whatever Revolutions happen in the World,' the hero of Ann Thomas' novel writes, signing a letter, 'you may always depend on the unalterable Friendship of . . . Adolphus de Biron' – a style of signing-off which explicitly links his personal and public loyalty. Indeed, Thomas' assurance that his personal constancy will be the basis for the public fidelity that will forestall revolution culminates in her conclusion to her novel, a novel which has taken the Revolution in France as its central theme, which warns Britons not of the need for any political rectitude nor religious probity, but asks simply but determinedly that they be wary of degenerating into licentiousness and vice.[108]

We have seen, then, the three threats that novelists chose to highlight as the great dangers facing Britain during the Revolution crisis, the three threats which, for them, largely constituted that crisis. It was straightforward to reprehend and to call for the repression of both levelling and nabobism, but it was the third danger, the corruption of the élite which posed the novelists, and indeed all anti-Jacobins, a serious problem. Such degenerate aristocrats threatened revolution every bit as much as levellers and nabobs could do, since in not fulfilling the duties incumbent upon them by virtue of their station they deprived the hierarchies of the nation of their very *raison d'être* and therefore of their sustainability. But unreservedly to attack the élite would have been almost tantamount to levelling, a point confirmed by the vituperation lavished on the so-called 'Methodists' in the Clapham Sect by the likes of the *Anti-Jacobin Review* or by some sections of the Established clergy in the late 1790s and early 1800s. The solution arrived at in the novels was to separate institutions from manners, to attack, and demand the reform of, the manners of the élite, or of clergymen, or lawyers or politicians or husbands, while defending the institutions of aristocracy, of the Church, of the law, of government, or of matrimony. And always, it was to be a reform that was to be achieved on a personal level, not by any attempt at the wholesale emendation of an entire organisation. Thus it is that some novelists can appear to have been making what seem revolutionary attacks on some of the most sacred areas of British society and state, and yet retain an undimmed conservatism. Their support for the institutions they appeared to be attacking remained indubitable, and, indeed, it was only their absolute faith in the rectitude and utility of those institutions which drove them so vigorously to seek their reformation.

CHAPTER 6

The creation of orthodoxy: constructing the anti-Jacobin novel

The Stagyrite, who rules from Nature drew,
Opinions gave, but gave his reasons too.
Our great Dictators, take a shorter way, –
Who shall dispute what the Reviewers say?
Their word's sufficient; and to ask a reason,
In such a STATE as theirs, is downright TREASON.

> Charles Churchill, *The Apology. Addressed to the Critical Reviewers* (1761), quoted by William Pontey, *The Rotten Reviewers; or, a Dressing for the Morbid Branches of the Anti-Jacobin and Critical Reviews* (1807?)

From the early 1790s onwards conservative novels consistently outnumbered the radical fictions that had provoked them into being, and by the turn of the century succeeded in almost entirely vanquishing *Things As They Are* and *Man As He Should Be* from the booksellers' lists and the circulating libraries' shelves. To be able to assess this literary phenomenon it has been necessary to consider at the outset exactly what defined the anti-Jacobin novel. Having done this, the more complicated question is, why did the anti-Jacobin novel achieve and sustain such prevalence? Why, in other words, were they written?

Implicit in my analysis of the anti-Jacobin novel has been the assumption that its popularity and eventual dominance is certainly a symptom, and perhaps also in a limited way, a cause, of the almost hegemonic political conservatism that characterised Britain from the mid 1790s until after Waterloo, strangely calm seas disturbed by only the occasional squall. We should be wary, though, of allowing such a view, however attractive, to answer the 'why' of anti-Jacobin fiction. When dealing with novels, as with any form of cultural production, a question concerning the rôle of the artist will always be posed, denying the possibility of an easy attribution of cause to effect. Is it in any way historically significant, for instance, that an individual author, no matter how meritorious intellectually

or artistically, responds in a particular way to his or her historical context? Each individual author will be affected by all sorts of
biographical conditions which interfere with the relationship between
historical circumstance and literary production, their subjectivity invali-
dating as unrepresentative any reaction in their work to what must remain
their own consciousness of an historical period. Even a text overtly positioned in an historical frame of reference, say Coleridge's 'France: An
Ode' (his recantation of support for the Revolution), cannot be seen as an
'effect' of historical events, as his own *Biographia Literaria* affirmed: 'The
'reality' that poems 'imitate' is not the objective world as such, but . . .
the consciousness of the poet himself in his encounters with the objective
world . . . the poet's only genuine subject matter is himself, and the only
ideas he presents will be ideas about the activity of consciousness in the
world around it.'[1] The author presents a reflection of his or her historical context but altered, often unrecognisably, in the mirror of his or her
own consciousness. For an historian to take any author, an anti-Jacobin
novelist say, as representative of a literary response would be as glaring a
synecdochic fallacy as for the literary critic to take a fictional character as
being representative of a real, historical group, taking George Walker's
Citizen Ego, say, to be a typical member of the London Corresponding
Society.

It might appear that there is something to be said for the significance
of several, even many, authors all writing similar sorts of things in response to their historical circumstances as they conceived them. That
Burns, Wordsworth and Coleridge all recanted their early support for
the French Revolution in the years 1795–1800 says something that is
more significant than the writings of any individual alone can ever be,
especially an individual such as Blake, to take an extreme example, whom
we might politely call 'eccentric'. By the same token, the publication of
some fifty or so anti-Jacobin novels between 1795 and 1805, years that
have been convincingly identified as a period of widespread counter-
revolutionary sentiment, is surely even more historically significant. Indeed, the basis of the preceding chapters has been that the anti-Jacobin
novels of the 1790s and beyond represented the emerging hegemony of
conservatism in Britain and that they clearly display what their authors
regarded as the composition of the Jacobinism against which they strove,
as well as what they considered to be its most vulnerable points. This, of
course, has been why I have insisted on regarding anti-Jacobin novels as
if they constituted a single text, as if they came from the pen of just one
aggregate author.

And yet just as the Burns–Wordsworth–Coleridge experience only really tells us of the response to the Revolution of young romantic poets, so the anti-Jacobin novels appear to tell us only about the reaction of a few individuals who it cannot be guaranteed accurately represented the society from which they came. It must remain a rather glib and unsatisfactory method of understanding anti-Jacobin fiction to surmise simply that the conservatism of the country as a whole in some nebulous way caused authors to write conservative novels which perfectly reflected the parameters, methods and values of that conservatism. But this is precisely the point where the form in which this anti-Jacobinism was carried, the popular novel, becomes so useful to historians. Much more than the poetry of Coleridge or Blake, for example, the popular fiction of the late eighteenth and early nineteenth centuries was written for its audience. It is not to denigrate the novels with which I have been dealing to point out that, as a whole, they were a commodity first, and an art-form second. In a fiercely competitive market there was no alternative. It is the willingness of these novelists to comply with what was expected of them that allows the historian to envisage the audience of novels, alongside their writers, as at least the co-authors of their composition. What we can detect in the fictional production of the 1790s and 1800s is a cyclical relationship between production and reception, a continuum in which authors refined their product according to what their readership demanded. It is the way in which this process operated which I will be exploring in this chapter.

This is not to say, however, that individual authors simply wrote what they thought their readers wanted. To an extent this was the case, but as we shall see in the sections that follow, there was a complex and well-established nexus of factors which mediated the demands of audience to authors, holding out the prospects of rewards if authors complied with the expectations of the society for which they were writing, and threatening any transgression with a variety of penalties: obscurity, poverty, opprobrium, or worse. As a result, the novelists of the late eighteenth and early nineteenth centuries overwhelmingly produced works which fell within what Hans Robert Jauss has called the 'horizon of expectations', both in artistic and ideological terms, responding in their continuing productivity to that which had been most successful, commercially and critically and thus ideologically too, in the recent past.[2] It is this quality that allows the historian to locate the reason for the production of so many anti-Jacobin novels – the *why* of conservative fiction – not in the internal and necessarily subjective volition of individual authors, but actually in the values and desires of the community for which those authors wrote. By demonstrating how fiction was purged of its radical content, and how it was forced into a conservative mould, we will be better able to speculate about why the ascendancy of the anti-Jacobin novel was born and sustained.

Because theirs was a new and potentially hazardous cause there has been an understandable tendency to view the radicals of the 1790s, in whatever sphere they were operating, as more committed than those who came to oppose them. Clearly, though, many anti-Jacobins were equally dedicated and equally willing to undertake their crusade against Jacobinism for no other reason than because they thought it imperative for the survival of all that they held sacred. This crusading fervour often existed irrespective of any external factors encouraging them to write as they did. Yet the facts that novelists often came to anti-Jacobinism in the midst of their careers, that an attempt at an anti-Jacobin production was sometimes only a once-off foray into political fiction before a return to less contentious material and that their anti-Jacobin works sometimes even represented a repudiation of previously held sentiments, all suggest that authorial volition was being filtered through, or even contaminated by, something alien to the purest well-springs of literary creation. Before looking at the nature of these factors affecting literary production, and then examining to what extent an anti-Jacobinism was, in fact, successfully imposed, it is important that we recognise fiction as a medium controlled by circumspection from within, as it were, rather than censorship from without.

British dramatists during the French Revolution were little short of unanimous in their retailing of a blatant and uncompromising conservatism but this is an unsurprising finding given that every play proposed for performance passed before the official Inspector of Plays, John Larpent, a man as proficient as he was willing in excising even the slightest sign of sedition or immorality.[3] There was no such control for novels, a cause of no little regret to some. 'Amicus' for one, perhaps a little behind the times with his letter to the *Gentleman's Magazine* in 1808, bitterly lamented that it was madness to persist in preserving the much-vaunted 'Liberty of the Press' in an age of circulating libraries when immorality could 'be circulated throughout the kingdom, and may enter every house, from the mansion to the cottage'.[4] But no censor of fiction was needed. The production of novels was controlled by the trepidation of the producers. First of all, a publisher willing to take on the manuscript was almost always required, which presupposed, though not always rightly, a public willing to buy or borrow the book. The novel was a commodity like any other, and few publishers or booksellers were prepared to flout the laws of the free market in its favour. That publishers could and did refuse to take on proffered novels is vividly depicted by the melancholy, and doubtless at least semi-autobiographical, tales which frequently find a place in the novels of the 1790s and 1800s – tales of penurious heroes and heroines hunting around Paternoster Row in the vain search for publishers willing to take on their manuscripts. Charlotte Smith's Marchmont provides an excellent example. He broods on the difficulty of maintaining any artistic integrity in a world where 'booksellers . . . [like] all men in trade regulate their offers of purchase by the necessities of the sellers'.[5] In such a climate, it would have been foolish in the extreme for any budding novelist not to have considered his or her potential publisher while writing. And whilst Marchmont and others wondered what they had done wrong, what they needed to remove from their manuscripts to make them acceptable to publishers, they would have been wise to ponder what they might have to add in order to guarantee quick and profitable publication. Indirectly, publishers encouraged certain elements in fiction, not censoring exactly, but shaping fiction none the less. That which publishers deemed profitable, novelists soon incorporated into their work. Mary Meeke, successful author of some thirty-four novels (including six in 1804 alone), many published at the Minerva Press, made no attempt to conceal this. Any author desirous of success, she advised in the introductory chapter to her *Midnight Weddings* (1802), would do well to 'consult the taste of her publisher', who, 'as being a more competent judge than herself of the prevalent taste', she ought to heed. 'Indeed,' Meeke continued,

> to secure their approbation is rather the general aim; for should you fail of meeting with a purchaser, that labour you hope will immortalize you is absolutely lost; a most mortifying circumstance in every sense of the word; and the gentlemen and ladies who sit in judgement upon the fine spun webs from the prolific brains of female authors, are very competent to decide upon the taste of the public.[6]

The publisher was the gatekeeper of literary success, and consequently, if fiction was to pass into the corporeal world of the booksellers and circulating libraries, authorial volition had to be circumscribed by their judgement. This judgement was almost always securely based on the laws of the market, which, as effectively as any parliamentary statute, curtailed the freedom of expression of novelists.

But even once published, there were other elements of this nexus exerting just as formidable a control over fiction, and which any aspiring author had to treat with equal respect. Chief amongst them were the

Reviews, a branch of literature's productive process that has only recently begun to receive the notice it deserves.[7] Not even William Lane at the Minerva Press could manage the market for novels without the assistance of the reviewers. The *Monthly*, the *Critical*, the *Analytical Reviews* and the *Gentleman's Magazine*, the *British Critic*, *Anti-Jacobin* and *Anti-Jacobin Review and Magazine*, their shorter-lived competitors, and, latterly, the *Quarterly* and *Edinburgh Reviews*, were the only means, save costly advertisements, of attracting potential readers' attention to particular productions amongst the mass of novels issuing from the presses. Certainly, the respect with which authors treated the Reviews testifies to their importance. The anonymous author of *Flights of Inflatus* regarded 'the whole tribe of Reviewers' not just as 'great and tremendous Law-givers', but as 'absolute monarchs over literary merit', and his obeisance took the form of a preface dedicated to their praise.[8] Exhibiting the same deference differently, it was only the paranoid exasperation of William Pontey, whose book, *The Forest Pruner* (1805?), had been savaged by the critics, that gave him the rash courage to replace obsequiousness with rebuke, knowing full well that it was within their unlimited power to answer him with more, and more detailed, asseverations of his folly and nefariousness (as indeed they did). 'Some idea may easily be formed of the state of *dependence* to which, it is intended, authors shall be reduced,' he wrote, advising hapless authors not to mourn their degradation, but 'ere you hope for fame and emolument from your labours, present yourselves, with due humility, before the *self-created, self-appointed WE!*'[9]

Charles Lloyd was another who refused to capitulate to the power of the reviewers, but he was happy to plead with them whereas Pontey had felt it beneath his dignity. His *Blank Verse* (with Charles Lamb, 1798) had been lambasted by the *Anti-Jacobin Review* and, according to Burton R. Pollin, Lloyd had produced what he considered to be the anti-Jacobin *Edmund Oliver* (1798) in response.[10] When Robert Bisset's review continued to malign his name, persisting with the charge that he possessed levelling tendencies, Lloyd felt compelled to publish the thirty-eight-page *Letter to the Anti-Jacobin Reviewers* (1799) in an attempt to clear his name, and appease the critics.[11] The attempt succeeded, and even after all this, indeed perhaps because of it, Lloyd remained convinced that the Reviews held the key to literary success, and in 1800 was demanding that friends in London enquire of the *British Critic* and the *Monthly Review* 'why they have not noticed Edmund Oliver'. Were they to do so, he explained, the copies that his Bristol printer still had in hand would be disposed of with ease.[12] If this was not quite *respect* for the reviewers, it was certainly a scrupulous deference.

For all the anecdotal evidence that even Wordsworth, Cowper or Southey, say, thought that reviews could make or break their careers, it can be still pointed out that consistently harsh reviews of Minerva novels did not seem to harm their sales.[13] Yet such is the circumstantial evidence of a universal trepidation amongst novelists with regard to reviewers that we are surely left in no doubt that fear of the reviewers exerted a very pervasive influence on what writers wrote and publishers published. Charlotte Smith privately professed that had she written a novel which she thought might be interpreted as even minutely immoral, 'I should not sleep for very horror of the next Reviews.'[14] Perhaps the reviewers did revel in their reputation for severity without being nearly so strict as they claimed to be, but authors were wholly complicit. 'If no *merit impure* they can glean from my page / To add to the *many* that sully this age,' pleaded the author of *The Misanthrope; or, the Guarded Secret* (1807), 'Then obscure in the rear of the novelist cluster / Should you deign to review me, O let me pass muster.'[15] Such sycophancy perpetuated the myth of critical consequence. And these almost mandatory pre-emptive, prefatorial pleas, supplicating for clemency and presenting every conceivable excuse for the presumption of attempting a novel, are testimony to an anxiety which persuaded authors to fashion their fiction to the designs of reviewers.

What criticism's real agenda was had long been a matter of conjecture among authors. Isaac D'Israeli, in his *Vaurien* (1797), depicted a spiteful cabal of London critics whose chief pleasure was to ridicule the privately published effusions of any hopeful country poet and whose chief motivation was simply to guard their own elevated station.[16] The uninhibited Pontey, concurring that there was some sinister conspiracy motivating the reviewers, accused them of being in the pay of particular booksellers, their only critical criterion being the interest of their paymasters.[17] Mr MacGowan, a reviewer in Smith's *Wanderings of Warwick*, was inexorable in his severity, unless, that is, 'the writer he reviewed was connected with some bookseller whose interest he had at heart, or was known to be of the party he espoused'.[18] This charge, that the Reviews were little more than booksellers' advertisements, a view supported by the fact that the major Reviews were at least partly owned by various publishers, has been convincingly repudiated at some length by Derek Roper.[19] Instead, what Roper identifies as the real 'bias' in the Reviews, is a concern for moral propriety, a concern that had become the chief criterion of criticism long before the 1790s.

Indeed, it had long been clear that moral rectitude could supersede literary merit as the chief criterion of criticism. Typically, in 1787, a review of Susannah Haswell's *Victoria*. *A Novel* had complimented the author for her attempt to inculcate filial piety and had shown no discomposure about any possible dereliction of duty in determining that 'In such a case Criticism soothes his brow, and takes off his spectacles, willing to see no fault. She who would support the cause of piety cannot err.'[20] For most critics, there was no split agenda, a moral appraisal being simply part of literary criticism. Even if anyone had questioned the non-literary agenda (which of course they could not do without incurring the wrath of the Reviews), the reason why such criteria were necessary lay within the novel form itself. The supposed reader of novels, young, female and very impressionable, a stereotype which had been painstakingly established over the last half century, provided the Reviews with their warrant for moral criticism. In the popular imagination, the novel not only found most of its readers amongst women, whose character was 'by nature, weak and exposed to temptation', but its readers, of both sexes, were, lacking in education, and therefore 'of a more ductile cast whose feelings are more easily interested, and with whom every impression is deeper, because more new'. In fact, 'so easily imposed upon' were they, that the *Quarterly* felt it incumbent upon itself to make its famous demand that the contents of the circulating libraries 'should be subject to the inspection of a *strict literary police*, and the standard of morality and sentiment kept as pure as the nature of things will admit'.[21]

The *Quarterly's* appeal was, at last, an open admission of at least this particular reviewer's determination to be the guardian of moral as well as literary probity, but it represented merely an articulation of a critical agenda that had long existed, an agenda of which any aspiring novelists who had ever perused the monthly catalogues of new novels that closed the Reviews were well aware. The reviewers had always been a literary police force, but it took the Revolution crisis to concentrate the attention of the critics. Returning to their posited novel-readers, and the critic's task to protect them, the *Edinburgh* in 1806 had reminded itself that extreme vigilance was the price of freedom: 'There can be no time, in which the purity of the female character can fail to be of the first importance to every community,' Jeffrey said, 'but it appears to us, that it requires at this moment to be more carefully watched over than at any other.'[22] More importantly, during the 1790s, the mission of the reviewers' policing rôle altered. The very name of the *Anti-Jacobin* is, of course, indicative of this new emphasis, although the rôle of this single, relatively small-scale and rather dilatory organ of the counter-revolution in defining the position of the literary establishment regarding dangerous fiction has perhaps been overestimated.[23] The *British Critic* had an equally well-known and specific remit to counter Jacobinism in all its forms, and, as testament to the popularity of this type of agenda, soon after its foundation could boast a circulation as large as the *Critical*.[24] So inextricably a part of what was still ostensibly literary criticism had this undeniably more political slant become, and so much a part of all the literary Reviews, not just those set up for a specifically anti-Jacobin purpose, that those who drew up the prospectus for a planned new periodical of 1799 felt obliged to garner support by promising that,

Though no arrogance will be indulged in this publication, whatever disturbs the public harmony, insults legal authority, outrages the best regards of the heart, invalidates the radical obligations of morality, attacks the vital springs of established functions of piety, or in any respect clashes with the sacred forms of decency, however witty, elegant, and well written, can be noticed only in terms of severe and unequivocal reprehension.[25]

Having read this, or simply having read the reviews of novels in the *Anti-Jacobin*, *British Critic* or any of the Reviews of the 1790s, any novelist must have realised that the way to gain credit with the critics was not to be 'witty', nor 'elegant', nor to write well, as the prospectus put it, but first to avoid any explicit or implicit clash with 'decency', whatever that might mean, and, second, to ensure that their work contained enough 'morality', 'piety' and perhaps loyalty too, to avert any remaining critical misgivings. They must have known, in the words of one novelist of 1805, that all literature was 'either entirely cried down, or else extolled to the skies, not according to its intrinsic merits or defects, but according to the speculative opinions which the writer of it is supposed to entertain'.[26] In this light, it is hardly surprising that after telling the reviewers that she held them in the greatest respect, and that she hoped to follow them in the paths of virtue, as they advised, Ann Thomas continued her preface with one further attempt to pre-empt their criticism: 'If an Apology be necessary for the political Part of the Novel, permit me to declare, that I could not lose the Opportunity of expressing my Gratitude for that Protection which every Individual enjoys under the British Constitution.'[27] The critics did not censor, then, but managed to maintain an effective control over the creativity of authors, or rather over that great majority of authors who wished to pursue the conventional channels to literary success. Just how effective they demonstrably were in instilling a determinedly *anti-Jacobin* agenda into novel-writing is a question to which I shall return, but, in their great quest to regulate literature, the Reviews were in any case aided by other, perhaps even more dedicated, agents.

The *raison d'être* of the *British Critic* had been clear right from its establishment, its manifesto being repeated in the preface to each succeeding edition and being evident from even the most cursory perusal of its articles. But when its editors proclaimed that their office was 'to wield the arms that we are competent to use, in defence of a pure church and wisely ordered state', this was a call to arms as well as a statement of intent.[28] It not only warned writers what they might expect from critics working for this Review, but it encouraged them to use the means at *their* disposal for the same ends, hoping to inspire these other writers to join the *British Critic's* crusade, to 'wield the pen, and shed the ink' now that Britain was in the most critical 'state of literary warfare'.[29] Many answered the call, or had already concurred with it, having made their own determination to contribute to the nation's security. Some of the most militant anti-Jacobin novelists did so – Bisset and Brydges for example – and attempted to use their fiction to scare other novelists into what they considered literary rectitude. So too did William Gifford, a man who even before editing the *Anti-Jacobin; or, Weekly Examiner* and the *Quarterly Review*, had written in a private capacity the *Baviad* (1791) and *Mæviad* (1795), dedicated to exposing what he regarded as the errors of modern poetic taste. Roper suggests that Gifford's attacks on the Della Cruscan school of poetry succeeded in educating reviewers in what their true office as 'official guardian of the public taste' should be. But attacks on pro-Revolutionary poems like *The Laurel of Liberty* (1790) by Robert Merry, leader of the Della Cruscans, also taught the effectual practice of political criticism.[30]

It was Gifford's friend and admirer, T. J. Mathias, who was to become the most striking amongst these autonomous literary vigilantes. His *Pursuits of Literature* (1794–7) was another verse satire of contemporary literature in which, its author was happy to admit, literary merit was entirely subordinate to literature's effect on 'publick order, regulated government, and polished society'. Mathias, like the *British Critic*, considered his undertaking as 'no longer a mere sport of the pen, a light skirmish, or a random shaft', as perhaps Gifford's satires had been, but as a literary crusade: 'our weapons must be instruments of war,' he insisted, 'able to break down the strong holds of anarchy, impiety and rebellion, and mighty to vindicate the powers of legitimate authority'. His satire was 'an instrument, and a powerful instrument, to maintain and enforce publick order, morality, religion, literature, and good manners, in those cases in which the pulpit and the courts of law can seldom interfere'.[31] As well as answering a call to arms, though, Mathias issued one of his own. 'We must *now* all assist in our various capacities, and feel and act as public men,' he said, demanding on the one hand an unprecedented level of watchfulness from 'all who are worthy to be called scholars', and on the other, a purity and probity of literature from any authors offering their productions to the public, a demand backed up by the threat of his condemnation, and if he had his way, that of the scholars and critics too.[32]

Mathias was even willing to have recourse to the law for authors who dared to transgress the boundaries which the need for good order imposed, but which he himself had designated. He brought the *Pursuits of Literature* to the zenith of its bombast by threatening Matthew Lewis, MP and author of *The Monk* (1796), with legal action. Yet, importantly, his 'discrimination' was not censorship. 'Toleration is fully granted to all opinions,' he stated in the first dialogue, though adding the proviso that this was subject to the laws. In the third dialogue, when he was really getting into his menacing stride, he even reiterated that, 'I am no enemy to the liberty of discussion, and the toleration of opinions; I am for NO literary prescription.'[33] Literature was theoretically free; the author's volition was uncurbed by any statute or censor; but its fate, at the hands of zealots such as Mathias or Gifford, or of the reviewers, was certain if it transgressed against the rules that they themselves had drawn up. What Mathias and Gifford, and what the reviewers also, were doing, was imposing censorship by proxy, a process which meant that authors, forming their novels under the influence of those that had most recently been in the public eye and conscious of how the critics had treated them, regulated their own output. As such, both the reviewers and the autonomous literary vigilantes like Mathias fit neatly into the conception of an ongoing cyclical relationship between authors, in their continuing productivity, and their reception as discussed at the beginning of this chapter. As a group, novelists modified their output according to the reception of fiction in the marketplace. That reception was most powerfully mediated through these two sets of critics, not only because, as they liked to think, they formed the public's taste, but also because, to the aspiring novelist, they were the most prominent indication of it.

Some novelists went further, not simply obeying the injunctions of the Reviews and independent critics, but answering the *British Critic's* call to arms themselves, taking responsibility for exposing dangerous novels, and using fiction for the same purposes that Mathias and Gifford had used verse. Robert Bisset, as might be expected of the writer who contributed more criticism to the *Anti-Jacobin Review* than anyone save its editor, provides a good example of this collusion between authors and critics. His *Douglas* (1800) and *Modern Literature* (1804) are saturated with admonitions to his errant fellow novelists, along with the occasional note of applause for practitioners whose morals and politics he allowed to pass muster. Even in 1793, Clara Reeve was also calling on her fellow novelists to enter the lists in the cause of political and moral probity, at the same time warning how cautious they must be, 'lest poison should be mixed with the food that is offered'. She was just as insistent as Mathias that 'Every one is answerable for the effects of their works', although her vigilance, unlike both his and Bisset's, was solely preventative, not punitive.[34] The influence of her literary reputation, which had not ceased to climb after her celebrated *Old English Baron* (1777), doubtlessly brought her strictures a resonance for aspirant novelists greater than that which either Bisset or Mathias could command. All, though, were collaborators in attempting to manage the production of fiction according to ordinances which they themselves had instituted.

The great lubricant of this self-censoring machine, the motivation for authors to obey the dictates of the self-appointed regulators of literature, was the desire of writers to succeed in their profession, whether their goal was remuneration or acclaim. The power of the critics, both reviewers and private vigilantes, was ultimately derived from their influence over those who could ultimately make a novelist rich or famous, the novel's consumers. To suppose that purchasers of novels always obeyed the dictates of the critics would be a mistake. Although the respect with which novelists generally treated them is immediately evident, there is little evidence to establish if the ordinary novel-reader showed similar deference. Equally, there is no reason to credit the reviewers' assertions that they were constantly struggling to impose some decency on the depraved appetites of novel-readers, and the question of the extent to which readers were influenced by critical opinion must remain obscure, there being scant testimony relating how individual readers responded to the critical decrees.[35] Yet it seems likely that novel-readers shared with the reviewers a taste for the morality that dominated criticism, and there were certainly few if any complaints about the policing rôle the critics took upon themselves. The success of the *British Critic* and *Anti-Jacobin Review*, with their specific agendas, also indicates a sympathy between readers and the trends of criticism of the 1790s and 1800s, even if those who bought the periodicals were not exactly the mainstay of the novel trade.

For the most part, critical and public opinion did coalesce. Even when they had initially failed to recognise its merits, critics (even Mathias and Bisset) would, given time, unerringly support the most popular fiction like that of Radcliffe or Burney.

Ultimately, what is important is that novelists were prepared to sub-ordinate their own artistic inclinations to the perceived will of their consumers and those critics who, operating at the interface between production and reception, seemed to be able to affect consumption. Charlotte Smith certainly moulded her fiction to the often fleeting de-mands of her intended audience. She continually railed against the con-ventions of popular fiction only ultimately to comply with them. Again and again she included the romantic storylines she claimed to abhor, the ruined castles she mocked and even her pet-hate, ghosts.[36] The ex-pectations of the audience were easy to identify. As Elizabeth Inchbald put it, novel-readers 'admire one novel because it puts them in mind of another, which they admired a few days before. By them it is required that a novel should be just like a novel.'[37] To defy these expectations of the audience was to invite the neglect of the public, something which the young romantic poets may have been content to risk, but which novelists could ill afford. To comply, on the other hand, was to do as much as an author could do to ensure success.

Inchbald's comment brings to mind nothing so much as Jauss' theory of the 'horizon of expectation', a concept he uses to define the formation of the literary canon, and the delineation of literary merit, in terms of the initial appearance of a work beyond the 'horizon' of what a readership expects from literature and the process by which it is gradually subsumed into their conception of what a literary work should be, ceasing to be challenging, and being absorbed into the canon of what is acceptable and desirable. Acute authors like Smith deliberately positioned their novels within this horizon, but, in the reality of late eighteenth- and early nineteenth-century fiction, most novelists fell into compliance with the norms of their chosen form by default. These works, which require 'no turn toward the horizon of yet-unknown experience', Jauss calls 'culinary' or entertainment art ('Unterhalungskunst' – what we could call 'kitchen fiction'), and he submits that such productions

can be characterized by an aesthetics of reception as not demanding any hori-zonal change, but rather as precisely fulfilling the expectations prescribed by a ruling standard of taste, in that it satisfies the demand for the reproduction of the familiarly beautiful; confirms familiar statements; sanctions wishful notions; makes unusual experiences enjoyable as 'sensations'; or even raises moral problems, but only to 'solve' them in an edifying manner as predecided questions.[38]

Surely, no literary works fit Jauss' notion of that which falls within the horizon of expectation better than the novels of the 1790s and 1800s, the proverbially popular and notoriously cloned productions of the Minerva Press and its many competing equivalents. And as his last phrase suggests, it was not merely the literary style and techniques which were endlessly recapitulated in these novels. In all respects, as we shall see, the 'kitchen fiction' of the Revolutionary era remained studiously committed to answering in full the expectations of its audience, both literary and moral-political.

As authors sought to emulate those novels which had been most successful most recently, and to avoid the blemishes of those which had failed, their work was continually being refined so as to fit the expectations and values of these influences. The production of novels was self-perpetuatingly controlled by a nexus of consumers, those who influenced consumption, and those who managed production, and their directives were constantly refining the demands made of authors, who were for the most part happy to collaborate with these pressures. It was thus that the individual volition of authors, as a group and in their continuing productivity, was being shaped by, and made to accord with, the wishes of society. It is this process, this complicity between authors and the nexus of influences exerting an effect on their writing, that allows us to speculate more fruitfully on the nature of the relationship between authors and the society out of which, and for which, they wrote, and moreover, to see their anti-Jacobin fiction as representative of something more than simply their own political opinions. Having considered the mechanics of the process of novel production in theory, it remains to consider whether, how and to what extent, the nexus of factors exerting a level of control over literary production, was able to impose a specifically conservative agenda on the popular novel.

The nexus of forces influencing literary production provided both carrots to promote anti-Jacobinism and sticks to deter radicalism, both of which were only effective when authors were responding to their own anxieties, whether principled or mercenary. We have already seen the incentives and deterrents with which those who controlled the circulation and response to literature could cajole authors, but there remains no way to determine to what extent these factors were acting in alignment with, or opposition to, each author's volition. Why, for instance, did Thomas Skinner Surr rework George Lillo's play, *The London Merchant*, of 1731, into an anti-Jacobin novel, *George Barnwell*, in 1798? Should we accept his own reason, that Mrs Siddons' performance as Miss Milwood so impressed him that he felt compelled to rewrite the piece to give the character she had played greater emphasis? Or, considering that the major changes to Lillo's plot lie in the introduction of the new philosopher, Mr Mental, requiring major reworking, should we conclude that Surr's real motivation was political? Surr was certainly worried about being thought a Jacobin – he included a note to accompany the statement of Mental's radicalism which painstakingly explained, for the benefit of any reader who might assume that he shared them, that 'it was not his wish to *disseminate* principles, which it is his intention to *destroy*' – but does this mean that he had been somehow wheedled into his anti-Jacobinism in an attempt to claim a safe and perhaps profitable political propriety?[39] Furthermore, if Surr himself either self-deludingly or deliberately disingenuously submitted Mrs Siddons as his inspiration, what chance do we have to discover whether it was political principle or pecuniary pragmatism that urged him to turn the frivolous comedy of Lillo into a dedicated satire of the radical danger to Britain? In any case, though, given that anti-Jacobin fiction, either conforming by default or by active endeavour, achieved an almost hegemonic prevalence by the end of the eighteenth century, an analysis of the effectiveness of the mechanisms of ensuring this conformity seems crucial.

Neither critics, publishers, nor readers had to dissuade Richard Cumberland, to take one example, from filling his novels with politics – he already objected to it on purely artistic grounds:

All I am bound to do as a story-maker, is, to make a story; I am not bound to reform the constitution of my country in the same breath, nor even (Heaven be thanked!) to overturn it, though that might be the easier task of the two, or, more properly speaking, one and the same thing in its consequences. Nature is my guide; man's nature, not his natural rights: the one ushers me by the straightest avenue to the human heart, the other bewilders me in a maze of metaphysics.[40]

Cumberland is being rather disingenuous here, his ostensible political ambivalence being underlaid by a carefully conspicuous conservatism. But just as he claimed not to be amenable to, or subject to, outside pressure urging him to introduce an ostentatious probity into his work, many authors who did produce actively anti-Jacobin novels likewise seem to have fallen into that rectitude without requiring external encouragement for their militant conservatism. Jane West, Elizabeth Hamilton, Robert Bisset and others, produced novels only of an anti-Jacobin tendency, and were generally congratulated on their orthodoxy, rather than converted to it, by the nexus. *Adolphus de Biron*, the loyal effort of Ann Thomas, did not even receive a review from the anti-Jacobin periodicals, but judging by her work, she was altruistically patriotic enough to consider herself well recompensed if she was able simply to contribute to the nation's safety. Her novel was published 'for the Authoress' at an obscure provincial press, and the conviction of her prose makes it evident that she picked up the pen primarily for the purpose of answering her own call to arms: 'When turbulent Men are so industrious in disseminating Sedition through the land,' she had one of her sagacious characters say, 'every good Subject, and every true Patriot ought to be vigilant to incite in himself, and in his Neighbour, that Obedience to the Laws, and Respect to the chief Magistrate, which may secure and promote Concord and Quiet.'[41]

Yet, if such authors as these were not actually persuaded into writing their anti-Jacobin fiction by external pressures, they nevertheless were able to benefit from sympathy towards their work. They must have known that they could hope for critical favour, or neutrality at least, and that their efforts in the cause of what they saw as the nation's good would not, unlike that of the radicals, attract only vilification instead of remuneration. Likewise, Surr, with his *George Barnwell*, cannot have been unaware that the introduction of anti-Jacobin characters and themes would, in 1798, procure him critical sympathy, and endow his fiction with a certain contemporaneity, not to say voguishness. Whether written for principle or profit, or more likely for both, it is difficult to believe that such a shrewd author as Surr later proved himself to be with his celebrated 'silver fork' novels could be unaware of the effects the inclusion of a host of topical concerns could have on a play almost seventy years old and as familiar to the literary public as any story outside Shakespeare and the Bible.

Indeed, some recent critics have contended that there was something more than voguishness to be gained by the introduction of an overt anti-Jacobin rectitude into fiction; that it could form a screen of correctness from behind which authors might be allowed to pursue their own, perhaps more radical, agendas unchallenged. Thus Claudia Johnson and Eleanor Ty have suggested that, amongst others, even the ultra-orthodox Elizabeth Hamilton filled her novels with an explicit, or perhaps even superficial, anti-Jacobinism so that she might delve behind the very code of gender propriety that she was ostensibly endorsing.⁴² If this is true, then Hamilton and others may be seen to have been deliberately importing an anti-Jacobin probity into their fiction as a response to outside pressures. But even if Johnson and Ty's proposition is questionable, the fact that authors displaying such a determined anti-Jacobin agenda were concerned with the mechanics of their work's reception, as well as its abstract worth, is evident from what we know of their relationships with their publishers. For example, it is illuminating that Hamilton gave her considered agreement to the opinion of George Robinson, the prospective publisher of her *Memoirs of the Life of Agrippina* (1804), when he suggested 'postponing the publication of a work totally unconnected with the objects that at present most powerfully engage the public mind'.⁴³ In agreeing with Robinson, Hamilton demonstrates that she was at least aware of the need to regulate her production by the exigencies of the market and not just allow her own preferences to hold sway. It was the publisher who held the reins of Hamilton's productivity, and she was a commercially successful author. After the author's own judgement, the publishers were the first line of the nexus controlling the authors.

That Robinson himself had made the recommendation not to publish the new work of a successful author as soon as it was ready for the press begs a number of questions. *Agrippina* was not another *Hindoo Rajah* or *Modern Philosophers*, and was in fact not particularly political at all, save by distant allegory. Had Robinson therefore wished to suggest that it might receive a better reception in a less highly charged political climate than was current in a nation just plunged back into war after the Amiens peace? Or did he wish to suggest that the time was riper for another explicitly anti-Jacobin work, either an entirely new production, or a new edition of one of Hamilton's former works? Indeed, Robinson did bring out another edition of *Modern Philosophers* in 1804, the fourth. In either case, the question of whether Robinson was making a narrowly commercial or a more patriotic decision remains unanswered. It is tempting, however, to consider concern about the publication of anti-Jacobin literature in general, and especially that published by Robinson, as purely financially motivated. His name was associated most with radical work, and why should a man who had shifted the *Critical* to a more Foxite stance after acquiring a stake in 1774, and had published William Godwin, Mary Wollstonecraft and Mary Hays, care personally about the effect *Agrippina* would have, or fail to have, on the public in 1804? He had even taken over the politically, if not commercially, risky publication of *Caleb Williams* for the second edition of 1796, and coming just two years before Joseph Johnson was gaoled for the best part of a year for publishing Gilbert Wakefield's supposedly seditious *Reply to the Bishop of Llandaff*, this is presumably indicative of either his radicalism, or his unstinting and fearless quest for a profit. Peter Garside has even hinted that Robinson might have deliberately taken up Hamilton's works in order to regain some vestige of respectability in conservative circles, presumably another commercial decision.[44]

Yet publishers on the whole, Robinson notwithstanding, were both ostensibly loyal, and apparently willing sometimes to allow their principles to prevail over their publishing interests, according to what they thought best for the nation, not best for their profits. Rivington's, for example, had been established under the sign of the Bible and Crown in 1711, and John Rivington, who having inherited the business from his father, ran it until his death in 1792, attended services at St Paul's twice a day, breakfasted every other Monday with the Archbishop of Canterbury and shut his shop every year on the anniversary of Charles I's execution. Moreover, he was prepared to regulate his publications by his beliefs, becoming official publisher for the Society for Promoting Christian Knowledge whilst staunchly refusing to publish Wesley, Whitefield, or the like.[45] The loyalism, or at least Pittitism, of William Lane of the Minerva, cannot be doubted either. Along with his fellow bookseller John Murray I (1745–93), Lane was accused, during the Regency crisis, of outright bias, their former printer accusing them of ordering him to 'support Mr PITT *through* THICK *and* THIN' and of sending him for printing 'a number of paragraphs, some of which were *wretchedly spelt, against* His ROYAL HIGHNESS the PRINCE OF WALES!'[46] Whilst the Minerva's initial advertisements spoke, somewhat conventionally, of limiting their productions to those 'such as are founded on the basis of virtue, and have tended to improve the understanding, and to amend the heart', by the middle of the 1790s a prospectus for the Minerva circulating libraries indicated a tighter, and more political, self-regulation: 'The printing department shall be open to such subjects as tend to the public good ... it shall never convey to the happy subjects of this kingdom false founded doctrines or opinions, but attached to the prosperity of the country, it shall be a barrier for its support.'[47] Still, though, we cannot be sure whether this was merely shrewd commercialism on the part of Lane, anxious no doubt to dispel his reputation for spawning novels furthering the progress of vice, of sedition even, or whether this really was the effusion of a deeply held principle. Perhaps an indication that his claims were really little more than a financially motivated rhetoric is to be found in the immediate citation of Robert Bage's *Man As He Is* (1792) as an example of this jealously guarded probity. And Lane's pledges, after all, did appear in an *advertisement*, a medium designed to influence potential patrons of his libraries and novels. Whatever their motives, Lane, Robinson and others, were in any case evidently exercising some degree of political regulation over what left their presses. If the house of Rivington had deliberately chosen to publish only 'good' books, then Lane had at least declared his intention of not publishing 'bad'. An anti-Jacobin publishers' list could be arrived at from either direction.

Bearing in mind the fear of insurrection and sedition and the consequent reaction into aggressive loyalism in the 1790s, it seems clear that political probity was a saleable commodity in the years of the Revolution Crisis. These advertisements produced by Lane were testament to this appeal, and marketability, of conservatism. Similarly, there seems to be no other obvious explanation for the sudden appearance of the imprint 'Printed at the Anti-Jacobin Press' than that it was hoped such a cachet would somehow impress prospective readers. At least six works appeared in 1799, with six more in 1800, with this imprimatur on their title page. Five of them were printed by one J. Plymsell and sold by C. Chapple, six printed by Thomas Crowder and published variously by Chapple, Longman and Rees, and Rivingtons. The works themselves are eclectic, ranging from William Jones' *Six Letters on Electricity* (1800) to Frederic Reynolds' highly successful and often reprinted play *How To Grow Rich* (1800). The Anti-Jacobin Press could, however, also boast of having produced works more in keeping with its name, and some initial connection with the *Anti-Jacobin Review* seems probable if not certain. John Gifford and Richard Polwhele, vehement opponent of Wollstonecraft and education for the poor, had work printed there, as was a report of the Committee of Secrecy of the House of Commons, the final leaf of which comprises a prospectus of the *Anti-Jacobin Review*. Robert Bisset had his anti-Jacobin novel *Douglas* (1800) printed there too. But any suggested connection does not explain why this particular name for the press was either invented or appropriated by Crowder, Plymsell, or anyone else, nor why the press was used by such an assortment of publishers or for such an assortment of works. Whilst any attempt at answering these questions must remain speculative, it seems not unlikely that the mere words 'Anti-Jacobin Press' were, in themselves, a kind of advert for what lay behind the title page on which they were printed, even if those pages sometimes contained nothing that, even using the loosest of definitions, could be denominated anti-Jacobin.

Both the advertisements of Lane at the Minerva and, quite possibly, the imprimatur of the Anti-Jacobin Press imprint, displayed an enviousness of the sort of favourable publicity that could accrue to publishers who had proved themselves properly principled. The *British Critic*, for instance, complimented 'Mr Longman's press' for 'what cannot be said of every other from which Novels are born' – certainly implying, if not naming, the Minerva, – 'that it does not send out anything offensive to good manners and pure morals'.[48] This was still a 'negative' compliment, though, and fear of censure not hope of praise, was probably a more effective check on publishers. The twin fears for publishers, and thus for their authors, were that a work would not sell, and that it would come to be regarded as seditious. Marchmont, in gaol and contemplating writing a novel to pay his debts, gave voice to Charlotte Smith's appreciation of this latter threat. Not only would publishers be unlikely to take on the work of an unknown, but,

It was besides very probable, that the principal dealers in literary traffic would hesitate at purchasing the work of a prisoner who was likely, besides the disgrace of the connection, to vent in his writing some part of the discontent that imprisonment is very apt to engender. – The passage from discontent to murmurs against the oppression, real or imaginary, is very short; and murmurs may savour of seditious notions, and seditious notions might carry a man nobody knew whither. What rich and substantial vendor would hazard anything like this in these times?[49]

What exactly it was that these publishers were afraid of Smith does not explain, or, at least, not here. The sort of prosecution Joseph Johnson's underwent was certainly one peril a publisher of subversive material might face. The author of *Memoirs of Planetes* feared that anyone publishing a description of a Godwinian utopia would 'be branded with the titles of visionary, and theorist, a disturber of the public peace, a jacobin, a democrat, and I know not what', and perhaps 'sent to a lunatic hospital, and ranked among the incurables'.[50] But there was also the more immediate danger to a publisher's business that the novel would not sell. Another fictional publisher, Mr Type in Edward Mangin's *George the Third* (1807), has learned this lesson by experience. Two years prior to the novel's present (*circa* 1792), he had taken on a novel by one of the 'enlightened gentlemen' of the age, but it had not sold at all, 'and no wonder', he recalls, 'half of it indeed was unintelligible, and might have gone down; but the rest was intolerable; nothing but sarcasms against intrigue and politeness; and in several parts of it the fellow had cast reflexions on kings and churchmen. – Never was I so taken in before; but I'm resolved the same shan't happen again!' For Mr Type, these two blades of the nexus are the same: Jacobinism means no sale and the possibility of an indictment, whether legal or social. He will publish anything now, he explains, so long as 'there was any chance of sale, and none of his being put in the pillory' – the two concomitant halves of the nexus of informal censorship by which public opinion and public legislation controlled the publisher, who controlled his authors.[51] It was a process illustrated well by Smith, who was never shy of complaining about her position as an author. In her *Banished Man*, she presented her readers with one Joseph Clapper, a bookseller, and evidently a pastiche of her former publisher, Joseph Bell. One of the many persecutors of another of Smith's pseudo-autobiographical characters, Mrs Denzil, Clapper clearly demonstrates the concerns of publishers as passed on to authors, demanding the speedy production of the next volume of her latest novel, and also, 'the Ode to Liberty, mentioned by you as a close to the same: but I shall change the tittle [*sic*] of that, having promis'd the trade that there shall be no liberty at all in the present work; without which assurance they would not have delt [*sic*] for the same'.[52] It should be noted, of course, that the changes Clapper suggests, or enforces, are purely cosmetic. His insistence that the name, rather than the substance, of the offending piece be altered, reveals Smith's opinion that the concern of at least this publisher that sedition should be absent from his publications, was not for the sake of principle, but merely a matter of business.

Even at the moment when Smith was using *The Banished Man* to clear her name of any taint of radicalism still adhering from the pro-Revolutionary *Desmond*, she was revealing, as an author subject to the constraints of the book trade, just how little choice she actually had in the matter. But publishers, even when, like the putative Clapper, they were dictating to authors what could and could not be allowed in their work, were the victims as well as the agents of the nexus influencing literary production. They were simply passing on the pressures which they detected in the marketplace to their authors. No matter what their own personal sentiments, publishers were concerned lest their productions were debarred an entrance into the marketplace or denied an unprejudiced response when they reached it. Ultimately, the reception of novels, however much publishers might wish to manage it by ostentatiously loyalist advertisements or imprints, lay with the buyers and borrowers in the marketplace, and with those who were in a position to influence their opinions, most notably the reviewers.

For all the power of the Reviews outlined earlier, we should not assume that they were in total control of literary production. It is tempting, for example, to regard the 'redemption' of Charlotte Smith, the complete transition from the radical *Desmond* to the anti-Revolutionary *The Banished Man*, as the result of the opinions of her readers transmitted through the comments of the reviewers, the most audible source of feedback. But such a causality is impossible to substantiate. Though her recantation would seem a perfect paradigm for the working of the nexus on an author's productivity, reviews of *Desmond*, though they found much to criticise, did not noticeably chide the author for her 'Jacobinism'.[53] Nor did the sales of *Desmond* conspicuously fail to meet expectations, even if it did make its first entrance into the world just as France had begun to consider exporting the Revolution abroad and eliminating the monarchy, the appearance of the second edition coinciding with the September Massacres. Smith's popularity may have been gradually diminishing after her earlier novels, but *Desmond* was certainly not shunned by a shocked public as some modern critics have asserted.[54] Another London edition appeared within a year, as was the case with most of the novels before 1795 (only *Celestina* had done better), and there were the customary Irish and French editions. The fact that Smith recanted, then, seems due to a personal conversion, made, like Coleridge's or Wordsworth's have long been held to have been, from a growing horror at unfolding events in France.

The *Monthly* evidently thought as much, its review of *The Banished Man* supposing that 'It is natural that her mind should revolt from the horrors committed in France; and it is equally natural for new converts to be zealous.'[55] The *British Critic* echoed the sentiments, but, significantly, added a note of censure for *Desmond* to its account of *The Banished Man*:

We must not close this article without congratulating the lovers of their King, and the constitution, in the acquisition of an associate like Mrs Charlotte Smith. Convinced by observation, that the changes in France have only produced rapine and murder, and that the most worthy among the French have been forced to quit the country to avoid inevitable slaughter, she makes full atonement by the virtues of the Banished Man, for the errors of Desmond. Such a convert gained, by fair conviction, is a valuable prize to the commonwealth.[56]

And such praise for *The Banished Man*, and retrospective criticism for *Desmond*, must have served as a potent example for any aspiring authors of the mid 1790s who had been aware of how one of the age's most prominent novelists was being treated. The *Critical's* review of *The Banished*

Man was quite unequivocal. She had written the novel, it said, first, to furnish her publisher with four more volumes, second, to give vent to her private grievances and third, 'to reinstate herself with the opinion of those who have been offended by the turn in her politics in a former publication, and to do away with suspicion of her having embraced the wrong side of the question'.[57] Amalgamating the first reason, which the reviewer called 'natural', with the third, called 'prudent' (and ignoring the second, the perennial failing of Smith in the eyes of the reviewers, who here called it 'unwise'), we see the effect at least this critic thought the market, goaded by critics, had on artistic production. If the four volumes that Smith presented to her publisher were to be a success, then they had to affirm a position demanded of each author by their potential consumers.

The reviewers, for their part, pursued their self-appointed task to ensure that no dangerous material reached the trusting reader, with an unrelenting vigour born of the same paranoia that fuelled the conspiracy theories of Barruel, Robison or Playfair. And as with the well-publicised fear of the Illuminati, the reviewers' apprehensions were, judging by their vehemence, both an expression of real dread and a rhetorical and somewhat insidious device to inspire in others a similarly zealous alacrity. The *Anti-Jacobin Review* held that literature had 'been rendered by the sceptical, schismatical and disaffected writers of the age, a vehicle for the promulgation of every false, bad, vicious principle, that can corrupt the heart or contaminate the mind of the present and rising generation'. And 'Our novels' in particular, said the same arbiter of taste, were 'often intentionally filled with poison of the most destructive kinds; with sedition, irreligion, and the grossest immorality'.[58] Starting from this premise, the rôle of the Reviews was clear, and their determination to succeed equally manifest: it was necessary to eradicate every trace of Jacobinism from the novel.

This politicisation of literary reviewing was not entirely new, for the older Reviews had never been renowned for keeping their politics out of their artistic judgements. Ralph Griffiths, owner and first editor of the *Monthly*, called himself 'an Old *Whig* and a consistent *Protestant*', and his son, and co-editor, became a colonel in the Volunteers, both infusing the oldest of the Reviews still appearing in the 1790s with a patriotic, if not quite conservative, sentiment. The *Critical*, meanwhile, had originally been known to take the yet more 'tory' side in any controversy, until taking a slightly more Foxite turn towards the end of the century.[59] But the roots of the *Anti-Jacobin* and *British Critic's* political criticism were not to be found in these antecedents, but rather in the traditional critical attitude to fiction. The novel, in the opinion of the reviewers, had fallen from the prelapsarian days of Richardson and Fielding, and carried the weight of its sin throughout its successive incarnations, the apparent expansion of its audience in the 1780s and 1790s only exacerbating the inherent evil. Only a handful of authors had managed to gain any lasting critical approval in the 1770s and 1780s, and although Burney, Reeve and Radcliffe, along with a few others, had been able to achieve a degree of success in the 1790s, the disdainful attitude of the *Anti-Jacobin* and *British Critic* was built upon this general antipathy to fiction. Their attitude that all novels were guilty until proven politically innocent, or even positively useful, was built upon the same tendency to write off all novels in literary terms until they had proved themselves to be of outstanding merit. There was, in other words, only a very small distance between the *Anti-Jacobin* telling its readers that all novels were written expressly for the purpose of undermining the political and moral health of the nation, and the reviewers of the *Monthly* or *Critical* expressing the opinion that 99 per cent of the novels received were not worth the paper they were written on. Either way, the novel was almost irredeemably flawed, and fully deserving of the most exacting scrutiny.

In the early days of the Revolution, in the heyday of the 'Jacobin novel', radicalism in fiction had been treated with ambivalence by the reviewers, a cause for comment but not necessarily for censure, as we have already seen to have been the case with Smith's *Desmond*. This had been helped, of course, by the fact that many of the Jacobin novels were written by authors not only possessed of talent, but also of strong connections with the Reviews themselves. The *Analytical*, not as radical in its reviewing as its reputation suggests, was perhaps typical in noting the politics of Holcroft's *Anna St Ives* (1792) – 'This novel appears to be written as a vehicle to convey what are called democratical sentiments', – but judging the work only in literary terms: 'Be that as it may, it contains many interesting scenes, which forcibly illustrate what the author evidently wishes to inculcate.'[60]

Perhaps the attention given by the critics to the novels of Holcroft and Bage, Smith and Inchbald, suggests that their literary quality was too rare a thing to be subordinated to narrow political concerns. If so, such indulgence was short-lived, for, by the middle of the decade, political ambivalence could find no place in the Reviews. It was still possible for Jacobin novels, in some few cases, to succeed as novels *in spite of* their politics. The *Critical*, for instance, thought Godwin's *Caleb Williams* (1794) on a par with the work of Fielding, Smollett and Burney, but dictated that any future edition must expunge the 'political reflections'. And even as late as 1798, the same periodical noted of Bage's *Hermsprong* (1796) that 'There is occasionally a little tincture of the new philosophy, as it is called, and a shade of gloom is thrown upon human life; but the writer is not unsuccessful in his humorous attempts; and, upon the whole, the reader has a chance of becoming wiser and better by a perusal of this work', the word 'but' here taking on a crucial significance.[61] Increasingly, though, literary merit was becoming subordinate to political propriety as the only criterion of criticism, and any taint of Jacobinism was enough to damn a novel irrespective of its artistic worth. The time-scale on which this was happening is apparent from Roper's survey of some twenty-eight reviews of what he calls 'reforming or revolutionary novels of purpose', all appearing before 1800. Only six were favourable, and three of these were for Bage's *Man As He Is* in 1792. After 1792, only the increasingly 'liberal' *Analytical* continued to praise any Jacobin novel, and then only the works of one author, Mary Hays.[62] As one might expect, the turn to a more scrupulous anti-Jacobinism in the Reviews coincided with the flurry of events in France and Britain at the end of 1792 and the beginning of 1793 that so demonstrably signalled the ascendancy of the counter-Revolutionary reaction in Britain. Or put another way, the shift in the attitudes of the *Monthly*, *Critical* and *Analytical* Reviews, with which Roper was most concerned, coincided more or less exactly with the birth of a new publication which embodied all the convictions slowly dawning on the older established organs of criticism, the *British Critic*.

It is immediately clear why the early attitudes of the older periodicals, still, in the early 1790s, attempting impartial criticism of what many thought an inherently seditious class of literature, must have been so provocative to the increasingly outraged reviewers who went on to contribute to the *British Critic* and *Anti-Jacobin*. That is not to say that both these Reviews were totally incapable of appreciating literature because of their political anxieties. The *British Critic*, unsurprisingly given that its staff were doubtlessly recruited in large part from existing periodicals, certainly began by affirming the old criteria of criticism – good novels existing 'where the imagination is not suffered to be licentious; where morality and virtue are the end and object; where probability is not violated, nor the passions improperly excited'.[63] It even seemed genuinely regretful that, because of the nation's present danger, it could not recommend what it knew to be fiction of uncommon quality. If Elizabeth Inchbald, for instance, 'had not met with some designing persons, who instilled unjust prejudices into her mind,' an editorial lamented, her *Nature and Art* could have received the acclaim it otherwise deserved.[64]

But when a reviewer took it upon him- or herself to revise the *British Critic's* manifesto of criticism five years later, a new emphasis had become evident, none of the qualities which good novels had previously required being quite jettisoned, but rather put into a new order. Unabashedly the reviewer told the Review's readers, including of course any potential novelists, that the recommendation of novels would be graded thus:

1st, those which are innocent, instructive, and well written; 2ndly, those which possess only two of these three properties, being deficient in the last mentioned; 3rdly, those which are pernicious in their tendency, whether they are well or ill written. Upon these, we shall set, as deeply as we are able, our mark of reprehension.[65]

And if any would-be novelist, publisher, or reader, wanted verification of this pledge, he or she needed only to wait until November of the same year for a clear example of the complete subordination of literary criticism to political considerations. With Alethea Lewis' novel, *Disobedience*, the reviewer seemed still inclined to favour the work, but obviously felt any such laxity would be a gross dereliction of duty:

There are many democratic traits in this piece, which highly deserve reprehension; and the disposition to decry and degrade the more elevated ranks of society, which forms part of the system of writers of a certain class, is sufficiently prominent in this novel. These very pernicious defects of course temper the commendation, which in other respects, we would gladly bestow.[66]

As for the *Anti-Jacobin Review*, one of its chief contributors, Robert Bisset, who had also been an editor of a literary periodical, made his critical method clear when he had the hero of his first novel become a reviewer and explain his views on the subject: 'the importance of works ought not to be rated by their literary excellence,' opined Douglas, for 'many productions, of no great intellectual force, were very beneficial, and others very hurtful to society'. It was, he added, 'the business of a reviewer to shew the good of the former, and expose the evil of the latter, according to the probability of their extensive operation'.[67]

However, the separation of literary merit and political defects evident in the *British Critic* and *Anti-Jacobin* ran counter to the tradition of criticism of fiction. Throughout its history, criticism of the novel had either condoned or condemned moral tendency at the same time as artistic value, the two criteria being inseparable. The great progenitors of the novel, it was held, had managed to combine virtue and entertainment, and it was only the Jacobins who had sundered the association by writing regrettably good novels with bad tendencies. Thus it was that reviewers, astonishingly given their antecedents and supposed rôle, evolved an ambivalence to literary merit. Indeed, an actual distrust of literary merit developed, a review of Godwin's *Caleb Williams*, for instance, opining that, 'When a work is so directly pointed at every bond which connects society, and at every principle which renders it amiable, its very merits become noxious as they tend to cause its being known to a wider circle.'[68] But if the gravity of the Revolution crisis, or the single-mindedness of the *British Critic*, caused criticism to depart from its tradition of seeing moral, and now political, rectitude as an indivisible part of artistic literary merit, the reviewers soon seemed to realise that the most efficacious way to attack Jacobin fiction must be to attack that quality which made *Caleb Williams* so dangerous, which caused it to be so attractive to readers, namely its literary merit.

At first, objections made on literary grounds became a shorthand for the more political concerns of the reviewers. The reviewer of Eliza Fenwick's *Secresy* (1795), for example, found it 'One of the wildest romances we have met with', with a catastrophe 'as deeply, as it is absurdly, unfortunate'. The novel surely attracted the epithets 'wild' and 'absurd' only because, as the reviewer later reveals, it brims with 'a morality, worthy enough of modern France, but far removed (we trust) from the approbation of Englishmen'.[69] Whilst the gap between literary and political criteria was maintained, any supposed low quality of fiction could be used by the reviewers as a stick to beat the Jacobin author. Thus a reviewer of Mary Robinson's *Walsingham* (1797), having scorned her perceived reproaches to the late French court and her encomiums of the virtue of the Revolutionaries, went on to lambast her imagery. In discussing Rousseau and Voltaire, Robinson excited the critic's ire by saying Britons 'vegetate in the glooms of ignorance'. But when the reviewer closed his or her review by lamenting 'When will authors . . . cease to surfeit us with such disgusting and depraved absurdities', it was, *ostensibly*, not Robinson's sentiments, but her metaphor, which was found so objectionable – for was not light, rather than gloom, the promoter of vegetation?

By 1800, the *British Critic* had refined its techniques of political criticism by proxy. Godwin's *St Leon* (1799) was castigated for its sterility, lack of originality and anachronisms, and the author's failure to depict the manners of the sixteenth century was remarked on at some length. But it was in the list of 'incorrect writing', in which the reviewer darted nimbly from highlighting grammatical errors and the misuse of words to the censure of Godwin's 'panegyric on prostitution' (page references helpfully supplied), that the technique reached its apogee. When the reviewer at length singled out the phrase 'the superfluidities of the rich are a *boon extorted* from the miseries of the poor' as particularly worthy of rebuke, it was only to add 'Who ever heard of a boon being extorted?'[70] Poor literary quality and radicalism had become synonymous.

Evidently, then, by the later 1790s, literary criticism was being used as a vehicle for censure of the politics of Jacobin fiction and the premise that Jacobinism and good literature were simply incompatible had been established. This message must have been very clear to any aspiring novelists. Any radicalism in their productions would not only be seized upon and execrated, but would invalidate the whole of their literary endeavours. In fact, the reviewers made it abundantly clear that it was Jacobinism itself that detrimentally affected literary quality.[71] Even the typographical mistakes of Edward Henry Illif's *Angelo* (1796) are adduced as indicative of its Jacobinism, and the heinous errors of vocabulary made by its author ('irrecovery', 'dubiety') are subject to the most withering animadversions of the critic: 'Reader, what language is this? It is the jargon of an unfortunate brain, never, undoubtedly, very strong, and entirely turned by the *perfectibility* system.'[72] Yet, once the reviewers had convinced themselves and, they must have hoped, their readers, that the merest taint of the new philosophy entirely undermined any incipient merit in a novel, the errors of a Jacobin novel became something to be grateful for. Iliff, indeed, was congratulated for the faults of his novel, his contempt for the laws of language, which according to the reviewer he gloried in despising as much as the laws of society, allowing the critic the luxury of noting 'were he intelligible, there would be no small danger in his rhapsodies'. The same baleful satisfaction at a novel's weaknesses, a strange inversion of the traditional values of the Reviews, could be found in the *British Critic's* appreciation of *The Life and Opinions of Sebaldus Nothanker* (1798), which, however pernicious its irreligion might have been on the Continent, was unlikely to interest anyone in Britain when translated so badly.[73]

But behind this flippancy lay an achievement of real significance. Having made an artistic crime of Jacobinism, having set it up in direct opposition to good taste and good writing, few authors, if designing to reach a wide audience, would consider writing a radical novel or even dare to submit their work to the public in a state which could possibly be interpreted as bearing any blemish of Jacobinism. Joseph Wildman's paranoid anticipation of what the critics might make of his *Force of Prejudice*

(1799) is typical of this minute circumspection with which the Reviews had so successfully imbued authors. Having reached the 'Conclusion' to his novel Wildman suddenly began to doubt whether his depiction of a character's descent into prostitution had not 'savoured too much of the philosophy of the *"New School"'*, and remembering the treatment that Kotzebue's plays had received in the periodicals for a similar violation of propriety, had felt it absolutely necessary to add – 'as it is possible the same critics may think the like observations may with equal justice, be extended to his [i.e. Wildman's] character of Augusta' – that his principles were derived only from the most respectable sources.[74] The reviewers, as both the manifestation of popular opinion most accessible to authors and publishers, and as the opinion-makers of the book-buying and borrowing public, had succeeded in ensuring that only those authors and publishers whose motivation for writing was actually deliberately and stubbornly Jacobin would continue to attempt to present a radical work before the public.

The concern of the reviewers for the eradication of any trace of Jacobinism from the novel was born out of their traditional suspicion for the novel. Their recognition that the novel could be a highly successful organ of anti-Jacobin propaganda was slower in materialising, and doubtlessly owed its emergence to the example provided not only by early anti-Jacobin novelists such as Sayer, Reeve, Pye and D'Israeli, but also by the Cheap Repository and the short fictions of Hannah More, Sarah Trimmer and others. I have already suggested that it was the recruitment of the novel for the anti-Jacobin cause that eventually did much to convince the suspicious of its validity as a literary form, and this is a process that becomes visible in the growing demands made on novels by the reviewers. In 1795, the *British Critic*, for instance, was chiding the author of *Such Follies Are* (1795) for daring to suggest 'That the pride of blood is contemptible', but went on to advise that positive restitution was possible and that the author, as one of the 'Public Instructors', should actively 'give such lessons as the exigencies of the times especially demand', 'namely, lessons of order, of just subjection, and of that rational *subordination*, which is so far from being unworthy of free men, that freedom itself cannot exist without it'.[75] By the mid 1790s, then, the Reviews were demanding of novelists not merely a negative rectitude, not merely the absence of discernible Jacobinism, but a deliberate, active and useful anti-Jacobinism.

The positive rewards that the reviewers held out for such zealous anti-Jacobinism seem designed to entice authors into compliance. For one thing, in an age when few novels, perhaps only three or four a year, were given the status of a full review, longer than a paragraph or two, a thoroughly anti-Jacobin novel could frequently demand prompt and extensive treatment, stretching over several pages and including lengthy quotation alongside sympathetic critical consideration. The *British Critic* accorded such privileged status to Hamilton's *Hindoo Rajah* (1796), Pye's *Democrat* (1795) and *Aristocrat* (1799), West's *Gossip's Story* (1796), *Tale of the Times* (1799) and *Infidel Father* (1802), Brydges' *Arthur Fitz-Albini* (1798) and Opie's *Adeline Mowbray* (1805), all anti-Jacobin novels, although the omissions from this list (for instance Walker's *Vagabond* (1799), D'Israeli's *Vaurien* (1797), Hamilton's *Modern Philosophers* (1800), all of which received favourable but short notices) demonstrate that even the most anti-Jacobin of novels could not be guaranteed the Reviews' full attention. Nevertheless, the record of anti-Jacobin novels in achieving substantial reviews was better than that of the doyenne of the age, Ann Radcliffe, for one, and the amount of praise bestowed on them in those reviews was second to none.

Clearly, it was the political content of these novels that won them such acclaim, and yet, as with novels possessed merely of a passively anti-Jacobin tendency, their political correctness was endorsed in terms of congratulation for their apparently discernible *literary* merit. The greatest praise bestowed on *Vaurien* by the *British Critic*, for example, was not that it would save the nation from the threat of the radicals or invasion by the French, but that it was 'evidently the performance of an able pen' and was 'certainly entertaining'.[76] Other classically anti-Jacobin novels received a similarly literary commendation rather than any direct reference to the political merits which had inspired the reviewers' praise. Could it really be the so much maligned and notoriously dreary Henry James Pye, and writing a Minerva novel too, whose *Aristocrat* (1799) was called 'agreeable', 'remarkably well-written', 'pleasing', 'the elegant amusements of a well-informed and accomplished writer', very refreshing after the usual 'trash which crowd the shelves of circulating libraries'? Even if the reviewer knew the author to be the Poet Laureate, these compliments were surely owing mostly to the 'religion, morality, good order, and true English loyalty' that the reviewers observed the author so strenuously asserting throughout, rather than to pure literary merit. Yet selecting quotations from the novel, and summing up the review, the critic chose to amplify not the political value, but the novel's elegance.[77]

On the few occasions that reviewers did separate the literary quality of a novel from its moral and political demeanour, it is clear which they regarded as more important. Ultimately, whereas literary merit, as we have seen, could not succeed without political probity, a forthright anti-Jacobinism could actually compensate for a lack of genius. Pye had surely benefited from this equation, and the *British Critic* eventually admitted that its darling, Jane West, had also not been judged entirely on the calibre of her novels. She could not be assigned a perpetual place by the side of Fielding, Smollett and Lesage, the reviewer confided in 1803, but with what the Review called 'more appropriate praise', praise of West's morality, religion and attacks on Voltaire and Rousseau as it turned out, it was able to continue in its applause for all her works.

Compared with the Reviews, the private, independent critics, who took it upon themselves to expunge all traces of Jacobinism from the novel, and to encourage an anti-Jacobinism as fervent as their own, could have only a much more limited effect on the production of novels. Both the number and quality of such satires were never very high in any case. Their attacks also reached a much smaller readership than the established Reviews and their opinions lacked the 'official' status of the major periodicals, however spurious that might have been. Indeed, the diatribes of individuals could always be attributed to motives little removed from personal animosity or admiration. Mathias, for instance, called his friend and rôle model William Gifford, 'the most correct poetical writer I have read, since the days of Pope', when no one else had been particularly anxious to draw such a grand comparison, and his enemies, men and women whom he made the object of a private crusade even if they had not originally been personal adversaries, remained figures of perpetual contempt.[78] Inchbald and Robinson, and even Smith, were never to redeem themselves, in his eyes, nor those of Bisset, after their initial identification as being 'tainted with democracy'.[79]

Yet, it was the personal and 'unofficial' nature of his satire that freed Mathias, and others, from any remaining scruples about having to treat writers with a vestige of fairness, especially in regard to their literary merits, a position the Reviews had been moving towards, but could never, without entirely defying their very *raison d'être*, achieve. For Mathias, Godwin was 'a monster whose faults are not compensated for by a single excellence', and his works were somehow both 'trite and dangerous' – a characteristically confused assertion of the necessary conjunction between the Jacobin and the poor writer.[80] Additionally, the tradition of the private satire sanctioned venomous attacks on individuals to an extent that the Reviews, at least before the *Anti-Jacobin* and *Edinburgh*, could or would not match. Just as Gifford's triumphant assaults on the

Della Cruscans had had no place in a periodical, so Mathias' most notable onslaught was also too personal for even the belligerent Reviews of the mid 1790s. Matthew Lewis' *The Monk* (1796) was the publication, 'too peculiar and too important to be passed over in a general reprehension', that excited Mathias' greatest ire, and it was to the law of the land that he turned as the ultimate sanction. 'I believe,' declared Mathias, that one particular passage in which Lewis had declared parts of the Bible to be too *risqué* for young readers, 'is indictable at common law', and he went on to suggest precedents for legal action on the grounds of blasphemy.[81] Lewis, even though an MP, could not withstand the threat of legal action, nor the infamy which had been generated, and as well as being forced out of politics, and eventually out of the country, by the scandal, he was never to write another novel.[82] It was in this sense, despite the poor quality, limited circulation and, probably, little credence given to these satires, that a figure like Mathias could exert an influence on aspiring novelists concerned with the reception of their own works. Anxious to avoid the fate of Lewis or Godwin, novelists could only have regarded the works of Mathias with a sense of circumspection almost certain to develop into self-censorship. Indeed, Mathias' calls for the 'Legislature and all the Magistrates of Great Britain' to control '*by the law* ... all the spawn of lewdness, infidelity, and democracy, in their vigour or in their dotage', and more particularly, 'to repress *by law* such popular works or novels as THE MONK', must have cast a shadow, almost as effectual as the substance, of government censorship of literature.[83]

That Mathias' call was heeded by at least one author is evident from the use, by George Walker, of a passage from *The Pursuits of Literature* as an epigraph for *The Vagabond* (1799). It is also a reminder that Mathias, like the other agents of the nexus, aimed not only to eradicate radicalism but to foster anti-Jacobinism. Walker allowed Mathias' words about 'The wayward nature of the time, and the paramount necessity of securing the kingdom her political and religious existence', which 'urged me to this endeavour to preserve them', to stand as an explanation of his own sudden conversion from the pseudo-Jacobinism of his *Theodore Cyphon; or, the Benevolent Jew* (1796), a novel unmistakably cast in the mould of *Caleb Williams*, to his next novel, the ultra-conservative *Vagabond* (1799).[84] The implication is that the author underwent a personal and heart-felt conversion, inspired by his realisation of the nation's peril. Yet with Walker, it is impossible to avoid speculating that there were more mercenary motivations at work, or, in other words, that his authorial volition was being swayed by external pressures, both dissuading him from radical fiction or encouraging him towards conservatism. Even in *Theodore Cyphon*, he had felt it necessary to insert a few scattered passages, unconnected to the narrative and running counter to the tenor of the novel, to evidence his disapproval of 'some modern reformers, who talk of liberty', presumably as a sop to those who might be offended at his picture of a hero's persecution under the British constitution.[85] Moreover, as Marilyn Butler has pointed out, Walker, as a shrewd London bookseller, 'evidently knew what sold', and his progression from Radcliffe-like fiction in the early 1790s, via a Godwinian novel in 1796, to a classically anti-Jacobin novel in 1799, must at least suggest that he altered his productions to suit the public's changing tastes.[86] With Walker, we realise that the commercial benefits of anti-Jacobinism were as important a factor as the disincentives to Jacobinism imposed by the concerted campaign of the Reviews or the ravings of Mathias.

Ultimately though, if Walker the bookseller imposed controls on Walker the writer, it was only in accord with his perception of the will of the public, for, by 1799, an almost hegemonic conservatism had asserted itself throughout Britain. I have argued that a nexus of forces exerting themselves on novelists not only reflected, but also passed on this domineering conservatism to authors, either forming their anti-Jacobinism by reflecting that of their market, or insisting on an anti-Jacobinism so vehemently that authors aspiring to success were afraid not to submit. And so successful was this nexus, comprised of critics, both public and private, and of those involved in bringing novels from the authors to their readers, that by the early years of the nineteenth century, the Jacobin novel was almost extinct and more than three dozen almost formulaic anti-Jacobin novels had appeared within eight years. Indeed, by Waterloo, satirists of modern literature could, almost with reluctance, dismiss the spectre of Jacobinism as unworthy of their attacks. George Daniel, for instance, author of *The Modern Dunciad* (1814), having first noted that the Della Cruscan Rosa Matilda's 'woeful madrigals' had ceased to be read and that Matthew Lewis no longer 'the tender maid affrights' – tributes to Gifford and Mathias respectively – was forced to ask himself what there was left that could possibly provoke his muse?

> – the blinded school,
> Whose greatest boast was that it err'd by rule
> That philosophic hoarde of fools and knaves
> Has fall'n – nor PAINE, nor PRIESTLEY raves;
> Repenting bigots bow and kiss the rod,
> And prostrate nations own the name of God.

Reason, that dang'rous pride of human kind,
For ever soaring, and for ever blind;
Prone to distrust when tardy to discern,
Too weak to compass, yet too proud to learn;
With shame reviews each ill-digested plan,
And turns with horror from 'THE RIGHTS OF MAN.'[87]

The novel had not only turned in horror from the rights of man, and from Rousseau and from Godwin, but had embraced enthusiastically a pervasive anti-Jacobinism. This was achieved neither because all novelists simultaneously underwent personal conversions, nor because they were subjected to censorship. Government had not been forced to legislate, nor had it offered bribes to novelists. Elizabeth Hamilton was apparently the only novelist to receive a government pension, and this was awarded after her anti-Jacobin novels had been written.[88] Mathias even went so far as to complain that Pitt was guilty of a 'systematick contempt and neglect of all ability and literary talent'.[89] Novelists had themselves regulated their fiction, but had done so according to the will of their readers transmitted to them, or perceived to be transmitted to them, through the nexus of critics and publishers, satirists and circulating library owners. At base, this was an economic process, and yet the nexus which acted as an interface between producers and consumers had been able to imbue it with an ideological significance that made novelists into propagandists. Their novels attempted to propagandise their readers, but they were doing so only because they, the authors, had already been proselytised by their readers and the society from which they came. This being the case, it is with a much greater degree of confidence that we can understand the anti-Jacobin novels that have been examined in the foregoing chapters to be an accurate reflection of the society from which they sprang.

CHAPTER 7

Conclusion

As to myself, after having for four years heard little else than the voice of commendation, I was at length attacked from every side, and in a style which defied all moderation and decency. No vehicle was too mean, no language too coarse and insulting, by which to convey the venom of my adversaries. The abuse was so often repeated, that at length the bystanders, and perhaps the parties themselves, began to believe what they had so vehemently asserted. The cry spread like a general infection, and I have been told that not even a petty novel for boarding-school misses now ventures to aspire to favour unless it contains some expression of dislike or abhorrence to the new philosophy, and its chief (or shall I say its most voluminous?) English adherent.

William Godwin, *Thoughts Occasioned by the Perusal of Dr Parr's*
Spital Sermon (1801)

The most crucial point to be made about anti-Jacobin novels is that they appeared in much greater numbers than has previously been thought. There were in excess of fifty novels published between 1790 and 1805 which were suffused with anti-Jacobinism, with perhaps as many again which were anti-Jacobin in parts or to a limited extent.

Yet this is a finding that has raised several difficult questions. As soon as an attempt is made to count these fictions, for instance, the problem of definition has arisen. The question of what actually constitutes an anti-Jacobin novel, although it has run through the whole of my analysis, can never be given a convincingly categorical answer. There were many more ways than one to skin a Jacobin cat, and although there can be no doubt that many novels shared the same basic strategies, strategies which I have isolated and examined in the preceding chapters, it is only superficially the case that 'Novel after novel unashamedly used the same structure,' as Marilyn Butler has argued.[1] If it were true, each anti-Jacobin novel might easily be identified, categorised and counted, but Butler's analysis overlooks the question of degree. Some novelists were clearly committed propagandists, straining to wring out the last drop of anti-Jacobinism from every character and twist of plot. Others were much less dedicated, and furnished their fiction with only snippets and shades of conservatism, their anti-Jacobinism appearing here and there but evidently not their primary concern. Indeed, if it was the case, as Butler suggests, that every anti-Jacobin novelist wrote to a formula then this only brings into question their anti-Jacobinism, for it would have been an easy matter to adopt that formula without possessing any of the ideological fervour which had originally animated it.

It is this problem of degree which also feeds into the most important question of all: why were so many anti-Jacobin novels produced and consumed in the 1790s and 1800s? It would be convenient, but misguided, to suggest that they were all designed as propaganda, written by committed individuals who wished to contribute their mite to the grand campaign against the Revolutionary menace. This was not the case, for, as we have seen, many authors produced work possessed of some distinctively anti-Jacobin motifs and characteristics whilst manifesting an ideological ambivalence, or even ambiguity, throughout the rest of their novel or novels. It would be equally convenient to suggest that what anti-Jacobin fiction represents is not propaganda, but an expression of a deeply pervasive, not to say hegemonic, conservative ideology which, co-opting authors into compliance, permeated their fiction without the necessity of working through their conscious volition. Such, after all, was what Godwin believed had happened, being convinced that the condemnation of himself and of new philosophy 'was so often repeated' that at length the whole nation began to believe what his original antagonists 'had so vehemently asserted'. Even petty novels for boarding-school misses, his perhaps understandable paranoia persuaded him, had succumbed to what he called this anti-Jacobin 'infection'.[2] Yet Godwin too, in insisting on both the sameness of the novels as well as their ubiquity, was demonstrably not entirely correct. For just as there were many conservative novels which made no mention of Godwin himself, nor even of new philosophy, so there were many novels published between the Fall of the Bastille and Waterloo which remained resolutely apolitical, lacking in any mention of any aspect of the ideological, moral, political or military war against Jacobinism–novels in which all the characters led 'calm lives' with no 'worries about the French Revolution, or the Napoleonic Wars', as Winston Churchill was to complain of Austen's fiction.[3] If this anti-Jacobin ideology was so pervasive, in other words, why did it not infiltrate these novels too?

More properly, then, anti-Jacobin fiction should be considered as the product of a combination of both the propagandistic intent of a few committed individuals and of the willingness of other authors to take up this ideological conviction despite lacking that underlying dedication to the conservative cause. It cannot be doubted, after all, that Robert Bisset, Elizabeth Hamilton, Jane West or Henry James Pye, to name just four, deliberately took up their pens so that they might contribute to the defeat of Jacobinism, however they individually conceived of it. Nor is it easy to dismiss the influence of the powerful and sophisticated nexus of factors pushing authors into an anti-Jacobin orthodoxy, something discussed in the last chapter. Authors, and their publishers and distributors, were both frightened out of producing anything savouring of Jacobinism, and emulous of the success achieved by other anti-Jacobins. They had before them the example of many who had succeeded in overcoming the lowly reputation of the novel form, and even of a woman using it, and had carved out for themselves careers that were both respected and prosperous. In a sense, this may be considered as the co-option of authors by a dominant ideology, for the values of the dominant groups in society were clearly imposed on those producing fiction to service it. But it was also a mercenary process, such as any other commodity might undergo, and one which coaxed authors into conservatism because of the financial rewards to be reaped there. But no one was actually forced into writing conservative fiction.

Irrespective of whether they were the product of pure conviction or of more tactical planning the conservative novels of the 1790s and 1800s provide a valuable insight into the conservatism of their age. Conservatism was not new to the 1790s of course. Scepticism and promiscuity, nabobs and corrupt nobles – these all had been the frequent themes of furious invective long before the Fall of the Bastille or the formation of the London Corresponding Society. Burke did not suddenly invent anti-Jacobinism in 1790, the conservatism of 1790s fiction being squarely founded on concerns evident for many decades already. But the Revolution crisis gave this conservatism a renewed urgency and vigour, which was largely responsible for enabling the novel to become a vehicle for its propagation, the contamination of fiction with politics having been previously regarded as something most earnestly to be avoided by orthodox opinion. Anti–Jacobinism was different from the conservatism of the 1770s and 1780s because of this sense of crisis, but also because, for the first time, conservatives had something around which they could organise themselves, something against which they could draw up their battle lines, something which endowed their cause with an energising sense of emergency–Jacobinism.

Yet Jacobinism, as we have seen, was the creation of the anti-Jacobins and this is where its great interest lies. The militant anti-Jacobin novelists chose to construct it in a form which they thought most likely to rouse their readers into the fierce loyalty, patriotism and piety which they thought so necessary for the preservation of the nation. Their conception of Jacobinism, therefore, reveals much about what British society thought most valuable and vulnerable about the *status quo*. Equally, those 'fellow travellers' who absorbed an almost perfunctory anti-Jacobinism into their work selected the most prominent and most easily assimilable aspects of the anti-Jacobin campaign for inclusion, again telling us much about how conservatism was conceived of by the more non-political public. I have spotlighted the main principles of literary anti-Jacobinism in the foregoing chapters, but two points are worth making more explicit here. First, the anti-Jacobins rarely identified Jacobinism as political in any strict sense. The radicals portrayed in the conservative novel, who in any case make only cameo appearances, seldom plot constitutional reform. Nor do they press for any specific measures such as religious relief or the abolition of the slave trade. When Godwin, Paine or Priestley feature it is not as legislative reformers, and Fox, Wyvill and Burdett scarcely figure at all. That this should be the case is partly due to the fact that fiction, as a medium, was much more geared to presenting the social and moral, rather than political, challenges to the nation. It was also enabled by events in France, which seemed less and less purely political in character, and by the British Jacobins, who, by the mid 1790s, had seemed to carry their attack to social proprieties, rather than the political establishment. Yet for anti-Jacobins to figure Jacobinism as an assault on the socio-moral fabric of Britain demonstrates that they wished to show the threat faced by Britain in the 1790s as unprecedentedly menacing, and far more so than any purely political movement. Additionally the anti-Jacobins sought to create as broad a base for their campaign as was possible. All could unite against the Jacobin monster they created. None of the traits they endowed it with were at all controversial in the sense that they might provoke a real debate, which was the very thing which anti-Jacobins most wished to avoid.

What is also clear is that the conservatism of the anti-Jacobin novel was only loosely connected with the specific issues of the day. The conservatism which crystallised in fiction had as its motivation the Revolution in France and the radicalism that sprang up in Britain in the early 1790s, but it soon veered away and constructed its own enemies. A few anti-Jacobin novels had been published during the heat of the Revolution debate in the early and mid 1790s, but they had been isolated and often rather primitive. By 1797, after the conservatives had essentially secured victory in the debate, a flood of sophisticated anti-Jacobin productions deluged the market, continuing until about 1804. Even in the years that followed, up until and beyond Waterloo, that flood did not quite abate, so that a generation after the Terror and the publication of the *Rights of Man*, discernibly conservative novels, still anti-Jacobin in terms of the Revolution debate, were able to find a niche for themselves in the market. Indeed, it is demonstrable that as the Jacobin danger became more distant, the bark of the anti-Jacobins became louder.

This is in keeping with the overall pattern of political responses to Jacobinism. It would be wrong to suggest that there was absolutely no revolutionary danger in Britain and Ireland around and after the turn of the century. But in general those episodes which are commonly taken to support the case for a sustained revolutionary peril after the mid 1790s and the Irish Rebellion of 1798 should more properly be considered as *responses* to perceived dangers rather than actual threats. The executions of Colonel Despard and Robert Emmet fall into this category, as do the many articles in the press warning of an abiding and impending revolutionary menace. So too do many anti-Jacobin novels. Thus, in Pye's *Democrat* and D'Israeli's *Vaurien*, published in 1795 and 1797 respectively, the two vaurien characters had criss-crossed Britain searching for indigenous Jacobins to launch a British revolution, but had found precisely none. In Walker's *Vagabond*, of 1799, and Bisset's *Douglas* and *Modern Literature*, of 1800 and 1804, however, genuine British Jacobins had abounded and, if we believe these fictions, then insurrection was imminent. With the most immediate danger of insurrection in Britain past, we realise, conservative authors found themselves more at liberty to talk up the Jacobin threat, and possibly thought it more essential that they did so in order to keep their readers from complacency. For their part, Pye and D'Israeli had been more anxious about Jacobinism, and more concerned to belittle its plausibility and the extent of its appeal.

This is an important point to be made about conservatism in general in Britain in the 1790s and 1800s. It is convenient to talk of a 'Revolution debate' or a 'Revolution crisis', but by the end of the century both the Revolution and radicalism had receded to the extent that conservatism broke free of its original mooring in real events and anxieties. This free-floating conservatism was then able to develop its own agenda,

separating itself from the concerns precipitated by the French Revolution
and returning to old, pre-Revolutionary battles, censuring the upwardly
mobile and the manners of the great, say, or arraigning the educators of
the poor or those who argued for sexual emancipation. It still claimed
Jacobinism as its extenuation but in reality it was fighting tangential
battles against social change which had little to do with the danger of
a Jacobin insurrection. Jacobinism, in other words, became a stalking
horse for whatever any conservative element within society wished to
denounce and attack. This 'liberation' of conservative ideology we can
see emerging in the anti-Jacobin novel.

That an anti-Jacobin residue remained in fiction long after the revolutionary threat had receded is also testament to the momentous effect
that the Revolution crisis had on the novel. Fiction had been pressed into
service to play its part in fighting the radical threat. Being employed in so
crucial and glorious a cause had endowed the novel with a respectability which it had not enjoyed since the days of Richardson and Fielding.
Once it had become clear that enlistment in this anti-Jacobin campaign
secured immunity from disdain, novelists were unwilling to relinquish
the source of their new-found regard, and hence, whether deliberately
or not, they perpetuated an ostentatious anti-Jacobinism long after it had
become ideologically obsolete. Many of the main enemies of fiction –
those critics who in the 1770s and 1780s had condemned the form for
its debilitating effects on, especially, women and the lower orders – were
at the forefront of the anti-Jacobin campaign in the 1790s. But many
were won over by the valiant part the novel appeared to play in staving
off the Jacobin menace. Those who had first commandeered the novel
for anti-Jacobinism, insisting that the political novel must be a lawful
instrument in such a time of danger (especially since the Jacobins were
assuredly using novels for their own purposes), had redeemed the novel
in the eyes of many of its most inflexible assailants. In literary terms this
was perhaps the most significant legacy of anti-Jacobin fiction. It is certainly true that the novel was gaining an unstoppable momentum by the
end of the eighteenth century in any case, but the reputation it was to
enjoy in the age of Scott was, at least to an extent, based on the success
of those conservative novelists who had imbued fiction with a sense of
purpose acceptable to even the form's sternest critics.

This, then, is one way in which the anti-Jacobin novel was successful.
Many novelists were ambitious for respectability, as well as profit, and
were able to accomplish it through their conservative fiction. In another
sense, though, it remains impossible to judge the achievement of the

anti-Jacobin novel, for there is little evidence to suggest that the novels actually succeeded as propaganda, helping to defeat the forces of radicalism and revolution. An enthusiastic biographer like Elizabeth Ogilvie Benger might insist that her subject, Elizabeth Hamilton, effected the reformation of a reader or two with her novels, but this is hardly a proof of any sustained efficacy.[4] After all, many more convincing explanations of the triumph of loyalism in the later 1790s have been proposed, and so it seems sufficient to suggest that conservative fiction played only a minor part in the anti-Jacobin campaign, simply opening up one more front. As a part of that campaign, though, however modest its success might have been, anti-Jacobin fiction shares the same motivating causes and the same major concerns, exhibiting them to our inspection with a transparency born of the fact that they were, sometimes very clumsily, transplanted into a literary form in which they remained conspicuous. Most usefully, then, in terms of the insight it provides into how politics was brought to the people, in terms of how those political ideas were constituted and in terms of its sheer extent, the anti-Jacobin novel offers a valuable perspective on the nature of the British response to the French Revolution.

Notes

INTRODUCTION

1 So reads the first sentence of what is still the standard survey of the fiction of the period, J. M. S. Tompkins' *The Popular Novel in England 1770–1800* (London: Methuen, 1932), p. 1.

2 Amongst the best of this work has been: Marilyn Butler, *Maria Edgeworth: A Literary Biography* (Oxford: Clarendon Press, 1972) and *Peacock Displayed: A Satirist in His Context* (London: Routledge and Kegan Paul, 1979); Warren Roberts, *Jane Austen and the French Revolution* (London: Macmillan, 1979); P. D. Tripathi, *The Doctrinal English Novel (Later Eighteenth Century). Middle-Class Consciousness in England During the American and French Revolutions* (Calcutta: Bagchi, 1977); David Durant, 'Ann Radcliffe and the Conservative Gothic', *Studies in English Literature 1500–1900*, 22 (1982), 519–30; Mary Poovey, *The Proper Lady and the Woman Writer. Ideology as Style in the Works of Mary Wollstonecraft, Mary Shelley, and Jane Austen* (Chicago: University of Chicago Press, 1984); Ann H. Jones, *Ideas and Innovations. Best-Sellers of Jane Austen's Age* (New York: AMS Press, 1986); Mary Anne Schofield and Cecilia Macheski (eds.), *Fetter'd or Free? British Women Novelists, 1670–1815* (Athens, OH: Ohio University Press, 1986); Margaret Anne Doody, *Frances Burney. The Life in the Works* (New Brunswick, NJ: Rutgers University Press, 1988); Kelvin Everest (ed.), *Revolution in Writing. British Literary Responses to the French Revolution* (Milton Keynes: Open University Press, 1991); Chris Jones, *Radical Sensibility. Literature and Ideas in the 1790s* (London: Routledge, 1993); Gary Kelly, *Women, Writing and Revolution 1790–1827* (Oxford: Oxford University Press: 1993); Mona Scheuermann, *Her Bread to Earn. Women, Money, and Society from Defoe to Austen* (Lexington: University Press of Kentucky, 1993); Eleanor Ty, *Unsex'd Revolutionaries. Five Women Novelists of the 1790s* (University of Toronto Press, 1993); and Loraine Fletcher, *Charlotte Smith. A Critical Biography* (Basingstoke: Macmillan, 1998). A fuller bibliographical survey than is presented in this chapter has already appeared: M. O. Grenby, 'The Anti-Jacobin Novel: British Fiction, British Conservatism and the Revolution in France', *History: the Journal of the Historical Association*, 83 (July 1998), 445–71.

3 Gregory, *The French Revolution and the English Novel* (New York: G. P. Putnam's Sons, 1915), pp. 134–60; Tompkins, *Popular Novel in England*, pp. 296–328;

Marilyn Butler, *Jane Austen and the War of Ideas* (1975; rpt. Oxford: Clarendon Press, 1987), pp. 88–123. See also A. D. Harvey, 'George Walker and the Anti-Revolutionary Novel', *Review of English Studies*, n.s., 28 (1977), 290–300 and Gary Kelly, *English Fiction of the Romantic Period* (London: Longman, 1989), pp. 59–64.

4 Peter H. Marshall, with his *William Godwin* (New Haven, CT: Yale University Press, 1984), has probably held the record for detecting anti-Jacobin novels with fifteen, all attacking the subject of his biography (pp. 211–33).

5 David McCracken, 'Godwin's Literary Theory: The Alliance Between Fiction and Political Philosophy', *Philological Quarterly*, 49 (1970), 120; Gary Kelly, *The English Jacobin Novel 1780–1805* (Oxford: Clarendon Press, 1976), p. 116.

6 Claudia L. Johnson, *Jane Austen: Women, Politics and the Novel* (Chicago: University of Chicago Press, 1988), p. xxi.

7 Gary Kelly, 'Jane Austen and the English Novel of the 1790s', pp. 285–306 in Schofield and Macheski (eds.), *Fetter'd or Free?*; Eleanor Ty, 'Female Philosophy Refunctioned: Elizabeth Hamilton's Parodic Novel', *Ariel. A Review of International English Literature*, 22 (1991), 111–29; Dale Spender, *Mothers of the Novel. 100 Good Women Writers Before Jane Austen* (London: Pandora Press, 1986), pp. 315–24. Claire Grogan, 'Introduction' to Hamilton's *Memoirs of Modern Philosphers* (Peterborough, Ontario: Broadview, 2000), especially pp. 12 and 21–6. See also Marilyn Butler's analysis of Maria Edgeworth's complex ideological ambitions in her broadly anti-Jacobin novel, *Leonora*: 'General Introduction' to *The Novels and Selected Works of Maria Edgeworth*, eds. Jane Desmarais, Tim McLoughlin and Marilyn Butler (London: Pickering and Chatto, 1999), I, lxx–lxxxi.

8 The same is true of some of the less well-known Jacobin novelists who could not have been more politically forthright. See for example the anonymous *The Excursion of Osman, the Son of Abdullah, Lord of the Vallies; A Political Romance: including Some Anecdotes relative to a Great Northern Family* (Liverpool, 1792) or Thomas Northmore's *Memoirs of Planetes, or a Sketch of the Laws and Manners of Makar* (London: J. Johnson and J. Owen, 1795).

9 Charles Lucas, *Gwelygordd; or, the Child of Sin. A Tale of Welsh Origin* (London: Minerva, 1820), I, 5.

10 West cites Hamilton's *Translations of the Letters of a Hindoo Rajah* (1796; 2nd edn, London: G. G. and J. Robinson, 1801) and Sophia King's *Waldorf; or, the Dangers of Philosophy* (London: G. G. and J. Robinson, 1798) as exactly parallel works whilst in *Memoirs of Modern Philosophers*, Hamilton, whose preface pretends that the manuscript of the novel was found and sent to the publisher by one Geoffrey Jarvis, uses Jarvis to compare favourably the work he has found to 'some other recent publications, which, like it, have avowedly been written in opposition to the opinions generally known by the name of the *New Philosophy*'. Jane West, *A Tale of the Times* (London: Longman and Rees, 1799), 'Advertisement'; Elizabeth Hamilton, *Memoirs of Modern Philosophers* (1800; 2nd edn, London: G. G. and J. Robinson, 1800),

I, xiii. The translator of the French edition of George Walker's *The Vagabond* also locates the work in a flourishing tradition of anti-Jacobin fiction, hoping that the flattering reception given to Brigitina (the anti-heroine of *Modern Philosophers*) will also greet Walker's characters (*Le Vagabond, ou La Rencontre de Deux Philosophes Républicains; Roman Philosophique, Traduit de l'anglais de Georges Walker...* (Paris: Hénée et Dumas, *et al.*, 1807), v–vi).

11 Hugh Murray, *Morality of Fiction; or, An Inquiry into the Tendency of Fictitious Narratives, with Observations on Some of the Most Eminent* (Edinburgh: A. Constable & Co., and London: Longman, 1805), pp. 8–9. Many reviews were also aware of the same two diametrically opposed schools of novel-writing (e.g. *The Monthly Mirror*, 10 (1800), 34), as was Anna Lætitia Barbauld: 'No small proportion of modern novels have been devoted to recommend, or to mark with reprobation, those systems of philosophy or politics which have raised so much ferment of late years.' She too groups West and Hamilton together as part of the 'light skirmishing troops' deployed 'with great effect' against Jacobinism. 'On the Origin and Progress of Novel-Writing' in *The British Novelists: with An Essay; and Prefaces* (London: F. C. and J. Rivington, 1810), I, 59.

12 P. A. Brown, *The French Revolution in English History* (1918; rpt. London: Frank Cass and Co., 1965); E. P. Thompson, *The Making of the English Working Class* (1963; rpt. Harmondsworth: Penguin, 1980); G. A. Williams, *Artisans and Sans Culottes: Popular Movements in France and England during the French Revolution* (London: Edward Arnold, 1968); Albert Goodwin, *The Friends of Liberty: The English Democratic Movement in the Age of the French Revolution* (London: Hutchinson, 1979).

13 E.g. A. B. Cobban (ed.), *The Debate on the French Revolution* (London: Nicholas Kaye, 1950); J. T. Boulton, *The Language of Politics in the Age of Wilkes and Burke* (London: Routledge and Kegan Paul, 1963); H. T. Dickinson, *Liberty and Property. Political Ideology in Eighteenth-Century Britain* (1977; rpt. London: Methuen, 1979); Marilyn Butler (ed.), *Burke, Paine, Godwin and the Revolution Controversy* (Cambridge: Cambridge University Press, 1984); Ian R. Christie, *Stress and Stability in Late Eighteenth Century Britain* (Oxford: Clarendon Press, 1984); Gregory Claeys, 'The French Revolution Debate and British Political Thought', *History of Political Thought*, 11 (1990), 59–80; Clive Emsley, 'The Impact of the French Revolution on British Politics and Society', pp. 31–62 in Ceri Crossley and Ian Small (eds.), *The French Revolution and British Culture* (Oxford: Oxford University Press, 1989); Ian Gilmour, *Riot, Risings and Revolution. Governance and Violence in Eighteenth-Century Britain* (1992; rpt. London: Pimlico, 1995), pp. 391–448.

14 See for instance, Alan Booth, 'Popular Loyalism and Public Violence in the North-West of England 1790–1800', *Social History*, 8 (1983), 295–313; Robert R. Dozier, *For King, Constitution, and Country: The English Loyalists and the French Revolution* (Lexington: University Press of Kentucky, 1983); J. C. D. Clark, *English Society 1688–1832. Ideology, Social Structure and Political Practice during the ancien régime* (Cambridge: Cambridge University Press, 1985);

Thomas Philip Schofield, 'Conservative Political Thought in Britain in Response to the French Revolution', *Historical Journal*, 29 (1986), 601–22; Gerald Newman, *The Rise of English Nationalism. A Cultural History 1740–1830* (London: Weidenfield and Nicolson, 1987), pp. 145–56 and 226–44; H. T. Dickinson, 'Popular Conservatism and Militant Loyalism 1789–1815', pp. 104–25 in Dickinson (ed.), *Britain and the French Revolution 1789–1815*, (Basingstoke: Macmillan, 1989), and *The Politics of the People in Eighteenth-Century Britain* (Basingstoke: Macmillan, 1995), pp. 255–86; Robert Hole, *Pulpits, Politics and Public Order in England 1760–1832* (Cambridge: Cambridge University Press, 1989); Mark Philp, 'Introduction', John Dinwiddy, 'Interpretations of Anti-Jacobinism' and David Eastwood, 'Patriotism and the English State in the 1790s', pp. 1–17, 38–49 and 146–68 in Philp (ed.), *The French Revolution and British Popular Politics* (Cambridge: Cambridge University Press, 1991); Mark Philp, 'Vulgar Conservatism, 1792–93', *English Historical Review*, 110 (1995), 42–69; Linda Colley, *Britons. Forging the Nation 1707–1837* (1992; London: Pimlico, 1994), pp. 195–319; J. J. Sack, *From Jacobite to Conservative: Reaction and Orthodoxy in Britain, c.1760–1830* (Cambridge: Cambridge University Press, 1993).

15 See M. Thomis and P. Holt, *Threats of Revolution in Britain 1789–1848* (London: Macmillan, 1977); J. Anne Hone, *For the Cause of Truth: Radicalism in London 1796–1821* (Oxford: Clarendon Press, 1982); Roger Wells, *Insurrection: the British Experience, 1795–1803* (Gloucester: Alan Sutton, 1983); H. T. Dickinson, *British Radicalism and the French Revolution 1789–1815* (Oxford: Blackwell, 1985); Iain McCalman, *Radical Underworld. Prophets, Revolutionaries and Pornographers in London, 1795–1840* (Cambridge: Cambridge University Press, 1988); John Stevenson, 'Popular Radicalism and Popular Protest 1789–1815', pp. 61–81 in H. T. Dickinson (ed.), *Britain and the French Revolution*; and E. P. Thompson, 'Hunting the Jacobin Fox', *Past and Present*, 142 (1994), 94–140.

16 See Susan Pederson, 'Hannah More Meets Simple Simon: Tracts, Chapbooks, and Popular Culture in Late Eighteenth Century England', *Journal of British Studies*, 25 (1986), 84–113. Well into the nineteenth century, the Eclectic Society regularly used the supposed growth of Jacobinism as the justification for its own decision to use the 'debased' form of popular literature as its means of instilling religion in the people. See *Eclectic Notes; or, Notes of Discussions on Religious Topics at the Meetings of The Eclectic Society, London, During the Years 1798–1814*, ed. John H. Pratt (London, 1865), p. 13.

17 Bisset in the *Anti-Jacobin Review*, 1 (1798), 223. The truculent John Thelwall was happy for himself and his colleagues to be called Jacobins precisely because 'it is fixed upon us, as a stigma, by our enemies'. The best he could come up with as a definition for his own Jacobinism was 'a large and comprehensive system of reform, not professing to be built upon the authorities and principles of the Gothic customary' – i.e. a system defined, once again, in terms of what it was not. John Thelwall, *Rights of Nature* (London: H. D. Symonds, 1796), II, 32.

18 It should not, however, be assumed that all who did so were necessarily committed anti-Jacobins. See Eugene Charlton Black, *The Association – British Extraparliamentary Political Organization, 1769–1793* (Cambridge, MA: Harvard University Press, 1963), pp. 233–74; Austin Mitchell, 'The Association Movement of 1792–93', *Historical Journal*, 4 (1961), 56–77; Donald E. Ginter, 'The Loyalist Association Movement of 1792–93 and British Public Opinion', *Historical Journal*, 9 (1966), 179–90; as well as Dozier, *For King, Constitution, and Country*; Dickinson, 'Popular Conservatism and Militant Loyalism 1789–1815', pp. 110–25; Philp, 'Vulgar Conservatism', pp. 62–3; and Colley, *Britons*, pp. 282–320.

19 Hannah More, *Remarks on the Speech of M. Dupont, with a prefatory Address in behalf of the French Emigrant Clergy* (1793) in *The Works of Hannah More* (London: Fisher, Fisher and Jackson, 1834), II, 406.

20 Dickinson, *The Politics of the People in Eighteenth-Century Britain*, p. 283.

21 Elizabeth Ogilvie Benger, *Memoirs of the Late Mrs Elizabeth Hamilton, with a Selection from Her Correspondence, and other Unpublished Writing* (London: Longman, 1818), I, 165.

22 Dickinson, *The Politics of the People in Eighteenth-Century Britain*, p. 256.

1 NOVELS REPROVED AND REPRIEVED

1 Whether this 'widened circle' of readers actually existed is another matter. Incontestably, more books, and especially novels, were being published as the century wore on, but we should be sceptical of claims – which have been made by modern scholars, as well as at the time – that this necessarily meant that more people were reading them. For a discussion of this question see Richard D. Altick, *The English Common Reader. A Social History of the Mass Reading Public 1800–1900* (Chicago: University of Chicago Press, 1957); R. K. Webb, *The British Working Class Reader 1790–1848. Literacy and Social Tension* (London: George Allen and Unwin, 1955); Paul Korshin (ed.), *The Widening Circle. Essays on the Circulation of Literature in Eighteenth-Century Europe* (Philadelphia: University of Pennsylvania Press, 1976); Jon P. Klancher, *The Making of English Reading Audiences 1790–1832* (Madison: University of Wisconsin Press, 1987); J. Paul Hunter, *Before Novels. The Cultural Contexts of Eighteenth-Century English Fiction* (New York: Norton, 1990); and James Raven, *Judging New Wealth. Popular Publishing and Responses to Commerce in England, 1750–1800* (Oxford: Clarendon Press, 1992).

2 Humphrey Repton, 'Advantages and Evils of Sunday Schools Considered' in *Variety: A Collection of Essays* (London: T. Cadell, 1788), p. 51–9. See Charlotte Smith, *The Old Manor House* (1793; rpt. Oxford: Oxford University Press, 1989, ed. Anne Henry Ehrenpreis), pp. 176–7, for a novelist's scorn of this attitude.

3 *Gentleman's Magazine*, 67 (1797), 820.

4 Anon., *Dorothea; or, A Ray of the New Light* (London: G. G. and J. Robinson, 1801), I, 2.

5 This figure is derived from *The Complete Writings of Thomas Paine*, ed. P. S. Foner (New York: Citadel Press, 1945), II, 910.

6 Robert Bisset, *Modern Literature. A Novel* (London: T. N. Longman and O. Rees, 1804), III, 147–8 and 156.

7 Samuel Horsley, 'Upon the Bill to Prevent the Increase in Papists, and to Regulate the Existing Monastic Institutions, July 10th 1800' in *The Speeches in Parliament of Samuel Horsley, Late Lord Bishop of St Asaph* (Dundee: Chalmers, 1813), p. 355.

8 William Hamilton Reid, *The Rise and Dissolution of the Infidel Societies in this Metropolis: Including, The Origin of Modern Deism and Atheism*... (London: J. Hatchard, 1800), rpt. in *Literacy and Society*, ed. Victor E. Neuburg (London: Woburn Press, 1971), p. 32. My emphasis.

9 William Roberts, *Memoirs of Hannah More* (London: Seeley and Burnside, 1834), II, 458.

10 'The Sunday School' (London, 1795?), repeated in *The Miscellaneous Works of Hannah More* (London: Thomas Tegg, 1840), I, 100–2. Compare Sarah Trimmer's earlier *Family Magazine; or a Repository of Religious Instruction*, the aim of which was also to provide reading matter for the poor which would reassure those 'who are fearful of trusting the common people with knowledge, lest they should misapply it' (I (1788), iii–iv).

11 Mark Philp has shown how the conservative tracts of the '90s cleverly avoided such an outrage: 'Vulgar Conservatism, 1792–93', *English Historical Review*, 110 (1995), 62–3.

12 Roberts, *Memoirs*..., II, 425–6.

13 *The Complete Collection of State Trials and Proceedings for High Treason*..., compiled by T. B. Howell and Thomas James Howell (London: Longman, 1817), XXII, 383.

14 See Joseph Bunn Heidler, *The History, From 1700 to 1800, of English Criticism of Prose Fiction* University of Illinois Studies in Language and Literature, 13 (Urbana: University of Illinois Press, 1928); W. F. Gallaway Jnr, 'The Conservative Attitude Toward Fiction, 1770–1830', *PMLA*, 55 (1940), 1041–59; John Tinnon Taylor, *Early Opposition to the English Novel. The Popular Reaction from 1760 to 1830* (Morningside Heights, NY: King's Crown Press, 1943); and Ioan Williams (ed.), *Novel and Romance 1700–1800. A Documentary Record* (London: Routledge and Kegan Paul, 1970).

15 *Gentleman's Magazine*, 57 (1787), 1048–9; Thomas Monro, *Olla Podrida*, 15 (1787), in Williams (ed.), *Novel and Romance. A Documentary Record*, pp. 349–50.

16 Charlton, *Rosella, or Modern Occurrences* (London: Minerva, 1799), IV, 113.

17 Anon., *The History of Sir George Warrington; or, the Political Quixote* (London: J. Bell, 1797), II, 83 and 93. My emphasis.

18 T. Harral, *Scenes of Life. A Novel* (London: B. Crosby, 1805), quoted in the *British Critic*, 26 (1805), 321. A remarkably early expression of this concern is to be found in the anonymous (but by P. Littlejohn?) *The Cipher, or The World as it Goes* (London: Minerva, 1791). I have not been able to see a copy, but, according to Allene Gregory, it has a preface 'bewailing the use of fiction

to corrupt the age with Revolutionary doctrines', although the novel itself apparently confines itself 'to common place morality'. Gregory, *The French Revolution and the English Novel* (New York: G. P. Putnam's Sons, 1915), p. 156.

19 T. J. Mathias, *The Pursuits of Literature. A Satirical Poem in Four Dialogues* (1794–7; 7th edn, London: T. Becket, 1798), 61n.c and 58n.zz.

20 Bisset, *Modern Literature*, III, 204–16. Jemima is the name of a protagonist in Wollstonecraft's *Maria* (1798). Those selected to be her lieutenants are a Mrs Sonnet, Mrs Egotist, Mrs and Miss Twostools, Miss Harry Clarendon and Miss Derwent Priory. *The History of Sir Henry Clarendon* was published anonymously in 1785 and *Derwent Priory* by A. Kendall in 1798. 'Sonnet', whose novels, according to Jemima, 'have proposed to decry existing institutions, exalt the philosophers of France, and to debase what is called female virtue, by an attempt to show that it depends on accident, and not principle', is doubtlessly Mary Robinson, who, as author of numerous poems lamenting the fate of Marie Antoinette and novels describing the horror of the Revolution in France, might very well have objected to being the constant butt of many anti-Jacobins' crusades. 'Egotist' is Charlotte Smith, who since 1794's *Banished Man* had adhered more or less to a conservative agenda, but who Jemima praises for encouraging filial disobedience, decrying every civil, ecclesiastical and political, as well as domestic, authority, and constantly reprehending what she calls 'the execrable and abominable constitutions which we are obliged to suffer in Britain'. In his *Douglas; or, the Highlander. A Novel* (London: 'Printed at the Anti-Jacobin Press', 1800), Bisset had already characterised Smith and Robinson as 'Charlotte Self-Praise' and 'Laura Maria', both parroting from Voltaire, Rousseau, Paine, Holcroft and Godwin all 'the badness of Kings, Priests, Nobles and Gentry,' and 'that all vice is owing to the distinction between rich and poor' (III, 38).

21 Bisset, *Modern Literature*, III, 181–2. See also the opinions of Bisset's hero's near namesake, William Hamilton Reid, who wrote in 1800 that 'the pernicious dogmas' of the Jacobins had 'captivated the attention, and were conveyed to the heart in the enchanting page of a novel, amidst the feigned adventures and passionate endearments of lovers'. *Rise and Dissolution of Infidel Societies*, p. 27.

22 Jane West, *Letters Addressed to a Young Man* (London: T. N. Longman and O. Rees, 1801), III, 185–6. See also Joseph Wildman, *The Force of Prejudice, A Moral Tale* (London: T. Barfield, 1799), I, 67–8.

23 Godwin, *Caleb Williams* (1794; rpt. Harmondsworth: Penguin, 1988, ed. Maurice Hindle), p. 3 and *British Critic*, 6 (1795), 94. Godwin's strategy is well lampooned in Edward Dubois' *St Godwin: A Tale of the Sixteenth, Seventeenth, and Eighteenth Century* (London: J. Wright, 1800), pp. 234–5.

24 Gilbert Imlay, *The Emigrants* (1793; rpt. Harmondsworth: Penguin, 1998, eds. W. M. Verhoeven and Amanda Gilroy), p. 1.

25 Ann Thomas, *Adolphus de Biron. A Novel. Founded on the French Revolution* (Plymouth: 'Printed . . . for the Authoress', 1795?), II, 74. Compare the sagacious Mr Denbeigh's similarly absolving advice to the autobiographical

protagonist of Elizabeth Hamilton's *Letters of a Hindoo Rajah* (1796; rpt. Peter-borough, Ontario: Broadview Press, 1999, eds. Pamela Perkins and Shannon Russell), pp. 302–3.

26 The idea that publication by women, especially on 'public' subjects, was a violation of strongly constructed female propriety is best set out in Mary Poovey, *The Proper Lady and the Woman Writer. Ideology as Style in the Works of Mary Wollstonecraft, Mary Shelley, and Jane Austen* (Chicago: University of Chicago Press, 1984). The foundation of the challenge to these ideas may be seen in Linda Colley, *Britons. Forging the Nation 1707–1837* (1992; rpt. London: Pimlico, 1994), pp. 237–81.

27 Thomas, *Adolphus de Biron*, I, v.

28 *The Minstrel; or, Anecdotes of Distinguished Personages in the Fifteenth Century* (London: Hookham and Carpenter, 1793), I, iii–iv. The records of Hookham's publishing firm suggest that the author was a Mrs Marriott and that the novel was actually published in 1794 irrespective of the date on the title page. See Jan Fergus and Janice Farrar Thaddeus, 'Women, Pub-lishers and Money, 1790–1820', *Studies in Eighteenth-Century Culture*, 17 (1987), 191–207, p. 202n.8.

29 Clara Reeve, *Memoirs of Sir Roger de Clarendon, the Natural Son of Edward Prince of Wales* (London: Hookham and Carpenter, 1793), I, xxii–iii, xvi and xvi–xvii, and *The Progress of Romance, Through Times, Countries and Manners, with Remarks on the Good and Bad Effects of It, on them respectively* (Colchester: 'printed for the author', 1785), I, vi.

30 King sought to justify her exercise in the gothic, *The Fatal Secret*, by ask-ing whether Godwin himself did not 'arbitrarily usurp and seize the fairy world of magic, wildly weaving, like the fatal sisters, a net to ensnare us' in his *St Leon*. Pye included in his *Aristocrat* a 'short digression on some of the novels of the present day' which specifically condemned *Caleb Williams* for its diabolical method of 'collecting and connecting every possible event in such a manner, as to produce a probable series of incidents that shall make mankind dissatisfied with their natural or political situation, or plead an excuse for the breach of fidelity and chastity'. Aware of the fact that he himself was using exactly the same technique, Pye wisely added that, on the other hand, 'commendable is such art when used to inculcate virtuous principles'. Sophia King, *The Fatal Secret, or, Unknown Warrior; a Romance of the Twelfth Century* (London: 'printed for the author', 1801), p. vi; Henry James Pye, *The Aristocrat: a Novel* (London: Sampson Low, 1799), I, 129, 131.

31 George Walker, *The Vagabond, a Novel* (3rd edn, London: G. Walker, 1799), I, vi.

32 Jane West, *A Tale of the Times* (London: Longman and Rees, 1799), III, 386–7.

33 Jane West, *The Infidel Father* (London: Longman and Rees, 1802), I, ii.

34 See Walker's *Vagabond*, I, iii; William Cole, *The Contradiction* (London: T. Cadell and W. Davies, 1796), pp. iv–v; Hugh Murray, *Morality of Fiction* (Edinburgh: A. Constable & Co., and London: Longman, 1805), p. 151n.; and (perhaps

with a touch of irony) Elizabeth Hamilton's *Memoirs of Modern Philosophers* (1800; 2nd edn, London: G. G. and J. Robinson, 1800), I, xv–xvi.

35 Charlotte Smith, *Desmond. A Novel* (London: G. G. J. and J. Robinson, 1792), 'Preface', I, iii.

36 For her horror of fiction see M. G. Jones, *Hannah More* (Cambridge: Cambridge University Press, 1952), p. 191.

37 Samuel Egerton Brydges, *Arthur Fitz-Albini. A Novel* (1798; 2nd edn, London: J. White, 1799), I, xiii.

38 Pye, *Aristocrat*, I, 54–6.

39 Hamilton, *Modern Philosophers*, II, 264–5. Cf. very similar episodes in *The History of Sir George Warrington*, I, 123–4, 107 and 119, and Bisset's *Douglas*, III, 86–7.

2 REPRESENTING REVOLUTION

1 Mary Meeke's tale of a contemporary France still dominated by monarchy and aristocracy, *Count St Blancard, or, the Prejudiced Judge, A Novel* (1795; rpt. New York: Arno Press, 1977) has prompted John Garrett to assert that 'Mrs Meeke's conservatism was based on a belief that the 1789 revolution was some sort of aberration of history' ('Introduction', I, xv).

2 E. J. Clery, *The Rise of Supernatural Fiction, 1762–1800* (Cambridge: Cambridge University Press, 1995), p. 172.

3 Margaret Anne Doody, *Frances Burney. The Life in the Works* (New Brunswick, NJ: Rutgers University Press, 1988), p. 318.

4 Charlotte Smith, *Desmond. A Novel* (London: G. G. J. and J. Robinson, 1792), I, iii and 105.

5 Edward Sayer, *Lindor and Adelaïde, a Moral Tale. In which are exhibited the Effects of the Late French Revolution on the Peasantry of France* (London: John Hockdale, 1791), pp. 323–25.

6 *Ibid.*, pp. 21n, vi–vii and 309–10.

7 *Ibid.*, pp. vii and 92.

8 Compare Smith in 1794: 'if I had been convinced I was in error in regard to what I formerly wrote on the politics of France, I should without hesitation avow it. I still think, however, that no native of England could help *then* rejoicing at the possibility there was that the French nation would obtain, with very little bloodshed, that degree of freedom which we have been taught to value so highly' (*The Banished Man* (London: Cadell and Davies, 1794), I, x–xi), with Coleridge after the French invasion of Switzerland, 1798: 'forgive me, that I cherished / One thought that ever blessed your cruel foes!' ('France: An Ode', lines 70–1, S. T. Coleridge, *Poetical Works*, ed. Ernest Hartley Coleridge (London: Oxford University Press, 1969), p. 246).

9 Smith, *Banished Man*, 'Preface', I, x–xi. Smith's intermediate novel, *The Old Manor House*, exhibits a mid-way stop on what seems the smooth transition between the pro-Revolutionary sentiments of *Desmond* and the anti-Jacobinism

of *Banished Man*. This movement towards the latter is again demonstrably determined by 'the *events* of the past Summer (*events* terrible enough God knows!)', whilst the former faith was not quite annihilated because of the recognition that all important historical processes, even those in which Britain is involved, will always be accompanied by *events* of cruelty which even 'exceed any thing that happened on the 10th of August, the 2nd September, or at any one period of the execrated Revolution in France' (*Old Manor House*, London: J. Bell, 1793; rpt. Oxford: Oxford University Press, 1989, ed. Anne Henry Ehrenpreis, p. 360n. My emphasis.).

10 Clara Reeve, *Memoirs of Sir Roger de Clarendon* (London: Hookham and Carpenter, 1793), III, 216 and 224.

11 Henry James Pye, *The Aristocrat. A Novel* (London: Sampson Low, 1799), I, 38.

12 John Moore, *Mordaunt. Sketches of Life, Characters, and Manners, in Various Countries...* (London: G. G. and J. Robinson, 1800), I, 66–7.

13 Anon., *History of Sir George Warrington* (London: J. Bell, 1797), II, 123 and III, 62.

14 R. C. Dallas, *Percival, or Nature Vindicated* (1801), in *Miscellaneous Works and Novels of R. C. Dallas, Esq.* (London: Longman, Hurst, Rees, Orme and Brown, 1813), III, 174, 177–8.

15 Charlotte Smith, *Marchmont: A Novel* (London: Sampson Low, 1796), III, 176–7 and 185.

16 Helen Craik, *Adelaide de Narbonne, with Memoirs of Charlotte de Cordet* (London: Minerva, 1800), III, 148.

17 Ann Thomas, *Adolphus de Biron. A Novel. Founded on the French Revolution* (Plymouth: 'Printed ... for the Authoress', 1795?), I, 147–8.

18 J. M. S. Tompkins, *The Popular Novel in England, 1770–1800* (London: Methuen, 1932), p. 135n.

19 Smith, *Banished Man*, III, 73–171, 195–224 and IV, 1–17.

20 Ronald Paulson, *Representations of Revolution (1789–1820)* (New Haven, CT: Yale University Press, 1983), pp. 60–3. See also James T. Boulton, *The Language of Politics in the Age of Wilkes and Burke* (London: Routledge and Kegan Paul, 1963), pp. 127–32.

21 Mary Charlton, *The Parisian; or, Genuine Anecdotes of Distinguished and Noble Characters* (London: Minerva, 1794), II, 140–3.

22 Moore, *Mordaunt*, II, 59–62. Burke had inveighed against dancing-masters in particular as the sort of person most likely to benefit from the French levelling system and to implant themselves into, and thus destroy, the old, hallowed family networks upon which society was based. *Letter to a Member of the National Assembly* (1791), pp. 294–335 in *The Writings and Speeches of Edmund Burke*, VIII, ed. L. G. Mitchell (Oxford: Clarendon Press, 1989), p. 317. See Craik, *Adelaide de Narbonne*, III, chs. 14–15, for a plan to spring Elizabeth from prison.

23 Smith, *Banished Man*, III, ch.8. Maria Edgeworth, 'Madame de Fleury', pp. 177–328 in *Tales of Fashionable Life* (London: J. Johnson, 1809), pp. 253–63.

24 Mary Robinson, *The Natural Daughter. With Portraits of the Leadenhead Family. A Novel* (London: T. N. Longman and O. Rees, 1799), II, 265–6.

25 Smith, *Banished Man*, IV, 7–8.

26 Robinson, *Natural Daughter*, I, 205. And lest we should think this is what France has always been like anyway, she immediately adds: 'I had passed a few days in Paris, two years before, in my *route* to Italy: the change was awful and impressive. I sighed when I recollected the causes of the metamorphosis, and I shuddered while I contemplated the effects.'

27 Edward Mangin, *George the Third. A Novel* (London: James Carpenter, 1807), II, 95–6.

28 Hugh Murray, *The Swiss Emigrants: A Tale* (London: T. N. Longman and O. Rees, 1804), pp. 79 and 96.

29 Mangin, *George the Third*, II, 120–4.

30 Anon., *Memoirs of M. De Brinboc: Containing Some Views of English and Foreign Society* (London: Cadell and Davies, 1805), II, 141. The only 'factual' basis for these 'severed head' episodes I have been able to find is in *The Times* of 20 July 1789, a not entirely reliable source of course, which describes how the mob beheaded the Governor and Commandant of the Bastille, 'stuck their heads on tent poles, and carried them in triumph to the Palais Royal, and through the streets of Paris'. Probably much more important in formulating such images was a passage in Burke's *Reflections* which reconstructed the events of 6 October 1789, telling of how the King and Queen left Versailles 'swimming in blood, polluted by massacre, and strewed with scattered limbs and mutilated carcasses' and were forced to watch as two gentlemen of birth and family, members of the royal bodyguard, were beheaded and 'Their heads were stuck upon spears', which were carried at the front of the procession conducting the royal captives to Paris. *Writings and Speeches of Edmund Burke*, VIII, 122.

31 *Memoirs of M. De Brinboc*, I, 5–6 and 6–8. My emphasis.

32 Louisa Sydney Stanhope, *The Nun of Santa Maria di Tindaro. A Tale* (London: Minerva, 1818), I, 138–9 and 203.

33 Frances Burney, *The Wanderer; or, Female Difficulties* (1814; rpt. Oxford: Oxford University Press, 1991), eds. Margaret Anne Doody, Robert L. Mack and Peter Sabor), p. 11, and *The Journals and Letters of Fanny Burney (Madame D'Arblay)*, ed. Joyce Hemlow *et al.* (Oxford: Clarendon Press, 1975), V, 232.

34 J. M. Roberts, *The Mythology of Secret Societies* (London: Secker and Warburg, 1972), p. 15. But see Clery, *Rise of Supernatural Fiction*, p. 162.

35 Sayer, *Lindor and Adelaïde*, pp. 4 and 145–68.

36 Anon., *The Siege of Belgrade: An Historical Novel. Translated from a German Manuscript* (London: H. D. Symonds, 1791), I, 47–8. See also Anna Maria Mackenzie, *Slavery: or, The Times* (London: G. G. and J. Robinson, 1792), II, 196.

37 Charles Lucas, *The Castle of St Donats; or, the History of Jack Smith* (London: Minerva, 1798), III, 120. Even having been forced to emigrate, these French aristocrats, for the most part, do not wish to see a return to the *ancien régime*,

a sign of the extent to which authors had drifted away from the Burkean standpoint – see H. J. Pye, *The Democrat* (1795; rpt. London: Minerva, 1796), I, 107–8.

38 Smith, *Banished Man*, III, 92. A particularly illuminating comparison, especially in regard to Smith's personal revolution, may be made with her *Desmond* of only two years earlier, in which D'Alonville's previous incarnation, the Marquis de Montfleuri, had been very much more sanguine about the Revolution precisely because it would remove these same oppressions: 'Enquire of them, whether they are or not better for being released from the *taille*, from the *gabelle*, from the imposts levied at the gates of every town, on every necessity of life ... Enquire of the citizen, the mechanic, if he reposes not more quietly in his house from the certainty that it is not now liable to be entered by the *marechaussées*, and that it is no longer possible for him to be forcibly taken out of it by a *lettre de cachet*, in the power of a minister, or his secretary, his secretary's clerk, or his mistress ...' (I, 132–4).

39 Mary Robinson, *Hubert de Sevrac, A Romance, of the Eighteenth Century* (1796; rpt. Dublin: B. Smith, C. Browne and H. Colbert, 1797), II, 6.

40 *Siege of Belgrade*, I, 48, II, 177–8 and IV, 130.

41 *Ibid.*, IV, 137–8.

42 Matthew Lewis, *The Monk* (1796; rpt. Oxford: Oxford University Press, 1990, ed. Howard Anderson), pp. 355–8; Elizabeth Helme, *The Farmer of Inglewood Forest, a Novel* (London: Minerva, 1796), II, 190–1.

43 Robert Bage, *Hermsprong* (1796; rpt. Oxford: Oxford University Press, 1985, ed. Peter Faulkner), pp. 225–6.

44 Helena Wells, *Constantia Neville; or, the West Indian. A Novel* (London: T. Cadell jun. and W. Davies, 1800), III, 100. Nor, for Jane West, can even Cromwell's republicanism justify lawlessness or rebellion: *The Loyalists: An Historical Novel* (London: Longman, Hurst, Rees, Orme and Brown, 1812), I, 138 and III, 69.

45 Thomas Skinner Surr, *George Barnwell. A Novel* (London: H. D. Symonds, 1798), I, 144–60. See also George Walker, *The Vagabond* (3rd edn, London: G. Walker, 1799), pp. 102–3.

46 Anon., 'A Disciple of the Old School', *The Chances; or, Nothing of the New School: A Novel* (London: Cuthell and Martin, 1803), III, 289–90, but cf. I, 277 when a party of horseguards does not intervene in a mob's attack on a homosexual libertine.

47 'I have studied the mobs of different nations,' says the conspirator, making the contemporary parallels obvious, 'and they are all alike.' Walker, *The Vagabond*, I, 134.

48 *History of Sir George Warrington*, II, 196–III, 50.

49 Moore, *Mordaunt*, I, 31. Marat and Robespierre, either separately or together, cut a dash across the action of Pye's *Democrat* (1795), Robinson's *Natural Daughter* (1799), West's *Tale of the Times* (1799), Dubois' *St Godwin* (1800), Moore's *Mordaunt* (1800), Craik's *Adelaide de Narbonne* (1800), Dallas' *Percival* (1801), Lucas' *Infernal Quixote* (1801), *Memoirs of M. De Brinboc* (1805), Mangin's *George*

the Third (1807), *Memoirs of Female Philosophers* (1808), Burney's *Wanderer* (1814) and Stanhope's *Nun of Santa Maria di Tindaro* (1818). In *The Natural Daughter* and *Adelaide de Narbonne* they even form, or attempt to form, libidinous relationships with principal characters.

50 See David Lodge, 'The French Revolution and the Condition of England: Crowds and Power in the Early Victorian Novel', pp. 123–40 in Ceri Crossley and Ian Small (eds.), *The French Revolution and British Culture* (Oxford: Oxford University Press, 1989), pp. 129–31.

51 Charles Lucas, *The Infernal Quixote. A Tale of the Day* (London: Minerva, 1801), I, 265. Charlotte Dacre ['Rosa Matilda'], *Confessions of the Nun of St Omer. A Tale* (London: J. F. Hughes, 1805), I, 129–30.

52 Craik, *Adelaide de Narbonne*, III, 266 and 167 n.; Anon., *Memoirs of M. De Brinboc*, II, 81.

53 Charlton, *The Parisian*, II, 50–1.

54 Moore, *Mordaunt*, II, 34.

55 *Ibid.*, I, 275–6.

56 Lucas, *Infernal Quixote*, I, 265–6.

57 Smith, *Banished Man*, II, 52 and III, 127. My emphasis.

58 Sayer, *Lindor and Adelaïde*, p. 313.

59 *Ibid.*, pp. 357–8.

60 Gerald Newman, 'Anti-French Propaganda and British Liberal Nationalism in the Early Nineteenth Century: Suggestions Toward a General Interpretation', *Victorian Studies*, 18 (1975), 386. See his *The Rise of English Nationalism. A Cultural History 1740–1830* (London: Weidenfield and Nicolson, 1987) and Linda Colley, *Britons. Forging the Nation 1707–1837* (1992; rpt. London: Pimlico, 1994).

61 Sayer, *Lindor and Adelaïde*, pp. 63–4.

62 Reeve, *Memoirs of Sir Roger de Clarendon*, I, xx. Thomas, *Adolphus de Biron*, II, 90–1.

63 Robinson, *Hubert de Sevrac*, II, 39; Walker, *Vagabond*, II, 264; John William Cunningham, *A World Without Souls* (1805; 2nd edn, London: J. Hatchard, 1806), p. 53.

64 Walker, *Vagabond*, I, 152–3.

65 Paulson, *Representation of Revolution*, p. 41.

66 Anon., *Dorothea; or, A Ray of the New Light* (London: G. G. and J. Robinson, 1801), II, 40–55.

67 Lucas, *Infernal Quixote*, III, 177–82, 168–9 and 182.

68 *Ibid.*, III, 263, 265–6 and 267.

69 Eaton Stannard Barrett, *The Heroine, or Adventures of a Fair Romance Reader* (1813; rpt. London: Henry Frowde, 1909, with an Introduction by Walter Raleigh), p. 217.

70 Robert Bisset, *Modern Literature* (London: T. N. Longman and O. Rees, 1804), III, 229, 231–4. Roger O'Rourke may be loosely based on Roger O'Conner, the prominent United Irishman and sceptic, and brother of Arthur O'Conner.

71 Doody, *Frances Burney*, pp. 318, 323 and 331. For Burney's anti-Jacobin portrayal of the Revolution, see Doody's 'Appendix 1' to *The Wanderer*, pp. 875–84.

72 Stanhope, *Nun of Santa Maria di Tindaro*, I, 119.

73 'I have heard that something very shocking indeed will soon come out of London . . . It is to be uncommonly dreadful. I shall expect murder and everything of the kind' – meaning a new gothic novel, but interpreted by Eleanor Tilney as civil unrest. Jane Austen, *Northanger Abbey* (1818; rpt. Harmondsworth: Penguin, 1985, ed. Anne Ehrenpreis), p. 126.

74 Pye, *The Aristocrat*, I, 192–203.

75 Sarah Wood, *Julia, and the Illuminated Baron. A Novel: Founded on Recent Facts, which have transpired in the course of the late Revolution of Moral Principles in France* (Portsmouth, NH: Charles Pierce, 1800), p. 284.

76 Mary Pilkington, *New Tales of the Castle; or, The Noble Emigrants, a Story of Modern Times* (1800; rpt. London: J. Harris, 1803), pp. 3–7.

77 Anon., *Memoirs of Female Philosophers . . . By a Modern Philosopher of the Other Sex* (London: Henry Colburn, 1808), I, 118–20.

78 Mangin, *George the Third*, II, 116–17.

3 THE NEW PHILOSOPHY

1 See, for instance, Robert Birley, *The English Jacobins from 1789–1802* (London: Oxford University Press, 1924); Philip Anthony Brown, *The French Revolution in English History* (1918; rpt. London: Frank Cass and Co., 1965); Marilyn Butler (ed.), *Burke, Paine, Godwin and the Revolution Controversy* (Cambridge: Cambridge University Press, 1984); Carl B. Cone, *The English Jacobins* (New York: Charles Scribner's Sons, 1968); H. T. Dickinson, *Liberty and Property. Political Ideology in Eighteenth-Century Britain* (1977; rpt. London, Methuen, 1979) and *British Radicalism and the French Revolution 1789–1815* (Oxford: Blackwell, 1985); Michael Freeman, *Edmund Burke and the Critique of Political Radicalism* (Oxford, Blackwell, 1980); Albert Goodwin, *The Friends of Liberty: The English Democratic Movement in the Age of the French Revolution* (London: Hutchinson, 1979); Edward Royle and James Walvin, *English Radicals and Reformers 1760–1848* (Brighton: Harvester, 1982); E. P. Thompson, *The Making of the English Working Class* (1963; rpt. Harmondsworth: Penguin, 1980); and Gwyn A. Williams, *Artisans and Sans-Culottes: Popular Movements in France and Britain during the French Revolution* (London: Edward Arnold, 1968).

2 Gary Kelly, *The English Jacobin Novel 1780–1805* (Oxford: Clarendon Press, 1976), pp. 1–2.

3 Emphasis added. Robert Bisset, *Douglas; or, the Highlander* (London, 'Printed at the Anti-Jacobin Press', 1800), I, 72–3; Samuel Horsley, 'The Charge of Samuel, Lord Bishop of Rochester, to the Clergy of his Diocese; Delivered at his second general Visitation, in the year 1800', *The Charges of Samuel Horsley* (Dundee: Chalmers, 1813), pp. 147–8; George III quoted in Gerald Newman, 'Anti-French Propaganda and British Liberal Nationalism

in the Early Nineteenth Century: Suggestions Toward a General Interpretation', *Victorian Studies*, 18 (1975), 391.

4 Ben Brierley, *Home Memories and Recollections of Life* (London: Marshall and Co., 1886), p. 6.

5 Francis Wollaston, *A Country Parson's Address to his Flock, to Caution them against being misled by the Wolf in Sheep's Clothing, or receiving Jacobin Teachers of Sedition . . .* (London: G. Wilkie, D. Bremner and J. Hatchard, 1799), pp. 16–17.

6 Mary Anne Burges, *The Progress of the Pilgrim Good-Intent, in Jacobinical Times* (London: John Hatchard, 1800), p. 181.

7 Joseph Wildman, *The Force of Prejudice, A Moral Tale* (London: T. Barfield, 1799), I, 66–7.

8 Mark Philp, 'Vulgar Conservatism, 1792–3', *English Historical Review*, 110 (1995), 42–69.

9 Anon., *Memoirs of M. De Brinboc: Containing Some Views of English and Foreign Society* (London: Cadell and Davies, 1805), II, 120.

10 Charles Lucas, *The Infernal Quixote. A Tale of the Day* (London: Minerva, 1801), II, 219 and 222–3.

11 Burke had lamented that the age of chivalry was gone, that the age of 'sophisters, oeconomists, and calculators' had succeeded, and novelists were pleased to demonstrate that, indeed, chivalry had been basely murdered by new philosophy. In *Memoirs of M. De Brinboc*, for instance, an elderly soldier is shocked to find that ten thousand swords did not leap from their scabbards to defend the honour of a beautiful young heroine and that he was the only man prepared to escort such a creature out of Revolutionary France: ' "In my juvenile days," continued the hoary warrior, 'half the garrison of Berlin would have set off at a moment's notice too [*sic*] rescue a weak female from the grasp of a villain; but we are all *philosophised*, I think they call it, and somehow or other we do not win so many battles as we used to do before we were philosophers." ' Burke, *Reflections on the Revolution in France* (1790) in *The Writings and Speeches of Edmund Burke*, vol. VIII, ed. L. G. Mitchell (Oxford: Clarendon Press, 1989), p. 127. Anon., *Memoirs of M. De Brinboc*, II, 256–7.

12 Ann Thomas, *Adolphus de Biron. A Novel. Founded on the French Revolution* (Plymouth: 'Printed . . . for the Authoress', 1795?), I, 157.

13 Thomas Skinner Surr, *George Barnwell. A Novel* (London: H. D. Symonds, 1798), I, 30.

14 Henry James Pye, *The Aristocrat, a Novel* (London: Sampson Low, 1799), I, 43–4. Cf. R. C. Dallas, *Percival, or Nature Vindicated* (London: Longman and Rees, 1801), I, 15–16.

15 Charles Lucas, *The Castle of St Donats; or, the History of Jack Smith* (London: Minerva, 1798), II, 220.

16 Lucas, *Infernal Quixote*, II, 225–94 and 297; Elizabeth Hamilton, *Memoirs of Modern Philosophers* (2nd edn, London: G. G. and J. Robinson, 1800), I, 66.

17 George Walker, *The Vagabond, a Novel* (London: G. Walker and Lee and Hurst, 1799), I, XI.

18 Burges, *Progress of the Pilgrim Good-Intent*, p. 45.

19 Anon., *Massouf, or the Philosophy of the Day. An Eastern Tale* (London: Minerva, 1802), p. 76.
20 For a full rendition of West's religious conception of new philosophy see her *Tale of the Times* (London: Longman and Rees, 1799), II, 272–4.
21 A. D. Harvey, 'George Walker and the Anti-Revolutionary Novel', *Review of English Studies*, n.s., 28 (1977), 290–300; Hugh H. MacMullen, 'The Satire of Walker's *Vagabond* on Rousseau and Godwin', *Publications of the Modern Language Association of America*, 52 (March 1937), 215–29. See also Gary Kelly, *Women, Writing and Revolution* (Oxford: Oxford University Press, 1993), pp. 140–1.
22 Peter H. Marshall, *William Godwin* (New Haven, CT: Yale University Press, 1984), pp. 211–33. See also, for example, Ford K. Brown, *The Life of William Godwin* (London: J. M. Dent and Sons, 1926), pp. 151–75, and Don Locke, *A Fantasy of Reason. The Life and Thought of William Godwin* (London: Routledge and Kegan Paul, 1980), pp. 113–14 and 148–59.
23 A sample of the citations of *Political Justice* may be found in Walker's *Vagabond*, I, 123n., Isaac D'Israeli's *Vaurien* (London: Cadell and Davies, 1797), I, 77n. and *Flim-Flams!* (London: John Murray, 1805), I, 80n., Elizabeth Hamilton's *Modern Philosophers*, I, 74n., Robert Bisset's *Douglas*, III, 84–100, Edward Dubois' *St Godwin* (London: J. Wright, 1800), p. 207n., and Anon., *Dorothea; or, A Ray of the New Light* (London: G. G. and J. Robinson, 1801), II, 24n., 29n. and 34n.
24 Bisset, *Douglas*, I, xxiv, and see Kelly, *Women, Writing and Revolution*, p. 143, for a summary of the angry accusations made by Hays that Hamilton had launched an unprovoked attack on her, and Hamilton's arch counter-claims that her satire was not so specific.
25 Identifications that seem reasonably safe are Joseph Priestley as Mr Mental in Surr's *George Barnwell* and as Dr Alogos in Walker's *Vagabond* (from the attacks on their laboratories); Thomas Holcroft as Tom Croft in Bisset's *Douglas* and Mr Allcraft in Dubois' *St Godwin* (for obvious reasons), and as Reverberator in D'Israeli's *Vaurien*, according to James Ogden, *Isaac D'Israeli* (Oxford: Clarendon Press, 1969), pp. 59–61, who also claims Rant to be John Thelwall (but ducks other identifications by not entirely correctly claiming that 'other characters are fairly easily identified by quotations from their writings'). Ford K. Brown thinks D'Israeli's Dr Bounce to be Samuel Parr – or possibly Joseph Fawcett – since we are told Bounce was a familiar figure at Old Jewry (*Life of William Godwin*, p. 161 and n.), whilst Marilyn Butler thinks him to be Richard Price, presumably for a similar reason (*Jane Austen and the War of Ideas* (1975; rpt. Oxford: Clarendon Press, 1987), p. 107). Mary Hays is clearly associated with Bridgetina Botherim in Hamilton's *Modern Philosophers* (by her squint and short stature as well as her principles), although Gary Kelly thinks of her as part Wollstonecraft too (*Women, Writing and Revolution*, p. 149). Notes citing *Memoirs of Emma Courtney* also suggest that Gertrude Sinclair in Charles Lloyd's *Edmund Oliver* may be based on Hays (*Edmund Oliver* (Bristol: Joseph Cottle, 1798), I, 36n. and 40n.). Wollstonecraft is evidently Jemima in Bisset's *Modern Literature*, is certainly behind the

portrait of Adeline Mowbray in Opie's novel of that name (see Dale Spender, *Mothers of the Novel* (London: Pandora Press, 1986), pp. 315–24, for a discussion of this), and seems to be a major part of the inspiration for the Goddess of Reason in Hamilton's *Modern Philosophers* (see Eleanor Ty, 'Female Philosophy Refunctioned: Elizabeth Hamilton's Parodic Novel', *Ariel. A Review of International English Literature*, 22 (1991), 116). According to Ernest Baker, Valloton [*sic*] in *Modern Philosophers*, with his 'Swiss name', is 'beyond all possibility of mistake' 'a scurrilous caricature of Rousseau' (*The Novel of Sentiment and the Gothic Romance*, vol. V of *The History of the English Novel* (London: H. F. and G. Witherby, 1934), p. 254), although Gary Kelly has other, and more convincing ideas (*Women, Writing and Revolution*, p. 150). As must be becoming apparent, these attributions may be strained almost to implausibility, something shown by the way in which almost every anti-Jacobin character may be said to be a travesty of Godwin. Ford K. Brown and Don Locke, in their biographies of Godwin, are particularly guilty of regarding him as virtually the sole subject of the anti-Jacobin novelists, and end up rather too over-zealously charting his 'appearances' in fiction (*Life of William Godwin*, pp. 31–32, 119, etc.; *A Fantasy of Reason*, pp. 113–14, 157–9, etc.). It is not stretching the bounds of possibility, though, to see him as Stupeo in Walker's *Vagabond* (although this is set *circa* 1780), as Subtile in D'Israeli's *Vaurien* and 'CACO-NOUS' in his *Flim-Flams!*, as Myope in *Modern Philosophers*, as the eponymous anti-hero of *St Godwin* (although mediated through Godwin's own character, St Leon) and as Subtlewould in *Douglas*. However, it is a salutary warning against reading too much significance into these glib identifications that *Douglas* also includes another, separate figure called simply 'Godwin' (e.g. III, 101). We should also bear in mind that in Elizabeth Helme's *The Farmer of Inglewood Forest* (London: Minerva, 1796), the honest, worthy and decidedly non-Jacobin country farmer of the title is actually called 'William Godwin' without there being the merest hint of any consciousness of, or correlation with, his real-life namesake.

26 Bernard Schilling, *Conservative England and the Case Against Voltaire* (New York: Columbia University Press, 1950), p. 296.

27 Edward Duffy, *Rousseau in England. The Context for Shelley's Critique of the Enlightenment* (Berkeley: University of California Press, 1979), p. 33.

28 MacMullen, 'The Satire of Walker's *Vagabond*', pp. 217 and 216–18.

29 *Writings and Speeches of Edmund Burke*, VIII, 219.

30 *Ibid.*, VIII, 314.

31 *Ibid.*, VIII, 313. Duffy, *Rousseau in England*, p. 41.

32 Sophia King, *Waldorf; or, the Dangers of Philosophy. A Philosophical Tale* (London: G. G. and J. Robinson, 1798), I, 46 and 74. The relationship between sensibility and Jacobinism is vexed and is open to various interpretations. Lok detests it as an obstacle to winning converts to his new philosophy, but other anti-Jacobins regard sensibility, at least in an exaggerated form, as a Jacobin trait – an affectation which, like new philosophy, found affliction or injustice where none in fact existed.

33 *Ibid.*, II, 199–200.

34 D'Israeli, *Vaurien*, I, 32–41. The same point is made more concisely by Thomas Love Peacock in his epigraph to *Headlong Hall* (1816; rpt. Oxford: Oxford University Press, 1987, eds. Michael Baron and Michael Slater): 'All philosophers, who find / Some favourite system to their mind / In every point to make it fit, / Will force all nature to submit.' That only some of the 'systems' that Peacock satirises could be described as 'Jacobin' should remind us that these techniques employed by the anti-Jacobin novelists were neither new nor necessarily to reach their apogee in conservative propaganda.

35 Anon., *Massouf*, pp. 29 and 31.

36 For this unusual kind of attack on specific points of Godwin's thought see Charles Lloyd, *Edmund Oliver* (Bristol: Joseph Cottle, 1798), II, 103–4 and Isaac D'Israeli, *Flim-Flams!*, III, 140.

37 Gary Kelly, in his *English Jacobin Novel*, has also concentrated on Godwinian Necessity as the underlying and unifying creed of radical novelists (especially pp. 15–16).

38 Dubois adds a note directing the reader to the relevant pages of Godwin's *Political Justice* and the hostile reviews that the work attracted. Dubois, *St Godwin*, pp. 206–7 and 207n.

39 D'Israeli, *Vaurien*, I, 71–84.

40 Elizabeth Hamilton, *Translation of the Letters of a Hindoo Rajah* (1796; 2nd edn, London: G. G. and J. Robinson, 1801), II, 191–205.

41 *Ibid.*, II, 200–1 and Surr, *George Barnwell*, I, 36–7.

42 Robert Bisset, *Modern Literature. A Novel* (London: T. N. Longman and O. Rees, 1804), III, 85–6.

43 Bisset, *Douglas*, II, 66–7.

44 *Ibid.*, I, 72; Kelly, *Women, Writing and Revolution*, p. 149.

45 Hamilton, *Modern Philosophers*, I, 331–4.

46 Sarah Green, *The Reformist!!! A Serio-comic political novel* (London: Minerva, 1810), I, 36.

47 Lucas, *Infernal Quixote*, II, 178–81.

48 Surr, *George Barnwell*, I, 62–96, 161–4 and 179.

49 Lloyd, *Edmund Oliver*, I, vii and vii–viii.

50 *Ibid.*, I, 35–6, 122–3 and 124.

51 Jane West, *The Infidel Father* (London: Longman and Rees, 1802), I, 269–72 and II, 221.

52 Bisset, *Douglas*, II, 143.

53 Walker, *Vagabond*, I, 180–1.

54 Lucas, *Infernal Quixote*, II, 176.

55 This is from the third, revised, edition of 1798, by which time Godwin had somewhat softened his stance on marriage. *Enquiry Concerning Political Justice*, ed. Isaac Kramnick (Harmondsworth: Penguin, 1985), 'Appendix' to bk. VIII, ch. viii, p. 763.

56 Anon., *Dorothea*, I, 109n.; Bisset, *Douglas*, III, 84–100; and Bisset, *Modern Literature*, III, 204–5.

57 See Ronald Paulson, *Representations of Revolution (1789–1820)*, (New Haven, CT: Yale University Press, 1983), pp. 60–4, for a discussion of Burke's use of this image, and Linda Colley, *Britons. Forging the Nation 1707–1837* (1992; rpt. London: Pimlico, 1994), pp. 253–6, who testifies to its impact on British women.

58 Kathryn Sutherland, 'Hannah More's Counter-Revolutionary Feminism', p. 34 in Kelvin Everest (ed.), *Revolution in Writing. British Literary Responses to the French Revolution* (Milton Keynes: Open University Press, 1991). Anon., *Dorothea*, I, 149–51; Helena Wells, *Constantia Neville; or, the West Indian* (London: T. Cadell jun. and W. Davies, 1800), I, 369. See also Lucas, *Infernal Quixote*, I, 135 and 171–3, and Bisset, *Douglas*, IV, 87.

59 When Elizabeth Hamilton actually considers Wollstonecraft's *Vindication*, she finds it an antidote to Rousseau's much worse views of women. *Modern Philosophers*, I, 196. Benjamin Silliman's *Letters of Shahcoolen, a Hindu Philosopher, residing in Philadelphia* (Boston, MA: Russell and Cutler, 1802), though it ruthlessly lampoons and reprehends Wollstonecraft's life and work, also acknowledges the reasonableness of some of her ideas and demonstrates an unusual level of familiarity with her writing.

60 Lloyd, *Edmund Oliver*, I, vii, 36n and 40n. Marilyn Brooks, 'A Critical Study of the Writings of Mary Hays, With an Edition of her Unpublished Letters to William Godwin', unpublished PhD thesis (University of London, 1995), pp. 96–115.

61 *Anti-Jacobin Review*, 3 (1799), 55.

62 Hamilton, *Letters of a Hindoo Rajah*, II, 218–19.

63 Amelia Opie, *Adeline Mowbray, or the Mother and Daughter: A Tale* (London: Longman, Hurst, Rees and Orme, 1805), III, 208, and see also the conventional, Burkean anti-Jacobinism of her death-bed retraction: III, 270.

64 Alethea Lewis, *Plain Sense. A Novel* (1795; rpt. London: Minerva, 1796), II, 228. Sir William Ackland, the speaker, goes on to say that he believes he and his wife 'were united upon the old terms [of marriage] of the wife's obedience and subordination'.

65 Anon., *Dorothea*, I, 1–2.

66 *Ibid.*, I, 150 and 146.

67 Edward Sayer, *Lindor and Adelaïde, a Moral Tale* (London: John Hockdale, 1791), pp. 285–8.

68 *Ibid.*, pp. 285–8n.

69 Harvey, 'George Walker and the Anti-Revolutionary Novel', p. 292.

70 'Rosa Matilda' [Charlotte Dacre], *Confessions of the Nun of St Omer. A Tale* (London: J. F. Hughes, 1805), I, 124–9, II, 71 and I, 89.

71 Anon., *The Citizen's Daughter; or What Might Be* (London: Vernor and Hood, 1804), p. 110.

72 Samuel Egerton Brydges, *Arthur Fitz-Albini, A Novel* (1798; rpt. London: J. White, 1799), I, 237 and 235–6.

73 Anon., *Memoirs of M. De Brinboc*, I, 136–9 and II, 102.

74 Hamilton, *Letters of a Hindoo Rajah*, II, 233–44.

75 Hamilton, *Modern Philosophers*, III, 26 and D'Israeli, *Vaurien*, I, 65–6 and 214–19.

76 Charles Lamb, *Letters of Charles and Mary Lamb*, ed. E. V. Lucas (London: Methuen, 1935), I, 237. See Godwin, *Political Justice*, pp. 169–71.

77 Lloyd, *Edmund Oliver*, I, 128–30.

78 Walker, *Vagabond*, I, 68–72.

79 Sarah Wood, *Julia, and the Illuminated Baron. A Novel* (Portsmouth, NH: Charles Pierce, 1800), pp. 253–4.

80 Hamilton, *Modern Philosophers*, I, 2, 30, 99, 102; Lucas, *Castle of St Donats*, II, 218. It seems that Lucas wishes it to appear that Pendragon has affected what his readers would recognise as the outfit of a Jacobin, for Surr's Mr Mental, for example, shares the same natural and adopted gaucheness: 'He was of large make, but thin; his face pale; his hair, a coal black, cropped short in the neck; his dress always the same, a suit of plain brown cloth' (*George Barnwell*, I, 30). Dwarfishness is just as much the sign of a new philosopher as the black, cropped hair. As well as Bridgetina, D'Israeli's Dr Bounce is described as of stunted growth in *Vaurien* (I, 51) and Halfaz is introduced as 'the minute philosopher' in *Memoirs of M. De Brinboc* (I, 135). More standard descriptions of new philosophers and Jacobins may be found in *The Citizen's Daughter's* Mr Mandred, a 'black-looking old toad of a man' with 'a person extremely plain, not to say disgusting, possessed of a disposition no less deformed, though concealed beneath a villainous cloak of learning and philosophy' (pp. 249 and 32), or in Helen Craik's description of one of the protagonists of her *Adelaide de Narbonne*, of whom she records that 'Nature had not been kind with Marat in point of looks – he has a face expressive of his disposition, he is little and cadaverous' (*Adelaide de Narbonne, with Memoirs of Charlotte de Cordet* (London: Minerva, 1800), III, 66). Craik acknowledged that she owed the characterisation to John Moore's *Journal*, and his portrait of Collot d'Herbois in *Mordaunt* is so similar as to suggest he had a fixed idea of the generic French Jacobin: 'His countenance was frightful. Children shut their eyes, and screamed at the sight of this man. His head sustained a frightful exuberance of bushy hair, black as tar, and stiff as the bristles of a hog; his complexion was cadaverous; his features haggard; his eyes sanguine: he looked very much like a villain and murderer; and he was a much greater villain and murderer than he looked like' (*Mordaunt* (London: G. G. and J. Robinson, 1800), II, 71–2).

81 D'Israeli, *Vaurien*, I, 51–2 and II, 257–8.

82 'Rosa Matilda' [Charlotte Dacre], *The Passions* (London: Cadell and Davies, 1811), II, 227.

83 Walker, *Vagabond*, I, 24–5 and 187.

84 Hamilton, *Letters of a Hindoo Rajah*, II, 344; Henry James Pye, *The Democrat* (1795; rpt. London: Minerva, 1796), II, 81–8.

85 Anon., *The History of Sir George Warrington* (London: J. Bell, 1797), I, 204–5, II, 17–18, etc; Sarah Green, *The Reformist!!!*, II, 143–4.

86 Samuel Egerton Brydges, *Le Forester, A Novel* (London: J. White, 1802), II, 25.

87 Hamilton, *Letters of a Hindoo Rajah*, II, 203–4.

88 Anon., *History of Sir George Warrington*, II, 17–18.
89 Anon., *Dorothea*, III, 51–6 and 84–93; Walker, *Vagabond*, II, 61–2; Opie, *Adeline Mowbray*, III, 160.
90 Anon., *Memoirs of M. De Brinboc*, III, 238–43.
91 Hamilton, *Letters of a Hindoo Rajah*, II, 215–16 and 273.
92 Hamilton, *Modern Philosophers*, III, 168–70.
93 Lloyd, *Edmund Oliver*, II, 86–7.
94 D'Israeli, *Flim-Flams!* (2nd edn, London: John Murray, 1806), I, 82–3.
95 Anon., *Massouf*, pp. 167–79.
96 Anon., *Berkeley Hall: or, the Pupil of Experience. A Novel* (London: J. Tindal, 1796), II, 338–73 and III, 35–97; Walker, *Vagabond*, II, 111–179.
97 Walker, *Vagabond*, II, 180, 187n., 190, 194–5 and 197–8.
98 *Ibid.*, II, 201–2n. and 196n, 241.

4 THE VAURIEN AND THE HIERARCHY OF JACOBINISM

1 Burke, *Reflections on the Revolution in France* (1790) *in The Writings and Speeches of Edmund Burke*, vol. VIII, ed. L. G. Mitchell (Oxford: Clarendon Press, 1989), p. 136.
2 Elizabeth Hamilton, *Translation of the Letters of a Hindoo Rajah* (1796; 2nd edn, London: G. G. and J. Robinson, 1801), II, 191–205; Anon., *The History of Sir George Warrington; or the Political Quixote* (London: J. Bell, 1797), I, 16–18; George Walker, *The Vagabond, A Novel* (3rd edn, London: G. Walker, 1799), II, 47–62; Anon., *Dorothea; or, A Ray of the New Light* (London: G. G. and J. Robinson, 1801), III, 51–6 and 84–93; Amelia Opie, *Adeline Mowbray, or the Mother and Daughter: A Tale* (London: Longman, Hurst, Rees and Orme, 1805), III, 160.
3 Helen Craik, *Adelaide de Narbonne, with Memoirs of Charlotte de Cordet. A Tale* (London: Minerva, 1800), III, 96; Mary Robinson, *Hubert de Sevrac, A Romance, of the Eighteenth Century* (1796; rpt. Dublin: B. Smith, C. Browne and H. Colbert, 1797), I, 10–39.
4 Elizabeth Helme, *The Farmer of Inglewood Forest, a Novel* (London: Minerva, 1796), IV, 34–5.
5 Sophia King, *Waldorf; or, the Dangers of Philosophy* (London: G. G. and J. Robinson, 1798), I, 118 and 131–2.
6 Anon, *History of Sir George Warrington*, II, 37.
7 *The Complete Collection of State Trials and Proceedings for High Treason . . .*, compiled by T. B. Howell and Thomas James Howell (London: Longman, 1817), XXII, 383.
8 Jane West, *The Infidel Father* (London: Longman and Rees, 1802), II, 307.
9 *Writings and Speeches of Edmund Burke*, VIII, 130.
10 Thomas Skinner Surr, *George Barnwell. A Novel* (London: H. D. Symonds, 1798), I, 145.
11 Anon., *Massouf, or the Philosophy of the Day. An Eastern Tale* (London: Minerva, 1802), pp. 146–7 and 201–5.
12 King, *Waldorf*, II, 199–200.

13 Walker, *Vagabond*, I, 88–95.

14 Anon., *History of Sir George Warrington*, I, 104 and 115.

15 *Ibid.*, I, 104 and 115.

16 Elizabeth Hamilton, *Memoirs of Modern Philosophers* (2nd edn, London: G. G. and J. Robinson, 1800), III, 56–7.

17 Isaac D'Israeli, *Vaurien: or, Sketches of the Times* (London: Cadell and Davies, 1797), I, 31–8.

18 Henry James Pye, *The Democrat: Interspersed with Anecdotes of Well Known Characters* (1795; rpt. London: Minerva, 1796), II, 90; Hamilton, *Letters of a Hindoo Rajah*, II, 344.

19 Burke, *Letter to a Noble Lord* (1796) in *The Writings and Speeches of Edmund Burke*, vol. IX, ed. R. B. McDowell (Oxford: Clarendon Press, 1991), pp. 180 and 173–4.

20 Hannah More, 'History of Mr Fantom' in *The Miscellaneous Works of Hannah More* (2 vols., London: Thomas Tegg, 1840), I, 1–2.

21 Anon., *History of Sir George Warrington*, I, 32–3 and 106.

22 *Ibid.*, II, 52–3.

23 *Ibid.*, II, 127–8, 194–7 and III, 33–8.

24 *Writings and Speeches of Edmund Burke*, IX, 174.

25 Anon, *Liberty and Equality; Treated of in a Short History addressed from a Poor Man to His Equals* (London: 'Printed for the Author, and sold by Hookham and Carpenter', 1792), pp. 21–2.

26 D'Israeli, *Vaurien*, II, 318 and I, 219.

27 John Gifford, *A Plain Address to the Common Sense of the People of England, Containing an Interesting Abstract of Pain's [sic] Life and Writing* (London: 'printed for the author', 1792). See also William Oldys [possibly a pseudonym for George Chalmers], *Life of Thomas Paine* (London?, n.d., but 1791?).

28 Pye, *Democrat*, I, 10–12.

29 *Ibid.*, I, 3–4 and 105–127.

30 Anon., *Dorothea*, II, 40–4 and I, 32–3.

31 *Ibid.*, II, 134.

32 *Writings and Speeches of Edmund Burke*, VIII, 102.

33 Pye, *Democrat*, II, 159.

34 Walker, *Vagabond*, II, 4; I, 79–83 and 88.

35 Anon., *Berkeley Hall: or, the Pupil of Experience* (London: J. Tindal, 1796), II, 338–73.

36 Samuel Egerton Brydges, *Arthur Fitz-Albini, a Novel* (1798; rpt. London: J. White, 1799), II, 40–2.

37 Sarah Green, *The Reformist!!! A Serio-comic political novel* (London: Minerva, 1810), I, iv.

38 Joseph Wildman, *The Force of Prejudice, A Moral Tale* (London: T. Barfield, 1799), II, 202–3.

39 Anon., *Dorothea*, II, 17–34.

40 Walker, *Vagabond*, II, 24 and 32–43.

41 Edward Sayer, *Lindor and Adelaïde, a Moral Tale* (London: John Hockdale, 1791), pp. 285–8.

42 Louisa Sidney Stanhope, *The Nun of Santa Maria di Tindaro. A Tale* (London: Minerva, 1818), III, 184.

43 Anon., *Memoirs of M. De Brinboc* (London: Cadell and Davies, 1805), I, 110–14 and II, 81.

44 Craik, *Adelaide de Narbonne*, III, 265–70.

45 John Moore, *Mordaunt. Sketches of Life, Characters, and Manners, in Various Countries* (London: G. G. and J. Robinson, 1800), II, 63–9.

46 Mary Robinson, *The Natural Daughter. With Portraits of the Leadenhead Family* (London: T. N. Longman and O. Rees, 1799), I, 209–13 and II, 266–7.

47 Helme, *Farmer of Inglewood Forest*, I, 211; Lloyd, *Edmund Oliver* (Bristol: Joseph Cottle, 1798), I, 35–36; Wildman, *Force of Prejudice*, II, 230–1.

48 Anon., *The Citizen's Daughter; or What Might Be* (London: Vernor and Hood, 1804), pp. 90–1 and 232.

49 Robert Bisset, *Douglas; or, the Highlander* (London: 'Printed at the Anti-Jacobin Press', 1800), III, 87–8; Charles Lucas, *Infernal Quixote* (London: Minerva, 1798), I, 134–6.

50 Surr, *George Barnwell*, II, 130 and 190.

51 Lloyd, *Edmund Oliver*, II, 76–7.

52 Anon., *Leonard and Gertrude. A Popular Story* (Bath: S. Hazard, 1800), pp. 48 and 272–3.

53 E.g. Charlotte Dacre, *Confessions of the Nun of St Omer* (London: J. F. Hughes, 1805), I, 89, 124–9, II, 70–1.

54 Walker, *Vagabond*, II, 176.

5 LEVELLERS, NABOBS AND THE MANNERS OF THE GREAT: THE NOVEL'S DEFENCE OF HIERARCHY

1 See for instance Charles Herbert Huffman, *The Eighteenth-Century Novel in Theory and Practice* (Dayton, VA: Ruebush-Kieffer, 1920), p. 114.

2 Edward Tatham, *Letters to the Right Honourable Edmund Burke on Politics* (Oxford: J. Fletcher, D. Prince and J. Cooke, and London: J. F. and C. Rivington and W. Richardson, 1791), p. 40.

3 Robert Hole, *Pulpits, Politics and Public Order in England 1760–1832* (Cambridge: Cambridge University Press, 1989), especially pp. 95–144; H. T. Dickinson, *Liberty and Property. Political Ideology in Eighteenth-Century Britain* (1977; rpt. London: Methuen, 1977), pp. 270–318, and *The Politics of the People in Eighteenth-Century Britain* (Basingstoke: Macmillan, 1995), pp. 264–70.

4 Hole, *Pulpits, Politics and Public Order*, p. 128 and see pp. 118–19.

5 Adam Ferguson, *Principles of Moral and Political Science; being chiefly a Retrospect of Lectures delivered in the College of Edinburgh* (London and Edinburgh: A. Strahan, T. Cadell and W. Creech, 1792), II, 442–3.

6 John Moore, *Mordaunt, Sketches of Life, Characters, and Manners, in Various Countries* (London: G. G. and J. Robinson, 1800), I, 39n.

7 Ferguson, *Principles of Moral and Political Science*, II, 371 and 423–4.

8 Clara Reeve, *Memoirs of Sir Roger de Clarendon* (London: Hookham and Carpenter, 1793), III, 228–9.

9 *Ibid.*, III, 229–30. Cf. Ann Thomas, *Adolphus de Biron. A Novel* (Plymouth: 'Printed . . . for the Authoress', 1795?), I, 225–6.

10 Hole, *Pulpits, Politics and Public Order*, p. 129. For an overview of the Church's defence of hierarchical society see R. A. Soloway, *Prelates and the People. Ecclesiastical Social Thought in England 1783–1852* (London: Routledge and Kegan Paul, 1969), pp. 55–74.

11 Elizabeth Hamilton, *The Cottagers of Glenburnie; A Tale for the Farmer's Ingle-Nook* (Edinburgh: Manners, Miller and S. Chapman, 1808), pp. 253 and 48–9.

12 Francis Lathom, *Men and Manners. A Novel* (London: J. Wright, 1799), IV, 155–6 and 174.

13 Charles Lucas, *The Castle of St Donats; or, the History of Jack Smith* (London: Minerva, 1798), III, 146.

14 Samuel Egerton Brydges, *Arthur Fitz-Albini, a Novel* (1798; rpt. London: J. White, 1799), I, 56–7.

15 T. Wright, *Solyman and Fatima; or, the Sceptic Convinced. An Eastern Tale* (London: John Bew, 1791), I, 22 and 2–3.

16 *Ibid.*, I, 22–3, 56, II, 14–15 and 87.

17 Anon., *Massouf, or the Philosophy of the Day. An Eastern Tale* (London: Minerva, 1802), p. 209.

18 Thomas, *Adolphus de Biron*, II, 129–34; Mary Charlton, *The Parisian; or, Genuine Anecdotes of Distinguished and Noble Characters* (London: Minerva, 1794), II, 192.

19 Charlotte Smith, *The Banished Man* (London: Cadell and Davies, 1794), I, 150.

20 Anon., *Massouf*, pp. 100–1.

21 Robert Charles Dallas, *Percival, or Nature Vindicated. A Novel* (London: Longman and Rees, 1801), II, 29. The 'nature' that was being 'vindicated' in Dallas' title was the unequal state of society innate in mankind since the Fall.

22 Mary Meeke, *Count St Blancard, or, the Prejudiced Judge, A Novel* (London: Minerva, 1795), III, 81.

23 Thomas, *Adolphus de Biron*, I, 155.

24 *Ibid.*, II, 70. C.f. Reeve, *Memoirs of Sir Roger de Clarendon*, III, 9.

25 Anon., *The Brothers; A Novel, for Children. Addressed to Every Good Mother* (Henley: G. Norton, 1794), chs.1–4.

26 Walker, *The Vagabond, a Novel* (3rd edn, London: G. Walker, 1799), I, 210–12.

27 Sarah Green, *The Reformist!!! A Serio-comic political novel* (London: Minerva, 1810), I, 20–1.

28 Dallas, *Percival*, I, 260.

29 Alethea Lewis, *Plain Sense. A Novel* (London: Minerva, 1796), I, 119.

30 Charles Lloyd, *Edmund Oliver* (Bristol: Joseph Cottle, 1798), II, 157.

31 Mary Meeke, *Conscience. A Novel* (London: A. K. Newman, 1814), quoted in John Garrett's introduction to Meeke's *Count St Blancard* (1795; rpt. New York: Arno Press, 1977), I, xxiii.

32 Jane West, *A Tale of the Times* (London: Longman and Rees, 1799), I, 27–8.

33 Brydges, *Arthur Fitz-Albini*, I, 11.

34 Charlotte Smith, *Marchmont: A Novel* (London: Sampson Low, 1796), II, 27.
35 Eliza Parsons, *Women As They Are. A Novel* (London: Minerva, 1796), III, 84–5.
36 Dallas, *Percival*, I, 239–42.
37 *Ibid.*, I, 231.
38 *Ibid.*, I, 238.
39 Mary Anne Burges, *The Progress of the Pilgrim Good-Intent, in Jacobinical Times* (London: John Hatchard, 1800), pp. 142–4.
40 Reeve, *Memoirs of Sir Roger de Clarendon*, I, xvi–xvii.
41 Anon., *The History of Sir George Warrington; or the Political Quixote* (London: J. Bell, 1797), I, 188.
42 Reeve, *Memoirs of Sir Roger de Clarendon*, I, xvii and xvi.
43 Hole, *Pulpits, Politics and Public Order*, p. 119. Thomas Spence was perhaps the most radical of British Jacobins, but even he 'did not advocate complete economic equality': H. T. Dickinson (ed.), *The Political Works of Thomas Spence* (Newcastle upon Tyne: Avero, 1982), p. xiii.
44 *To the Parliament and People of Great Britain* (London, 1795), quoted in Dickinson, *Liberty and Property*, p. 255.
45 Henry James Pye, *The Democrat: Interspersed with Anecdotes of Well Known Characters* (1795; rpt. London: Minerva, 1796), I, 3–4, 10–12.
46 Walker, *Vagabond*, I, 10. See Dickinson, *Liberty and Property*, pp. 251–4, and *Politics of the People*, pp. 184–5, for discussions of the limited extent to which any demand for rights for women featured on the radical agenda.
47 Henry James Pye, *The Aristocrat. A Novel* (London: Sampson Low, 1799), II, 193.
48 Susanna Pearson, *The Medallion* (London: G. G. and J. Robinson, 1794), quoted in *The Critical Review*, n.s., 12 (1794), 99–101.
49 Helen Craik, *Adelaide de Narbonne, with Memoirs of Charlotte de Cordet. A Tale* (London: Minerva, 1800), I, 208–10, 219 and 218.
50 Anon., *Massouf*, p. 177.
51 Moore, *Mordaunt*, I, 39n.
52 Walker, *Vagabond*, II, 270.
53 Edmund Burke, *Reflections on the Revolution in France* (1790) in *The Writings and Speeches of Edmund Burke*, vol. VIII, ed. L. G. Mitchell (Oxford: Clarendon Press, 1989), p. 100.
54 Hamilton, *Cottagers of Glenburnie*, pp. 320–1.
55 Thomas, *Adolphus de Biron*, II, 115–19.
56 Edward Sayer, *Lindor and Adelaïde, a Moral Tale* (London: John Hockdale, 1791), pp. 5–11.
57 Elizabeth Hamilton, *Translation of the Letters of a Hindoo Rajah* (1796; 2nd edn, London: G. G. and J. Robinson, 1801) defended Hastings, but cf. George Walker's *Theodore Cyphon; or, the Benevolent Jew* (1796; rpt. London: A. K. Newman, 1823), II, 189–98. For defences of slavery see Anon., *The Chances; or, Nothing of the New School* (London: Cuthell and Martin, 1803), I, 134 and James Barton, *The Remorseless Assassin; or the Dangers of Enthusiasm* (London: J. F. Hughes, 1803), II, 70–3.

58 Eliza Parsons, *Woman As She Should Be; or, Memoirs of Mrs Menville. A Novel* (London: Minerva, 1793), III, 86. Cf. Isaac D'Israeli, 'The Daughter; or, A Modern Romance' in *Romances; Second Edition Corrected. To which is now added 'A Modern Romance'* (London: Murray and Highley, 1801), p. 218.

59 Smith, *Marchmont*, III, 58.

60 Robert Bisset, *Douglas; or, the Highlander* (London: 'Printed at the Anti-Jacobin Press', 1800), IV, 375. Cf. Hamilton, *Cottagers of Glenburnie*, p. 286.

61 Reeve, *Memoirs of Sir Roger de Clarendon*, I, 67.

62 Lloyd, *Edmund Oliver*, II, 109; Lathom, *Men and Manners*, I, 131–4; Mary Robinson, *The Natural Daughter* (London: T. N. Longman and O. Rees, 1799), I, 145.

63 See, for example, Bisset, *Douglas*, II, 39–40 and 171–4 or Anon., *The History of Sir George Warrington*, III, 125–55.

64 Elizabeth Hamilton, *Memoirs of Modern Philosophers* (2nd edn, London: G. G. and J. Robinson, 1800), I, 3; Lathom, *Men and Manners*, I, 150–1.

65 Samuel Egerton Brydges, *Mary de Clifford. A Story* (1792; rpt. London: Clarke's Home Library, 1845), pp. 5–6 and 56.

66 Brydges, *Arthur Fitz-Albini*, II, 110–11.

67 *Writings and Speeches of Edmund Burke*, VIII, 102–3 and 101–2.

68 Samuel Egerton Brydges, *Le Forester, A Novel* (London: J. White, 1802), I, 227; *Arthur Fitz-Albini*, I, 257 and II, 44–5.

69 Brydges, *Arthur Fitz-Albini*, I, 297.

70 Anon., *Berkeley Hall: or, the Pupil of Experience. A Novel* (London: J. Tindal, 1796), II, 74.

71 Dickinson, *Politics of the People*, p. 265.

72 Smith, *Marchmont*, I, 296.

73 Anon., *Berkeley Hall*, II, 73.

74 Thomas Skinner Surr, *George Barnwell. A Novel* (London: H. D. Symonds, 1798), III, 144–5.

75 Brydges, *Arthur Fitz-Albini*, I, xv–xvi. My emphasis.

76 Meeke, *Conscience* (1814), quoted in John Garrett's introduction to Meeke's *Count St Blancard*, I, xxiii.

77 Brydges, *Arthur Fitz-Albini*, I, 77–8.

78 Joanna Innes, 'Politics and Morals. The Reformation of Manners Movement in Later Eighteenth-Century England' in Eckhart Hellmuth (ed.), *The Transformation of Political Culture. England and Germany in the Later Eighteenth Century* (Oxford: Oxford University Press, 1990), pp. 60–1. See also V. Kiernan, 'Evangelicalism and the French Revolution', *Past and Present*, 1 (1952), 44–56.

79 Gerald Newman, *The Rise of English Nationalism. A Cultural History 1740–1830* (London: Weidenfield and Nicolson, 1987), p. 234.

80 West, *Tale of the Times*, II, 274–5.

81 Jane West, *The Infidel Father* (London: Longman and Rees, 1802), I, 145–6.

82 E. g. Charles Lucas, *The Infernal Quixote. A Tale of the Day* (London: Minerva, 1801), I, 11.

83 Surr, *George Barnwell*, II, 8–11.

84 Lucas, *Infernal Quixote*, I, 48.
85 Charlotte Smith, *The Young Philosopher: A Novel* (London: T. Cadell jun. and W. Davies, 1798), III, 10–11 and n.
86 West, *Tale of the Times*, II, 126–8.
87 Smith, *Marchmont*, III, 61–4.
88 Dallas, *Percival*, I, 310.
89 Pye, *The Aristocrat*, I, 16.
90 Mary Robinson, *Hubert de Sevrac, A Romance, of the Eighteenth Century* (1796; rpt. Dublin: B. Smith, C. Browne and H. Colbert, 1797), II, 6–7.
91 Mary Charlton, *Rosella, or Modern Occurrences* (London: Minerva, 1799) II, 134, 138–40.
92 Newman, *Rise of English Nationalism*, p. 235.
93 Jane West, *A Gossip's Story, and a Legendary Tale* (1796; rpt. London: T. N. Longman, 1798), I, 116.
94 West, *Infidel Father*, II, 67–8.
95 Bisset, *Douglas*, III, 74 and 118–19.
96 *Ibid.*, II, 54.
97 West, *Tale of the Times*, III, 18.
98 West, *The Loyalists: An Historical Novel* (London: Longman, Hurst, Rees, Orme and Brown, 1812), III, 346–7; Anon., *Such Follies Are: A Novel* (London: Minerva, 1795), I, 137–8.
99 Anon., *Such Follies Are*, I, 30–1 and 63.
100 Smith, *Marchmont*, II, 100, 214–15 and III, 29. But compare IV, 39–40.
101 Hamilton, *Hindoo Rajah*, I, 21–9, 20 and 127.
102 Newman, *Rise of English Nationalism*, p. 235. Emphasis *sic*.
103 *Writings and Speeches of Edmund Burke*, VIII, 72.
104 Pye, *Democrat*, I, 89.
105 Lloyd, *Edmund Oliver*, I, 178 and 183–5.
106 Edmund Marshall, *Edmund and Eleonora: or Memoirs of the House of Summerfield and Gretton* (London: Jonh Stockdale, 1797), I, 229, 264–8 and 311.
107 Lewis, *Plain Sense*, II, 228.
108 Thomas, *Adolphus de Biron*, I, 13 and II, 194.

6 THE CREATION OF ORTHODOXY: CONSTRUCTING
THE ANTI-JACOBIN NOVEL

1 Quoted in C. M. Wallace, *The Design of Biographia Literaria* (London: Allen and Unwin, 1983), p. 113.
2 Hans Robert Jauss, *Towards an Aesthetic of Reception*, trans. Timothy Bahti (Brighton: Harvester Press, 1982).
3 See Theodore Godfrey Grieder, Jnr, 'The French Revolution in the British Drama: A Study in British Popular Literature of the Decade of Revolution' (Unpublished PhD thesis, Stanford University, 1957), especially pp. 6–7.
4 *Gentleman's Magazine*, 78 (September 1808), 782–83.
5 Charlotte Smith, *Marchmont* (London: Sampson Low, 1796), II, 226–9 and IV, 329. See also Charlotte Smith, *The Wanderings of Warwick* (London: J. Bell,

1794), ch.7; Robinson, *The Natural Daughter* (London: T. N. Longman and O. Rees, 1799), II, ch.31; Francis Lathom, *Men and Manners* (London: J. Wright, 1799), IV, ch. 26; but compare the more optimistic Robert Bisset, *Douglas; or, the Highlander* (London: 'Printed at the Anti-Jacobin Press', 1800), IV, 372.

6 Mary Meeke, *Midnight Weddings. A Novel* (London: Minerva 1802), I, 4.

7 See James Raven, *Judging New Wealth. Popular Publishing and Responses to Commerce in England, 1750–1800* (Oxford: Clarendon Press, 1992), especially p. 67; Jon P. Klancher, *The Making of English Reading Audiences 1790–1812* (Madison: University of Wisconsin Press, 1987), especially pp. 19–26; Derek Roper, *Reviewing Before the 'Edinburgh' 1788–1802* (London: Methuen, 1978); Joanne Shattock, *Politics and Reviewers: The 'Edinburgh' and the 'Quarterly' in the Early Victorian Age* (Leicester: Leicester University Press, 1989); and Frank Donoghue, *The Fame Machine. Book Reviewing and Eighteenth-Century Literary Careers* (Stanford, CA: Stanford University Press, 1996).

8 Anon., *Flights of Inflatus; or, the Sallies, Stories, and Adventures of a Wild-Goose Philosopher* (London: C. Stalker, 1791), I, v.

9 William Pontey, *The Rotten Reviewers; or, a Dressing for the Morbid Branches of the Anti-Jacobin and Critical Reviews: Being an Exposition of the Extreme Modesty, Spotless Purity, Mature Judgement, and Strict Impartiality of Certain Writers in these Reviews. . .* (Huddersfield: T. Smart, n.d., but 1807?), pp. 12–13.

10 Burton R. Pollin, 'Charles Lamb and Charles Lloyd as Jacobins and Anti-Jacobins', *Studies in Romanticism*, 11 (1973), 639.

11 The review of *Edmund Oliver, Anti-Jacobin Review*, 1 (August 1798), 176–80, is attributed to Robert Bisset in Emily Lorraine de Montluzin, *The Anti-Jacobins, 1798–1800. The Early Contributors to the 'Anti-Jacobin Review'* (Basingstoke: Macmillan, 1988), p. 166.

12 BL Ashley MSS. collection, As.B.1005, Charles Lloyd to Thomas Manning, 2 June 1800.

13 Roper, *Reviewing Before the 'Edinburgh'*, p. 26 and De Montluzin, 'Jacobinism and the Reviewers. The English Literary Periodicals as Organs of Anti-Jacobin Propaganda. 1792–1832' (Unpublished PhD thesis, Duke University, 1974), pp. 75–9.

14 Charlotte Smith to Sarah Farr Rose, 4 July 1804. Quoted in Alan Dugald McKillop, 'Charlotte Smith's Letters', *The Huntingdon Library Quarterly*, 15 (1952), 255.

15 Quoted in the *British Critic*, 30 (December 1807), 677.

16 Isaac D'Israeli, *Vaurien; or, Sketches of the Times* (London: Cadell and Davies, 1797), I, 8–11.

17 Pontey, *Rotten Reviewers*, p.4.

18 Smith, *Wanderings of Warwick*, p. 276. Compare Lathom, *Men and Manners*, III, 70 and Thomas Love Peacock, *Headlong Hall* (1815; rpt. Oxford: Oxford University Press, 1987, eds. Michael Baron and Michael Slater), p. 22.

19 Roper, *Reviewing Before the 'Edinburgh'*, pp. 27–8 and 30–6.

20 *Critical Review*, 63 (January 1787), 76–7.

21 *British Critic*, 13 (April 1799), 438; *Quarterly Review*, 3 (August 1809), 146.

22 *Edinburgh Review*, 8 (July 1806), 459.

23 By Marilyn Butler for example: *Jane Austen and the War of Ideas* (1975; rpt. Oxford: Clarendon Press, 1987), pp. 88–95.

24 Roper, *Reviewing Before the 'Edinburgh'*, p. 23.

25 'Prospectus' for the *New London Review; or Monthly Report of Authors and Books* (1799), quoted in Walter Graham, *English Literary Periodicals* (New York: T. Nelson and Sons, 1930), p. 225.

26 Anon., *Memoirs of M. De Brinboc: Containing Some Views of English and Foreign Manners* (London: Cadell and Davies, 1805), II, 211.

27 Ann Thomas, *Adolphus de Biron* (Plymouth: 'Printed ... for the Authoress', 1795?), I, v. See also the preface to Mrs Marriott's *The Minstrel; or, Anecdotes of Distinguished Personages in the Fifteenth Century* (London: Hookham and Carpenter, 1793), which puts Thomas' anxieties in an even clearer light, especially as regards the paradoxical position of a woman writing anti-Jacobin fiction, such a public and political enterprise constituting, for many, a transgression against the very conservative orthodoxy they were upholding.

28 *British Critic*, 'Preface', 16 (July–December 1800), iii.

29 *British Critic*, 'Preface', 18 (July–December 1801), i.

30 Roper, *Reviewing Before the 'Edinburgh'*, p. 79.

31 T. J. Mathias, 'An Introductory Letter to a Friend' (1798), pp. 12–13 and 9, and 'Preface' to 'Dialogue the First' (1794), p. 42 in *The Pursuits of Literature. A Satirical Poem in Four Dialogues. With Notes* (7th edn, London, T. Becket, 1798).

32 *Ibid.*, 'Preface' to 'Dialogue the First', p. 44, and 'Preface' to 'Dialogue the Third' (1796), p. 162.

33 *Ibid.*, 'Dialogue the First', p. 61 n.c, and 'Preface' to 'Dialogue the Third', p. 162.

34 Clara Reeve, *Memoirs of Sir Roger de Clarendon* (London: Hookham and Carpenter, 1793), III, 231.

35 See John Clive, *Scotch Reviewers: the 'Edinburgh Review', 1802–1815* (London: Faber and Faber, 1957), pp. 12–13 and De Montluzin, 'Jacobinism and the Reviewers', pp. 75–6, for a discussion of this problem.

36 Charlotte Smith, *The Banished Man* (London: Cadell and Davies, 1794), II, vi; Smith to Sarah Farr Rose, 30 July 1804, in McKillop, 'Charlotte Smith's Letters', p. 246.

37 Elizabeth Inchbald, from an article in *The Artist* (June 1807), reprinted in William Mckee, *Elizabeth Inchbald, Novelist* (Washington DC: Catholic University of America, 1935), pp. 156–7.

38 Jauss, *Towards an Aesthetic of Reception*, p. 25.

39 Thomas Skinner Surr, *George Barnwell. A Novel* (3 vols., London: H. D. Symonds, 1798), I, 'Advertisement' and 36n.

40 Richard Cumberland, *Henry* (London, 1795), quoted in Ioan Williams (ed.), *Novel and Romance 1700–1800. A Documentary Record* (London: Routledge and Kegan Paul, 1970), p. 413.

41 Thomas, *Adolphus de Biron*, II, 74.

42 Claudia L. Johnson, *Jane Austen. Women, Politics and the Novel* (Chicago: University of Chicago Press, 1988), p. 21; Eleanor Ty, 'Female Philosophy Refunctioned: Elizabeth Hamilton's Parodic Novel', in *Ariel. A Review of International English Literature*, 22 (1991), 111–29 and *Unsex'd Revolutionaries. Five Women Novelists of the 1790s* (Toronto: University of Toronto Press, 1993), pp. 13–30.

43 NLS MS.585, ff.48–49, Letter from Elizabeth Hamilton to George Robinson, 29 November 1803.

44 Peter Garside, 'Introduction' to Elizabeth Hamilton, *Memoirs of Modern Philosophers* (London: Routledge and Thoemmes, 1992), I, xi.

45 De Montluzin, 'Jacobinism and the Reviewers', pp. 24–5. The firm was the natural publisher for the *British Critic*.

46 Dorothy Blakey, *The Minerva Press, 1790–1820* (London: The Bibliographical Society, 1939), p. 13.

47 *Ibid.*, pp. 16–18; and 'Prospectus of the Minerva Library Repository, &c.' in the *Morning Advertiser*, 10 February 1794, p. 1; rpt. in facsimile, 8 February 1894.

48 *British Critic*, 12 (July 1798), 74.

49 Smith, *Marchmont*, IV, 329–30.

50 'Phileleutherus Devoniensis', i.e. Thomas Northmore, *Memoirs of Planetes, or a Sketch of the Laws and Manners of Makar* (London: J. Johnson and J. Owen, 1795), p. 128.

51 Edward Mangin, *George the Third. A Novel* (London: James Carpenter, 1807), I, 147–8 and 148.

52 Smith, *The Banished Man*, II, 231. Compare Smith's *Marchmont*, II, 229.

53 *Monthly Review*, n.s., 9 (December 1792), 406; *Critical Review*, n.s., 6 (September 1792), 100; *European Magazine*, 20 (July 1792), 22–3; *Analytical Review*, 13 (August 1792), 428–35.

54 Roper, *Reviewing Before the 'Edinburgh'*, p. 130. Florence Hilbish, *Charlotte Smith, Poet and Novelist (1749–1806)* (Philadelphia: University of Pennsylvania Press, 1941), p. 147, and Judith Phillips Stanton, 'Introduction' to Charlotte Smith, *The Old Manor House*, ed. Anne Henry Ehrenpreis (Oxford: Oxford University Press, 1989), p. xix.

55 *Monthly Review*, n.s., 16 (February 1795), 135.

56 *British Critic*, 4 (December 1794), 623.

57 *Critical Review*, n.s., 13 (March 1795), 275.

58 *Anti-Jacobin Review* 15 (May 1803), 41, and 19 (December 1804), 424. For earlier examples of this paranoia, the prefaces to each volume of the *British Critic* may be consulted.

59 Roper, *Reviewing Before the 'Edinburgh'*, p. 21.

60 *Analytical Review*, 13 (May 1792), 72.

61 *Critical Review*, n.s., 11 (July 1794), 290, and 23 (June 1798), 234.

62 Roper, *Reviewing Before the 'Edinburgh'*, p. 159.

63 *British Critic*, 3 (March 1794), 279.

64 'Preface' to *British Critic*, 7 (January-June 1796), xviii.
65 *British Critic*, 11 (March 1798), 316.
66 *British Critic*, 12 (November 1798), 543.
67 Bisset, *Douglas*, IV, 31–2.
68 *British Critic*, 4 (July 1794), 71.
69 *British Critic*, 6 (November 1795), 345.
70 *British Critic*, 15 (January 1800), 47–52.
71 See the *British Critic* on Mary Hays and Anne Plumptre for instance: 9 (March 1797), 315 and 11 (May 1798), 563.
72 *British Critic*, 7 (May 1796), 552.
73 *British Critic*, 10 (June 1798), 680.
74 Joseph Wildman, *The Force of Prejudice, A Moral Tale* (London: T. Barfield, 1799), II, 307.
75 *British Critic*, 6 (August 1795), 189.
76 *British Critic*, 9 (March 1797), 317.
77 *British Critic*, 13 (March 1799), 297–302.
78 Mathias, *Pursuits of Literature*, p. 155.
79 *Ibid.*, p. 58n.zz.
80 *Ibid.*, p. 367n.r.
81 *Ibid.*, pp. 246, 239, and 239n.
82 See André Parreaux, *The Publication of 'The Monk.' A Literary Event, 1796–1798* (Paris: Librarie Marcel Didier, 1960).
83 Mathias, *Pursuits of Literature*, p. 366n.
84 George Walker, *The Vagabond, a Novel* (3rd edn., London: G. Walker, 1799), I, iii.
85 George Walker, *Theodore Cyphon; or, the Benevolent Jew* (1796; rpt. London: A. K. Newman, 1823), III, 209n.
86 Butler, *Jane Austen and the War of Ideas*, p. 111.
87 George Daniel, *The Modern Dunciad, A Satire; with Notes, Biographical and Critical* (1814?; 4th edn, corrected and enlarged, London: Effingham Wilson, 1816), pp. 9–10.
88 Elizabeth Ogilvie Benger, *Memoirs of the Late Mrs Elizabeth Hamilton, with a Selection from her Correspondence, and other Unpublished Writing* (London: Longman, 1818), pp. 165 and 165n.
89 Mathias, *Pursuits of Literature*, p. 126. In fact, Elizabeth Hamilton's biographer records a pension granted to her after the publication of her first two novels, 'as an acknowledgement that her literary talents had been meritoriously exerted in the cause of religion and virtue', and she assures us that 'the prime minister paid a complimentary tribute to her talents, which enhanced the value of the gift' (Elizabeth Ogilvie Benger, *Memoirs of the Late Mrs Elizabeth Hamilton*, pp. 165 and n.). Such a pension must have been a powerful contribution to the nexus of factors encouraging anti-Jacobinism in fiction, but this is the only recorded instance I have found of government intervention in the production of novels.

7 CONCLUSION

1 Marilyn Butler, *Jane Austen and the War of Ideas* (1975; rpt. Oxford: Clarendon Press, 1987), p. 88.

2 William Godwin, *Thoughts Occasioned by the Perusal of Dr Parr's Spital Sermon, being a Reply to the Attacks of Dr Parr, Mr Mackintosh, the Author of An Essay on Population, and others* (London, G. G. and J. Robinson, 1801), pp. 21–2.

3 Quoted in Warren Roberts, *Jane Austen and the French Revolution* (London: Macmillan, 1979), p. 5.

4 According to Benger, *Memoirs of Modern Philosophers* (1800) caused one of its readers instantly to abjure the follies and absurdities which she had shared with Bridgetina Botherim. *Memoirs of the Late Mrs Elizabeth Hamilton* (London: Longman, 1818), I, 133.

Select bibliography

1 ANTI-JACOBIN NOVELS AND TALES

Anon., *Dorothea; or, A Ray of the New Light* (3 vols., London: G. G. and J. Robinson, 1801).

Anon., *Massouf, or the Philosophy of the Day. An Eastern Tale* (1 vol., London: Minerva, 1802).

Anon., *Memoirs of M. De Brinboc: Containing Some Views of English and Foreign Society* (3 vols., London: Cadell and Davies, 1805).

Anon., *Berkeley Hall: or, the Pupil of Experience. A Novel* (3 vols., London: J. Tindal, 1796).

Anon., *The Chances; or, Nothing of the New School: A Novel. In Three Volumes. By A Disciple of the Old School* (3 vols., London: Cuthell and Martin, 1803).

Anon., *The Citizen's Daughter; or What Might Be* (1 vol., London: Vernor and Hood, 1804).

Anon., *The History of Sir George Warrington; or, the Political Quixote. By the Author of the Female Quixote* (3 vols., London: J. Bell, 1797).

Anon., *The Siege of Belgrade: An Historical Novel. Translated from a German Manuscript* ('4 vols. in 2', London: H. D. Symonds, 1791).

Bisset, Robert, *Douglas; or, the Highlander. A Novel* (4 vols., London: 'Printed at the Anti-Jacobin Press', 1800).

Modern Literature. A Novel (3 vols., London: T. N. Longman and O. Rees, 1804).

Brydges, Sir Samuel Egerton, *Mary de Clifford. A Story. Interspersed with Many Poems* (1 vol., London: H. Symonds, 1792; rpt. London: Clarke's Home Library, 1845).

Arthur Fitz-Albini, a Novel (2 vols., London: J. White, 1798; rpt. London: J. White, 1799).

Le Forester, A Novel. By the Author of Arthur Fitz-Albini (3 vols., London: J. White, 1802).

Burges, Mary Anne, *The Progress of the Pilgrim Good-Intent, in Jacobinical Times* (1 vol., London: John Hatchard, 1800).

Charlton, Mary, *The Parisian; or, Genuine Anecdotes of Distinguished and Noble Characters* (2 vols., London: Minerva, 1794).

Craik, Helen, *Adelaide de Narbonne, with Memoirs of Charlotte de Cordet. A Tale* (4 vols., London: Minerva, 1800).

Dallas, Robert Charles, *Percival, or Nature Vindicated. A Novel* (4 vols., London: Longman and Rees, 1801).

D'Israeli, Isaac, *Vaurien: or, Sketches of the Times: Exhibiting Views of the Philosophies, Religions, Politics, Literature, and Manners of the Age* (2 vols., London: Cadell and Davies, 1797).

'The Daughter; or, A Modern Romance' in *Romances. Second Edition, Corrected. To which is now added, 'A Modern Romance'* (1 vol., London: Murray and Highley, 2nd edn, 1801).

Flim-Flams! or, The Life and Errors of My Uncle, and the Amours of my Aunt! With Illustrations and Obscurities, by Messieurs Tag, Rag, and Bobtail. With an Illuminating Index (3 vols., London: John Murray, 1805; 2nd edn, London: John Murray, 1806.)

Dubois, Edward, *St Godwin: A Tale of the Sixteenth, Seventeenth, and Eighteenth Century. By Count Reginald De Saint Leon* (1 vol., London: J. Wright, 1800).

Edgeworth, Maria, *Leonora* (2 vols., London, 1806; rpt. 1 vol., ed. Marilyn Butler and Susan Manly, London: Pickering and Chatto, 1999).

'Madame de Fleury', in *Tales of Fashionable Life* (3 vols., London: J. Johnson, 1809), pp. 177–328.

Hamilton, Elizabeth, *Translation of the Letters of a Hindoo Rajah; Written Previous To, and During the Period of his Residence in England* (2 vols., London: G. G. and J. Robinson, 1796; 2nd edn, 2 vols., London: G. G. and J. Robinson, 1801; rpt. 1 vol., eds. Pamela Perkins and Shannon Russell, Peterborough, Ontario: Broadview Press, 1999).

Memoirs of Modern Philosophers (3 vols., London: G. G. and J. Robinson, 1800; rpt. London: Routledge and Thoemmes, 1992; rpt. 1 vol., ed. Claire Grogan, Peterborough, Ontario: Broadview Press, 2000).

Harral, Thomas, *Scenes of Life. A Novel* (3 vols., London: B. Crosby, 1805).

Helme, Elizabeth, *The Farmer of Inglewood Forest, a Novel* (4 vols., London: Minerva, 1796).

King, Sophia, *Waldorf; or, the Dangers of Philosophy. A Philosophical Tale* (2 vols., London: G. G. and J. Robinson, 1798).

The Fatal Secret, or, Unknown Warrior; A Romance of the Twelfth Century, with Legendary Poems (1 vol., London: 'Printed for the author', 1801).

Lloyd, Charles, *Edmund Oliver* (2 vols., Bristol: Joseph Cottle, 1798).

Lucas, Charles, *The Castle of St Donats; or, the History of Jack Smith* (3 vols., London: Minerva, 1798).

The Infernal Quixote. A Tale of the Day (4 vols., London: Minerva, 1801).

Mackenzie, Anna Maria, *Slavery: or, The Times* (2 vols., London: G. G. and J. Robinson, 1792).

Mangin, Edward, *George the Third. A Novel* (3 vols., London: James Carpenter, 1807).

Marriott, Mrs, *The Minstrel; or, Anecdotes of Distinguished Personages in the Fifteenth Century* (3 vols., London: Hookham and Carpenter, 1793).

Moore, John, *Mordaunt. Sketches of Life, Characters, and Manners, in Various Countries; including the Memoirs of a French Lady of Quality* (3 vols., London: G. G. and J. Robinson, 1800).

Murray, Hugh, *The Swiss Emigrants: A Tale* (1 vol., London: T. N. Longman and O. Rees, 1804).

Opie, Amelia, *Adeline Mowbray, or the Mother and Daughter: A Tale* (3 vols., London: Longman, Hurst, Rees and Orme, 1805; rpt. 1 vol., eds. Shelley King and John B. Pierce, Oxford: Oxford University Press, 1999).

Pearson, S[usanna], *The Medallion* (3 vols., London: G. G. and J. Robinson, 1794).

Pye, Henry James, *The Democrat: Interspersed with Anecdotes of Well Known Characters* (2 vols., London: Minerva, 1795; rpt. London: Minerva, 1796).

The Aristocrat, a Novel (2 vols., London: Sampson Low, 1799).

Reeve, Clara, *Memoirs of Sir Roger de Clarendon, the natural son of Edward Prince of Wales, commonly called the Black Prince; with anecdotes of many other eminent persons of the fourteenth century* (3 vols., London: Hookham and Carpenter, 1793).

Robinson, Mary, *Hubert de Sevrac, A Romance, of the Eighteenth Century* (3 vols., London: Hookham and Carpenter, 1796; rpt. 2 vols., Dublin: B. Smith, C. Browne and H. Colbert, 1797).

The Natural Daughter. With Portraits of the Leadenhead Family. A Novel (2 vols., London: T. N. Longman and O. Rees, 1799).

Sayer, Edward, *Lindor and Adelaïde, a Moral Tale. In which are exhibited the Effects of the Late French Revolution on the Peasantry of France . . . By the Author of 'Observations on Doctor Price's Revolution Sermon'* (1 vol., London: John Hockdale, 1791).

Silliman, Benjamin, *Letters of Shahcoolen, a Hindu Philosopher, residing in Philadelphia; to his friend El Hassan, an inhabitant of Delhi* (1 vol., Boston, MA: Russell and Cutler, 1802; rpt. 'Introduction' by Ben Harris McClary, Gainsville, FL: Scholars Facsimiles and Reprints, 1962).

Smith, Charlotte, *The Banished Man. A Novel* (4 vols., London: Cadell and Davies, 1794).

Marchmont: A Novel (4 vols., London: Sampson Low, 1796).

Stanhope, Louisa Sidney, *The Nun of Santa Maria di Tindaro. A Tale* (3 vols., London: Minerva, 1818).

Surr, Thomas Skinner, *George Barnwell. A Novel* (3 vols., London: H. D. Symonds, 1798).

Thomas, Ann, *Adolphus de Biron. A Novel. Founded on the French Revolution* (2 vols., Plymouth: 'Printed by P. Nettleton for the Authoress', n.d. but 1795?).

Walker, George, *The Vagabond, a Novel* (2 vols., London: G. Walker and Lee and Hurst, 1799; rpt. 3rd edn, 'with notes', London: G. Walker, 1799).

Le Vagabond, ou La Rencontre de Deux Philosophes Républicains; Roman Philosophique, Traduit de l'anglais de Georges Walker . . . (1 vol., Paris, Hénée et Dumas, *et al.*, 1807).

Wells, Helena, *Constantia Neville; or, the West Indian. A Novel* (3 vols., London: T. Cadell jun. and W. Davies, 1800; rpt. 2nd edn, London: T. Cadell jun. and W. Davies, 1800).

West, Jane, *A Gossip's Story, and a Legendary Tale. By the Author of Advantages of Education* (2 vols., London: T. N. Longman, 1796; rpt. London: T. N. Longman, 1798).

A Tale of the Times; By the author of A Gossip's Story (3 vols., London: Longman and Rees, 1799).

The Infidel Father; By the author of A Tale of the Times, A Gossip's Story, &c (3 vols., London: Longman and Rees, 1802).

The Loyalists: An Historical Novel. By the author of 'Letters to a Young Man', 'A Tale of the Times', &c. (3 vols., London: Longman, Hurst, Rees, Orme and Brown, 1812).

Wildman, Joseph, *The Force of Prejudice, A Moral Tale* (2 vols., London: T. Barfield, 1799).

Wood, Sarah Sayward Barrell Keating, *Julia, and the Illuminated Baron. A Novel: Founded on Recent Facts, which have transpired in the course of the late Revolution of Moral Principles in France. By a Lady of Massachusetts* (1 vol., Portsmouth, NH: Charles Pierce, 1800).

Wright, T., *Solyman and Fatima; or, the Sceptic Convinced. An Eastern Tale* (2 vols., London: John Bew, 1791).

2 OTHER NOVELS CITED

Anon., *Asmodeus; or, the Devil in London: A Sketch* (3 vols., London: J. F. Hughes, 1808).

Anon., *Flights of Inflatus; or, the Sallies, Stories, and Adventures of a Wild-Goose Philosopher* (2 vols., London: C. Stalker, 1791).

Anon. (Anne Hughes?), *Jemima, a Novel* (2 vols., London: Minerva, 1795).

Anon., *Memoirs of Female Philosophers, in Two Volumes. By a Modern Philosopher of the Other Sex* (2 vols., London: Henry Colburn, 1808).

Anon., *Such Follies Are: A Novel* (2 vols., London: Minerva, 1795).

Anon., *The Bastile. Or the History of Charles Townley, a man of the world* (4 vols., London: Minerva, 1789; rpt. 3 vols., Dublin: George Grierson, 1789).

Anon., *The Brothers; A Novel, for Children. Addressed to Every Good Mother, and Humbly Dedicated to the Queen* (1 vol., Henley: G. Norton, 1794).

Anon., *The Chateau de Myrelle, or Laura. A Novel* (1 vol., London: Hookham, 1791).

Anon., *The Excursion of Osman, the Son of Abdullah, Lord of the Vallies; A Political Romance: Including Some Anecdotes relative to a Great Northern Family* (1 vol., Liverpool, 'Printed by T. Schofield', 1792).

Anon., *The Invasion; or, What Might Have Been* (2 vols., London: H. D. Symonds, 1798).

Anon., *The Irishmen; a Military-Political Novel, wherein the idiom of each character is carefully preserved, & the utmost precaution taken to render the ebullitionary phrases, particular to the sons of Erin, inoffensive as well as entertaining . . . By a Native Officer* (2 vols., London: Minerva, 1810).

Anon., *The Last Man, or Omegarus and Syderia, A Romance in Futurity* (2 vols., London: R. Dutton, 1806).

Anon. (J. H. Pestalozzi?), *Leonard and Gertrude. A Popular Story, Written Originally in German . . . and Now Attempted in English; With the hope of its being useful to the Lower Orders of Society* (1 vol., Bath: S. Hazard, 1800).

Anon., *The Magnanimous Amazon; or Adventures of Theresa, Baroness Van Hoog. With Anecdotes of other Eccentric Persons* (1 vol., London: Vernor and Hood, 1796).

Anon. (John Davis?), *The Post-Captain; or, the Wooden Walls Well Manned; Comprehending a View of Naval Society and Manners. By the Author of 'Edward;' 'A View of Society in France;' &c.* (1 vol., 'third edition', London: Thomas Tegg, 1808).

Anon. (M. Harley?), *Priory of St Bernard; an Old English Tale . . . Being the First Literary Production of a Young Lady* (2 vols., London: Minerva, 1786; rpt. New York: Arno Press, 1977).

Austen, Jane, *Northanger Abbey* (2 vols., London: John Murray, 1818; rpt. 1 vol., ed. Anne Henry Ehrenpreis, Harmondsworth: Penguin, 1985).

Bage, Robert, *Hermsprong; or, Man As He Is Not* (3 vols., London: Minerva, 1796; rpt. 1 vol., ed. Peter Faulkner, Oxford: Oxford University Press, 1985).

Barrett, Eaton Stannard, *The Heroine, or Adventures of a Fair Romance Reader* (3 vols., London: Henry Colburn, 1813; rpt. 1 vol., London: Henry Frowde, 1909, with an introduction by Walter Raleigh).

Barton, James, *The Remorseless Assassin; or the Dangers of Enthusiasm* (2 vols., London: J. F. Hughes, 1803).

Beckford, William ('J. A. M. Jenks'), *Azemia, A Novel: Containing imitations of the manner, both in prose and verse, of many of the authors of the present day; with political strictures* (2 vols., London: Sampson Low, 1797).

Burney, Frances, *The Wanderer; or, Female Difficulties* (5 vols., London: Longman, Hurst, Rees, Orme and Brown, 1814; rpt. 1 vol., eds. Margaret Anne Doody, Robert L. Mack and Peter Sabor, with an introduction by Margaret Anne Doody, Oxford: Oxford University Press, 1991).

Charlton, Mary, *Rosella, or Modern Occurrences* (4 vols., London: Minerva, 1799).

Cole, Rev. William, *The Contradiction* (1 vol., London: T. Cadell and W. Davies, 1796).

Combe, William, *The Devil Upon Two Sticks in England* (6 vols., London: 'printed at the Logographic Press', 1790–1).

Cunningham, John William, *A World Without Souls* (1 vol., London: J. Hatchard, 1805; rpt. 1 vol., London: J. Hatchard, 1806).

Dacre, Charlotte, *Confessions of the Nun of St Omer. A Tale. By Rosa Matilda* (3 vols., London: J. F. Hughes, 1805).

The Passions. By Rosa Matilda (4 vols., London: Cadell and Davies, 1811).

Dallas, Robert Charles, *Aubrey: a Novel* (4 vols., London: T. N. Longman, 1804).

The Miscellaneous Works and Novels of R. C. Dallas, Esq. (7 vols., London: Longman, Hurst, Rees, Orme and Brown, 1813).

Godwin, William, *Caleb Williams* (3 vols., London: B. Crosby, 1794; rpt. 1 vol., ed. Maurice Hindle, Harmondsworth: Penguin, 1988).

St Leon (4 vols., London: G. G. and J. Robinson, 1799; rpt. 1 vol., ed. Pamela Clemit, Oxford: Oxford University Press, 1994).

Graves, Richard, *Plexippus: or, the Aspiring Plebian* (2 vols., London: J. Dodsley, 1790).

Green, Sarah, *The Reformist!!! A Serio-comic political novel* (2 vols., London: Minerva, 1810).

Hamilton, Elizabeth, *Memoirs of the Life of Agrippina, the Wife of Germanicus* (3 vols., Bath and London: G. G. and J. Robinson, 1804).
  The Cottagers of Glenburnie; A Tale for the Farmer's Ingle-nook (1 vol., Edinburgh: Manners, Miller and S. Chapman, 1808).
Imlay, Gilbert, *The Emigrants* (London: A. Hamilton, 1793; rpt. 1 vol., eds. W. M. Verhoeven and Amanda Gilroy, Harmondsworth: Penguin, 1998).
Lamb, Caroline, *Glenarvon* (3 vols., London: Henry Colburn, 1816; rpt. 1 vol., ed. Frances Wilson, London: Everyman, 1995).
Lathom, Francis, *The Midnight Bell* (3 vols., London: H. D. Symonds, 1798; rpt. 1 vol., with an introduction by Lucien Jenkins, London: Skoob Books, 1989).
  Men and Manners. A Novel (4 vols., London: J. Wright, 1799).
Lewis, Alethea, *Plain Sense. A Novel* (3 vols., London: Minerva, 1795; rpt. London: Minerva, 1796).
Lewis, M. G., *The Monk. A Romance* (3 vols., London: J. Bell, 1796; rpt. 1 vol., ed. Howard Anderson, Oxford: Oxford University Press, 1990).
Littlejohn, P. (?), *The Cipher, or The World as it Goes* (3 vols., London: Minerva, 1791).
Lucas, Charles, *Gwelygordd; or, the Child of Sin. A Tale of Welsh Origin* (3 vols., London: Minerva, 1820).
Marshall, Edmund, *Edmund and Eleonora: or Memoirs of the Houses of Summerfield and Gretton* (2 vols., London: John Stockdale, 1797).
Meeke, Mary, *Count St Blancard, or, the Prejudiced Judge, A Novel* (3 vols., London: Minerva, 1795; rpt. 'Introduction' by John Garrett, New York: Arno Press, 1977).
  Midnight Weddings. A Novel (3 vols., London: Minerva, 1802).
  Conscience. A Novel (4 vols., London: A. K. Newman, 1814).
More, Hannah, *Coelebs in Search of a Wife* (2 vols., London: Cadell and Davies, 1809).
Northmore, Thomas ('Phileleutherus Devoniensis'), *Memoirs of Planetes, or a Sketch of the Laws and Manners of Makar* (1 vol., London: J. Johnson and J. Owen, 1795).
Opie, Amelia, *Valentine's Eve* (3 vols., London: Longman, Hurst, Rees, Orme and Brown, 1816).
Palmer, Charlotte, *It Is, and It Is Not. A Novel* (2 vols., London: Hookham and Carpenter, 1792).
Parsons, Eliza, *Woman As She Should Be; or, Memoirs of Mrs Menville. A Novel* (4 vols., London: Minerva, 1793).
  Women As They Are. A Novel (4 vols., London: Minerva, 1796).
Peacock, Thomas Love, *Headlong Hall* (1 vol., London: T. Hookham jun., 1816; rpt. eds. Michael Baron and Michael Slater, Oxford: Oxford University Press, 1987).
  Nightmare Abbey (1 vol., London: T. Hookham, 1818; rpt. ed. Raymond Wright, Harmondsworth: Penguin, 1986).
Pilkington, Mary, *New Tales of the Castle; or, The Noble Emigrants, a Story of Modern Times* (1 vol., London: Vernor and Hood, 1800; rpt. London: J. Harris, 1803).

Porter, Anna Maria, *The Hungarian Brothers* (3 vols., London: Longman, Hurst, Rees and Orme, 1807).

Radcliffe, Mary Anne, *The Female Advocate; or An Attempt to Recover the Rights of Women from Male Usurpation* (1 vol., London: Vernor and Hood, 1799; rpt. 1 vol., ed. Jonathan Wordsworth, Oxford: Woodstock Books, 1994).

Reeve, Clara, *The Old English Baron* (1 vol., London, 1777; rpt. ed. James Trainer, Oxford: Oxford University Press, 1967).

Robinson, Mary, *Walsingham; or, the Pupil of Nature* (4 vols., London: T. N. Longman, 1797).

Roche, Regina Maria, *The Children of the Abbey. A Tale* (4 vols., London: Minerva, 1796).

Sands, James, *Monckton; or, The Fate of Eleanor. A Novel ... To which is prefixed, A General Defence of Modern Novels* (3 vols., London: G. and J. Robinson, 1802).

Mary Martha Sherwood, *The Traditions, a Legendary Tale* (2 vols., London: Minerva, 1795).

Smith, Catharina, *The Misanthrope Father; or, the Guarded Secret* (3 vols., London: Appleyards, 1807).

Smith, Charlotte, *Desmond. A Novel* (3 vols., London: G. G. J. and J. Robinson, 1792).

   The Old Manor House (4 vols., London: J. Bell, 1793; rpt. 1 vol., ed. Anne Henry Ehrenpreis; 'Introduction' by Judith Phillips Stanton, Oxford: Oxford University Press, 1989).

   The Wanderings of Warwick (1 vol., London: J. Bell, 1794).

   The Young Philosopher: A Novel (4 vols., London: T. Cadell jun. and W. Davies, 1798).

Stanhope, Louisa Sidney, *Treachery; or, the Grave of Antoinette. A Romance* (4 vols., London: Minerva, 1815).

Summersett, Henry, *Leopold Warndorf. A Novel* (2 vols., London: Minerva, 1800).

Surr, Thomas Skinner, *A Winter in London; or, Sketches of Fashion* (3 vols., London: Richard Phillips, 1806).

   The Magic of Wealth, an Antibank Novel (3 vols., London: T. Cadell and W. Davies, 1815).

Thelwall, John, *The Daughter of Adoption; A Tale of Modern Times* (4 vols., London: R. Phillips, 1801).

Trimmer, Sarah, *The Servant's Friend. An Exemplary Tale; Designed to Enforce the Religious Instruction Given at Sunday and other Charity Schools ...* (1 vol., London: Longman, Robinson, Johnson, 1787).

Walker, George, *Theodore Cyphon; or, the Benevolent Jew* (3 vols., London: B. Crosby, 1796; rpt. London: A. K. Newman, 1823).

Walpole, Horace, *The Castle of Otranto. A Story* (1 vol., London: Thomas Lownds, 1764; rpt. James Ballantyne and Co., 1811; rpt. ed. W. S. Lewis, Oxford: Oxford University Press, 1969).

William, Helen Maria, *Julia, a Novel. Interspersed with some Poetical Pieces* (2 vols., London: T. Cadell, 1790).

3 MANUSCRIPT SOURCES

British Library
Add. MSS.   37,914
Add. MSS.   42,577
BL Ashley MSS.   As.B.1005

National Library of Scotland
NLS MS.585

4 NEWSPAPERS AND PERIODICALS

Analytical Review; or, History of Literature Domestic and Foreign
Anti-Jacobin Review and Magazine; or, Monthly Political and Literary Censor
British Critic, a New Review
Critical Review; or, Annals of Literature
Edinburgh Review, or Critical Journal
European Magazine and London Magazine
The Family Magazine; or a Repository of Religious Instruction
Gentleman's Magazine
The Lounger
The Microcosm: a Periodical Work
Monthly Review (or Literary Journal)
Morning Advertiser
Morning Herald
New London Review; or Monthly Report of Authors and Books
Olla Podrida: a Periodical Work
Quarterly Review

5 OTHER PRIMARY SOURCES (FIRST PUBLISHED BEFORE 1860)

Anon. (Michael Nash?), *Gideon's Cake of Barley Meal. A Letter to the Rev. William Romaine, on his Preaching for the Emigrant French Clergy; with some Strictures on Mrs Hannah More's Remarks* (London: J. S. Jordan, 1793).

Anon., *A Letter to a Country Parson, or, Reply to the Rev. F. Wollaston's Address* (London: Matthews, n.d.).

Anon., *Liberty and Equality; Treated of in a Short History addressed from a Poor Man to His Equals* (London: 'Printed for the Author, and sold by Hookham and Carpenter', 1792).

Anon., *To the Parliament and People of Great Britain, an explicit declaration of the principles and views of the London Corresponding Society* (London, 1795).

Ashhurst, Justice, *Mr Justice Ashhurst's Charge to the Grand Jury for the County of Middlesex* (London?, 1792).

Barbauld, Anna Lætitia, *The British Novelists: with An Essay; and Prefaces, Biographical and Critical, by Mrs Barbauld* (London: F. C. and J. Rivington, 1810).

Beattie, James, *Dissertations Moral and Critical* (Dublin: Exshaw, Walker, *et al.*, 1783).

Benger, Elizabeth Ogilvie, *Memoirs of the Late Mrs Elizabeth Hamilton, with a Selection from Her Correspondence, and other Unpublished Writing* (2 vols., London: Longman, 1818).

Bowles, John, *A Letter to Samuel Whitbread, Esq. MP in Consequence of the Unqualified Approbation Expressed by Him in the House of Commons of Mr Lancaster's System of Education . . .* (London: Hatchard, 1807).

Brydges, Sir Samuel Egerton, *Autobiography, Times, Opinions, and Contemporaries of Sir Samuel Egerton Brydges* (London: Cochrane and M. Crone, 1834).

Burke, Edmund, *An Appeal from the New to the Old Whigs, in Consequence of Some Late Discussions in Parliament, relative to the 'Reflections on the French Revolution'* (London: J. Dodsley, 1791).

Correspondence of Edmund Burke, ed. Lucy S. Sutherland (Cambridge: Cambridge University Press, 1960).

Reflections on the Revolution in France (1790) in *The Writings and Speeches of Edmund Burke*, vol. VIII, ed. L. G. Mitchell (Oxford: Clarendon Press, 1989), pp. 53–293.

Letter to a Member of the National Assembly (1791) in *The Writings and Speeches of Edmund Burke*, vol. VIII, ed. L. G. Mitchell (Oxford: Clarendon Press, 1989), pp. 294–335.

Letter to a Noble Lord (1796) in *The Writings and Speeches of Edmund Burke*, vol. IX, ed. R. B. McDowell (Oxford: Clarendon Press, 1991), pp. 145–87.

Burney, Frances, *The Journals and Letters of Fanny Burney (Madame D'Arblay)*, ed. Joyce Hemlow *et al.* (12 vols., Oxford: Clarendon Press, 1975).

Cheap Repository for Moral and Religious Publications, *Cheap Repository Tracts. Collected edition for 1795* (London: Marshall and Hazard, n.d.).

Coleridge, Samuel Taylor, *Poetical Works*, ed. Ernest Hartley Coleridge (London: Oxford University Press, 1969).

Dallas, R. C., *Miscellaneous Writings: consisting of Poems; Lucretia, a Tragedy; with a Vocabulary of the Passions* (London: T. N. Longman, 1797).

D'Israeli, Isaac, *Curiosities of Literature* (3rd edn, London: J. Murray, 1793).

Curiosities of Literature (5th edn, 'with large additions and improvements', London: John Murray, 1807–17).

Romances (London: Cadell and Davies, 1799).

Daniel, George, *The Modern Dunciad, A Satire; with Notes, Biographical and Critical* (4th edn, corrected and enlarged, London: Effingham Wilson, 1816).

Ferguson, Adam, *Principles of Moral and Political Science; being chiefly a Retrospect of Lectures delivered in the College of Edinburgh* (2 vols., London and Edinburgh: A. Strahan, T. Cadell and W. Creech, 1792).

Gifford, John, *A Plain Address to the Common Sense of the People of England, Containing an Interesting Abstract of Pain's [sic] Life and Writing* (London: 'printed for the author', 1792).

Godwin, William, *Enquiry Concerning Political Justice and its Influence on Modern Morals and Happiness* (London: G. G. J. and J. Robinson, 1793; rpt. third edn, ed. Isaac Kramnick, Harmondsworth: Penguin, 1985).

Thoughts Occasioned by the Perusal of Dr Parr's Spital Sermon, being a Reply to the Attacks of Dr Parr, Mr Mackintosh, the Author of An Essay on Population, and others (London: G. G. and J. Robinson, 1801).

Hard, Josiah, *Imposture Exposed, in a few Brief Remarks on the Irreligiousness, Profaneness, Indelicacy, Virulence of certain Persons, who style Themselves Anti-Jacobin Reviewers* (Cambridge: J. Deighton, n.d. but 1801?).

Horne, George, *Sunday Schools Recommended in a Sermon Preached at the Parish Church of St Alphage, Canterbury, on Sunday, December the Eighteenth, MDCCLXXXV* (Oxford: Clarendon Press, 1786).

Horsley, Samuel, *The Charges of Samuel Horsley* (Dundee: Chalmers, 1813).

The Speeches in Parliament of Samuel Horsley, Late Lord Bishop of St Asaph (Dundee: Chalmers, 1813).

Howell, T. B., and Howell, Thomas James (eds.). *The Complete Collection of State Trials and Proceedings for High Treason . . .* (London: Longman, 1817).

Knox, Vicissimus, *Essays Moral and Literary* (London: Charles Dilly, 1778–9).

Lackington, James, *Memoirs of the Forty-Five First Years of the Life of James Lackington* (London: 'printed for the author', 1791).

The Confessions of J. Lackington, Late Bookseller, At the Temple of the Muses (London: J. Lackington, 1804).

Lamb, Charles, *Letters of Charles and Mary Lamb*, ed. E. V. Lucas (London: Methuen, 1935).

Mackintosh, Sir James, *Memoirs of the Life of the Right Honourable Sir James Mackintosh*, ed. *Robert James Mackintosh* (London: E. Moxon, 1835).

Mangin, Edward, *An Essay on Light Reading* (London: James Carpenter, 1808).

Mathias, T. J., *The Pursuits of Literature. A Satirical Poem in Four Dialogues. With Notes* (1794–7; 7th edn, London: T. Becket, 1798).

Moore, John, *The Works of John Moore, M.D. with Memoirs of His Life and Writings*, ed. Robert Anderson (7 vols., Edinburgh: Stirling and Slade *et al.*, 1820).

More, Hannah, *The Works of Hannah More* (4 vols., London: Fisher, Fisher and Jackson, 1834).

The Miscellaneous Works of Hannah More (2 vols., London: Thomas Tegg, 1840).

More, Martha, *Mendip Annals: or, a Narrative of the Charitable Labours of Hannah and Martha More in their Neighbourhood. Being the Journal of Martha More*, ed. Arthur Roberts (London: James Nisbet and Co., 1859).

Murray, Hugh, *Morality of Fiction; or, An Inquiry into the Tendency of Fictitious Narratives, with Observations on Some of the Most Eminent* (Edinburgh: A. Constable and Co. and J. Anderson, and London: Longman, Hurst, Rees and Orme, 1805).

Oldys, William (pseud.: George Chalmers?), *Life of Thomas Paine* (London?, n.d., but 1791?).

Paine, Thomas, *Rights of Man* (London: J. S. Jordan, 1791–2; rpt. ed. Henry Collins, Harmondsworth: Penguin, 1982).

Complete Writings of Thomas Paine, ed. P. S. Foner (New York: Citadel Press, 1945).

Pontey, William, *The Rotten Reviewers; or, a Dressing for the Morbid Branches of the Anti-Jacobin and Critical Reviews: Being an Exposition of the Extreme Modesty, Spotless Purity, Mature Judgement, and Strict Impartiality of Certain Writers in these Reviews*... (Huddersfield: T. Smart, n.d., but 1807?).

Reeve, Clara, *The Progress of Romance, Through Times, Countries and Manners, with Remarks on the Good and Bad Effects of It, on them respectively* (Colchester: 'printed for the author', 1785).

Reid, William Hamilton, *The Rise and Dissolution of the Infidel Societies in this Metropolis: Including, The Origin of Modern Deism and Atheism*... (London: J. Hatchard, 1800).

Repton, Humphrey, *Variety: A Collection of Essays* (London: T. Cadell, 1788).

Roberts, William, *Memoirs of Hannah More* (4 vols., London: Seeley and Burnside, 1834).

Robinson, Mary, *Impartial Reflections on the Queen of France* (London: John Bell, 1791).

    Perdita. The Memoirs of Mary Robinson (4 vols., London: G. Lister, 1801; rpt. 1 vol., ed. M. J. Levy, London: Peter Owen, 1994).

    The Poetical Works of the Late Mrs Robinson (3 vols., London: R. Phillips, 1806).

Search, Sappho (pseud.: Rev. John Black?), *A Poetical Review of Miss Hannah More's Strictures on Female Education: in a series of anapestic epistles* (London: T. Hurst, 1800).

Sheridan, R. B., *Sheridan's Plays*, ed. Cecil Price (Oxford: Oxford University Press, 1975).

Smith, Adam, *An Inquiry into the Nature of the Wealth of Nations* (2 vols., London: W. Strahan and T. Cadell, 1776; rpt. ed. Edwin Cannan, London: Methuen, 1920).

Smith, Charlotte, *Rural Walks: in Dialogues. Intended for the Use of Young Persons* (2 vols., London: Cadell and Davies, 1795).

    What is She? A Comedy, in five acts (1799; rpt. London: T. N. Longman and O. Rees, 1800).

Society of Clergymen in Dumfries-shire, *The Scotch Cheap Repository Tracts: containing Moral Tales for the Instruction of the Young* (Edinburgh: Oliphant, Waugh and Innes, 1815).

Spence, Thomas, *The Political Works of Thomas Spence*, ed. H. T. Dickinson (Newcastle upon Tyne: Avero, 1982).

Spencer, Edward, *Truths Respecting Mrs Hannah More's Meeting House, and the Conduct of Her Followers; Addressed to the Curate of Blagdon* (Bath, 1802).

Stone, Francis, *An Examination of the Right Hon. Edmund Burke's Reflections on the Revolution in France* (London: Robinson, Johnson, et al., 1792).

Tatham, Edward, *Letters to the Right Honourable Edmund Burke on Politics* (Oxford: J. Fletcher, D. Prince and J. Cooke, and London: J. F. and C. Rivington and W. Richardson, 1791).

Thelwall, John, *Rights of Nature* (London: H. D. Symonds, 1796).

Trimmer, Sarah, *The Oeconomy of Charity; or, an Address to Ladies; Adapted to the Present State of Charitable Institutions in England: with a Particular View to Cultivation of*

Religious Principles, Among the Lower Orders of People (2 vols., London: J. Johnson, F. and C. Rivington, and W. Richardson, 1801).

Instructive Tales (London: F. C. and J. Rivington, 1810).

'Unus Solus', *A Letter, Addressed to the Rev. R. Polwhele, Vicar of Manaccan. To which is subjoined An Appendix, containing Miscellaneous Remarks, on the Ignorance, Arrogance, and Scurrility of the Anti-Jacobin Reviewers* (Bristol: W. Bulgin, 1800).

West, Jane, *Letters Addressed to a Young Man* (London: T. N. Longman and O. Ress, 1801).

Wollaston, Francis, *The Origin and Insidious Arts of Jacobinism: A Warning to the People of England . . .* (London: G. Wilkie, D. Bremner and J. Hatchard, 1799).

A country Parson's Address to his Flock, to Caution them against being misled by a Wolf in Sheep's Clothing, or receiving Jacobin Teachers of Sedition, who intrude themselves under the Specious Pretence of Instructing Youth and Preaching Christianity (London: G. Wilkie, D. Bremner and J. Hatchard, 1799).

Wyvill, Christopher (ed.), *Political Papers, chiefly respecting the Attempt of the County of York, and other Considerable Districts . . . to effect the Reformation of the Parliament of Great Britain* (4 vols., York and London: J. Todd and J. Johnson, 1794).

6 SECONDARY SOURCES (PUBLISHED AFTER 1860)

Adams, M. Ray, *Studies in the Literary Backgrounds of English Radicalism* (Lancaster, PA: Franklin and Marshall College, 1947).

Aers, David, Cook, Jonathan and Punter, David, *Romanticism and Ideology. Studies in English Writing 1765–1830* (London: Routledge and Kegan Paul, 1981).

Allen, B. Sprague, 'The Reaction Against William Godwin', *Modern Philology*, 16 (1918), 225–43.

'William Godwin's Influence upon John Thelwall', *Publications of the Modern Language Association of America*, 37 (1922), 622–82.

Altick, Richard D., *The English Common Reader. A Social History of the Mass Reading Public 1800–1900* (Chicago: University of Chicago Press, 1957).

Armstrong, Nancy, *Desire and Domestic Fiction: A Political History of the Novel* (New York; Oxford University Press, 1987).

Atherton, Herbert M., 'The British Defend their Constitution in Political Cartoons and Literature' in Harry C. Payne (ed.), *Studies in Eighteenth-Century Culture* (Madison, WI: 1982), II, 3–31.

Baker, Ernest, *The Novel of Sentiment and the Gothic Romance* (London: H. F. and G. Witherby, 1934), vol. V of *The History of the English Novel*.

Bartolomeo, Joseph F., 'Subversion of Romance in *The Old Manor House*', *Studies in English Literature 1500–1900*, 33 (1993), 645–57.

Bellanger, Terry, 'Publishers and Writers in Eighteenth-Century England' in Isabel Rivers (ed.), *Books and Their Readers in Eighteenth-Century England* (Leicester: Leicester University Press, 1982), pp. 5–25.

Bender, John, *Imagining the Penitentiary: Fiction and the Architecture of the Mind in Eighteenth-Century England* (Chicago: University of Chicago Press, 1987).

Birley, Robert, *The English Jacobins from 1789–1802* (London: Oxford University Press, 1924).

Black, Eugene Charlton, *The Association – British Extraparliamentary Political Organization, 1769–1793* (Cambridge, MA: Harvard University Press, 1963).

Blakey, Dorothy, *The Minerva Press, 1790–1820* (London: The Bibliographical Society, 1939).

Booth, Alan, 'Popular Loyalism and Public Violence in the North-West of England 1790–1800', *Social History*, 8 (1983), 295–313.

Botting, Fred, 'Reflections of Excess; *Frankenstein*, the French Revolution and Monstrosity' in Alison Yarrington and Kelvin Everest (eds.), *Reflections of Revolution. Images of Romanticism* (London: Routledge, 1993), pp. 26–38.

Boulton, J. T., *The Language of Politics in the Age of Wilkes and Burke* (London: Routledge and Kegan Paul, 1963).

Bowstead, Diana, 'Charlotte Smith's *Desmond*. The Epistolary Novel as Ideological Argument' in Mary Anne Schofield and Cecilia Macheski (eds.), *Fetter'd or Free? British Women Novelists, 1670–1815* (Athens: Ohio University Press, 1986), pp. 237–63.

Brailsford, H. N., *Shelley, Godwin and Their Circle* (1913; rpt. London: Oxford University Press, 1951).

Brierley, Ben, *Home Memories and Recollections of Life* (London: Marshall and Co., 1886).

Bronowski, Jacob, *William Blake and the Age of Revolution* (1944 as *A Man Without a Mask*; rpt. London: Routledge and Kegan Paul, 1972).

Brown, Ford K., *The Life of William Godwin* (London: J. M. Dent and Sons, 1926).

Brown, Philip Anthony, *The French Revolution in English History* (1918; rpt. London: Frank Cass and Co., 1965).

Butler, Marilyn, *Maria Edgeworth: A Literary Biography* (Oxford: Clarendon Press, 1972).

  Peacock Displayed: A Satirist in His Context (London: Routledge and Kegan Paul, 1979).

  Romantics, Rebels and Reactionaries. English Literature and its Background 1760–1830 (Oxford: Oxford University Press, 1981).

  Jane Austen and the War of Ideas (1975; rpt. Oxford: Clarendon Press, 1987).

  'General Introduction' to *The Novels and Selected Works of Maria Edgeworth*, eds. Jane Desmarais, Tim McLoughlin and Marilyn Butler, in vol. 1 (London: Pickering and Chatto, 1999).

Butler, Marilyn (ed.), *Burke, Paine, Godwin and the Revolution Controversy* (Cambridge: Cambridge University Press, 1984).

Byatt, A. S., *Wordsworth, Coleridge and Their Time* (London: Thomas Nelson and Sons, 1970).

Campbell, Clarissa (ed.), *Wollstonecraft's Daughters. Womanhood in England and France 1780–1920* (Manchester: Manchester University Press, 1996).

Campbell, Ian, 'Glenburnie Revisited' in Joachim Schwend, Susanne Hagemann and Hermann Völkel (eds.), *Literatur im Kontext – Literature in*

Context. Festschrift für Horst W. Drescher (Frankfurt am Main: P. Lang, 1992), pp. 71–90.

Carnall, Geoffrey, *Robert Southey and His Age. The Development of a Conservative Mind* (Oxford: Clarendon Press, 1960).

Christie, Ian R., *Stress and Stability in Late Eighteenth-Century Britain* (Oxford: Clarendon Press, 1984).

Claeys, Gregory, 'The French Revolution Debate and British Political Thought', *History of Political Thought*, 11 (1990), 59–80.

Clark, Anna, 'The Politics of Seduction in English Popular Culture, 1748–1848' in Jean Radford (ed.), *The Progress of Romance. The Politics of Popular Fiction* (London: Routledge and Kegan Paul, 1986), pp. 47–70.

Clark, J. C. D., *English Society 1688–1832. Ideology, Social Structure and Political Practice during the ancien régime* (Cambridge: Cambridge University Press, 1985).

Clery, E. J., *The Rise of Supernatural Fiction, 1762–1800* (Cambridge: Cambridge University Press, 1995).

Clive, John, *Scotch Reviewers: the 'Edinburgh Review', 1802–1815* (London: Faber and Faber, 1957).

Cobban, A. B. (ed.), *The Debate on the French Revolution* (London: Nicholas Kaye, 1950).

Cole, Lucinda, '(Anti)Feminist Sympathies: The Politics of Relationship in Smith, Wollstonecraft, and More', *ELH*, 58 (1991), 107–40.

Colley, Linda, *Britons. Forging the Nation 1707–1837* (1992; rpt. London: Pimlico, 1994).

Cone, Carl B., *The English Jacobins* (New York: Charles Scribner's Sons, 1968).

Cornwell, J., *Coleridge, Poet and Revolutionary, 1772–1804. A Critical Biography* (London: Allen Lane, 1973).

Crawford, Thomas, *Boswell, Burns and the French Revolution* (Edinburgh: Saltire Society, 1990).

Cross, Nigel, *The Common Writer. Life in Nineteenth-Century Grub Street* (Cambridge: Cambridge University Press, 1985).

Cutting, Rose-Marie, 'A Wreath for Fanny Burney's Last Novel: *The Wanderer*'s Contribution to Women's Studies', *Illinois Quarterly*, 37 (1975), 45–64.

Davidoff, Leonore and Hall, Catherine, *Family Fortunes: Men and Women of the English Middle Class, 1780–1850* (London: Hutchinson, 1987).

De Montluzin, Emily Lorraine, *The Anti-Jacobins, 1798–1800. The Early Contributors to the 'Anti-Jacobin Review'* (Basingstoke: Macmillan, 1988).

Dickinson, H. T., *Liberty and Property. Political Ideology in Eighteenth-Century Britain* (1977; rpt. London: Methuen, 1979).

British Radicalism and the French Revolution 1789–1815 (Oxford: Blackwell, 1985).

'Popular Conservatism and Militant Loyalism 1789–1815' in Dickinson (ed.), *Britain and the French Revolution 1789–1815* (Basingstoke: Macmillan, 1989), pp. 104–25.

'Popular Loyalism in Britain in the 1790s' in Eckhart Hellmuth (ed.), *The Transformation of Political Culture. England and Germany in the Later Eighteenth Century* (Oxford: Oxford University Press, 1990), pp. 503–33.

The Politics of the People in Eighteenth-Century Britain (Basingstoke: Macmillan, 1995).

Dickinson, H. T. (ed.), *Britain and the French Revolution 1789–1815* (Basingstoke: Macmillan, 1989).

Dinwiddy, John, 'Interpretations of Anti-Jacobinism' in Mark Philp (ed.), *The French Revolution and British Popular Politics* (Cambridge: Cambridge University Press, 1991), pp. 38–49.

Donoghue, Frank, *The Fame Machine. Book Reviewing and Eighteenth-Century Literary Careers* (Stanford, CA: Stanford University Press, 1996).

Doody, Margaret Anne, *Frances Burney. The Life in the Works* (New Brunswick, NJ: Rutgers University Press, 1988).

Dozier, Robert R., *For King, Constitution, and Country: The English Loyalists and the French Revolution* (Lexington: University Press of Kentucky, 1983).

Duffy, Edward, *Rousseau in England. The Context for Shelley's Critique of the Enlightenment* (Berkeley: University of California Press, 1979).

Durant, David, 'Ann Radcliffe and the Conservative Gothic', *Studies in English Literature 1500–1900*, 22 (1982), 519–30.

Eagleton, Terry, 'Aesthetics and Politics in Edmund Burke', *History Workshop*, 28 (1989), 53–62.

Eastwood, David, 'Patriotism and the English State in the 1790s' in Mark Philp (ed.), *The French Revolution and British Popular Politics* (Cambridge: Cambridge University Press, 1991), pp. 146–68.

'Robert Southey and the Meanings of Patriotism', *Journal of British Studies*, 31 (1992), 265–87.

Emsley, Clive, 'The Impact of the French Revolution on British Politics and Society' in Ceri Crossley and Ian Small (eds.), *The French Revolution and British Culture* (Oxford: Oxford University Press, 1989), pp. 31–62.

Espinasse, Francis, 'Histories of Publishing Houses – No. II: The House of Longman', *The Critic*, 20 (1860), 366–86.

Everest, Kelvin (ed.), *Revolution in Writing. British Literary Responses to the French Revolution* (Milton Keynes: Open University Press, 1991).

Fergus, Jan and Thaddeus, Janice Farrar, 'Women, Publishers and Money, 1790–1820', *Studies in Eighteenth-Century Culture*, 17 (1987), 191–207.

Fischer, David Hackett, *Historians' Fallacies: Towards a Logic of Historical Thought* (New York: Harper and Row, 1970).

Fletcher, Loraine, *Charlotte Smith. A Critical Biography* (Basingstoke: Macmillan, 1998).

Foster, James R., 'Charlotte Smith, Pre-Romantic Novelist', *Publications of the Modern Language Association*, 43 (1928), 463–75.

Freeman, Michael, *Edmund Burke and the Critique of Political Radicalism* (Oxford: Blackwell, 1980).

Friedman, Barton R., *Fabricating History. English Writers on the French Revolution* (Princeton, NJ: Princeton University Press, 1988).

Fry, Carroll Lee, *Charlotte Smith* (New York: Twayne, 1996).

Gallaway, W. F., Jnr., 'The Conservative Attitude Toward Fiction, 1770–1830', *Publications of the Modern Language Association*, 55 (1940), 1041–59.

Gilmore, William J., *Reading Becomes a Necessity of Life. Material and Cultural Life in Rural New England, 1780–1835* (Knoxville: University of Tennessee Press, 1989).

Ginter, Donald E., 'The Loyalist Association Movement of 1792–93 and British Public Opinion', *Historical Journal*, 9 (1966), 179–90.

Goodwin, Albert, *The Friends of Liberty: The English Democratic Movement in the Age of the French Revolution* (London: Hutchinson, 1979).

Graham, Walter, *English Literary Periodicals* (New York: T. Nelson and Sons, 1930).

Gregory, Allene, *The French Revolution and the English Novel* (New York: G. P. Putnam's Sons, 1915).

Grenby, M. O., 'The Anti-Jacobin Novel: British Fiction, British Conservatism and the Revolution in France', *History: the Journal of the Historical Association*, 83 (July 1998), 445–71.

Grylls, R. G., *William Godwin and His World* (London: Odhams Press, 1953).

Gunn, J. A. W., *Beyond Liberty and Property. The Process of Self Recognition in Eighteenth-Century Political Thought* (Kingston, Ontario: McGill-Queen's University Press, 1983).

Hahn, H. George and Behm, Carl, *The Eighteenth-Century British Novel and its Backgrounds: an Annotated Bibliography and Guide to Topics* (Metuchen, NJ: Scarecrow, 1985).

Hall, K. G., *The Exalted Heroine and the Triumph of Order. Class, Women and Religion in the English Novel 1740–1800* (Basingstoke: Macmillan, 1993).

Harden, O. Elizabeth McWhorter, *Miss Edgeworth's Art of Prose Fiction* (The Hague: Mouton, 1971).

Harvey, A. D., *English Poetry in a Changing Society 1780–1825* (London: Allison and Busby, 1980).

Harvey, A. D., 'George Walker and the Anti-Revolutionary Novel', *Review of English Studies*, n.s., 28 (1977), 290–300.

Heidler, Joseph Bunn, *The History, From 1700 to 1800, of English Criticism of Prose Fiction*, University of Illinois Studies in Language and Literature, 13 (Urbana: University of Illinois Press, 1928).

Hilbish, Florence, *Charlotte Smith, Poet and Novelist (1749–1806)* (Philadelphia: University of Pennsylvania Press, 1941).

Hole, Robert, 'British Counter-revolutionary Popular Propaganda in the 1790s' in Colin Jones (ed.), *Britain and Revolutionary France: Conflict, Subversion and Propaganda* (Exeter: University of Exeter Press, 1983), pp. 53–68.

Pulpits, Politics and Public Order in England 1760–1832 (Cambridge: Cambridge University Press, 1989).

Hone, J. Anne, *For the Cause of Truth: Radicalism in London 1796–1821* (Oxford: Clarendon Press, 1982).

Houston, R. A., 'Literacy, Education and the Culture of Print in Enlightenment Edinburgh', *History*, 78 (1993), 373–92.

Literacy in Early Modern Europe (London: Longman, 1988).

Huffman, Charles Herbert, *The Eighteenth-Century Novel in Theory and Practice* (Dayton, VA: Ruebush-Kieffer, 1920).

Hunter, J. Paul, *Before Novels. The Cultural Contexts of Eighteenth-Century English Fiction* (New York: Norton, 1990).

Innes, Joanna, 'Politics and Morals. The Reformation of Manners Movement in Later Eighteenth-Century England' in Eckhart Hellmuth (ed.), *The Transformation of Political Culture. England and Germany in the Later Eighteenth Century* (Oxford: Oxford University Press, 1990), pp. 57–118.

Jacobs, Edward, 'Anonymous Signatures: Circulating Libraries, Conventionality, and the Production of Gothic Romances', *ELH*, 62 (1995), 603–29.

James, Louis (ed.), *English Popular Literature 1819–1851* (New York, Columbia University Press, 1976).

Jauss, Hans Robert, *Towards an Aesthetic of Reception*, trans. Timothy Bahti (Brighton: Harvester, 1982).

Jewson, C. B., *The Jacobin City. A Portrait of Norwich in its Reaction to the French Revolution 1788–1802* (Glasgow: Blackie, 1975).

Johnson, Claudia L., *Jane Austen: Women, Politics and the Novel* (Chicago: University of Chicago Press, 1988).

Jones, Ann H., *Ideas and Innovations. Best-Sellers of Jane Austen's Age* (New York: AMS Press, 1986).

Jones, Chris, *Radical Sensibility. Literature and Ideas in the 1790s* (London: Routledge, 1993).

Jones, M. G., *The Charity School Movement* (Cambridge: Cambridge University Press, 1938).

Hannah More (Cambridge: Cambridge University Press, 1952).

Kaufman, Paul, *Libraries and Their Users* (London: Library Association, 1969).

Kelly, Gary, *The English Jacobin Novel 1780–1805* (Oxford: Clarendon Press, 1976).

'Jane Austen and the English Novel of the 1790s' in Mary Anne Schofield and Cecilia Macheski (eds.), *Fetter'd or Free? British Women Novelists, 1670–1815* (Athens: Ohio University Press, 1986), pp. 285–306.

English Fiction of the Romantic Period (London: Longman, 1989).

'Enlightenment and Revolution: The Philosophical Novels of Dr John Moore', *Eighteenth-Century Fiction*, 1 (1989), 219–37.

Women, Writing and Revolution 1790–1827 (Oxford: Oxford University Press, 1993).

Kiernan, V., 'Evangelicalism and the French Revolution', *Past and Present*, 1 (1952), 44–56.

Klancher, Jon P., *The Making of English Reading Audiences 1790–1832* (Madison: University of Wisconsin Press, 1987).

Korshin, Paul (ed.), *The Widening Circle. Essays on the Circulation of Literature in Eighteenth-Century Europe* (Philadelphia: University Of Pennsylvania Press, 1976).

Landon, Richard G., 'Small Profits do Great Things: James Lackington and Eighteenth-Century Bookselling', *Studies in Eighteenth-Century Culture*, 5 (1976), 387–99.

Laqueur, Thomas Walter, *Religion and Respectability. Sunday Schools and Working Class Culture. 1780–1850* (New Haven, CT: Yale University Press, 1976).

Lloyd, Pamela, 'Jane West', *Notes and Queries*, 229 (1984), 469–71.

Locke, Don, *A Fantasy of Reason. The Life and Thought of William Godwin* (London: Routledge and Kegan Paul, 1980).

Lodge, David, 'The French Revolution and the Condition of England: Crowds and Power in the Early Victorian Novel' in Ceri Crossley and Ian Small (eds.), *The French Revolution and British Culture* (Oxford: Oxford University Press, 1989), pp. 123–40.

MacCarthy, B. G., *The Female Pen. Women Writers and Novelists 1621–1818* (1944–7; rpt. Cork: Cork University Press, 1994).

Mackee, William, *Elizabeth Inchbald, Novelist* (Washington, DC: Catholic University Press of Amercia, 1935).

MacMullen, Hugh H., 'The Satire of Walker's *Vagabond* on Rousseau and Godwin', *Publications of the Modern Language Association of America*, 52 (March 1937), 215–29.

Marshall, Peter H., *William Godwin* (New Haven, CT: Yale University Press, 1984).

Maxted, Ian, *The London Book Trade 175–1800, a Preliminary Checklist of Members* (Folkestone: Dawson, 1977).

McCalman, Iain, *Radical Underworld. Prophets, Revolutionaries and Pornographers in London, 1795–1840* (Cambridge: Cambridge University Press, 1988).

McCracken, David, 'Godwin's Literary Theory: The Alliance Between Fiction and Political Philosophy', *Philological Quarterly*, 49 (1970), 113–33.

'Godwin's Reading in Burke', *English Language Notes*, 7 (1970), 264–70.

McKillop, Alan Dugald, 'Charlotte Smith's Letters', *The Huntingdon Library Quarterly*, 15 (1952), 237–55.

Mitchell, Austin, 'The Association Movement of 1792–93', *Historical Journal*, 4 (1961), 56–77.

Money, John, 'Freemasonry and the Fabric of Loyalism in Hanoverian England' in Eckhart Hellmuth (ed.), *The Transformation of Political Culture. England and Germany in the Later Eighteenth Century* (Oxford: Oxford University Press, 1990), pp. 235–71.

Moore, Catherine E., "Ladies... Taking the Pen in Hand". Mrs Barbauld's Criticism of Eighteenth-Century Women Novelists' in Mary Anne Schofield and Cecilia Macheski (eds.), *Fetter'd or Free? British Women Novelists, 1670–1815* (Athens: Ohio University Press, 1986).

Myers, Mitzi, 'Hannah More's Tracts for the Times: Social Fiction and Female Ideology', in Mary Anne Schofield and Cecilia Macheski (eds.), *Fetter'd or Free? British Women Novelists, 1670–1815* (Athens: Ohio University Press, 1986), pp. 264–84.

'Reform or Ruin: A Revolution in Female Manners', *Studies in Eighteenth-Century Culture*, 11 (1982), 199–216.

Neuburg, Victor E. (ed.), *Literacy and Society* (London: Woburn Press, 1971).

Popular Literature. A History and Guide (London: Woburn Press, 1977).

Newman, Gerald, 'Anti-French Propaganda and British Liberal Nationalism in the Early Nineteenth Century: Suggestions Toward a General Interpretation', *Victorian Studies*, 18 (1975), 385–418.

The Rise of English Nationalism. A Cultural History 1740–1830 (London: Weidenfield and Nicolson, 1987).

Ogden, James, *Isaac D'Israeli* (Oxford, Clarendon Press, 1969).

Orians, G. Harrison, 'Censure of Fiction in American Romances and Magazines, 1789–1810', *Publications of the Modern Language Association*, 52 (1937), 195–214.

Orr, Leonard, *A Catalogue Checklist of English Prose Fiction, 1750–1800* (Troy, NY: Whitson Publishing Co., 1979).

Parreaux, André, *The Publication of 'The Monk.' A Literary Event, 1796–1798* (Paris: Librairie Marcel Didier, 1960).

Paulson, Ronald, *Representations of Revolution (1789–1820)* (New Haven, CT: Yale University Press, 1983).

Pederson, Susan, 'Hannah More Meets Simple Simon: Tracts, Chapbooks, and Popular Culture in Late Eighteenth-Century England', *Journal of British Studies*, 25 (1986), 84–113.

Phillips, Judith Stanton, 'Charlotte Smith's "Literary Business": Income, Patronage and Indigence', *The Age of Johnson: A Scholarly Annual*, 1 (1987), 375–405.

Phillipson, Nicholas and Skinner, Quentin (eds.), *Political Discourse in Early Modern Britain* (Cambridge: Cambridge University Press, 1993).

Philp, Mark (ed.), *The French Revolution and British Popular Politics* (Cambridge: Cambridge University Press, 1991).

'Vulgar Conservatism, 1792–93', *English Historical Review*, 110 (1995), 42–69.

Pickering, Samuel, Jnr, 'The Cheap Repository Tracts and the Short Story', *Studies in Short Fiction*, 12 (1975), 15–21.

The Moral Tradition in English Fiction 1785–1850 (Hanover, NH: University Press of New England, 1976).

Pollard, Graham, 'The English Market for Printed Books: *The Sanders Lectures, 1959*', *Publishing History*, 4 (1978), pp. 7–48.

Pollin, Burton R., 'Charles Lamb and Charles Lloyd as Jacobins and Anti-Jacobins', *Studies in Romanticism*, 11 (1973), 633–47.

Poovey, Mary, *The Proper Lady and the Woman Writer. Ideology as Style in the Works of Mary Wollstonecraft, Mary Shelley, and Jane Austen* (Chicago: University of Chicago Press, 1984).

Pratt, John H. (ed.), *Eclectic Notes; or, Notes of Discussions on Religious Topics at the Meetings of The Eclectic Society, London, During the Years 1798–1814* (London, 1865).

Prickett, Stephen, *England and the French Revolution* (Basingstoke: Macmillan 1989).

Quennell, P., *Byron: A Self-Portrait in Letters and Diaries* (London: John Murray, 1950).

Quinlan, Maurice J., *Victorian Prelude. A History of English Manners 1700–1800*, Columbia University Studies in English and Comparative Literature, no. 155 (New York: Columbia University Press, 1941).

Raven, James, *British Fiction, 1750–1770: a Chronological Checklist of Prose Fiction Printed in Britain and Ireland, 1750–1770* (Newark University of Delaware Press, 1987).

Judging New Wealth. Popular Publishing and Responses to Commerce in England, 1750–1800 (Oxford, Clarendon Press, 1992).

'Selling One's Life: James Lackington, Eighteenth-Century Booksellers, and the Design of Autobiography' in O. M. Brack Jnr (ed.), *Writers, Books, and Trade. An Eighteenth-Century Miscellany for William B. Todd* (New York: AMS, 1994), pp. 1–24.

Rendall, Jane, 'Writing History for British Women: Elizabeth Hamilton and the *Memoirs of Agrippina*' in Clarissa Campbell (ed.), *Wollstonecraft's Daughters. Womanhood in England and France 1780–1920* (Manchester: Manchester University Press, 1996), pp. 79–93.

Renwick, W. L., *English Literature, 1789–1815. The Rise of the Romantics 1789–1815. Wordsworth, Coleridge and Jane Austen* (Oxford: Clarendon Press, 1963), vol. XI of *The Oxford History of English Literature*.

Rigby, Brian, 'The French Revolution and English Literary Radicals: the Case of the *Analytical Review*' in H. T. Mason and W. Doyle (eds.), *The Impact of the French Revolution on European Consciousness* (Gloucester: Sutton 1989), pp. 91–103.

Rivers, Isabel (ed.), *Books and Their Readers in Eighteenth-Century England* (Leicester: Leicester University Press, 1982).

Roberts, J. M., *The Mythology of Secret Societies* (London: Secker and Warburg, 1972).

Roberts, M. J. D., 'The Society For the Suppression of Vice and Its Early Critics, 1802–1812', *The Historical Journal*, 26 (1983), 159–176.

Roberts, Marie, *Gothic Immortals. The Fiction of the Brotherhood of the Rosy Cross* (London: Routledge, 1990).

Roberts, Warren, *Jane Austen and the French Revolution* (London: Macmillan, 1979).

Roe, N., *Wordsworth and Coleridge, the Radical Years* (Oxford: Clarendon Press, 1988).

Rogers, Katharine M., *Feminism in Eighteenth-Century England* (Brighton: Harvester, 1982).

'Fanny Burney: The Private Self and the Public Self', *International Journal of Women's Studies*, 7 (1984), 110–17.

Roper, Derek, *Reviewing Before the 'Edinburgh' 1788–1802* (London: Methuen, 1978).

Rosa, M. W., *The Silver Fork School: Novels of Fashion Preceding 'Vanity Fair'*, Columbia University Studies in English and Comparative Literature, no. 123 (New York: Columbia University Press, 1936).

Royle, Edward and Walvin, James, *English Radicals and Reformers 1760–1848* (Brighton: Harvester, 1982).

Sack, J. J., *From Jacobite to Conservative: Reaction and Orthodoxy in Britain, c. 1760–1830* (Cambridge: Cambridge University Press, 1993).

Sales, Roger, *English Literature in History 1780–1830: Pastoral and Politics* (London: Hutchinson, 1983).

Sanders, Andrew, ' "The French are Always at it" – the Impact of the French Revolution on Nineteenth-Century English Literature, 1815–1870' in H. T. Mason and W. Doyle (eds.), *The Impact of the French Revolution on European Consciousness* (Gloucester: Sutton, 1989), pp. 104–16.

Sanderson, Michael, *Education, Economic Change and Society in England 1780–1870* (Basingstoke: Macmillan, 1991).

Schilling, Bernard, *Conservative England and the Case Against Voltaire* (New York: Columbia University Press, 1950).

Schofield, Mary Anne, and Macheski, Cecilia (eds.), *Fetter'd or Free? British Women Novelists, 1670–1815* (Athens: Ohio University Press, 1986).

Schofield, R. S., 'The Measurement of Literacy in Pre-Industrial England' in Jack Goody (ed.), *Literacy in Traditional Societies* (Cambridge: Cambridge University Press, 1968), pp. 310–25.

Schofield, Thomas Philip, 'Conservative Political Thought in Britain in Response to the French Revolution', *Historical Journal*, 29 (1986), 601–22.

Schnorrenberg, Barbara B., with Hunter, Jane E., 'The Eighteenth-Century Englishwoman' in Barbara Kanner (ed.), *The Women of England. From Anglo-Saxon Times to the Present* (London: Mansell Information Publishing, 1980), pp. 183–228.

Scott, Iain Robertson, "Things As They Are": the Literary Response to the French Revolution 1789–1815' in H. T. Dickinson (ed.), *Britain and the French Revolution 1789–1815* (Basingstoke, Macmillan, 1989), pp. 229–49.

Shattock, Joanne, *Politics and Reviewers: The 'Edinburgh' and the 'Quarterly' in the Early Victorian Age* (Leicester: Leicester University Press, 1989).

Shepperson, Archibald, 'Gothic Nonsense' in Thomas Meade Harwell (ed.), *The English Gothic Novel: A Miscellany in Four Volumes, Salzburg Studies in English Literature: Romantic Reassessment,* ed. James Hogg (Salzburg: Salzburg University Press, 1986), I, 237–51.

Smith, Olivia, *The Politics of Language 1791–1819* (Oxford: Clarendon Press, 1984).

Soloway, R. A., *Prelates and People. Ecclesiastical Social Thought in England 1783–1852* (London: Routledge and Kegan Paul, 1969).

Spender, Dale, *Mothers of the Novel. 100 Good Women Writers Before Jane Austen* (London: Pandora Press, 1986).

Spinney, G. H., 'Cheap Repository Tracts: Hazard and Marshall Edition', *The Library*, 4th ser., 20 (1939), 295–340.

Spring, David, 'The Clapham Sect: Some Social and Political Aspects', *Victorian Studies*, 5 (1961), 35–48.

Stephens, F. G. and George, M. D., *Catalogue of Political and Personal Satires Preserved in the Department of Prints and Drawings in the British Museum* (11 vols., London: British Museum, 1870–1954).

Stevenson, John, 'Popular Radicalism and Popular Protest 1789–1815' in H. T. Dickinson (ed.), *Britain and the French Revolution 1789–1815* (Basingstoke, Macmillan, 1989), pp. 61–81.

Stone, Lawrence, 'Literacy and Education in England, 1640–1900', *Past and Present*, 42 (1969), 69–139.

Sutherland, Kathryn, 'Hannah More's Counter-Revolutionary Feminism' in Kelvin Everest (ed.). *Revolution in Writing. British Literary Responses to the French Revolution* (Milton Keynes, Open University Press, 1991), pp. 27–63.

Taylor, John Tinnon, *Early Opposition to the English Novel. The Popular Reaction from 1760 to 1830* (Morningside Heights, NY: King's Crown Press, 1943).

Thomis, M. and Holt, P., *Threats of Revolution in Britain 1789–1848* (London: Macmillan, 1977).

Thompson, E. P., *The Making of the English Working Class* (1963; rpt. Harmondsworth: Penguin, 1980).

'Hunting the Jacobin Fox', *Past and Present*, 142 (1994), 94–140.

Todd, F. M., *Politics and the Poet* (London: Methuen, 1957).

Tompkins, J. M. S., *The Popular Novel in England, 1770–1800* (London: Methuen, 1932).

Tripathi, P. D., *The Doctrinal English Novel (Later Eighteenth Century). Middle Class Consciousness in England During the American and French Revolutions* (Calcutta: Bagchi, 1977).

Ty, Eleanor, 'Female Philosophy Refunctioned: Elizabeth Hamilton's Parodic Novel', *Ariel. A Review of International English Literature*, 22 (1991), 111–29.

Unsex'd Revolutionaries. Five Women Novelists of the 1790s (Toronto: University of Toronto Press, 1993).

Uphaus Robert W., 'Hazlitt, the Novel, and the French Revolution', *Studies in Eighteenth-Century Culture*, 17 (1987), 217–27.

Varma, Devendra P., *The Evergreen Tree of Diabolical Knowledge* (Washington, DC: Consortium Press, 1972).

Vincent, David, 'Reading in the Working-Class Home' in John K. Walton and James Walvin (eds.), *Leisure in Britain 1780–1939* (Manchester: Manchester University Press, 1983), pp. 207–26.

Literacy and Popular Culture. England 1750–1914 (Cambridge: Cambridge University Press, 1989).

Von den Steinen, Karl, 'The Discovery of Women in Eighteenth-Century Political Life' in Barbara Kanner (ed.), *The Women of England. From Anglo-Saxon Times to the Present* (London: Mansell Information Publishing, 1980), pp. 229–58.

Wallace, C. M., *The Design of Biographia Literaria* (London: Allen and Unwin, 1983).

Watson, J. Steven, *The Reign of George III, 1760–1815* (Oxford, Clarendon Press, 1960).

Webb, R. K., *The British Working-Class Reader, 1790–1848. Literacy and Social Tension* (London: George Allen and Unwin, 1955).

Weiss, Harry B., *Hannah More's 'Cheap Repository' Tracts in America* (New York Public Library, 1946).

Wells, Roger, *Insurrection: the British Experience, 1795–1803* (Gloucester: Alan Sutton, 1983).

Wiles, Roy McKeen, 'The Relish for Reading in Provincial England Two Centuries Ago' in Paul Korshin (ed.), *The Widening Circle. Essays on the Circulation of Literature in Eighteenth-Century Europe* (Philadelphia: University of Pennsylvania Press, 1976), pp. 85–115.

Williams, Gwyn A., *Artisans and Sans-Culottes: Popular Movements in France and Britain during the French Revolution* (London: Edward Arnold, 1968).

Williams, Ioan (ed.), *Novel and Romance 1700–1800. A Documentary Record* (London: Routledge and Kegan Paul, 1970).

Winans, Roberts, 'The Growth of a Novel-Reading Public in Late Eighteenth-Century America', *Early American Literature*, 9 (1975), 267–75.

Woodworth, Mary Katherine, *The Literary Career of Sir Samuel Egerton Brydges* (Oxford: Basil Blackwell, 1935).

Zimmerman, Sarah, 'Charlotte Smith's Letters and the Practice of Self Presentation', *Princeton University Library Chronicle*, 53 (1991), 50–77.

7 UNPUBLISHED DISSERTATIONS

Brooks, Marilyn, 'A Critical Study of the Writings of Mary Hays, with an Edition of her Unpublished Letters to William Godwin' (PhD, University of London, 1995).

De Montluzin, Emily Lorraine, 'Jacobinism and the Reviewers. The English Literary Periodicals as Organs of Anti-Jacobin Propaganda. 1792–1832' (PhD, Duke University, 1974).

Hamlyn, Hilda M., 'The Circulating Libraries of the Eighteenth Century' (MA, University of London, 1948).

Gregory, Philippa, 'The Popular Fiction of the Eighteenth-Century Commercial Circulating Libraries' (PhD, University of Edinburgh, 1985).

Grieder, Theodore Godfrey, Jnr, 'The French Revolution in the British Drama: A Study in British Popular Literature of the Decade of Revolution' (PhD, Stanford University, 1957).

Pendleton, Gayle Trusdel, 'English Conservative Propaganda During the French Revolution, 1789–1802' (PhD, Emory University, 1976).

Schofield, Thomas Philip, 'English Conservative Thought and Opinion in Response to the French Revolution 1789–1796' (PhD, University of London, 1984).

Scott, Iain Robertson, 'From Radicalism to Conservatism: the Politics of Wordsworth and Coleridge, 1797–1818' (PhD, University of Edinburgh, 1987).

Index

CAMBRIDGE STUDIES IN ROMANTICISM

GENERAL EDITORS

MARILYN BUTLER, *University of Oxford*
JAMES CHANDLER, *University of Chicago*